Negotiation and Conflict Management

This book presents a series of essays by I William Zartman outlining the evolution of the key concepts required for the study of negotiation and conflict management, such as formula, ripeness, prenegotiation, mediation, power, process, *intractability*, escalation, order. Responding to a lack of useful conceptualization for the analysis of international negotiation, Zartman has developed an analytical framework and specific concepts that can serve as a basis for both study and practice.

Negotiation is analyzed as a process, and is linked to other major themes in political science such as decision, structure, justice and order. This analysis is then applied to negotiations to manage particular types of conflicts and cooperation, including ethnic conflicts, civil wars and regime-building. It also develops typologies and strategies of mediation, dealing with such aspects as leverage, bias, interest, and roles.

This book of essays by the leading exponent of negotiation and mediation will be of great interest to all students of negotiation, mediation and conflict studies in general.

I William Zartman is the Jacob Blaustein Distinguished Professor of International Organization and Conflict Resolution at the Nitze School of Advanced International Studies of The Johns Hopkins University. He is author of over 20 books on conflict management and negotiation.

Security and conflict management
Edited by:
Fen Osler Hampson
Carleton University, Canada
Chester Crocker
Georgetown University, Washington DC
Pamela Aall
United States Institute of Peace, Washington DC

This series will publish the best work in the field of security studies and conflict management. In particular, it will promote leading-edge work that straddles the divides between conflict management and security studies, between academics and practitioners, and between disciplines.

Negotiation and Conflict Management

Essays on theory and practice

I William Zartman

Routledge
Taylor & Francis Group

LONDON AND NEW YORK

First published 2008
by Routledge
2 Park Square, Milton Park, Abingdon, Oxon OX14 4RN

Simultaneously published in the USA and Canada
by Routledge
270 Madison Ave, New York, NY 10016

Routledge is an imprint of the Taylor & Francis Group, an informa business

© 2008 I William Zartman

Typeset in Baskerville by Wearset Ltd, Boldon, Tyne and Wear
Printed and bound in Great Britain by TJI Digital Ltd, Padstow,
Cornwall

British Library Cataloguing in Publication Data
A catalogue record for this book is available from the British Library

Library of Congress Cataloging in Publication Data
A catalog record has been requested for this book

ISBN10: 0-415-42950-1 (hbk)
ISBN10: 0-203-94525-5 (ebk)

ISBN13: 978-0-415-42950-4 (hbk)
ISBN13: 978-0-203-94525-4 (ebk)

Contents

Illustrations

Figures

Tables

Introduction

International security is achieved by conflict management, and conflict management is accomplished above all by negotiation. It is not the expensive military hardware that assures the security of a state and its inhabitants, but the diplomacy associated with its use and non-use. Insecurity arises from problems unsolved and conflicts unmanaged; it is the solution of problems and the resolution of conflicts that bring security to states in their relations with each other and to the populations they contain. Only when insufficient attention and effort are devoted to solutions and resolutions, are defense and armaments – *ultima ratio regis* ("the king's final argument") as a seventeenth-century cannon bore on its barrel – brought into action. At that point, even military means may not assure security, and in any case, negotiation and management of conflict are more necessary than ever.

Hence negotiation has a role to play in three acts – in the "prologue," when the conflict is merely an issue or a problem, to prevent it from getting worse; during the conflict if the first has failed, to provide solutions and resolutions; and in the crisis, if the first two have failed, to bring the escalation and violence to an end. Negotiation is a calling for all seasons, the means of devising cooperative solutions to problems and political alternatives to violence. For conflict situations are omnipresent in human and social relations. Conflict refers simply to an incompatibility of positions, a static situation when mutually exclusive views are present. Escalation is dynamic conflict, an effort to prevail in a contest between those incompatible positions. When one party decides to increase its efforts, the other may decide to give in or to increase its own efforts too. And so it goes. In either case, negotiation is needed to bring the conflict to an end, to decide the terms of the outcome jointly whether one party prevails or all parties stalemate in their efforts to prevail.

Thus, negotiation is a universal and fascinating topic. But it is more. Conflict too is universal and inherent in social activity, and deadlock and violence – escalated conflict (Chapter 12) – are frequent, instinctive possibilities, despite their cost, pain and ultimate ineffectiveness. Some things are worth that escalation and not everything is negotiable, but for the most part there is a practical as well as moral obligation to investigate the path of negotiation so as to widen it and better enable it to lead to satisfactory outcomes. By definition, "satisfactory" means "mutually satisfactory," so that both parties have an interest in outcome durability. And so there is a moral as well as practical opportunity to develop a better understanding of the negotiation process.

New fields to discover

Negotiation is the process of combining of divergent/conflicting positions through communication into a joint decision. It takes up the major part of all international relations and foreign affairs. It has prevented literally innumerable conflicts from escalating into violence, insecurity and newspaper headlines; it has been used to resolve important problems and day-to-day issues; it has brought an end to the exceptional conflicts that rivet attention – sometimes after a rapid escalation, sometimes after long periods of intractability. Negotiation means giving something to get something. It is the process of determining the price and the currency in a barter, where both the purchase and the price are indeterminate and must be brought into concordance with each other. (Many negotiators in foreign policy forget that if they want something, right is not enough: they have to either take it or buy it; if they can't take it, they must buy it; and if they have to buy it, they have to pay for it, by giving something in exchange).

Yet the striking fact is that little attention has been devoted to analyzing and understanding the process of negotiation. This neglect begins – or perhaps ends – with the meager funds assigned to the diplomatic side of states' foreign relations compared to their defense budgets. It continues into the weak preparation and formation of public opinion for an understanding of diplomacy and negotiation, both through the media and through the schools. Newspapers focus on the momentary crisis; when they turn to negotiations, they expect quick results, based on expectations of immediate movement (usually by the other party) and disparagement of "concessions" and "compensations" (in the wake of the pre-World War II devaluation of "appeasement"). Education has moved away from history-by-battles but has not yet moved to history-as-agreements and especially not to the process of attaining them. Diplomatic academies have only occasional courses in negotiation, believing that skill only comes by doing and that good doers have untransmittable skills. Public schools are slow and sporadic in adding conflict management to their curricula (it is not considered an "academic subject" even in the schedules of educational reforms such as the "No Child Left Behind" program of the 2000s).

It is in the area of higher education, where public understanding and professional reflexes are formed, that the inattention to negotiation and conflict management/resolution is most critical.[1] Survey texts in international relations (IR) give comparatively little space to diplomacy and frequently omit negotiation altogether. Foundation support for conflict management has dried up, while security studies with its national defense focus continues to thrive, in writing and funding. The dominant international relations paradigm of realism can only explain conflict, not its resolution or cooperation, and has no place for negotiation. Competing paradigms such as liberalism and constructivism have more room for both but have done little to fold negotiation into their premises. Furthermore, realism is taught and analyzed as a form of structural determinism, leaving no room to explain ways of getting out of its grasp and of managing conflict. The forces – although not the processes – of conflict become so well explained that there is no explanatory room left for doing something about them. And this is the analytical base on which professionals in the foreign policy business ground their reflexes when they arrive in influential positions, either as commentators or as actors.

Unfortunately, analytical work on the process of negotiation has also contributed to this neglect, in both its quantity and its quality. To begin with, systematic negotiation analysis is a new field, although recognition of negotiation itself is as old as Abraham (in his negotiation with the Lord over the fate of Sodom [Genesis 18:23–33], from which conceptual lessons can still be drawn). Negotiation has been practiced for millennia, but until the current era the treatment was neither systematic nor process-oriented but focused simply on historical outcomes and commonsense advice. The seventeenth and eighteenth centuries saw a series of important international negotiations in Europe and a corresponding spate of works on the subject – notably de Callières (1963[1716]) – that can be characterized as "books of proverbs," insightful but often contradictory pieces of wisdom that are still relevant but scarcely analytical and do not tell the *which when why* of the many things they advise. Two centuries later, economists developed highly theoretical models of bilateral monopoly (notably Zeuthen 1930), but they are limited in their applicability because of their restrictive assumptions of fixed openers and linear concession rates. They were followed by the development of basic models in game theory (notably Nash 1950), again highly systematic but free of any consideration of process as practiced in negotiation. Even more seriously, neither line of analysis has room for power and its adjunct, persuasion, not in its restrictive military sense (again a problem for the realists) but in the more accurate and broader political sense as measures to move the other party in an intended direction. As a result they were not much help either in the understanding or in the practice of negotiation in international relations (or other relations, for that matter), where political power is all.

The systematic study of the negotiation process itself began with some salient works in the 1960s – Schelling's *The Strategy of Conflict* (1960), Ikle's *How Nations Negotiate* (1964), and Walton and McKersie's *A Behavioral*

Theory of Labor Negotiations (1965) – all reactions to the opportunity for accurate conceptualization of the process. Schelling's discussion of elements of power, Ikle's characterization of different types of process, and Walton and McKersie's typology of process-driven outcomes gave important impetus to the field. They broke away from case histories, from simple characteristics of a good negotiator, and from idealized theory distant from the real process, and opened the way to more systematic analysis of conflict resolution and problem-solving and to the pursuit of many paradoxes and puzzles lying within the subject.

One of the exciting things about working on the subject of negotiation is that it is a vast field of discovery, where new concepts, regularities, behaviors and strategies await identification. These are more than just intellectual challenges (if that were not enough) because negotiation is practiced every day by everyone, basically in the same ways, sometimes clothed differently in different cultures, but similar in its basics to the practice on the highest levels of Big Politics. We learn by observing ourselves. Thus there is a conceptual world to invent and discover around us, and inside us all as well. I like to think that I have been part of that exploration and naming process, for the benefit of others as well as for my own manifest enjoyment.

My own path in the field

My own path into this developing field began in area studies, specifically in writing a book on negotiations between Africa and the European Economic Community (EEC), where I found myself dissatisfied with the state of negotiation theory as a deductive guide to understanding the real world (Chapter 1). As a result, I set out to generalize regularities from the experiences I observed, with both a critical evaluation of the shortcomings of current theory and a layout of a different way of conceptualizing the negotiation process. Instead of a series of concessions from fixed positions to a point of convergence, actual negotiations begin with the establishment of a formula of broad principles, and then turn to their application in the determination of the details of the agreement (Chapters 2 and 3). This led me into a series of adventures, working on the internal or logical development of those generalized regularities or concepts for deductive purposes and also on the actual practice of negotiations and its lessons for inductive purposes. The two served as a correction on each other, using concepts (theory is too big a word for the current state of knowledge on negotiation [Chapter 7]) and practice as "two connected servomechanisms," to use Alan Coddington's (1969) phrase about the negotiation process itself. In the following selections, I have generally kept the original text, despite some partial repetitions, to show the evolution of thinking.

The reason why negotiation eludes a fully fledged theory, despite the efforts of economists, operations researchers, game theorists, social psychologists, and political scientists, is that it is hung on a paradox, the Toughness or Negotiator's Dilemma, to which there is no answer. "If I am Tough, I increase the chances of a favorable agreement but decrease the chances of any agreement at all, whereas if I am Soft, I increase the chances for an agreement but decrease the chances for a favorable one." The fact that both parties face this dilemma only increases its potency. The search for answers proceeds through the most important question of social analysis: *which when why?* In this way, concepts – the naming of regularities – are refined and help us work out of that dilemma (Zartman 2005).

Several such puzzles invited elucidation, often to clear up commonly held notions which lack a conceptual basis. What is the role of justice in this process, if at all, or is the process entirely dominated by power (in the political sense) (Chapters 4 and 5)? And in power relation, what is the effect of inequality, since in reality – contrary to classroom experiments – pure symmetry is never obtained (Chapters 6, 7 and 11)? What happens before negotiations begin, when in fact do they begin, and what relation does this have to the formula-detail model (Chapters 7 and 11)? What effect does conflict escalation have on negotiation, and when and how can escalation facilitate rather than impede negotiation as we usually think (Chapter 12)? What does the presence of a third party have to do with the negotiation process? Is mediation negotiation? Must a mediator be impartial or are mediator's interests also present (Chapter 10)? And most importantly, *when* can negotiations take place – just anytime or at specific, identifiable moments during a conflict (Chapters 2, 11 and 14)? Since many of the answers to these questions are ambiguous, as exemplified previously in the Toughness Dilemma, how can they be sorted out?

Other puzzles come from the side of practice, in the form of topical issues where negotiation came into play and where better conceptualization could make its contribution, not only to an understanding of the use and process of negotiation but also to the practical solution and resolution of problems and conflicts. The original inquiry – on how the weak confront the strong in the African–EEC negotiations – did not answer all the questions associated with asymmetry in problem-solving or cooperative negotiations, particularly pressing in the 1970s and 1980s: how and why do the weak and strong negotiate in order to come to a mutually acceptable agreement, and why do they do so anyhow, if the strong is strong and the weak weak, the Structuralist's Paradox (Chapters 6, and 11)? In the 1980s and 1990s the topic of conflict management and resolution, particularly in internal and ethnic conflicts, came to the fore, a situation that, despite basic differences is also asymmetrical in nature. How do rebels over come their asymmetry and how can the conflicting parties reach an equitable result (Chapters 11, 12 and 15)? Most recently, another topic of asymmetry came (back again) on the table, that of terrorism: since, despite policy refusals and denials, governments often do negotiate with terrorists, when and how do they do so (Chapter 15) – again the *which when why?* question.

While the selections presented here are primarily articles and chapters, they had generally led in turn to authored and edited books that expand the inquiry, often in a team effort. The path that began with a review of the current state of the literature led to the formula/detail approach (Zartman 1971, 1978, 1987) (Chapters 1, 2 and 3), and then grew with the addition of the pre-negotiation functions to make the *diagnosis/formula/detail model* (Chapter 7). Formula, the innovative central notion, is defined as a common definition of the problem and its solution, identification of the terms of trade, and/or a jointly determined sense of justice to govern the exchange. The latter element raises a further issue: is there a single criterion of justice applicable to negotiated outcomes or processes, or in its absence is justice absent from negotiations? In a collaborative project, the Washington Interest in Negotiation (WIN) Group found reality in a third option: as part of the formula phase, negotiators themselves determine the definition of justice that will govern their subsequent negotiations on the details of the issue (Chapter 4). The search for an agreeable principle of justice, as well as the principle (formula) itself, then become specific components of the process (Chapter 5). But then another dilemma remains: how to reconcile justice with peace in negotiation, when the two often conflict? A broad study of historic cases point to a sequenced answer that maximizes both values (Zartman and Kremenyuk 2005)

The characteristic asymmetry of any negotiation poses intriguing questions, but also provides its own answers when examined closely. The ways in which weaker parties can and do negotiate with stronger parties invites an examination of best practices, distilled into generalized regularities or concepts, and then played back as recommendations for better negotiations in the future. This was the question pursued from the beginning in examining African and European behaviors (Chapter 1), and then in a more controlled comparison of near symmetrical and clearly asymmetrical contexts (Chapter 6). In the end, the findings showed that contrary to assumed wisdom, clearly asymmetrical negotiations were the most efficient and effective, that nearly symmetrical (inconclusively asymmetrical) negotiations were the least so, and that purely symmetrical negotiations, although optimal, were a figment of controlled experiments, unobtainable in the real world. They also developed categories of best tactics for the weaker, all variations on the practice of borrowing power from some source – the context, the process, the opponent, or third parties.

This inquiry also spread in two other directions. One was purely conceptual, born of a dissatisfaction, from the earliest studies (Zartman 1971, 1976, 1978) (Chapters 1 and 2) with the two predominant and competing definitions of power. The structural definition – power as resources – led to the *paradox*; the behavioral definition – power as an ability – is tautological and conclusionary. But when defined as measures to move a party in an intended direction, power can be measured against both its source and its result, providing a concept useful for testing and for practice (Chapter 6).

The other direction leads to multilateral negotiations and of their use in building regimes. Many cases and plenty of counsel had characterized studies of multilateral negotiations, but no attempt had been made to conceptualize the process. Negotiation theory is almost exclusively bilateral, whereas multilateral negotiations are above all matters of coalition, of parties, issues and roles. A contest organized among competing theoretical approaches for the best explanation of multilateral processes and outcomes focused on the concept of managed complexity (Zartman 1994), and in turn led to a tenth-anniversary presentation of new studies based on the original work (Crump and Zartman 2003). At the same time, the management of complexity was used to frame the first conceptual analysis of the UN Conference on Environment and Development in Rio de Janeiro in 1993 (Spector *et al.* 1994) and then a decade later to challenge the current interpretation of regime-building as a legislation-and-compliance process (Spector and Zartman 2003). Introducing a new conceptualization based on an empirical record of regimes not available when the subject was launched twenty years earlier, the study argues that regimes are recursive negotiations for periodic review and adjustment rather than one-shot rules for compliance (Chapter 13). Most broadly, this path of inquiry has lead to a rapprochement of the two concepts of cooperation and conflict management (Zartman 2007), tying together two basic IR concepts which have long run parallel to each other without identifying their conditional overlap.

While much of this work has focused on cooperative negotiations, negotiations to manage and resolve violent conflicts also pose intriguing questions, primarily focusing on the role of external parties. Collaboration with Saadia Touval on questions of mediation began early to produce a basic work (Touval and Zartman 1985) and alternating authorships have produced successive studies in pursuit of further answers to the topic (Touval and Zartman 1989, 2001; Zartman and Touval 1996, 2007): Mediation is catalyzed negotiation, helping the parties do what they cannot do alone by overcoming identifiable types of obstacles; the mediator has its own motivating interests and need not be impartial but is expected to deliver to the side toward which it is biased (Chapter 10). Along with this collaboration, another important question arose, concerning when to mediate and negotiate. A comparative study of four African cases in search for an appropriate formula for resolution found instead that the key to success in getting conflicting parties to negotiate lay in the conflict itself: when parties found themselves in a Mutually Hurting Stalemate (MHS) and perceived the possibility of a negotiated Way Out (WO), the conflict was ripe for talks about resolution (Zartman 1985, 1989) (Chapter 14). A second controlled comparison of eleven cases contrasted those which had reached some settlement (actually in the course of preparing the manuscript) with those that had not, to find ripeness a crucial element in starting negotiations and to press further the identification of appropriate tactics and outcomes that could take advantage of the ripe moment (Zartman 1995). Ripeness provides the answer to the contribution of escalation to producing a negotiable situation, when escalation leads to an MHS (Zartman and Faure 2005) (Chapter 12, building on Zartman and Aurik 1991). The notion of ripeness has been further developed to complement the push-effect of the MHS into negotiations with a pull-effect of the WO as a Mutually Enticing Opportunity (MEO) that draws negotiations to a successful conclusion (Chapter 14).

As noted the exciting attraction of the field is the continual array of new challenges for explanation and new topics to be addressed. The latest work shows the diversity of the challenge. The notion of intractability has long posed an existential conundrum: is it only momentary, however long the moment, or is it a permanent conditionof certain conflicts? When defining elements of intractability are identified, negotiators can whittle away at the supporting conditions (Zartman 2005). In another direction, the challenge of knowing how, when and why to negotiate with terrorists, since such negotiations do take place, requires a definitional distinction among types of terrorists and then an application of normal negotiating tactics – either lower or change the terms of trade – in an unusually difficult situation (Zartman 1990, 2003, 2006; Zartman and Alfredson 2003, Zartman and Faure 2006) (Chapter 15)

All of these topics of inquiry seek answers to negotiation puzzles by sharpening old concepts and creating new ones, developing them inductively and testing them deductively on cases and applications. In addition to such inquiries within the topic there are intellectual opportunities to locate the topic within larger fields. Again, both practice and theory have offered fruitful terrains. While negotiation is a principal method for conflict resolution and problem solving, its role "in the prologue" in preventing conflict and preempting problems invites analysis, differentiated for the first time according to the way it operates in different issue areas and held together by strategies to change stakes, values and attitudes (Zartman 2000, 2005). Theoretically, negotiation has been identified as one of only five ways of social decision-making, along with voting, judication, force, and chance (Chapters 2 and 3), but it is also one of a number of forms of order, a basic concept of political science, with its own differentiating characteristics (Chapter 9).

However, while proposing new ideas and answers, this work also enters the methodological debate with a reaffirmation of an established and refined research approach in contrast to newer ones with still unaddressed problems. In the search for scientificity through quantification, contemporary methods have lost the sensitiveness of data and the appropriateness of questions that only multiple comparative case studies can handle (Chapter 16).

This collection documents the evolution of some of these concepts – formula, ripeness, prenegotiation/diagnosis, mediation, power, process, intractability, escalation, order, and others – and of a richer understanding of negotiation. It also shows their application to different contexts where negotiation has taken place – internal conflicts, interstate conflicts, cooperation and regime-building, and lately terrorism. The articles are reproduced with very few changes, in order to show that evolution, at the cost of a few repetitions or more usually elaborations. The writings presented here make no claims of exhausting the subject. They do aspire to invite and encourage more efforts to explore and develop it, in the final goal of generating greater creativity in its practice, for the more satisfactory resolution of conflict and the peaceful accomplishment of change, two permanent conditions of human life.

Fellow wayfarers on the path

A review of this activity would not be complete with a collegial bow to the collaboration that this interest has fostered.[2] Since the beginning of the 1980s the interdisciplinary, inter-university WIN Group has met at the School of Advanced International Studies of The Johns Hopkins University to review research in negotiation, and to produce results of its own (Chapter 5). It also edits an international peer-reviewed journal, *International Negotiation*, published three times a year by Brill (http://interneg.org/in/) in its tenth year in 2006. An extraordinary international, inter-disciplinary program has been conducted since 1987 by the Processes of International Negotiation (PIN) Group at the International Institute of Applied Systems Analysis (IIASA) housed in Maria Theresia's Summer Palace in Laxenburg, outside Vienna, a symbolically perfect site for the study of negotiation. PIN has produced a book a year (including Zartman 1994, 2000; Zartman and Rubin 2000; Zartman and Faure 2005; Zartman and Kremenyuk 2005, Faure and Zartman 2007; Avenhaus and Zartman 2006), contributing enormously to the pursuit of intellectually challenging questions in the field of negotiation, and is not running out of topics. The standard concluding chapters of the books edited by PIN are "Lessons for Theory" and "Lessons for Practice," the same face-off between concepts and applications necessary to understanding the subject. In addition to its published work, PIN organizes road-shows on negotiations in inviting institutions, sideshows at conferences of parties (COPs) of international regimes, a biennial newsletter *PINPoints*, and CaspiLog, a Track 2 (NEGO-led) discussion around the Caspian Sea (pin@iiasa.ac.at). It is gratifying to know that others share the same passion and intellectual challenge in this field, which is of such salience in human activity and importance to world peace, problem-solving and conflict reduction.

Part I

Negotiations in concept

1   The study of negotiation[3]

Considering the length of time that states have bargained with each other, it is surprising that there has been so little analysis of the process of negotiation. Lately, however, there has been a sudden flurry of interest. Yet most of the new material is either a continuation of or an overreaction to old ways of looking at diplomacy. Assuming that purposefulness is as characteristic of students as of practitioners of diplomacy, the inadequacy of most current writing suggests that the subject is highly resistant to systematic study. The tendency of some writers to continue in the same old vein might also be taken to suggest that the traditional study of diplomacy fills a need, even if it does not satisfy the equally important necessity for analysis of negotiations. On the other hand, some current reactions to the old diplomatic studies do attempt to provide systematic negotiations analysis, but they seem to be one of current political science's "huge missteps in the right direction." (Hoffmann 1960).

Diplomacy and bargaining

Any attempt at a systematic study begins with precise use of terms. A distinction has been implied between "study of diplomacy" and "analysis of negotiations," even though in the past "diplomacy" and "negotiations" were often used synonymously and without too much confusion. Yet, it is important to make a distinction. Diplomacy is an art or a skill, and the term will be used here to mean the pursuit of national policy goals through international communication. The study of diplomacy is essentially a prescriptive study. The great writers on diplomacy – Thucydides, Machiavelli, de Callières (1963[1716]), Pecquet (1738), de Felice (1978[1778]), Nicolson (1963) – amassed suggestions for effective behavior on the part of diplomats. The diplomatic historians attempted to describe the application of these principles in specific cases. Neither tried to analyze the dynamics of a negotiation process in any abstract or rigorously comparative sense. What is more significant is that the contemporary students of diplomacy – Morgenthau (1960), Aron (1966), Lall (1966), Ikle (1964), Fisher (1969) – have also sought to establish, or to confirm by new methods, prescriptive principles for successful diplomacy. They may have brought new wisdom, benefited from new methodology on detailed aspects, or uncovered new situations and characteristics in the world of the cold war and the United Nations, but they are still studying diplomacy and its principles.

Such studies are helpful, and they move far toward the limits of what is realistically possible. Particularly if the analysis starts from behavioral principles, it can at best conclude that these principles were unevenly observed and that success or failure is attributable to tactical ploys or mistakes of varying degrees. If the analysis is made from the basis of power principles, success or failure is *prima facie* evidence of observance or disregard of the proper relation between ends and means. Behavioral principles may go no further than Dale Carnegie in pinstripe; yet, admittedly, as long as de Callières and Nicolson are not applied with perfection, admonitions to do so can be very useful to a state's diplomatic agents. Power principles can also be useful, by reminding states to keep their bank balances big enough to cover their shopping lists.

If both types of principles' approach lead to circular or at least commonplace conclusions – the one that failure results from lack of skill, and the other that failure results from lack of capability – it is because analysis on this level can only go so far. The behavioral principles approach permits detection of national styles and perhaps a balance sheet of skills and weaknesses, but it does not permit analysis of confrontations or negotiating processes. The power principles approach would lose some of its tautology if notions of power, capability, means, and influence were further analyzed to show how outcomes were brought about. The first approach does not even permit this, for it is dealing not with unifying concepts but with noncomparable principles – as sound as the Book of Proverbs but often as contradictory.

If there is a criterion for analysis in either form of the principles approach, it is that of success or failure. Yet it is illusory as a central concept, for it provides no help in making fine analytical distinctions. Analyzing diplomacy on the basis of success or failure is as insightful as analyzing coalition or legislative behavior on the basis of bills passed. The referents are so relative, the participants so fluid, and the relevant area of analysis so much larger than the terrain chosen for study that only a little is learned. In sum, the principles approach to the study of diplomacy provides useful lessons for diplomats, but little in the way of analysis of the negotiating process (how outcomes are attained).

The implication is that negotiation analysis offers something different. Analysis is systematic, comparative, and at least somewhat replicable, even if not fully "scientific." Negotiation is the process of combining divergent viewpoints to produce a common agreement. While more precise than "diplomacy," it is broader than "bargaining," and therein lies the problem of approach. In reaction to the inadequacies of the diplomatic principles approach, there has been a recent spurt of effort to analyze bargaining through the use of game theory and matrix methodology (Rapoport 1960, 1966; Schelling 1960; Midgaard 1968). To the extent that this type of analysis deals with strategies for chosing precisely quantifiable alternatives, it is valuable. Some analysts have found it to be applicable to labor-management negotiations over wage increases, even if such important corollaries as strike costs and fringe benefits are recognized to be quantifiable but less easily relatable (Walton and McKersie 1965; Siegel and Fouraker 1960). To the extent that game theory allows the formulation of hypotheses and principles that can then be essayed in negotiations analysis, it is also useful. But for the most part, matrical analysis cannot be directly applied to international negotiations. Where the study of diplomatic principles was too broad and too fluid to answer questions of "how" and "why," game theory, by its very precision, is too narrow.

This judgment can be examined in greater detail by reviewing the assumptions of the approach. One is that quantitative utilities can be assigned to alternative positions or outcomes. In fact, many positions in most negotiations cannot be expressed either as a single quantifiable item or as several quantifiable and relatable items; as long as one of a complex of subjects under negotiation cannot be reduced to quantifiable, relatable form, it is hard to see how the whole process of choice can be matrically expressed, let alone determined.

Furthermore, even if at some point alternatives could be described as utilities, the process of reaching that point – as much or more a part of negotiations than the rest – is excluded from the analysis.[4] Since the process of nailing down general principles is usually a major problem in negotiations, and since even quantifiable utilities are often finally reconciled on the basis of midpoint, other reference points, or criteria that have a contextual significance other than their innate utility, quantitative analysis is of limited value. In this situation, it seems difficult to reduce a negotiations set to a succession of matrices, let alone a single matrix. Game theory is useful in analyzing the choice of whether to negotiate or not; once negotiations have started, it is not directly applicable to an analysis of the process – even idealized – of arriving at an agreement.[5]

A second assumption also runs up against the "process nature" of negotiations. Game theory strategies are often based on noncommunicative negotiation, or alternatively, on an assumption that when communication is present the major problem is one of trust. It is perhaps paradoxical that "prisoners' dilemmas" are more common in diplomacy, as defined, than in negotiations. Although motives may be suspect, information incomplete, secrecy broken, and leaks and indirect outside pressures part of the negotiations process – all indicating that communication may be only partial and always open to interpretation and evaluation – communication is an essential part of negotiation. But the problems it poses in most negotiations primarily concern interpretation, not trust.[6]

A third assumption is that of rationality and conservatism. There is no intent here to reopen the roving debate on the meaning and reality of rationality. If the term refers to a logical, purposeful, and informed decision, the point can quickly be made that, even if purposeful, negotiators' decisions are not always logical or informed and that purposes vary and even combine, there is no guarantee that a negotiator can prefer a single outcome over all others, that he can choose such an outcome in any but a tautological way, or that his ability to do so is a necessary assumption for the analysis of negotiations. In other words, negotiators often do not – even unconsciously – make a matrix for themselves and systematically line up their alternatives. To the extent that this is true, game theory strategies are an element of prescriptive, not descriptive, analysis and thus are not helpful for analyzing what actually happened or will happen. Nor even what should happen, for not all negotiators are willing or able to choose a single fixed strategy, or to replay the game often enough to choose a mixed strategy. In fact, a negotiator may well gamble: he can gamble that the other side will, or does not see the matrix as they may do, that they can change their alternatives and even reverse their choices at a later moment, or simply that irrational elements – such as an ideologically "predictable" wave of history or an eventual change in situational realities or the rules of the game – will save them from the unfavorable portions of their chosen outcome. Idealized situations of pure strategy can produce indirect insights of great value, but their very idealization (or theoretical nature) removes the element that makes them directly applicable to negotiations. Mainly because of these problems, the systematic tools that are being developed for the analysis of games of pure strategy have not found useful application in the analysis of real cases of negotiations. To repeat, however, this does not mean that such analysis is useless; its value is simply limited.

The main question to answer in a comprehensive analysis of negotiation, it seems, should be: *how* are divergent viewpoints combined to produce a common agreement?[7] If Lasswell's definition of politics applied to "negotiation" is set up as an equation to be solved for an unknown, X marks the "how" (Zartman 1974). "Who" refers to the parties negotiating, "what" refers to the outcome, and "when" refers to the end of the process. "Who?", "What?" and "When?" are simple factual questions that can be answered in any set of negotiations. Finding the answer to "How?" depends on a further breakdown of analytical questions, and leads to an investigation of power in the context of negotiation, since the combining of divergent viewpoints is an exercise in "the process of affecting the policies of others with the help of (actual or threatened) ... deprivations [or gratifications] for non – conformity," i.e., power (Lasswell and Kaplan 1951, p. 76; cf. Bacharach and Baratz 1970). Several schematic answers can be essayed, to suggest an approach.

Alternatives

The first answer to the question "How?" suggests that *divergent positions are combined by limiting alternatives.* Negotiation is a process of defining and reducing alternative positions until a unique combination is reached that is acceptable to all parties; it is a collective decision-making process with discrete "sides," since a decision is "a choice among alternative modes of action." (Rossi 1958, p. 364). The value of this conceptual approach is that it focuses on choices and the means of arriving at a result, thus approximating the real process pursued by the participants. Its limitation is that it does not indicate any dynamic in the process of negotiation; although this approach answers "How," it does not tell why one particular means of limiting alternatives is chosen over another (except in some form of the commonplace observation that one means seems to be "most applicable").

There are four ways of limiting alternatives. One is to make one alternative appear more attractive than others, either by promising additional side effects or by predicting benefits inherent in the favored alternative. A second is to make one alternative appear less attractive than others, either by threatening sanctions if it is chosen or by warning of inherent or associated deprivations (Rapoport 1966, p. 129). The third is by making one alternative appear to be already chosen, through the use of commitments and obligations. The last is by making some alternatives appear to be already eliminated, either by fait accompli or by simple incapacity:

The first pair of means for limiting alternatives is *promise* and *prediction* (cf. Sawyer and Guetzkow 1965, pp. 480, 483–4; Schelling 1960, pp. 43–6). Both involve future gratification, but *promise* refers to a volitional adjunct to agreement whereas *prediction* provides gratification through the agreement itself. The terms are used here in a more precise sense than commonly understood, so that analytical distinctions may be presented. Although the European Six made greater use of promises than the Africans (since they had more to promise), each Association Convention concluded with a number of ancillary engagements or promises from both sides: the Africans promised not to recognize East Germany, the Six promised the African Eighteen to study means of increasing consumption of tropical products, and the French promised to continue supports and supplement aid on a bilateral basis when possible. In negotiations with Libya and Spain for military bases, the US has used promises of aid to make the rest of its terms acceptable to the other side. The North African states have continually predicted outcomes in the interest of the Six by showing how the development and unification of the Maghreb would follow EEC Association.

The second pair is *threat* and *warning* (cf. Ikle 1964, pp. 62ff.; Schelling 1960, pp. 35–43, 103ff., 123ff.; Rapoport 1966, pp. 93, 125; Sawyer and Guetzkow 1965, pp. 480, 483–4). Both involve future deprivations, but a *threat* is volitional whereas a *warning* refers to future consequences beyond the warner's control. In both Yaoundé negotiations, the African states frequently warned of the political instability that would occur if Europe did not aid their economic development; they threatened not to enter a new Association that did not satisfy their demands, but the threat was not convincing. Indeed, even when talks temporarily broke down – in the Yaoundé, Maghreb, and East African sets – the parties were at pains to state that they were not threatening rupture, i.e., that break up was not a real alternative. Africa, including the Maghreb and Commonwealth countries, used warnings more frequently than threats in dealing with the Six, since their signature was just about the only item of value that they could voluntarily withhold. The Europeans made crucial use of threats (in the guise of warnings) when they told the Eighteen that rejection of European packages would weaken the position of the Africans' friends among the Six and result in a worse offer.

The third pair consists of *commitment* and *obligation* (cf. Ikle 1964, pp. 65–8, 175 on countertactics; Schelling 1960, passim). Both involve publicly tying the hands of one party: a *committed* party ties its own hands whereas an *obligated* party has its hands tied by another. Both constitute a presumed preselection imposed on the chooser. The process of negotiations itself builds up a structure of commitments and obligations as it goes along. Some of the commitments in the Eurafrican negotiations were arrived at before the negotiations ever began, by far the most important being the Europeans' commitment to unity. The Rome Treaty and the 1957 (North Africa) and 1963 (Commonwealth) Declarations of Intentions implicitly or explicitly committed the Six to "success" (i.e., an agreement) once negotiations had started. GATT and UNCTAD also served as commitments, although their precise nature remained open to interpretation. Again, the terms of the Yaoundé agreement acted as a commitment for the Six in the Lagos and second Yaoundé negotiations since Europe could not give Nigeria better terms than it had given the Eighteen, nor could it let the Eighteen's terms fall substantially.

Obligation is a subtler matter. While the Six had committed themselves to some sort of agreement with various African groups, the Africans tried to turn this general commitment into an obligation to a particular agreement by saying that anything less would not satisfy the terms of the original commitment. They also tried to create an obligation out of their inherited economic situation – the ex-French colonies tried to pin the obligation for maintaining their price support system on the metropole which had begun it, and the Commonwealth and other nondiscriminatory states tried to oblige the Six not to ask more concession than their former metropoles had sought. *Richesse oblige* was little invoked during the Yaoundé negotiations but rose in importance in the institutional interim between the 1962 and 1968 negotiations.

The final pair of means for limiting alternatives is *fait accompli* and *simple incapacity* (cf. Sawyer and Guetzkow 1965, p. 485 on fait accompli;

Schelling 1960, p. 37, on coercive deficiency as simple incapacity). Unlike the previous pair, these means impose their preselection on the object. Both remove the possibility of accomplishing alternatives, the first by eliminating them directly (things that cannot be undone) and the second indirectly by showing that they are unfeasible (things that cannot be done). When the Six gradually reduced the benefits of Algeria's *de facto* status they were in fact narrowing the *status quo* which Algeria could eventually seek to restore by finally deciding to negotiate a de jure relation. In its bilateral postcolonial relations Algeria is an extreme but typical case of the use of nationalization as a fait accompli. When the French agreed to eliminate subsidies as a part of the EEC internal agreement, the Eighteen found that a fait accompli had eliminated one alternative that they might have preferred. A fait accompli can also be imposed by outside forces rather than deliberate state action, the only element of the latter being the decision to sit back and await the outcome. Thus, by waiting, the EEC allowed the changing commercial situation to alter attitudes in Nigeria and East Africa toward Association. It is therefore possible to divide *faits accomplis* into those accomplished deliberately by a party, those accomplished by a third party, and those resulting from outside forces, but the effect is the same – alternatives are eliminated.

Simple incapacity also achieves the same effect. The Six let Africa know that they "could not" give a billion dollars in aid in 1962 (although they "could" in 1969), and the Africans let Europe know that they "could not" do without aid. For economic and administrative reasons, the Africans "could not" immediately align their tariffs and give preferences. For economic and political reasons, the Six "could not" offer aid to Commonwealth countries. The distinction between "could not" and "would not" is thin; like many of the other means of limiting alternatives, *simple incapacity* depends to a large extent upon one party's ability to convince the other of its weakness.

Each of these "four pairs" relates in some way to interests and may be termed substantive criteria for decisions. Frequently, at some moment in the negotiations, enough points of agreement have been reached and enough alternatives eliminated so that remaining differences no longer involve interests, substantive criteria, and various forms of power. Instead, procedural or mechanical justifications of choice are used, such as midpoints, initial offers, round figures, previous agreements, and other *reference points* whose justification lies in their existence rather than in their innate content or value (Ikle 1964, pp. 212–13). (Sometimes, commitments and obligations can serve as reference points, when there is agreement, not on their merits, but simply on their presence and the need to respect them.) There were many reference points in the Eurafrican negotiations: midpoints and round figures (focal points) were used in the FED negotiations, initial offers (despite the absence of round figures) served to limit alternatives in the Nigerian negotiations, previous agreements on the

FEDOM figure and the price support figure were used in the FED negotiations, and round figures (both as attainable and as unattainable ceilings) played the most important role in the second FED negotiations. Procedural reference points are usually called into play only after substantive criteria have narrowed alternatives to the point where the difference can be "split" but where such criteria themselves have been ineffective in eliminating the final gap.

Theoretically, negotiations begin with an infinite field of alternatives open for the choosing. In fact, the "terrain" of the negotiations is first defined, that is, the choice of subjects and a broad span of possibilities, followed by a number of key questions and principles which help narrow the choice of subjects. Thereafter, the process of limiting alternatives begins, as outlined, through the communication of future deprivations and gratifications, and present possibilities, until any remaining differences can be split by procedural means. Each side tries to show that its possibilities plus associated gratifications are more beneficial to the other side than their proposals (which are either impossible or associated with deprivations), and are surely more beneficial than no agreement at all.

Convergence

The second approach to the question of reconciling divergent viewpoints is structural, through the convergence of positions. Instead of focusing on an unlimited field of substantive alternatives and analyzing how they are reduced to a unique combination, the second approach takes the initial positions as a starting point and asks how they are brought into convergence. Instead of a vast contracting field, an analytical model would show broken lines drawn from the initial points to the point of convergence, and then investigate what brought these lines closer and closer to final coincidence. The advantages of this conceptual approach lie in its ability to show which side gave in most or moved furthest from its original position and to indicate clearly the relationship of one party's moves to those of the other. This approach does not deal as much with the substance of the debate as with the tactical process, which the previous approach has already shown to be important.

The disadvantages of this approach lie in part in the obverse of the advantages. Convergence analysis can be combined with an analysis of alternative limitation to bring out substantive and power considerations; alone, however, convergence analysis plays down the substantive arguments in order to bring out procedure and so may give a false impression of the negotiation process.

There is another operational disadvantage, however. The analysis of the FED negotiations – where, if anywhere, this approach should be most clearly applicable – has shown that even monetary matters are in fact not simply reducible to quantitative terms. The FED negotiations – even when isolated somewhat arbitrarily from other considerations – began on a split level of quantitative and nonquantitative positions, where principles and figures were mixed. Once bargaining got down to purely mathematical components, there was continual shifting back and forth between reference figures and nonmathematical criteria, and even on the lever of figures, there were important shifts of attention from one component to another. A simple analysis that dealt only with total figures would never provide genuine insight into the real determinants. These problems will be taken into account, following a discussion of the mechanics of the procedural model.

There are five ways of arriving at convergence from initial positions; as follows from the original notion, distinctions essentially concern the relation of moves to each other. The first may be called *simple coincidence* of initial positions, and it takes place most frequently at the beginning and the end of negotiations. A proposal from one party may be accepted by the other (someone, after all, must be the first to voice the position), or both parties may discover that their initial proposals (brought with them to the negotiating table or perhaps previously discussed in the press, parliament, or other public forums) are identical. The Yaoundé agreement on advantages "at least equivalent" to the Rome Treaty or the Lagos agreement not to include aid are cases in point, as are some of the concluding provisions to both Conventions that were arrived at after the "crest" of the negotiations had been concluded.

A second way of arriving at convergence can be called *concession* because one party gives in to the other (Ikle 1964, pp. 104, 206–7). Although the history of negotiation may provide more examples of partial concession, where one party moves unilaterally toward the position of the other without actually reaching it, there are also cases of full *concession*. The Eighteen conceded to the Six on the principles of market guarantees and co-management, while at another time the Six conceded that reciprocal preferences would not be required from the nondiscriminatory states among the Eighteen.

Concessions are often coupled with a third category, *counterconcessions* or *compensation,* in which the party that has received a *concession* explicitly makes one of its own in return, but on another matter. Thus, in negotiating with North Africa, the Europeans in principle conceded Tunisian and Moroccan demands for industrial preferences (the inter-Community regime). In turn, they asked for and received some kind of interim preference for their industrial goods on the North African market before a full free-trade area would go into effect toward the end of the agreement; this exchange of *concession* and *counterconcession* is likely to be repeated in negotiations on agricultural goods. In intra-European negotiations, France agreed to the Nigerian mandate at the price of an agreement to the Maghreb mandate (albeit partial) from the rest of the Six.

A fourth way of arriving at convergence is through *compromise* or joint concession, whereby both parties give some ground to arrive at a point somewhere between both of their initial (or latest) positions. Final convergence on the FED figure appears to be an example of *compromise*, for Africans and Europeans moved from their latest positions of $810 million and $780 million respectively to *compromise* on a round figure of $800 million. When the process is analyzed, however, it shows up clearly as one of concession and counterconcession, for the Six accepted the African figure of $230 million for the supplement but required an African concession on the figure of $570 million for the base. Thus, a better example of *compromise* is the Europeans' earlier convergence on the supplemental (and round) figure of $200 million and on the total of $780 million. In general, however, reference points lend themselves best to use in *compromises*.

The final way of arriving at convergence is, paradoxically, to avoid it, in a process that may be termed *understanding* (Ikle 1964, pp. 14–22). In this process, explicit convergence is bypassed and the debate goes on to implement an ambiguity. A few illustrations should clarify this artifice. Before the Yaoundé negotiations began, France and the Netherlands disagreed over the legal basis of the continued Association, France holding that the new Association was a continuation of the old as provided under Rome IV and the Netherlands maintaining that the new Association was indeed a new chapter to be negotiated under Article 238 of the Rome Treaty. The communiqué announced that the Association would continue *"jusqu'à nouvel ordre,"* a phrase which meant that it would continue as long as it would continue, with no reference to the legal basis. Later, when negotiations began, the problem arose again, and again the communiqué (and the new Convention's text) provided for this continuation "in conformity with the principles of the Treaty," without reference to the Article. Both parties could claim victory before their respective parliaments, and the negotiations and subsequent Association could proceed because an *understanding* had been reached. Many such *understandings* took place over principles in the Yaoundé negotiations, permitting principles to flow from details, rather than the reverse procedure used in the Lagos negotiations. *Understanding* was also used to begin negotiations between the US and Panama over a new Canal Zone Treaty when, on 3 April 1964, a joint declaration provided for "procedures" but never mentioned "canal," "negotiations," or "treaty." Similarly, the Security Council resolution on Palestine in November 1967 used "secure frontiers" and "agreement" as an *understanding* for "pre-June boundaries" and "direct negotiations," although the understanding came undone under duress.

These five means of achieving convergence can also be used to evaluate Eurafrican negotiations. The Eighteen conceded much in the early stages of the Yaoundé negotiations, and only entered into the process of counterconcession and compromise at the end. The apparently complex nature of the negotiations was also a result of the frequent use of coincidence, understanding, and the induction of principles from details. In the Lagos negotiations, concessions and counterconcessions were more equally balanced, coincidence more frequent, the need for compromise arose less often, and the negotiations were basically deductive in nature. The final convergence points in the Yaoundé set were closer to the Europeans' initial positions than to the Africans', whereas in the Lagos set convergence was not far from the Nigerians' position and not far from the Europeans' either; in the second case, however, the range of positions was narrower than in the first.

In a word, the Eighteen gave in more but also got more, while the Nigerians gave in less and got less. This paradox raises an important warning about the use of the convergence approach. Convergence covers the process of negotiations, but not the value of the final accord. Although the Nigerians did better in terms of departures from their original positions, their final package – which contained no aid and only limited preferences – was smaller than the Eighteen's. Perhaps the Nigerians were able to strike a harder bargain (i.e., move less from their original positions) because they were asking for so little in comparison with the Eighteen. Tentative as this conclusion must be, it is significant because it suggests the reverse of the commonly held notion that a party which starts from an extreme position has more influence in shaping a favorable outcome. Many of the Eighteen's extreme demands (extreme in comparison with the result, not with their needs) were simply irrelevant to the negotiating process, since the package resulted from a decisive convergence among the Six. The 1967 Panama Canal Zone Treaty closely resembled the initial American position of 1964–5 (with implementing details added) rather than Panama's total demands, although these demands were necessary to bring about negotiations, and hence the American position. The degree and mechanics of movement from initial points to convergence tells much more about the negotiating process than a simple evaluation of final results.

On the other hand, it would be dangerous to take movement toward convergence too mathematically. To begin with, initial positions are tactical stands, whether played close or wild, and do not necessarily represent the intrinsic value that their content may suggest. Nigeria played close, moved little, and its inability to concede acted as a commitment and an incapacity that could not be shaken. The Eighteen played wild and were probably less committed to their initial stand; their position increased in value to them as they moved toward convergence. Values (utilities) change with movement, although this does not imply that they increase at some fixed rate as they approach convergence.

In addition, there is simply no way of ascribing finite – let alone comparative – value to positions, either initial or subsequent. The problem of combining quantitative and nonquantitative positions has already been noted; but even quantitative positions are only indices, not fixed utilities.

This is true even in the case of a "purely quantitative" matter such as the FED, where monetary sums have a utility not only in terms of their exchange rate but also in terms of a particular state's ability to pay its share, in terms of its previous outlays, and in terms of its expected – but at least partially unquantifiable – results, and probably other considerations as well. This is especially true of commercial matters. "A precise appreciation of tariff cuts is, however, very difficult. No satisfactory method of measurement of concessions has yet been evolved ... Indeed, [GATT has] decided after careful investigation that quantitative estimates of concessions are practically impossible." (Curzon 1965, p. 80). Convergence analysis permits greater understanding of a process, but not measurement of gains and losses.

With all these caveats – and with the problem of the shifting levels of analysis mentioned earlier – taken into consideration, what value is left in the convergence approach? The value it seems lies in isolating those points where changes in positions occurred and in bringing out the important shifts both for tactics and for analysis – on the way to convergence. The approach tells what to look for and where to look, and it flags the important procedural element of the negotiations process. It recognizes the "process" nature of negotiations, rather than focusing on single-session confrontations or simply on final results.

Thus there are many "hows." "How" can mean "in what way?" or "by what means?" It can refer, then, to either procedural or substantive factors. The implication is that the two approaches should be combined for a more complete analysis of the negotiations process. In fact, the two approaches fit together quite well. When convergence analysis has indicated at what point a change in positions has occurred, the limitations approach can be utilized to investigate what uses of power accomplished the result.

Propositions

The preceding discussion has centered on an analytical approach to the process of negotiation. Can this approach be carried a step further toward the development of a theory of negotiations? Theory has many meanings. For present purposes, it will be used rather precisely for an explanatory hypothesis that contains a dynamic or projective element. A theory should be able to indicate that under certain conditions, a certain outcome is likely to occur for certain reasons. Using the limitation and convergence approaches, a theory should indicate that a particular convergence point would result under identifiable conditions, including the application of particular uses of power (ability to use certain criteria decisively) at specific junctures.

At the present stage, attempts at theorizing based on the outlined systematic approaches appear to be inconclusive, despite their value for analysis, for reasons to be explained. One potential formula – inherent in the principles approach discussed at the beginning of this chapter – hangs on the word "successful." Thus (1), "the side which most successfully brings applicable uses of power to bear on the convergence process will swing the convergence point closer to its initial position," which is an accurate summary of the Yaoundé negotiations. Or (1a), "A convergence process which is successfully played through to the end will produce agreement, and one where one party has not been successful in eliminating the other's conflicting alternatives will not produce agreement", which is an accurate but definitional description of the two sets of Commonwealth African negotiations. Or (1b), "when there is prior commitment to agreement the party that can hold out the longest will bring convergence closest to its initial point," which is an accurate portrayal of the Arusha and Maghrebi negotiations, but a terrible tautology. Whether the word "successful" is used or implied, this type of statement is only a commonplace, for it equates the conditional and the predictive parts of the "theory."

Such statements, however, do have illustrative value. As one seeks to sharpen them by pinning down the conditions, it becomes evident that much depends on the effective use of tactics, or the willingness to compromise, or the ability to make one's inflexible stand credible and acceptable to the other party. All of these elements of "success" lead back to the principles of skillful negotiation and to the fact that negotiators are human beings with greater or lesser skills and with fortuitous elements aiding or hindering them. The inability to theorize on this level reinforces the continuing – if limited – usefulness of the principles approach.

These statements, however, can be pursued one step further. A key phrase in the first formula is "applicable uses of power," suggesting that each party must identify the supports for the other's stand in order to weaken them. In the Yaoundé set, the Europeans' strength lay largely in their commitment to unity and in their control over such items as disposable financial aid and market guarantees. The Africans were unable to shake the Europeans' position significantly on these matters, that is, they were unable to muster the kind of power that would eliminate the Europeans' alternatives. Isolating these elements in a particular set of negotiations tells something about the process and its outcome. It also tells negotiators where to aim their guns, and possibly even what kinds of ammunition to use, as the arguments in the subsequent institutional debate show. However, isolating these elements does not help much in building a theory of negotiations.

Another aspect brought out by the convergence and limitation approach might be stated as proposition (2):

> negotiation is a process of limiting alternatives until agreement is reached on a single position; the process continues as long as there is

hope of convergence at a point acceptable to both sides. Acceptability is a function, not of parties' initial positions, but of their estimate of cost and gain applied at any moment to the foreseeable convergence point as compared to no agreement.

For all its accuracy as a summary, this statement recalls a number of interpretive limitations mentioned earlier. Such notions as cost and gain estimates cannot be taken strictly or quantitatively, for there is little evidence that parties actually do add up a mathematical balance sheet and much more evidence that such a balance sheet, involving many non quantitative and noncomparable items, cannot be precisely drawn. For this reason, among others, a general description of the negotiation process is preferable to such strictly quantitative notions as contract curves and contract areas. In addition, it must be remembered that different parties will generally ascribe different estimates (utilities) to the same points and positions, and that those estimates may vary during the negotiations – either because of changing evaluations or changing conditions – to the point where it is usually meaningless to think in terms of fixed minimum points or resistance points. Changing estimates can readily be seen in the various sets of Eurafrican negotiations: the shifting economic situation of the Maghreb and the declining advantages of Algeria's "status," the re-estimates made by East Africa of its goal and of its cost/gain, the extremely fluid desiderata of the Yaoundé Eighteen, their evaluation of advantages in and out of Association and their decision not to break off negotiations. In sum, the second proposition replaces the "soft" terms of the first formula – "success" and "applicable" – with slightly "harder" terms – "acceptability" and "estimate" – that refer to perception. There is a dynamic element to this type of theoretical statement, but not a predictable element, for the blanks cannot be filled in advance.

In most of the sets of negotiations under analysis, the question was less one of "success" (i.e., final agreement at some point) than of where the convergence point would be. The theoretical statement above focuses mainly on final agreement; can it be reformulated to explain where the agreement will lie? Or, in other words, is there a theoretical statement that can be made about the use of power during negotiations that will tell how convergence will be shaped?

The completed sets of EEC–African negotiations that have been analyzed are of two types: those that covered a narrow range of alternatives and whose convergence point fell somewhere in between the positions of the two sides (Lagos), and those that covered a broad range of alternatives and whose convergence point was distinctly closer to the initial position of one party than that of the other (Yaoundé I and II, Maghreb and Arusha). Perhaps the negotiations among the Europeans in all the Eurafrican sets should be considered as well, in which case it would form a third category where the range of alternatives can vary but where the final balance sheet of convergence points is somewhere in between the initial positions. These cases, then, suggest that mere diversity in the range of alternatives is not relevant in determining the convergence point, but that two convergence patterns can be discerned: a symmetrical one, where concessions come from all sides, and an asymmetrical one where one party gives in noticeably more than the other. Obviously, these two archetypes represent poles of a continuum, with mixed cases of varying degrees in the middle.

From what has been said, then, a further proposition can be advanced (3):

> convergence will be asymmetrical toward one party's position if it is considered preferable to no agreement by the other party, and if the one party shows that their real alternatives are worse for the other party. There will be no convergence if one party holds to positions not considered by the other party to be preferable to no agreement. Convergence will tend to be symmetrical if the two parties' positions are coincident, complementary, or if both parties prefer an agreement to holding out on unacceptable positions.

Another proposition will add (4):

> the closer one party holds to its own positions, the greater the risk of rupture but the greater the chance of gain. The party can aim for convergence asymmetrical to its side when the risk of rupture is small, that is, when the other side values an agreement more than a particular position, or when the value of agreement as compared with no agreement is slight.

As a result in negotiations it seems to be less important to sell one's own position than to eliminate alternatives, either by showing why the other party's positions are unacceptable or why one's own only real alternatives are worse than its current positions – in other words, by showing that better alternatives are impossible and possible alternatives are worse for the other party. Commitments and obligations, promises and predictions, faits accomplis and incapabilities are evoked to indicate what is possible; threats and warnings are used to show what is less favorable.

It has been possible to advance a few propositions by using the concepts, "alternatives," "convergence," and "symmetry/asymmetry." Clearly, these have not led far toward a comprehensive theory of negotiations, but, hopefully, they have opened a path of some usefulness and greater promise. These propositions are still close to the notion of "success," and hence recall the need for paying attention to the "principles" school of diplomacy. Just as advances in the physical study of impact on objects and the biochemical study of muscles have not outmoded lessons on how to play tennis, so the principles approach in negotiations will continue to be important for the foreseeable future even though a systematic theory of negotiations' may be constructed. But hopefully the alternative/convergence approach to the study of negotiations and the theoretical propositions derived from it can be used to understand better the confrontation of diplomatic skills.

Weak and strong

The original question was: how can the weak negotiate with the strong, considering that the weak are both weak and needy and the strong are both strong and rich (For relevant cases, see Nogee 1963; Zartman 1964a, 1964b; Friedheim 1965; McWhiney 1966; Houben 1967). To this question was added the suggestion that the weak in fact do have ways of finding strength in negotiations, or at least, have ways of turning their weakness to their advantage. The results of their negotiations, as reviewed here, confirm that the weak can win a good deal, not necessarily in comparison with their endless growing needs, but in more relevant comparisons with what other rich states were doing, or with what the weak states had before, or with various initial points in the negotiations. A review of these negotiations has also suggested ways of analyzing negotiations in general, which can then be played back and reapplied to give some answers to the original question.

Even at this point, however, the analysis brings out some caveats. "Strong" and "weak" are of course caricatures, as are the other pairs of words used to describe the two sides: "old"–"new," "developed"–"underdeveloped," "large"–"small," "colonial"–"anticolonial," "rich"–"poor." Better would be a mammoth matrix combining all these variables and checking their coincidence with various types of behavior.) (cf. Rosenau 1967). But even this would not give a proper answer on power, since power is relative and situational, leaving the relation and the situation to be defined. The cases studied here are both similar and different enough to be comparative; yet they are not typical of all weak/strong confrontations in negotiations. The relations between the sides were friendly; the stakes were mostly positive-sum and hence the negotiations were of the extension-innovation type (Ikle 1964); there was a commitment to success (but not time limit); there was no military pressure behind the negotiations; there was scarcely any "East–West" ingredient. On the other hand, the negotiations were typical of a large span of postcolonial and developmental relations; the issues were political as well as economic, and were strongly "North–South" in nature.

The eight paired ways of limiting alternatives line up rather neatly into strong and weak state columns, with only one surprise. Strong states tended to make more use of volitional means of gratifying and depriving – promise and threat whereas weak states relied on nonvolitional means – prediction and warning. The reason is obvious, almost circular: strong states had the goods to deliver, whereas weak states could only point to new gratifications created by the agreement itself or deprivations that would be the dire consequences of *force majeur*. Similarly, the strong states used commitments more frequently and more successfully, while the weak states invested more successful energies into obligating others than in committing themselves. This use was dictated more by the direction of demands than by the balance of strength: as givers, the strong states could both afford and hide behind commitments, while the weak states were askers and were more interested in tying down the others. The surprise comes with the last pair. It might first be expected that the weak states would plead simple incapacity and the strong states use fait accompli, by their very natures. On the contrary, the strong states frequently tried to plead simple incapacity, since they were the ones being asked to make an effort for the others, while the weak both practiced fait accompli – a sign of new sovereignty that it would have been impolitic to contest – and suffered from it (usually at the hands of time, as they waited for the strong to make up their minds).

A bit fuller description will put some of these means into more recognizable garb. The obligations that the weak states attempted to impose on the strong were moral in nature, and evidenced moral power (Feld 1966, p. 580). How much power, of course, depends on the standard of comparison: perhaps the strong states "should" do more, but at least they do do something. France was able to make a commitment to inaction that repelled any attempt at obligation in regard to Guinea, but such a case is unique. While it is true that one never knows if moral obligations are "real" motivations, since man has a habit of couching his motivations in moral terms in order to hide crasser reasons, such behavior is by the same token no proof that crasser reasons are "real" either and that soul-saving is not the "realest" reason of all. A sounder level of analysis indicates that weak states in fact tried to pin moral obligations on the strong (not having any other kind), and the strong repeated the same reasoning when acting.

Similarly, the threats that the strong used took the form of the take-it-or-leave-it packages with which the weak were presented. The strong states certainly had no intention of handing ultimatums to the weak; the package came out of the dynamics of the three-dimensional negotiations, in which the strong had to agree among themselves before facing the weak. A Senegalese is supposed to have said (and in any case a Nigerian quoted): "When Europe is divided, Africa pays; when it is united as now, Africa also pays." (Witkin 1969). African unity was under terrible strains, including those of newness, poverty, competitiveness, and the pressure to unite initially around "more" (since they were generally the askers) while the strong states were coming together about "less" (since they were the givers and since their viability, stability, and development were not at stake). Thus, the weak were constantly forced to reverse and water down, as they were drawn toward the convergence point of the strong, who were bound to unanimity. The strong's commitment backed the threat that accompanied their promise.

Unity was also related to alternatives, in a curious way. It is no coincidence that the single weak state had the greatest freedom of choice and the largest group had the fewest alternatives. Unity reduces alternatives, even though it can strengthen commitment to a single choice. Any one weak state could find security for itself in the wake of some other strong state. But no strong state could take on a new responsibility for a whole group, which would bring more needs than assets. The rule appears to be almost mathematical from the four cases: the two groups of three states had considerably (sixfold?) more latitude than the Eighteen and (a third?) less than the one; one of the groups of three maintained a high degree of latitude through disunity, and the other lost flexibility and time through the need to agree among themselves.

In the process of convergence, understandings and coincidence both came into use, but the typical pattern of agreement involved mostly concessions and counterconcessions. This pattern generally began with a weak state demand, which was met by a strong state offer involving some concession from the publicly announced initial points of the component members. The weak states then made a counterconcession, involving an acceptance of the offer under protest or after several rejections; the strong state move was then a slight improvement of the offer without changing the basic terms of reference. The alternative pattern was a series of coincidences, in which both weak and strong whittled at the common position, although in the case where this occurred, weak and strong were more nearly equal since the weak side needed agreement less than the strong side felt it did. During this process, negotiations also move through different levels, normally from principles through questions and answers to details. In this change of levels, the strong states also had control. If there was no coincidence or convergence on the principles, they reversed the order and turned to details until the principles fell into place.[8] The weak states could always break off talks, although that was a rather minimal exercise of power if it did not force the other side to give in (as it did not). Not only were the weak unable to bend the strong significantly by walking out; in addition, it was actually the weak that felt the pressure of passing time more painfully than did the strong. Thus, rather than being able to boycott tactically, the weak had to press for procedural speed as well as substantive benefits, adding to the burden of their demands.

Where then does the power of weak states lie? In three areas, all of them procedural, and in one context. The context is the positive-sum negotiation. When there is a fixed pie to be redistributed, the weak are bound to lose. It is always in their interest to seek a non-zero-sum terrain for negotiations, where even if they get less than they think they deserve, they at least get something more than they had in the beginning. The three areas of strength suggest that the weak states do have the power to choose their terrain, the choice being a procedural matter.

First, weak states can provoke an encounter. By their mere existence and membership in the world community and its organizations, they can influence agendas. Whether the question is independence and decolonization, or fair-trade practices, or the negotiation of an agreement, they can raise the point. Second, they can put forward their needs, with all the self-generating pressures that such demands arouse in a world convinced of its problem-solving role. Needs tend to have an almost self-negotiating power; they become a challenge, a moral pang of practical dimensions that is quite different from the humanitarian heartburn of the past century. Such a characteristic must not be exaggerated, of course, but it contains an essential truth. Third, weak states have the power to agree, which means the power to gratify both in the psychological sense and the sense of bringing into being the newly allocated pie. Without their signature, neither the problem-solving satisfactions nor the material benefits can be achieved. Toward strong states, which feel they have a role as well as an opportunity and which have made initial commitments to success, such power is real. It represents, after all, the only expenditure that the weak states made in the negotiations studied. They gave no aid, lost no income, and probably even lost no real opportunities for industrial development. For the price of a diplomatic staff in Brussels,[9] they provoked an encounter, made their demands, and accepted what was offered to them, removing any tinge of mendacity by seriously proclaiming it was not enough, figures in hand. That is a respectable exercise of power by the weak over the strong.

2 The 50% solution[10]

Ours is an age of negotiation. The fixed positions and solid values of the past seem to be giving way, and new rules, roles, and relations have to be worked out. The hard lines and easy cognitive recognition systems of the Cold War have first multiplied and then melted, revealing the necessity and the possibility of talking things over and out. Even lesser conflicts whose issues used to be nonnegotiable and where friend and enemy once were easily identifiable – such as those of the divided nations, the Indians and the Pakistanis, even the Arabs and Israelis – are showing themselves susceptible to discussion. It has been asserted that ideology is waning, which means that dogmatic formulas, strong feelings of righteousness, black-and-white perceptions, beliefs in historical inevitability, and disinclinations to compromise are all being softened. Instead, people become aware that they share both goals and problems, and that a useful way of achieving separate as well as joint ends is through discussion and bargaining. People and nations who, it was said, knew their place, before are questioning that concept, and individuals and countries who were inclined to put others in their place in the past are no longer sure of their power or of the proper order of things. New orders must therefore be defined.

Two types of situations characterize this age. One involves a transition from one order of things to another. When existing systems prove inadequate for current needs, replacements must be devised or defined, invented or discovered. Either relations need restructuring to meet some future image of desirable affairs, or their new form must be ratified to reflect real changes that have already taken place. Conceptually, these efforts are shaped by justice, as the basis of the future ideal, and by power, as the past determinant of reality, and so justice and power become basic elements in the process of negotiation that characterizes the transition. Few would doubt that the current age is one of transition, although a transition to what is not always clear. From bipolarity to polycentrism, from colonialism to independence, from nuclear stalemate to disarmament, from a single gold standard to floating currencies – these are all changes, none of them yet completed, that were in process when the fourth quarter of the last century began and are still present as the first quarter of the new millennium begins. The transition, in each case, requires negotiation.

The other type of situation involves a change from fixed rules and roles to flexible ones. If the existing order proves inadequate, the replacement may be not a new order but an absence of set systems, a "transition" so prolonged as to appear permanent. The shift to a dynamic from a static system characterizes many current developments. Those who see permanent revolution in the American or Russian system, or in the cultural revolution of China, identify this type of change. The process of economic development, with its takeoff and self-sustaining growth, incorporates such a dynamic equilibrium, and to the extent that political or social development can be conceived on a parallel image, it too involves a shift from defined to continually redefined relations. Even within established institutions, the dominant *modus operandi* is often one of bargaining and accommodation, as studies of the World Court, the World Bank, and the American foreign policy process have shown (Gross 1962; Coplin 1969; Baldwin 1965; Allison 1971). In such cases, negotiation becomes not a transition but a way of life, with a continuing role for power and justice.

These characteristics, and the associated process of negotiation, are often identified with diplomacy and international relations, as many of the examples illustrate, but the age of negotiation extends deeper down into domestic life. The most obvious occurrence is in labor relations, where collective bargaining has overtaken the unilateral use of power – through edict or strike – to determine wages and working conditions. But negotiation has replaced other decision-making processes in other areas of domestic governance than simply labor relations. Adversary pleading and adjudication have been joined and partially replaced by plea bargaining in the courts and negotiated settlements out of court. Even the bureaucratic domain has been invaded by demonstrations and sit-ins that require explanation and group decision-making. Election and legislation still remain important parts of governance, but behind each lies a process of bargaining and horse-trading that is clearly negotiatory. Indeed, in the wake of Watergate, President Gerald Ford proclaimed a motto of "communication, conciliation, compromise, and co-operation," negotiation politics more appropriate to this era than the politics of victory and defeat.

More surprising is the new predominance of negotiation as a form of decision-making in nonpolitical areas where other orders have traditionally reigned. "Rapping" has crept into American life at all levels. Wherever action was designated by command – in the schoolroom, the family, the hospital, even the Army – new styles have added more collective and participatory ways of arriving at decisions. Followers, obeyers, conformers, and workers have become demanders, discussants, contestants, and participants in a shift of roles and processes that clearly reflects a shift in rules and accepted ways and orders.

Indeed, some have seen such changes as particularly characteristic of all America. Herbert Gans, writing in the New York *Times Magazine* (6 February 1972), noted that in America the gap between aspirations and expectations was closing, but the gap between expectations and achievement has increased.

As a result, matters previously decided by fiat, consensus or the application of traditional values now have to be negotiated, and in many ways America has become a negotiating society ... Politicization and the demand for negotiation not only complicate the life of the political decision-maker but also contribute to the malaise. They bring political conflict out in the open, raising popular awareness of the conflict, and increasing the dissatisfaction of those on the losing end. In this view, the current concern with conflict-solving processes only increases conflict.

Yet the age of negotiations continues. On a "typical" day such as 27 March 1973, when the lead story in the newspaper was about the final agreement for the release of the Vietnam prisoners negotiated by the Four-party Joint Military Commission in Saigon, other front-page news included the failure of the Saigon and Vietcong delegations to agree on an agenda for negotiations leading to a national election, the opening of the twenty-state ministerial commission in Geneva to negotiate world monetary reform, and the agreement of striking students to begin negotiations of grievances with university authorities in Athens. Other stories in the same issue of the newspaper noted that public protest over the Forest Hills housing project had abated in a year of negotiation and compromise, lawyers for Joan Baez and David Harris were negotiating a divorce settlement, Connecticut bus service was restored after a new agreement was negotiated, and "the atmosphere of the National Invitation Tournament is becoming more and more like a high pressure market place where college basketball scholarships are up for grabs, coaches are job-hunting, and agents and pro scouts are in almost constant negotiation."

At the end of the year, on the day the world prepared to commemorate the Armistice negotiated to end World War I, the French newspaper *Le Monde,* in another "typical" day's reporting, carried articles on the acceptance of the Kissinger plan by Egypt and Israel, the consideration of periodical European Community summit meetings, a negotiating session between Chancellor Brandt and President Sadat, a schedule for Nixon Round tariff negotiations, the breakdown of collective bargaining in the Netherlands, and, in France, attempts by professional unions to negotiate with government representatives, by trade unions and left-wing parties to reach an agreement on priority goals, and by strikers at the Renault factory to win a raise. Other such typical days could be chosen at random to show that the age of negotiations is worldwide.

If negotiation is such a pervasive aspect of modern life, it is important to understand what goes on in the process, what the accompanying characteristics are, and how outcomes are determined. Since the process is not a new invention, one would expect to find a good deal of study and wisdom accumulated on the subject, and indeed there is. At the same time, however, more recent modes of scholarship have only begun to develop to their fullest in the analysis of negotiation, since its pervasive characteristic is only a recent phenomenon. It is therefore appropriate to turn attention to this important political process, first to understand its nature and then to examine the various ways in which it has been analyzed. In the end, we are interested in understanding how the political process works and how negotiators make their decisions – as distinguished from other political processes or ways of making decisions – or at least in learning what we have left to learn to find out these answers.

We are also interested in providing analytical tools and examples to facilitate further work by others for the analysis of the variety of negotiating experiences in more helpful terms. The most striking fact about the subject is the small number of studies available, and the large communications gap between those who practice negotiations and those who study it. The two aspects are related. Most works today fall into two categories: the descriptive account of the encounter and the abstract conceptual study or experiment on the theoretical phenomenon. The first is often uninteresting to the scholar, and the second is incomprehensible to the negotiator. Perhaps even more striking, there has been little attempt to bring the two together, as people or as studies. Possibly because the theoretical, conceptual, and methodological work has only been establishing itself with some confidence in the 1950s and 1960s, there have been very few studies of real-life encounters that use or test notions derived from theoretical or experimental studies.

This collection is compiled in the hope of inspiring or challenging further work in this direction. It would be comforting to be able to note that the two traditional areas of interest in negotiation – diplomacy and labor relations – provide enough solid studies for students to be able to proceed to newer subjects. Yet this is not so: few diplomatic encounters have received adequate study, and there are almost no detailed accounts of labor-management negotiation cases. Access to information, as much as conceptual sophistication, remains a problem in both areas. In the area of newer subjects, the family as a negotiating situation, hostage and holdup bargaining, the drafting of a resolution in committee, patterns of market haggling, comparative typologies of colonial independence negotiations, commodity agreements, and auction behavior can all be studied with rigor and imagination within a negotiation framework of analysis.

Negotiation defined

Negotiation has been defined in many ways, but most of the definitions contain common components. To begin with, negotiation is considered one of the basic processes of *decision-making*, along with legislation and adjudication, among others (see Dahl 1955; Coddington 1973). That is to say, it is a dynamic or moving event, not simply a static situation, and an event concerning the selection of a single value out of many for implementation and action. This decision-making event is a sociopolitical process involving several parties, and not simply one individual's making up their mind.

But now three additional components of this process-event have been brought to the light. One is the *parties* or sides that engage in the process as actors. Whether groups or individuals, they may be conceived of as having their own internal dynamics, but it is the interaction among parties that interests the analyst of negotiations in the first place. Second is the element of *values* or interests or demands presented by the parties for the purpose of collective choice. Such values are "things" that matter to the parties and may be positive or negative, as benefits and costs. Third is the *outcome*, which presents a slightly more complicated matter to conceptualize. Negotiations may be successful or unsuccessful, depending on whether or not a single agreed value has been chosen as the result of the process; an agreement is acceptable as *prima facie* evidence of "success," since it can be assumed that no party would agree to a value that they viewed as being worse than the value of nonagreement. But successful or unsuccessful, any negotiation has an outcome, in the sense of an agreed, jointly-determined value, even if that outcome is only the breakoff of negotiation and the agreement to disagree. (Unilateral break off, however, may prove a special case.) This view of outcomes raises further problems, which will be dealt with later, but it is a helpful and logical component of the present definition.

A final logical element is *mutual movement,* the beginning point in the process and one that is conceptually necessary only to separate the event from a mere situation. It will be assumed that negotiation begins when some movement has taken place from the parties' initial positions, since it is common sense that merely stating positions does not constitute negotiation, much as it may lead to it. However, once admitted, this assumption creates other definitional limitations that will prove useful to analysis. It means that if one side does not give in at all but forces the other side to make all the concessions, *diktat* and not negotiation has taken place, even though other elements of the definition appear to apply (see Lall 1966, p. 288). Actually, this assumption is not as restrictive as might appear, since there are few such encounters in the real world in which one side does not give in a little, even if the other does give in a lot.

These four elements – parties, values, outcomes, and movement – are crucial to an understanding of negotiation, but they do not distinguish it from other basic political processes. All four are common to the two other modes of decision-making – legislation and adjudication – but other elements mark the difference. Legislation or voting involves a twofold choice (pass–fail) and so represents a zero-sum situation; values are constant, and decision is made by aggregating a larger number of the parties on one side than on the other; the immediate source of power is therefore found in numbers of parties (and size, in weighted-vote situations) and their order of appearance. Adjudication or choosing involves a single choice out of a plural or infinite field; there is only one party involved in the choosing, and so there is a conflict only in values, not in parties. It should be clear that these terms are being used as conceptual labels for separate theoretical modes of decision-making and not as descriptive summaries for all that goes on in a parliament or a court, for, as already suggested, these bodies in the real world engage in mixed processes. In order for the distinction to be pursued, it is necessary to identify the additional elements that are peculiar to negotiation, assumptions that both definitionally and operationally provide the necessary and sufficient conditions for its occurrence (for a similar exercise, see Rapoport 1966, pp. 18–21).

The first assumption is the *mixed-motive* nature of the process. Most studies of negotiations, from the implicit wisdom of de Callières and De Felice to the explicit analysis of Nash and Rapoport, note that negotiations take place when common and conflicting goals are present among the parties. If the situation were only one of conflicting goals, it would be impossible for the process to begin and hence impossible to analyze it. The moment there is a decision to negotiate, there is *prima facie* evidence of at least one common goal (the agreement itself). On the other hand, if the situation were one of common goals only, it would be uninteresting. At most, agreement would be a matter of discovery, and although discovery is a common aspect of the negotiation's interchange of views, it is scarcely the only component of the process. There is also a third category of values (beyond the residual category of those things that neither side cares about), which may be termed complementary, values that matter only to one side or to the other but not to both, and that can be used as tradeoffs against each other during the negotiating process. Some such values are sometimes called side payments by game theorists, but too little attention has been paid to them within the process of negotiations.

Although it is in both parties' interest to reach agreement on an acceptable reallocation of values, it is also in the interest of each to end up with as much of the pile as it can or to give up as little and gain as much as possible, depending on whether the reference is to a single contested value or to several exchangeable or complementary values. Nevertheless, as the previous assumption on satisfactory outcomes indicated, the expected value of the outcome to each side, and hence the total value of the outcome, must be positive, or there would be no incentive to engage in negotiations or to accept the outcome. In negotiations, both parties win (are better off than at no agreement) or they would not come to agreement; they are not competing for an unsharable victory, as in a vote. Each party wants the other to be satisfied too, not because they care about each other per se, but so that the other will make and keep the agreement that gives the first party its share. Thus, the second assumption is the *nonzero-sum* nature of the encounter.

To yield a non-zero sum, either things must be valued differently by the different parties or there must be side payments that are newly available because of the agreement. In the first case, each party presumably gives up its less valued items in exchange for items it values more, or gives up a part of the single value it prizes in order to get (as it otherwise would not) the remainder, again depending on whether it is complementary or contested values that are at stake. As Homans' (1961, p. 62) maxim has it:

> The more the items at stake can be divided into goods valued more by one party than they cost to the other and goods valued more by the other party than they cost to the first, the greater the chances of successful outcome.

In the second case, the agreement itself must be counted as a good, since it is the successful outcome that creates the situation for the realization of the other positive values. "The goal of the participants in a mixed-motive or bargaining situation," according to Gruder (in Swingle 1970, p. 111), "is to reach some agreement as to how to divide between themselves the total outcome available from their relationship." In many cases, the "opportunity benefit" 'of the agreement (as opposed to opportunity costs) is the most important value, since the absence of a peace treaty or cease-fire would mean more war.

It may be easier to portray this assumption by a few examples. The simplest situation for negotiation is the one where a quantity of goods is made available to two parties provided they can agree on an acceptable allocation of the goods between themselves. It may be a matter of a handful of candy offered to John and Mary or of Algeria's iron deposits at Tindouf, which are only economically available if they can be evacuated through neighboring Morocco. If we stick with John and Mary as a schematic example, we might imagine initially that every piece of candy won by Mary would be a piece of candy lost to John, a typically zero-sum situation (line A–B in Figure 2.1). But that is not the whole story. It is more likely that both John and Mary would consider that any deviation to the advantage of the other party from an equitable standard such as a fifty-fifty division of the candy pile would require some additional compensation for the party with the smaller pile; this compensation could be made either through side payments, such as marbles, or through nonmaterial additions to the values involved, such as appeals to rights and to reason. *The farther the deviation from the solution of justice, the more side payments required,* resulting in a nonzero-sum situation. Thus a contested-value encounter is likely to give a concave negotiations front (line M–N).

A more complex situation – if only because there are more values involved – concerns the complementary values encounter. If Bill and Jack decide to barter their prized possessions, they will do so only if and in ways that each will be better off at the end (Nash 1950). Unlike the encounter as described between John and Mary, Bill and Jack can be better off

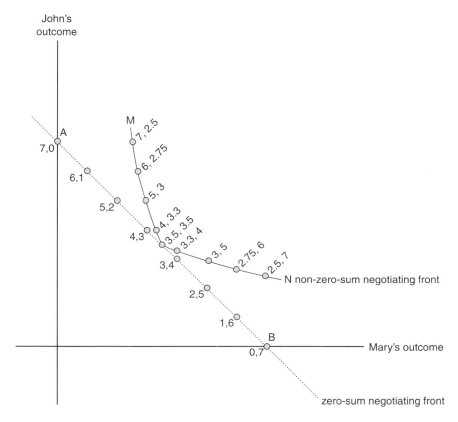

Figure 2.1 Negotiating fronts.

because they value the goods involved differently; Jack can buy some things he values highly with goods that he values less than those he receives, and vice versa. An evaluation or utility scale might look as follows:

Using the same device, there are two ways of portraying this situation. The origin of the graph can be put at zero, as in John and Mary's encounter. But unlike John and Mary, Jack and Bill have a fallback position – a security or threat point (A in Figure 2.2) – that is, greater than zero, since even with no agreement they have goods – valued at 6 and 12, respectively. In the second portrayal, the origin can be placed at the security point, and the graph will portray value gains or losses. Again, however, the negotiation's front or indifference curve will be positive, although this time convex.

If negotiation were merely a matter of arriving at an acceptable reallocation of a given set of values between their owners, two simple utility scales listing how much each value is worth to each party would show a clear result in most cases. This result (point M in Bill's and Jack's horse trading) is known as the Nash Point and is located at the place where the

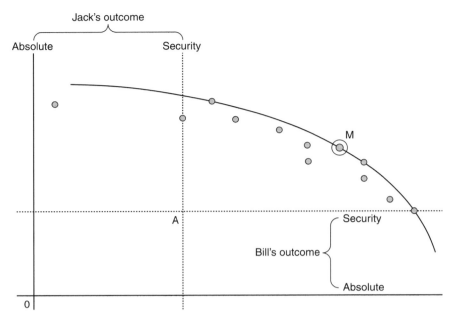

Figure 2.2 Pareto-optimality and the negotiating front. Outcomes not on the negotiating front are not Pareto-optimal since one party can improve its positions – by advancing to the front – without depriving the other.

product of the parties' values is the greatest. Under such assumptions, the study of negotiation could be reduced to a study of outcome and ignore process. But reality is not that simple, and it is three additional complexities that separate the study of negotiations from the current body of efforts to analyze a more stylized type of bargaining. Since it is in each party's interest to get a little more while giving a little less, and, in Homans' terms, to value the things it is giving a little less than those it is getting, it is also in each party's interest to control each other's knowledge of its own utility lists. Thus, a third assumption is *imperfect information*, with the amount of information and its veracity under control of the parties involved. Indeed, since negotiation is by nature a communications encounter, not a physical encounter (like war) or a mechanical encounter (like voting) or some other sort, the controlled exchange of partial information is the very essence of its decision-making process.

The verbal encounter of the process is not designed to reveal a given reality, in this case a fixed hierarchy of utilities. Instead, it is designed to shape a new reality, for the values in question are at least partially alterable as well as partially unknown. While many parties enter negotiations with a rather firm notion of what they want under what terms, they are quite unlikely to come out of the encounter with all of these values intact.

More precisely, it is definitionally impossible that both sides emerge with both their shopping lists and budgets filled. If they do, it is not negotiations that will have taken place, but, again, simple discovery. If controlled communication is the essence of negotiation, the essence of that communication is *variable values*, the fourth assumption of negotiation. As a result, it unfortunately becomes very difficult to portray the process analytically as a simple matter of scales and curves (see Valavanis 1958; Ikle and Leites 1962). The single-function negotiation curve or frontier or set so commonly used is at best an illustration, not a depiction, and a misleading one at that, for – like the other commonly used device, the matrix – it shows value choices as unalterable givens. Such illustrations are graphic and convenient, and have heuristic value, but must be used advisedly lest they be taken literally to the point of distorting the analysis. Thus, John might well be able to convince Mary that she doesn't like chocolates in red wrappers or, in the old days, that as a male he deserved or needed more chocolates than she, and Bill would try to persuade Jack that one can play ball without a bat or read a book without a whip. Kissinger has said that the main obstacle to agreement in the Nixon–Brezhnev summit conference of 1974 on permanent limitations for offensive nuclear arms was the difficulty of agreeing upon how to balance missile vs. warhead totals (*New York Times,* 5 July 1974). Such problems must be portrayed through new value diagrams, assuming it is possible in the first place to give accurate portrayals to evaluations, for they represent efforts to alter rather than work within the given negotiation set.

But even within the given evaluations, Mary might decide that she doesn't want John to have more than a particular number of chocolates because they are bad for his health (without her valuing them more highly for herself), and Bill might discover that he would be better off if he didn't give up his ball in exchange for the pen, toy, and knife, just as Jack would be better off if he didn't give up his knife in order to get the book, whip, ball, and bat. These new problems in the negotiation process introduce the most important and most misunderstood element, the matter of *power*.

In the verbal and nonverbal exchanges that comprise negotiation, information is manipulated for the purpose of changing the other party's evaluation of the values involved, in order to bring about convergence or agreement at a point more favorable to one side than to the other. Power is defined as the volitionally controlled ability of one party to produce such movement or re-evaluation on the part of the other party, often more generally as the ability of one party to cause another to change behavior in an intended direction. Such a definition indicates neither a thing nor a variable, nor even a thing symbolizing a relationship, but an "ability." It is merely a label for a causal relation, an area for inquiry rather than a concept of inquiry. Hence, on the first round, the identification of power as an assumption of negotiation has led back simply to a search for a causal explanation for the movement that produces outcomes.

The matter should be pursued further, however. There are at least two ways of handling the assumption that outcomes do not just happen but are caused. One is to rephrase the question as, What is the best variable to explain outcomes and to look for a causal theory. There is no overabundance of such theories, but a few of them have been devised, notably those in terms of concession rates and utilities (Cross 1969; Edgeworth 1881; Zeuthen 1930). These will be reviewed at appropriate places following. Their general characteristic, within this discussion, however, is that, paradoxically, they have no place for the connotations of will and skill that hover about the term "power." Quite the opposite, as all the causal theories and explanatory variables devised to date are "cataclysmic," in Coddington's word (1968, p. 79); once the process has been set into motion, it runs its course and determines its outcomes, impervious to any human tinkering. (Another generic criticism that can be made, as Hamermesh has done in this volume, is that the variables in terms of which the theory explains outcomes are inoperationalizable, a separate point that will also be taken up later.) There is one set of theories that is not impervious to human hands in the same sense, however, since they depend entirely on choice strategies. But these, the game theory explanations of outcomes, cannot answer the original question about the cause of outcomes, either, since they have nothing to do with process; they explain only why a particular choice is made (in terms of their assumptions about rationality) among given values, not the process of changing behavior by altering those values. They too are cataclysmic, since the choice is determined by an array of potential outcomes that is given.

The other way of meeting the causal question in terms closer to the common-sense connotations of "power" is to identify the types of human behavior, the settings in which they are effective, and the resources they use, in causing other human behavior to change. The operational assumption of this approach is that bargaining behavior causes and is caused by other bargaining behavior, and so the main variable is identified. The qualifications – type, setting, and source – are important, since they break down the concept of power into analytical components, permitting refinement and testing of the general proposition that certain types of action, employing certain resources in certain situations, have certain effects on the other party (who in turn initiates and responds with actions that can be analyzed in the same way).

This restatement of the problem also gets over the major conceptual dispute over power as a possession and power as a relation. It has already been seen that power is neither a thing nor a variable. Contrary to common usage, power is not something one "has." In this sense, the original definition is misleading, since grammatically one can "have" a capability. Indeed, too many of the standard discussions of power, such as Dahl's or March's or Harsanyi's, say that it is something "A *has* over B" (in Bell *et al.* 1969, pp. 80, 181, 239). However, there is something that a negotiator can have in regard to power, and that is resources, which they use in a particular way to create a causal relationship. Thus it is more nearly correct to say that power is a relation. Yet within even that understanding, what the analyst really wants to know is what causes the relation or the effect of one party on the other. To be complete, an explanation must not merely correlate effects or assert a causative relation, but also must, in its chosen terms, tell what it is in one element that causes another. Hence the identification of "power" as a causative relation leads one back to the search for components and variables, such as resources (base), their use (means), and the setting. In this circular confusion, it is as much the common-sense vs. the analytical semantics of the term that causes the trouble as anything else. What is idiomatic ("to have power over someone") is not scientific, and what is scientific ("to be in power" – i.e., a causal relationship – toward someone) is hardly idiomatic.

The last aspect of the power confusion relates to the setting of process vs. outcomes. "Power is present" in a negotiation situation when one party shifts another from its initial positions and toward the positions of the first party, because the first party has caused the second to move. Such a notion allows the analyst to compare the amount of movement effected by each party, as an index of the ability of each to cause the other to change, or, in other words, of their power. But effect is not cause, only an indicator of it (just as, in regard to power as a possession, resources are not use, but only a basis for it). From movement, one can infer a motivating force, but one cannot tell what it is in the "ability" that causes the movement. To do so, the analyst must look into the process, not simply the outcomes.

Furthermore, it has already been seen that there are some theories that explain "natural" outcomes through a cataclysmic process, without taking power into account. Thus, there are already partial explanations accounting for some of the movement, rendering an examination of outcomes alone a poor measure of power. It may therefore be more useful to the understanding of the role of agent causality to explain deviation from cataclysmic processes and outcomes rather than simply change from initial positions.

In summary, the recognition that there is a volitional causal relationship between parties negotiating over values that accounts for movement from beginning to outcome leads to a search for explanatory elements in the type, basis, and setting of related behaviors. It is only by looking into negotiators' behavior that negotiated outcomes can be explained. The operational problem that remains is how to translate different types of behavior, using different resources very differently, into comparable elements for analysis.

Outcomes explained

The problem of explaining the outcomes of negotiation has intrigued students for centuries, but little progress toward a solution has been achieved until recently. Probably the reason is that for a long time analysts asked their questions and sought their answers in terms of single cases and so were thrown back to situational and historical descriptions of essentially unique events. Only with the attention that economists brought to more abstract analysis of general situations in symbolic or mathematical language has the interest turned to theoretical answers and to the analysis of negotiation rather than the study of particular negotiations. These attempts have been a step in the right direction, but they pose two further questions: what is the best variable for analyzing the process? How can theoretical variables be translated into practical terms? In their search for the proper variable in terms of which to explain the process, modern analysts have produced a number of different approaches to analysis and theory. That search continues, for, despite all claims, there is not yet a satisfying theory of negotiation and, perhaps even more important for the present discussion, there is still no explanation in terms of fully operationalizable variables that can be applied to real cases.

The interesting questions are simple enough. What caused a particular outcome? This is the basic challenge underlying any account of negotiations. Generalized into a more abstract analytical inquiry, the question becomes, what causes particular outcomes? When a complete answer to this question has been devised, it can be said that the outcomes are determinate within a theory or causal explanation. If the answer can be calculated in probabilities, the outcomes can be called partially determinate within a stochastic theory.

The problem of determinate models, like the problem of any theory, is that explanations must be given in terms of relevant variables – variables that are independent, meaningful, applicable, and evaluable (even if not necessarily measurable). There are perfectly sound explanations of winning at negotiations "because the winner is stronger" or "because the winner is more skillful." But even if they were not circular, these would not tell us much, since it has been impossible thus far to operationalize "strength" or "skill" satisfactorily. Thus, de Callières (1963[1716], p. 42), one of the best early analysts of negotiating skills, advises every student of negotiation to read the Letters of Cardinal Arnaud d'Ossat (1698),

> one of the most profitable readings I know for this purpose ... He will see how Monseigneur d'Ossat profited by everything, how he is firm as a rock when necessity demands, supple as a willow at another moment, and how he possessed the supreme art of making every man offer him as a gift that which it was his chief design to secure.

Unfortunately, we still do not know when necessity demands rockiness and when it demands willowiness, or of what is composed that admittedly crucial art.

There is a way in which clearer distinction can be forced on common-sense concepts, and that is through comparison or the use of parallel cases. By conducting several case studies, chosen for their similarity in a number of important aspects, the analyst can relate the differences in outcome to the remaining differences in "input" into the cases. Such attempts at control are simply efforts to move a bit closer toward the scientific experiment, sacrificing some science for realism without any of the reverse. Such studies as Young's (1968) on a series of international crises, Randle's (1973) on ending hostilities, George *et al.* (1971) on coercive diplomacy, or Zartman's (1971) of five rounds of Eurafrican negotiations allow concentration on a few variables, while others are held constant or controlled. They try to avoid being dominated by the event rather than by the analysis, as they do something more than simply letting the whole encounter speak for itself in terms of its intuitively most striking features. They follow a selective focus on variables identified beforehand, and hence are attempts to answer the causal question in chosen terms, while operating within the explanatory chronology of the historical event.

Attainment of outcomes

In the end, outcome can never be understood without an investigation of the means by which negotiating positions are inflected. The point missed by both strategic and processual models is that the participating parties to negotiations are people making decisions on how to change the others' stands and undergoing the effects of the others' decisions for the same purpose. The process is neither a matter of independent choices nor one of inexorable mechanisms but one of choice and mechanism related. For this, more work is needed in the aspect of power that is most relevant to negotiations, that of political persuasion.

Persuasion involves *contingent gratification and deprivation*. While immediate gratification and deprivation are occasionally used in negotiation, primarily to change reality or confirm credibility as an adjunct to bargaining (see George *et al.* 1971; Schelling 1966), delayed obligation imposed by a present agreement for future benefits is more common. Even where past events *(faits accomplis)* are used for persuasion, it is the implicit idea of gratification or deprivation involved in undoing them that provides the element of contingency. ("You know I can't do that" means "I want you to believe that the cost would be too high for me to do that.") It is this contingency that makes persuasion a matter of *commitment* (of one's self) or *obligation* (of the other), arid hence a matter of some uncertainty. (On the importance of uncertainty, see Schelling 1966.)

Contingent sanctions used for persuasion fall further into two types, those referring to volitional acts and those referring to nonvolitional events. The difference between volitional *threats* ("I'll cut off your cabbage supply if you don't come to terms") and nonvolitional warnings ("Your people will starve if you don't come to terms") has been more frequently analyzed than the corresponding difference between *promises* ("I'll open up a cabbage credit for you if you come to terms") and *predictions* ("Your economy will prosper if you come to terms"). The threats and promises cited here have been stated as commitments, tying our hands; they can also be used as obligations, tying the other party's hands ("You announced that rejection of *your* association would mean exclusion from the cabbage trade," and "You have always extended massive cabbage credits to friendly countries," respectively). Interestingly, the common form of warnings and predictions is obligatory, constraining the other party, but these too can be stated as commitments, the one sometimes termed coercive deficiency ("My economy will collapse if you don't come to terms") and the other as yet unnamed ("My people will finally be able to defend themselves [against the common foe, for example] if you come to terms").

There are many advantages to a typological exercise of this kind. By isolating the exercise of persuasion within the power question, one is able to distinguish the use of specific tactical devices from the general search for causal explanations. Then again, the identification of such types of persuasion enables further inquiry into their properties such as that pursued by Schelling (1960, 1966), Fisher (1969), Lockhart (1974), Deutsch (1974), and Baldwin (1971c). The notion, for example, that "promises tend to cost more when they succeed, while threats tend to cost more when they fail" (Baldwin 1971c, p. 28) is an important implication of the original distinction that reveals in turn further, often paradoxical implications: bigger threats are cheaper than bigger promises, overthreat devalues credibility but overpromise devalues currency; bluff is an element of threat, not promise; gratification tends to lead to sympathy, continuity, exploitation, and blackmail, whereas deprivation tends to imply hostility, avoidance, and conditioning. Other propositions on the appropriateness of the various types of persuasion and their implications can be developed. Since theory involves the discovery of regular relationships among concepts, work of this type is a further step toward theory.

Furthermore such concepts have an important place in the total grasp of the negotiation process. If negotiation can be conceived as a process of mutually adjusting cost/benefit conditions or of inflecting utility curves, then the different means of persuasion can be portrayed as positive or negative values to be added onto the evaluations of the stakes under discussion. A threat to cut off the cabbage supply represents a presumably large negative increment to the threatened and probably a small negative increment to the threatener as well, whereas a promise to open a cabbage credit contains a presumably large positive increment for the promisee and a variable increment for the promisor. The side payments of persuasion attached to the original stakes become part of them. This formulation is not a theory, nor is it a recipe for assigning quantitative values to apples and oranges. But it is a conceptual means of handling both power and interest on the same plane, an important step toward the analysis of – the negotiation process.

The notion of contingency also allows further conceptual thinking about response and countermoves, as well as initial offers. On one hand, any offer can be met with a response that is either a defense or an attack. The defense would be to heighten the element of contingency or doubt about implementation. This could take the form of moral impediments at the sources ("You wouldn't do a thing like that because of your concern for your reputation") or physical impediments at the target ("You couldn't do a thing like that because we no longer eat cabbages" or "... because we grow our own"). The attack would take the form of a different means of persuasion launched to annul the initial move ("We will decrease – or increase – our supply to you of inkwells"). Particular means of persuasion are susceptible to particular forms of response, under certain conditions, providing hypothetical relations for research to verify.

A further possibility for analysis can also be introduced by identifying more clearly the value forms or "pressure points" to which the means of persuasion are applied. Any negotiator has three "points" in mind, his offering point and his acceptance point – the point of his current public bid for agreement and the minimum point that he would accept – plus his threat point or security point – the quantity available at no agreement.

But they are also aware that these three points are on the mind of the other party as well. Each party is therefore juggling their own offer, acceptance, and security points and their estimate of the other party's three points. Furthermore, these points are potentially movable, and hence defensible. A serious error of many portrayals of negotiation (and of some practitioners as well) has been to consider one or more of these points as fixed, thus missing an understanding both of the nature and of the opportunities of the process. It is the job of the means of persuasion to bring about – that is, to cause – this movement, against any defense or counter-move. By being attached, or added, to the latest bid (offering point) to make it more expensive or more rewarding to the bidder, to the other party's acceptance point to reduce their expectations, or to the security point to make their no-agreement position less satisfying than it originally appeared, the means of persuasion raise or lower the value of various alternatives and related reference points, and render other alternatives relatively more or less attractive. Negotiation then is a matter of bringing several "images into focus" by adding values to the original offers until desires and offers on both sides coincide, a much more complex reality than that analyzed by models based on concession rates or other changes in offering points alone.

Justifying outcomes

The discussion so far has been in Morgenthalian terms of power and interest, looking at actors and interactions and looking for the explanation of outcomes in party and process, structure and communication. But it has not provided any over arching criterion by which to judge negotiations, negotiators, or negotiated outcomes. Is there no justice? Earlier parts of the discussion have suggested that there is, and that it serves along with power as a limit to negotiation. In fact, there are several types of justice, each with a special type of limiting relationship to the process, although it will be seen that this very plurality reflects and expresses the basic impossibility of any overarching criterion, equivalent on its level to the absence of any underlying determinacy.

One kind of justice, the kind most frequently referred to, may be called substantive or partial justice. In any negotiating situation, each side believes that it represents the just solution, that the best outcome in a perfect world would be the adoption of its position, and that negotiation and compromise are necessary in the first place only because the forces of error, if not of evil, have enough power to prevent true justice from being enacted. Such a description is no caricature, and it is necessary to remind too fervent partisans of negotiation – from de Callières' gentlemen to Nicolson's shopkeepers to Morton Deutsch's cooperative personalities – that negotiation is required precisely because both sides think that they are right and the other wrong. Such feelings often interfere with analysis as well, when students of the process develop overly strong sympathies with one side and so have difficulty admitting that the "bad" side has used skills, strategies, or strengths that have enabled it to outdo the "good guys." Analytically, the argument enters the old and unnecessary domain of value-free research. There is a time for objective analysis of the negotiating process, like any other political process, in order to understand how it works. There is also a time for taking sides on substantive issues and using the analytical knowledge gained to good purpose. If "good purpose" may appear obvious in some situations, however, there are far many more over which there is never agreement or on which agreement changes with the context and the age. It is in the nature of the bumpy world that truths about the best way to achieve outcomes through negotiation will be available to good guys and bad alike, and that the "bad" may occasionally be "better" in procedural skills. That would seem to be all the more reason to find out how and why.

Substantive justice legitimizes inputs, but it does not explain outcomes. If presented as an explanation, it would exclude power, obviate process, and invalidate negotiation. As an ingredient among others in the process, however, it mobilizes power, and screens the use of the means of persuasion. It thus becomes very important to analysts and practitioners alike, as a source of power (as Underdal [1973] and others discuss). As a single explanatory or evaluative referent external to decision-making, justice has its own process, called adjudication, that is not negotiation but an alternative to it, with its own assumptions and analysis. (It should be noted that there is both a real and an analytical difference as well between two closely associated variants on these processes: arbitration, a form of adjudication, and mediation, a special catalytic form of negotiation – negotiation *à trois,* in which the third party has only procedural interests. A special literature has grown up on the subject of mediation but is not treated here; see Edmead 1971.)

There is, however, another kind of justice, which may be called procedural or impartial. Procedural justice is quite different from substantive, and if anything is more important to the negotiating process, it is the justice of the conciliator, the structural justice drawn from the basic equality of the parties found in the ideas of democracy and the Enlightenment, and it is antithetical to any notion of inherent or substantive justice in the stand of one party or the other. If substantive justice says one side, or each, is right and therefore deserves the entire outcome, procedural justice-recognizing the claims of both sides-says that the just solution lies in the middle. A number of studies have shown split-the-difference or its variants to be a "natural" solution and one that responds best to demands for a meeting of the minds or a reference point when all arguments have been exhausted and an equitable outcome is sought (Schelling 1960; Nash 1950). Yet the impartial justice of the midpoint is also an alternative to negotiation, a pure cooperation point in contrast to the pure conflict solutions of partial justice, the solution of Good Guys and Shopkeepers in a world free of Bad Guys and Warriors (Young 1968, pp. 25–6; Cross 1969, p. 42). Like the pure solution of partial justice, therefore, it can also serve analysis as a baseline or ideal solution, and is even more useful in this light since it represents a point of high legitimacy, deviation from which can be accounted for by the exercise of power.

The final aspect of justice is that it represents its own undoing: Evoked in a search for an overarching criterion for judging negotiations, it gradually leads the analyst into the same paradoxes, dilemmas, and components as did the study of power and interest. It has been seen that the study of justice must begin with a recognition of the claims to partial justice on each side, and must then proceed by reaction to the substantive incompatibility of these claims to a recognition of impartial justice in the middle. But just as impartial justice is an answer to the internal incompatibility of partial justice, so the search continues for an answer to the incompatibility of partial and impartial justice; one can no more enforce the two at the same time (and there is something to say – some justice – for each) than one can enforce both elements of partial justice at the same time. The search for an agreed *Olympian* solution has only complicated the problem. The answer then comes in a third and fourth type of solution, beginning first with an outcome of distributive justice. Combining elements of procedure and substance, this says that the outcome should be split, not equally, but according to need (Homans 1961). Distributive justice is antithetical to both partial and impartial justice, and its outcome – is not as immediately obvious as the other two. Since need is vulnerability and weakness, it is the strategy of the weak and seeks to use weakness as the basis for power – as a referent for the means of persuasion. The final type of solution should now be evident: it is the mirror image of distributive justice, and it says that the outcome should be split, neither equally nor by need, but according to the parties' ability to do without or according to their fallback position, or in other words according to their power (Shapley 1953). By now it can be seen that the argument has come full circle. The search for an irrefutable criterion for the right solution has led right back to the analysis of negotiation as an arena of power, in which legitimacy and process, need and power, are essential elements.

Thus to say that there is no just solution is in itself justification for negotiation, but it is also quite similar to saying that there is no determinate outcome. Indeed, it is quite impossible – or it is not yet possible – to indicate that, given X, a particular outcome will or should be attained, unless there is agreement beforehand on the assumptions of power and/or justice. Yet to obtain such agreement would mean merely transferring the negotiating problem to its analytical components and would neither determine nor justify anything at all. At the present point, barring new analytical breakthroughs, the process of negotiation remains operative within two limits that have been previously identified as running through the concepts of power, justice, and process itself. On one hand, negotiators seek to increase common interests and expand cooperation in order to broaden the area of agreement to cover the item under dispute. On the other, each seeks to maximize his own interest and prevail ill conflict, in order to make the agreement more valuable to themselves. No matter what angle analysis takes, it cannot eliminate the basic tension between cooperation and conflict that provides the dynamic of negotiation.

3 Negotiation as a joint decision-making process[11]

Negotiation is one of a limited number of decision-making modes whose characteristics, taken as assumptions, are not compatible with most of the theoretical work on negotiation to date. The concession/convergence approach has problems of symmetry, determinism, and power, but above all fails to reflect the nature of negotiation as practiced. Negotiators begin by groping for a jointly agreeable formula that will serve as a referent, provide a notion of justice, and define a common perception on which implementing details can be based. Power makes the values fit together in the package and timing is important to making the formula stick. The article provides examples from cases and experiments are discussed, including the results of a new survey of UN ambassadors using miniscenarios. Finally, the strengths and weaknesses of the formula/detail approach are assessed.

In attempting to develop scientific comprehension of a subject, it is as important to understand the nature of the subject itself as it is to develop theories to explain how it works. Different theoretical approaches developed independently of the subject can generate counterintuitive insights and original explanations, but such explanations are not applicable unless they relate to its true nature. Such an observation may seem so obvious as to be puzzling, and over time it is self-enforcing. In the long run, theories that misapprehend reality show themselves to be incapable of explanation and prediction and are abandoned (Kuhn 1962). But in the short run they may prove tenacious, as students debate whether the theory is inapplicable or merely in need of further refinement. The theory takes on its own life and attractiveness and its proponents develop an investment in the given approach. It is therefore important to continue to pose the question of correspondence between theory and reality, while still pursuing the debate over the internal development and consistency of current theory. Even an "as if" approach only assumes but does not establish that particular correspondence and may in fact be very misleading; "as if" needs to be related to "as is."

There are two sides to this effort. One is an independent examination of the subject to discover its nature, properties, and processes, to serve as the basis of a reality test for theory. The other is a formulation of theory in terms that can be identified, applied, and tested in observation and experiment, to provide for the operationalization of the theory. Much has been written about the relationship of reality and operationalization to theory; it need not be repeated here. The present discussion will proceed to a review of these two criteria in regard to a particular area of theory.

The argument in this essay is that negotiation is one of a limited number of decision-making modes. As such, it has a set of characteristics which identify and distinguish it from the other modes, and which, taken as assumptions, are not compatible with much of the theoretical work on negotiation to date. Instead, there are distinct patterns which appear in the actual practice of negotiation and which can be used as a basis for new directions in theoretical analysis.

Political science can be reduced to a study of structural modes of decision-making. The study of politics as choice or decision has advanced a good deal in recent years but unevenly, and few authors have looked specifically at negotiation in this context. Twenty years ago, Robert Dahl embarked in an interesting direction by identifying four types of decision-making processes based on leader-nonleader relations and meeting two conceptual requirements: "categories should actually fit governmental behavior [and] should not be incompatible with one another" (Dahl 1955, p. 47). The four types were democratic (upward control), hierarchical (downward control), bargaining (reciprocal control), and price (self-control). Unfortunately, the typology was not pursued in his later work and is unmentioned in *Modern Political Analysis* (Dahl 1976). Kenneth Arrow also identifies a number of decision-making systems based on the degree of centralization and the coincidence (identity) of both information and interests. (Arrow 1974, p. 69) His typology is threefold-authority, bargaining, and consensus – but the implications of the categories are not developed. Anatol Rapoport more fully explores three modes of conflict – fights, games, and debates – that can also be regarded as decision-making modes, the decision being made by eliminating, outwitting, or convincing the opponent, respectively (Rapoport 1960). In international relations, EH Carr (1949, p. 218) found three processes of peaceful change, two presupposing a political order and one not. They are the judicial process among parties of equal status and no power, the legislative process among parties with power but subordinate to legislative authority, and the bargaining process in which the parties have both equality and power and when all decisions are unanimous. All of these typologies have common elements which, added to others, can provide the essential characteristics for analyzing the basic processes of decision-making

There are at least three identifiable modes of social decision-making. The first may be called *coalition*,[12] the process of making a choice by numerical aggregation, involving voting majorities, rules of collective choice, arid legislation. Decision by coalition is a zero-sum process in that one side wins and the other loses. The winners win by being more numerous than the losers; there are many parties, fixed values, and a twofold choice (yes or no) on any given proposal. Neither side has any power over the other outside of the process of choice itself, if only because each side only exists through the act of constituting itself to make the choice. Thus, any side can make the decision alone, if it is big (powerful) enough, with power being associated with size and its ramifications (position in building up a majority winning coalition, for example).

Obviously, coalition is the basic component of real events such as voting and legislating, although the real events are much less pure and neat than their abstract core. This complexity, however, does not prevent their analysis in terms of the concept. In fact, even though coalition and legislating are two different orders of things, it is not only the power and logic of the former but also the correspondence between coalition theory and the essential nature of legislation that allows the former to be so useful in explaining much of the latter. Each one of these elements could be elaborated on (see Riker 1992; Brams 1975); together they form the assumptions that identify coalition as a decision-making process and the categories in which other assumptions must be made to distinguish other modes of decision-making.

Judication differs from the others in that it is a hierarchical process, during which parties plead before a single judge or executive who aggregates conflicting values and interests into a single decision that may or may not favor one of the parties more than the other(s).[13] It is hard to conceive of decision-making by a single judging individual in terms of sums; there is one deciding party, variable values which are combined into a decision, and a one-fold choice on any given subject (i.e., the judicator picks their decision, which is made decisive by their choice). They do not even cast their vote for the position of one party or another, thus creating a majority, since they are free to invent their own position which their vote alone turns into a decision. Since the process is hierarchical, one side has all the power to make the decision and the parties before the judicator can only avail themselves of the means of persuasion, to reason, plead, and promise (and their correlates) in order to affect the decision. It should be emphasized that, like the other processes discussed here, judication refers to social or collective decision-making. As an individual, non-collective process, it is the only form of decision-making, since, whether a part of coalition, judication or negotiation, the individual person must make up his mind alone. Here, however, the social unit included a number of parties not just the judge-executive but also the contending parties before the judicator.

The third mode of social decision-making, *negotiation,* differs from the other two on most counts. Negotiation is a process of two (or more) parties combining their conflicting points of view into a single decision (for similar attempts to identify characteristics, see Young 1975; Tracy

1978; Zartman 1974; Kelley 1970). It is a *positive-sum* exercise, since by definition both parties prefer the agreed outcome to the status quo (i.e., to no agreement) or to any other mutually agreeable outcome. Both sides come off better in the agreement than in the absence of the agreement, or else they would not agree (a point that is theoretically true but may have some exceptions in reality and even some complications in theory in regard to threats). There are *fixed parties* and *flexible values;* a decision is made by *changing the parties' evaluation* of their values in such a way as to be able to combine them into a single package, by persuasion, coercion or force (on the first two, see Zartman 1971 [Chapter 1] and Zartman 1976; and George *et al.* 1971). In the process, the parties exercise a *threefold choice* (yes; no; maybe or keep on talking). Choice is neither numerical (the size of the parties does not matter to the outcome) nor hierarchical (parties are formally or procedurally equal and fixed). Both sides have *power over each other.* This latter characteristic is evident in two important ways: negotiation takes place when stalemate occurs or, otherwise stated, when a decision is impossible by other means, and hence when in some sense the parties have equal stalemating power; and negotiation is a joint decision-making process in which both parties are necessary to the decision or, otherwise stated, in which each party has veto power. In addition, the parties have mixed motives, so that it is impossible to speak of a winner and a loser as in coalition, or of a pleader and a decider as in judication; both parties have reasons to agree and to disagree, to cooperate and to conflict, to concede and to compel.

Within these characteristics, then, the important theoretical questions to explain become: how are decisions made by negotiation; i.e., how are values combined in order to produce a single, joint, agreeable outcome; and, are there unique outcomes which are the foreseeable (predictable, determinant) result of the process defined in some particular terms? (For similar attempts to pose key questions, see Coddington 1968.) It should be noted that the questions require two answers relating to the way things are done (reality) and their conceptual explanation (theory).

From these summary characteristics it is easy to see that the three modes lend themselves differently to theorization. It does not minimize the work of the imaginative scholars who have worked on the problem to note that coalition is clearly the process most susceptible of theoretical treatment. It deals with numerical aggregation, twofold choice and zero-sums. Judication is much more difficult, as the work on judicial decision-making shows. Although it may be possible to forecast the decisions of given individuals on the basis of their past actions, there is no theoretical approach that has proven capable of handling the judication process itself, for its characteristics do not easily lend themselves to theory. The process of negotiation lies in between. A growing amount of theory has been developed, capitalizing on the aspects of the process that appear to be most amenable to theorization. Although eight different approaches to the study of negotiation have been identified (Zartman 1976; and Tracy 1975), four deserve brief mention here because of their theoretical development. The following paragraphs are not meant to contain a full critique but merely to present a few summary ideas as background to the subsequent discussion.

First mention should be made of the personality or psychological approach that looks at the decision makers themselves more than at the process. It seeks to explain bargaining effectiveness at conflict resolution in terms of such variables as the behavioral characteristics of the negotiators and their perceived and actual use of interpersonal strategies (Deutsch 1973; Spector 1978; Swingle 1970; Druckman 1973; Rubin and Brown 1975). Admittedly, in one sense this approach is the most appropriate to the analysis of negotiation and is certainly more applicable than it would be to coalition, for example. It focuses on the fixed element of the process – the parties – and their ability or propensity to modify the variable element – the values at stake. In terms of the criteria mentioned earlier, the psychological approach does well. It deals with realistic aspects of negotiation using concepts that are possible – even if not always easy – to operationalize.

However, by the same token, to analyze the agent rather than the process is to focus on the secondary rather than the primary element of decision-making, whether the process be negotiation or judication. In a crude simile, the driver, marksman, and cook are important ingredients in their respective processes, but they are secondary or ancillary to matters of mechanics, ballistics, and recipes. In any case, it is not yet possible to give a full evaluation of the psychological approach since its findings have not yet been combined into a general theory of negotiation or even reduced to the identification of a few key variables (see Rubin and Brown 1975, pp. 299 ff.).

Second is the economic approach with characteristics that are quite the opposite of the psychological. The economic approach does not lack putative theories, but their determinacy above all depends on artificial constructs and unoperationalizable concepts, such as indifference curves, negotiating fronts, and pareto-optimality (Young 1975; Coddington 1968 and 1973). Theories of bilateral monopoly seek to explain a jointly determined outcome in terms of the rational tendencies of the parties to reach an optimal point of intersection on their lists of interchangeable preferences. The problem is not one of identifying the wrong processes, but rather of assuming away all the interesting elements that make the process work and would make it understandable. Component assumptions – interchangeable preferences, a specific type of rationality, power-free determinacy – are neither real nor operationalizable, and attempts to add new aspects of preference – such as ophelimity (Pen 1975[1952]) or reciprocal demand intensities (Wade and Curry 1971) bring the approach closer neither to reality nor to operationalization.

The economic theories' determinant outcomes have little or no predictive power (Hamermesh 1973; Young 1975, pp. 143, 287), for their very determinacy makes them count as irrationality any element of power, persuasion, or coercion that could cause deviation from the predicted result. These criticisms are not directed against the internal consistency of the theories, which has already been the subject of a good deal of debate, but rather against their usefulness in understanding reality. Not surprisingly, economic theories of negotiation have mainly been confined to citing labor bargaining as an example, but they have been no better in explaining such outcomes than they have in improving understanding of other types of negotiations.

A third approach, the strategic, involves similar problems. Game theory seeks to explain negotiated outcomes in terms of rational choice behavior toward a given array of values. The approach is an important part of coalition theory and can also provide important insights into the process, and it is particularly well-suited to analyze the decision whether to negotiate or not (see Rapoport 1966, 1974; Brams 1975), notably in Prisoners' – and Chicken-Dilemma-type situations. It is, however, unsuited for analysis of the negotiation process. Reference to the characteristics of the decision-making modes exhibits the reasons. Negotiation is the process of varying values, and game theory deals with fixed values in which outcome is inherent in their structure. Therefore, it can show the array of values and the outcomes of choice at any given moment, but it cannot show the essential characteristic of negotiation, the process of their changing. Game theory mistakes repetitive strategy for interactive strategy in which parties use various means of persuasion to modify the others' values. Even its determinism proves its own undoing in predicting results for there are a number of persuasive theories establishing different determinant outcomes, each a function of its particular assumptions.

The approach that has come closest to grasping the nature of negotiation is process analysis, most developed in the study of concession/convergence (three excellent works are Siegel and Fouraker 1960; Cross 1969; Bartos 1974; see also Cross 1977; Bartos 1977; Hopmann and Smith 1977). This approach views negotiation as a learning process in which the parties react to each other's concession behavior. The approach responds to an intuitive understanding of many examples of negotiations, such as wage bargaining, rug buying, and territorial concessions, and is particularly attractive because it is amenable to addressing the age-old concerns of writers on negotiations: how to bargain best (see de Callieres 1963[1716]; Pecquet 1738; De Felice 1978[1778]; Nicolson 1964)? The approach has provided some of the most imaginative, rigorous, and useful work both in theory and in experimentation on the subjects of negotiations.

But there are problems. First, the approach cannot overcome the problem of symmetry on several levels. Because the findings of the convergence/concession approach are available to both parties, there is no advice on how to bargain best that is not equally accessible to the other side, leading the parties back to the stalemate that characterizes the situation ripe for negotiation! The very nature of the approach keeps it from answering the question that it addresses. There have been attempts to overcome this problem by recognizing the possibilities of short-term or tactical asymmetries. "In other words, one should be soft against an opponent likely to be tough, tough against one likely to be soft" (Bartos 1967a). But this conclusion, supported by logic and experimental evidence, is based on one crucial assumption: that agreement is preferred to nonagreement. Thus, against a "softie" one may be tough and win more, but against a "toughie" one can only be soft if any agreement is to be reached at all. Such advice follows directly from the assumptions of the convergence/concession approach but is only mildly helpful in understanding negotiations and scarcely helpful at all as a form of advice.

Second, the approach cannot – or has not – overcome the problems of determinacy (see Coddington 1973; Tracy 1975). Convergence/concession has been developed as a determinant theory that eliminates certain problems of advice. But again the learning process, as a key to the analysis of negotiation, raises other problems of applicability, although their solution can be found within the general approach. To begin with, concession rates are as difficult as indifference curves to locate in the real world. If understanding an outcome depends on pre- or post-diction from a known behavior expressed with mathematical precision as a concession rate, it hangs on the dubious assumptions that such a rate can in fact be calculated from the past and that it will hold in the future. Thereafter, the theory runs afoul of the basic characteristics of the negotiations process, for, like any determinant theory, it leaves no room for skill, tactics, and power. Once set in motion, running like a machine to a given conclusion; the approach has appropriately been termed "cataclysmic" (Coddington 1968).

There is a way out of this problem within the approach itself, and that is to turn the learning theory into a teaching theory, that is, to recognize that behavior not only responds to behavior – an error activated case of infinite regress in extreme, as has been pointed out but, because of that fact, behavior can be used to evoke responsive behavior. In this way, learning theory could be used to incorporate the necessary element of power in negotiation, since the role of the parties is to change the values of the other in order to bring about a mutually agreeable result. But in the process, the insights of the determinant theory are exploited but the determinacy is lost. The challenge remains, for learning theorists to meet.

But there is a further problem about convergence/concession analysis. It has been mentioned that, intuitively and experimentally, it corresponds to identifiable cases of negotiation. But does it capture the essence of the process? Does it reflect the nature of negotiation as found in the majority of real cases? In a word, is negotiation, as it is practiced in many forms, a matter of two parties arriving at their joint decision by inching incrementally toward each other from specific initial positions? Or if certain unreal assumptions have to be made to handle the problem theoretically, do these assumptions respect the nature of the process or do they depart from that very nature?

The problem has already been recognized (see Raiffa 1953; Braithwaite 1955; Landsberger 1955; Douglas 1957; Coddington 1966; Zartman 1971; Bartos 1974). Writers have identified a phenomenon of mixed rates, or endgame, in which the parties both act tough in order to test each other and then jump to a proposed agreement, moving in such a way as to present an outcome that is favorable to the proposer but agreeable to the other party as well. The party that jumps first is able to formulate the terms of an agreement and therefore seize the edge of advantage between favorable and agreeable. Such behavior is especially characteristic of deadline bargaining but is also found in cases where no formal deadline exists. Such behavior has been analyzed within the context both of concession/convergence and of strategic models, but there is some real question as to whether it represents incremental inching toward an agreement or rather a different behavior more appropriately described as jumping.

On the other hand, as already noted, concession/convergence analysis depends on the identification of specific positions. It is therefore limited in its application to quantifiable cases of the types suggested – wages, rugs, boundaries – and perhaps even in those cases there are other topographical elements which affect the inching process in a way that is not revealed in the theories and experiments.

The problem with any of the existent schools of analysis which deal with the structure of process and making decisions out of values i.e., all but the psychological school among the ones discussed aboveis that they have to assume a fixed array of items with precise and intrinsic values under discussion, like Bill's and Jack's treasures in Nash's (1950) example. This assumption contains two digressions from reality. It first ignores the fact that the very list of items under negotiation is a matter of negotiation; it may often be possible to come to an agreement about specific items under discussion only by packaging some of them together and ignoring others. The second error is to consider changes affected in the evaluation of these items to be purely a tactical matter, accomplished without reference to any other underlying values which give the original items their worth. In other words, it considers the stakes in negotiation to be "inchable" values composed of discrete increments in such a way that a little more or a little less can be independently determined and does not affect the nature of the item itself.

If these two aspects of the finite value assumption were incidental to a basic process of making decisions by negotiation, deviance from reality would be unimportant, at least for the initial formulation of the theory.

But they are matters which are crucial to the nature of the process itself. Because of this fact, negotiations in the real world are generally not matters of incremental convergence – despite all the images of the parties "coming closer together" in common parlance – but of something else. In other words, the trouble with concession/convergence theory, its inability to explain real events, lies not in its internal development as theory, but in its lack of corespondence with the way things take place.

Since this assertion is the major thrust of the rest of this chapter, it needs a good deal of support. This will be developed in three different ways: by an identification of the types of negotiation processes, by examples from actual cases, and by reference to data generated in current research. Rather than a matter of convergence through incremental concessions from specific initial positions, negotiation is a matter of finding the proper *formula* and implementing *detail*. Above all, negotiators seek a general definition of the items under discussion, conceived and grouped in such a way as to be susceptible of joint agreement under a common notion of justice.[14] Once agreement on a formula is achieved, it is possible to turn to the specifics of items and to exchange proposals, concessions, and agreements. Even then, details are resolved most frequently in terms of the referents that justify them and give them value rather than in their own intrinsic values. This means that convergence does not take place by inching from fixed positions toward the middle, but rather by establishing a referent principle from which the value of the detailed item will be derived.

It is still not clear whether formula/detail is the only pattern of negotiation, or merely the dominant one. Admittedly, there are cases when the items under negotiation are well enough established through prior agreement to enable convergence/concession bargaining to take place. Moreover, a third type of negotiation, which can be called progressive construction, can also take place when parties are not ready to handle items as a group but would rather deal with them seriatim, or when negotiations on a broad subject are viewed over a long time span as in disarmament. But since the convergence/concession types that do exist usually only take place when a formula has already been adopted, and since progressive construction negotiation frequently either operates within a formula or, over a long time period, contains a succession of formulae, this paper will concentrate on formula and detail as being the most typical and most important type of negotiations.

This is no place to indulge in lengthy diplomatic histories. But a brief discussion and a few references will help point out that major negotiations of recent years – Cuba, Vietnam, Middle East – are best analyzed from the formula/detail approach.

Cuba has been subject to a number of different analyses from two angles: one involves competing models purporting to provide the best explanation of events (Allison 1971; Holsti 1972; Forward 1971); the other involves competing definitions of the proper range of items to be covered by an agreement in the 1962 missile crisis (Bernstein 1976; Marshall 1965). The two analyses do not speak to each other or to common concerns. The first assumes that what happened was uniquely reasonable and successful" and therefore provides a nearly perfect case study for inductively derived models; the revisionists (of both right and left) discuss, or more frequently contest, whether the appropriate items were exchanged.

One of the studies of the confrontation has sought to make use of one of the theoretical approaches described above, presumably because none was found to be helpful in explaining outcomes. Interestingly enough, a concession/convergence model could have been applied, complementing Holsti's and Forward's communications models, to show how alternatives were narrowed to a final outcome that, predictively, may well have been a good bet but was certainly not necessarily a sure thing. However, it is stretching the concession/convergence approach from a precise model to a literary allusion to try to make it fit such an uneven series of events as a strategic choice of ends and means, a quarantine announcement, retraction of a naval perimeter, and acceptance of a specific exchange of contingent actions, to mention only the concessions on the American side.

It is more appropriate to consider the Cuban crisis within the framework of formula/detail. In this approach, the two types of analyses can be brought together; the problem to be solved was the discovery of a formula that could include items of sufficient importance to both sides to be accepted by them. The various revisionist formulae were considered at the time and can be considered in the analysis, but they did not fit the requirements of the definition. The idea of including missiles only and not Castro, and of accepting no counterpart such as Turkey or Berlin, on the American side, and the idea of extracting a counterpart promise on the invasion of Cuba, on the Soviet side, were parts of the definition of an acceptable formula, which finally appeared in the exchange of letters of 26–27 October 1962. The subsequent incident concerning the Ilyushin bombers as offensive weapons was part of the detail phase. At the same time, analysis of the Cuban missile crisis as an attempt to find a mutually agreeable formula also leaves an important place for the study of power, the ability of the parties to modify the other's evaluation of the items at stake. To be sure, this process is akin to the one described by Zeuthen (1930, p. 106; cf. Young 1975. pp. 80, 134, 147, 184), involving a continual comparison between the expected values of settlement and the expected values of conflict, but it leads to a search for an appropriate formula and then for accurately implementing details, not to successive exchanges of concessions.

The Paris negotiations to end the Vietnam war have already been analyzed in terms of alternative models, showing that the concession/convergence model is neither useful in analysis nor accurate in reflecting the actual course of events (Zartman 1976). Again, the model could be stretched to fit: if the stalemate occurred because both sides insisted on negotiated victory on their terms, concessions on both sides provided an intermediate position finally agreeable to both sides. If this accurately represents the outcome, it does not reflect the process. The Paris negotiations involved a two-year period of American attempts to propose various formulae (October 1970 to October 1972), followed by a period of joint search for details, during which proposals were accepted or rejected rather than incrementally modified. If concessions were made, they were for the most part whole concessions exchanged rather than partial concessions to a midpoint, as is usually meant. Again, power was an important and controversial aspect of the process. If a concession/convergence approach could be modified to take the various forms of power employed into account, it would not, however, show any direct relation between the use of power and the making of concessions – even in the case of the Christmas 1972 bombing of Hanoi. But in the search for a formula, and in the maintenance of that formula during the search for details, force, coercion, and persuasion did contribute to the process by modifying or supporting such elements as territorial referents, credibility, deadlines, and the weights given to the component elements of the agreement.

The final example to be cited in passing is the case of the Kissinger rounds in the Middle East. At first glance, it might appear that such territorial negotiations in which two incompatible concepts on a new withdrawal line were brought gradually into coincidence would be prime instances of concession/convergence. Yet even here, the appearance of inching is misleading. Instead of making successive changes in the location of a withdrawal line in response to specific means of persuasion, the parties cast about for a formula for an agreement that would contain a particular location for the line and also the principles that justified that location. Here formula and detail were closely related in time as well as in concept, and at some point specific spots – such as Quneitra or the three hills in the Golan sector – became details to be settled within the formula already adopted rather than elements of the formula itself.

Further confirmation of the usefulness of the formula/detail approach comes from a high official commenting recently on the way to get negotiations moving again on the Palestine problem.[15] He said that decisions were first needed on the "negotiability" and the "terms of reference" of the issue, and when asked to elaborate on the latter notion he indicated a need to "spell out a formula under which Palestinians and Israelis could negotiate together comparable to Resolution 242," indicating the "purpose of the negotiations, e.g., the purpose of both sides is to restore peace … The recognition could follow." Such a description clearly indicates negotiation by formula and detail, not by concession and convergence.

The negotiation process

In sum, even a cursory reference to the three major negotiations of recent times shows that they were conducted through a search for a single formula satisfactory to both sides, followed by a further search for the implementation of this formula through specification of the details necessary to affect the agreement. In no case was the process one of exchanging small concessions that modify opposing positions until they come into coincidence. The reasons are clear. Concession/convergence would be most likely to yield an incoherent agreement, a mosaic made up of little pieces chipped down to size in order to fit but providing no overall pattern. Concession/convergence implies that the variable value in question is the concession rate rather than the items at stake, that the item itself has no intrinsic value, and that a little more or a little less does not affect the nature of the item. While this assumption may not be totally inaccurate in regard to used-car haggling or rug buying, it is not even accurate in regard to other apparently similar negotiations such as wage bargaining or aid determination (see Hammermesh 1973; Zartman 1971, pp. 67–74), and even less so when it comes to less simple, quantitative stakes.

The substantive incoherence of the concession/convergence approach is also visible in the experiments that are designed to test it (cf. Bartos, 1974 pp. 377–89; Winham, 1977a, pp. 15–17). When players are called on to bargain an agreement in which it is a simple aggregate payoff and not the substance of the agreement that matters, their actions reflect these conditions: the results lend themselves to a concession/convergence interpretation because there is no substance to the negotiations to impose a more realistic pattern; the reports of caucus and negotiating sessions show an absence of coherence and reasons for action. When experimental subjects are given a chance to define their own stakes and control their value rather than accept fixed, externally determined values, however, they tend: (1) to invent a formula first to cover their own positions and then to provide the basis for a mutually satisfactory agreement, and (2) increase their satisfaction with the results to the extent that they do develop such a formula. This is evident in preliminary results from team runs of Spector's Camp Game (adapted from Spector 1975), where two teams negotiate the allocation of seven facilities in a summer camp that they have jointly purchased (Zartman 2005c). A final example of an experimental situation of bargaining that throws some light on competing interpretive approaches is the Fermeda Workshop. In this simulated attempt that was ultimately unsuccessful, it is clear from accounts (Walton 1970) that there was no inching, concession or convergence, but rather a number of attempts to find a formula – that failed.

The importance of formula/detail to the negotiation process is currently the subject of investigation of a survey-research project designed to test the theoretical findings of students of negotiation against the experience of seasoned diplomats, and at the same time to tap the instincts of the diplomats in such a way as to make their experience available to others in assimilable form. More generally, the project seeks to bridge the gap between theory and reality.

One set of surveys in the research project involves the use of miniscenarios, short, two-person narrative games in which the interviewer reveals preprogrammed moves successively in response to the answers of the interviewee. The scenarios are constructed to contain a number of theoretical propositions or questions, translated into narrative terms. The first question is whether negotiators follow a concession/convergence or formula/detail approach. The second is whether concessions they might make follow a regular and intrinsic pattern, or whether they are determined by other referents. The third concerns the relation between the two negotiating parties' concession rates: one set of theories suggests that the relation is *reciprocal* and that concessions from one side will be met by concessions of equal magnitude on the other (Deutsch 1973). Another set of theories suggests that the relation is *exploitive,* and that concessions on one side will engender concessions of opposite magnitude on the other (Siegel and Fouraker 1960; Bartos 1974). A third set suggests that the relation is *unresponsive* and that negotiators will hold tight until they get close to a deadline and then seek to force the other party into a favorable final concession (Douglas 1957; Coddington 1966). A fourth set suggests that the relation is projective and that both parties naturally aim at a target point between their two initial positions and concede in such a way as to arrive at that point at the same time (Nash 1950; Shapley 1953; Rapoport 1966; Young 1975).

Two scenarios, among others, are used to test these notions.[16] They differ in the degree to which specific increments are identifiable in the stakes. One scenario casts the negotiator as a representative of a school board negotiating with the union for a teachers' pay raise; stakes here are precise monetary values with concessions expressed either as regular increments in money or in percentages. The other scenario concerns a piece of territory left in disputed ownership between two countries by a shifting river boundary; stakes here are discrete components of the disputed territory (city, suburbs, rice field, oil fields, amenable to sectoring by the shape of the riverbeds), but the sense of absolute or relative increments is not as immediately apparent. Interviewees are first asked how they would approach the problem. They are then given an opening bid from the other side and asked for a response, an estimated reaction, and an expected outcome. Following these steps, they are given a new bid (reflecting one or more of the above theories) and the game proceeds. Mini-scenarios were run with UN diplomats at the ambassadorial level. Complete results are reported elsewhere (Zartman and Berman 1982), but summary answers can be given to the three research questions.

The 50 interviews show first that most of the respondents look at negotiations as a matter of finding an appropriate formula and its implementing details, rather than of converging on a point through incremental
concessions. Support of the proposition is relative rather than absolute,
however. In the territorial negotiations where the increments are less
apparent and the nature of the conflict already defined, there is hardly
any concession/convergence behavior, but in the wage dispute it is much
more frequent. However, concession/convergence behavior in the latter
case is generally associated with passive negotiation in which the party
merely reacts from frame to frame, whereas formula/detail behavior is
associated with an active search for a solution. Hence, as seen in the Camp
Game cited previously, formula/detail is associated with greater satisfaction with the solution. This is not surprising since the approach pays
greater attention to substance and content and seeks an outcome which
respects the concerns of both sides as much as possible.

Second, even the concession/convergence behavior is governed to a
large extent by external referents rather than simply responses to the
other party's concession rate. Thus, most of the diplomats who responded
incrementally to the other party's wage concessions still did so with reference to a cost-of-living figure, and the much smaller number who
responded incrementally to territorial concession's were trying to find a
stable equilibrium point in terms of referents that would hold an agreement into place – a behavior closer to a successive submission of formulae
than to pure concession behavior.

Third, whatever the approach to the negotiation scenarios, the respondents generally reacted similarly toward the other party's opening level
and concession behavior. One common pattern was to return toughness
for toughness and softness for softness: when the programmed party conceded regularly, the interviewee also made concessions, although at a
slower rate. Another pattern saw a higher opener to produce a higher
result, although not proportionally so. The "outlandishly high" openers in
the territorial and wage disputes produced both a higher expected
outcome in the eyes of the respondent and a higher negotiated outcome
in their behavior, but in addition yielded a higher incidence of breakdown.

Finally, many respondents made a concession – often only a symbolic
move – at the end when they felt agreement was in sight and they believed
that the other side would accept their package. This behavior occurred
whether the interviewee had been making regular concessions or whether,
as was more frequently the case, they had been holding firm on their
opening bid up to the final point. Yet this final concession also had
another nature. It was part of a move to jump to an agreement, as already
noted in the theoretical literature, but was usually not simply an isolated
figure but part of a package that tied down all the items at stake within a
comprehensive justification. In other words, the final concession generally

appeared as a detail within a winning – or presumably winning – formula. Thus, even what seemed to be concession/convergence behavior is better understood as formula/detail.

Conclusions

The argument presented here is summarized as follows: current theoretical approaches to the study of negotiations do not correspond to the conceptual characteristics or assumptions of the subjects as a mode of decision-making and do not deal with the process as it is actually practiced. In the hands of the more experienced and more successful negotiators, negotiation tends to be a matter of finding a formula encompassing the optimum combination of interests of both parties and then of working out the details that implement these principles. Both a practical understanding and a theoretical explanation of the negotiatory mode of decision-making must therefore deal with the process as a matter of formula and detail.

This conclusion masks one major problem and a large number of advantages. The problem is important: unlike the concession/convergence approach to negotiation or the strategic approach to coalition, formula/detail does not lend itself readily to theorization. Although a few stabs have been made at developing a new approach to handle such types of problems, none has gone very far (e.g., Boulding 1956). The difficulties are formidable. A theory of negotiation must encompass an infinite number of possible combinations of items with variable evaluation attached to them, and include as well the impact of the exercise of power. It must also deal with multiple optimal timing, and strategic advantage and reasons for rational choice nonoptimal. A theory that indicates the best possible combination of values would be useful, even though it did not predict which would be chosen. However, such a theory is difficult to envisage at this point (cf. Druckman 1977; Tracy 1978).

If social science were replete with effective theories explication most of its processes, such a problem would be a major drawback. However, considering the state of theory in social science in general such difficulties are not unusual. And despite their presence, there is a good deal to be gained, beyond simple fidelity, by recognizing the real nature of the negotiatory process.

The first advantage is that the approach shows that, for conceptual reasons, and in any useful terms, negotiation is not a determinate process. The latter qualification is important since theoretical formulations could be made in unoperationalizable or artificial terms. But negotiation involves not merely a reaction to past moves from the other side but also the initiation of forward-oriented moves to guide the other party toward the preferred target. It also involves subjective responsiveness to both parties' exercise of power. For these reasons, a determinate outcome is conceptually impossible, both the concession/convergence and the formula/detail approach. At best, either can indicate ways of calculating optimal points or tactical insights showing how to play better, even if not best (as in Nash 1950; Cross 1969; Schelling 1960; Rapoport 1974). Since they could be of practical use to negotiators and could enable both practitioners and analysts to judge outcomes and seek reasons for deviation from the ideal, such findings would be extremely useful.

Second, the formula/detail approach guides further study. Among all the possible formulae one could find in a particular encounter, the question always arises, "why this one at this time?" leading to the practitioner's form of the question, "how to find the best formula and make it stick?" (Zartman and Berman 1982). Although others have alluded to a notion of a formula before without specifically identifying its nature or importance (e.g., Schelling 1960, p. 104; Burton 1969, pp. 83–7) no one has yet worked out conceptual means of handling the aggregation of different quantities of divergent elements into various packages, and then of relating these calculations to the right moment. Clearly, in the process of jumping or proposing the winning formula, there is some importance to doing it at the right time and there is also importance in being able to hold out or force out further proposals. The second element has been touched on in some concession/convergence studies but as assumptions rather than as calculations and as an aspect of concession, not of formula (cf. Young 1975, pp. 145–63, 183–90, 253–66).

Third, in addition to providing a more accurate portrayal of reality, formula/detail also forms a general approach in which both psychological and concession/convergence findings have their place. The former, in dealing with the characteristics of the agent, can provide useful information on the relation between agent behavior and the process of finding a formula and its implementing details (Spector 1978). Since it is at the point – once the terms of reference of the agreements have been decided – that convergence through incremental concessions is possible in some types of subjects, concessions) convergence findings are compatible with the detailed phase of formula/detail. Some negotiations do proceed in this fashion in particular areas, under a governing formula or as part of a larger process, and the negotiators' behavior can be analyzed somewhat by the model.

Fourth, the formula/detail approach also has room for the analysis of power as added value. As yet, no theory of negotiation has included power, thus making it difficult for theories to explain negotiation as a political process. It is only by conceptualizing power as a modifier (negative and positive addition) to the original value of the items at stake that one can explain how formerly incompatible elements can be combined to fit into a formula acceptable to both sides (Zartman 1974, pp. 397f.). The process of finding an acceptable formula involves two types of actions: a selection of values for inclusion in the proposal and a modification of these values through persuasion coercion, and force. If no modification were necessary, negotiation would be merely a matter of discovery and no conflict would be present.

Fifth, the formula/detail approach is able to meet the ancient problem of prescription as no other approach has been able to do. The presumed determinism and symmetry of the concession/convergence approach has been its prescriptive undoing. If the outcome were determinate, no advice would be given to the parties' as to how best negotiate. If any advice were available to both parties in the game against each other, then no one could be told how to upgrade their tactics. But if the nature of negotiations is understood as formula and detail, then it becomes possible to advise both parties to devise an optimum formula in such a way as to benefit both parties, thus stimulating the development of tactical means of improving the package for one or both parties.

Finally, the formula/detail approach permits a more healthy and constructive public attitude toward negotiation. At present the public tends to look at negotiation as a matter of concessions, rather like an athletic match, in which our concessions are losses and theirs are gains ("We conceded the point but rallied in the next round.") (Kahneman and Tversky 1979). As a result, negotiation loses its positive-sum character and negotiators are under pressure to hold out and to devise bargaining chips. Negotiation as a search for a formula and its details permits a more positive and creative attitude to the resolution of conflict and the making of decisions.

4 Negotiation as a search for justice[17]

Negotiation is one of the basic modes of social decision-making, a crucial element in commerce, diplomacy, law and everyday international (and other) life, but we are still surprisingly far from a theory about how people negotiate. Negotiated outcomes are achieved by the combined and competing efforts of parties holding initially conflicting positions. But they are not merely the results of a contest of countervailing wills and power nor of a confrontation of skills and tactics. Rather, the range of potential agreements and the shape of the final outcome are determined in large part by underlying notions of fairness or justice

Despite some semantic debates that undoubtedly have importance in some other contexts, the two terms are used interchangeably here. This article reviews current attempts to answer the basic analytical question of how negotiated outcomes are obtained and explained, and presents growing research on an alternative explanation: in the process of negotiating the exchange or division of the items contested between them, negotiators come to an agreement on the notion of justice which will govern this disposition; if they do not, negotiations will not be able to proceed to a conclusion. Unlike other explanations, the renewed focus on justice as a parameter not only explains how and why negotiations proceed, but also why they fail

Fairness and justice are a major motivating force in all human decision-making and hence in negotiation (Lerner 1975; Deutsch 1985; Wilson 1993); indeed there is evidence that getting a fair deal is often more important than getting the best deal (Lind and Taylor 1988). "It seems that wherever one finds people who want something (are there are other kind?), whenever there are desired resources to distribute, the preeminent factor in the decision process appears to be one of the various facets of justice – fairness, rights, deserving, etc." (Lerner 1975, p. 1). "[C]laims will not be successful unless they embody a bona fide ideal of distributive justice" (Elster 1992, p. 5).

The concern with justice goes back to initial thinking about negotiation, which present research – as is often the case with scientific inquiry – revives in a new light. To the earliest writers on negotiation (Genesis

18:16–33; Thucydides 1963), negotiation was a means of achieving an outcome based on a principle of justice. Later (but still long ago), the key to negotiation was seen as the ability to harmonize the interests of the parties (de Callieres 1963[1716], p. 110), with no mention of justice, and economic (Nash 1950), sociological (Homans 1961), and labor (Walton and McKersie 1965) analysis has followed the spoor. The renewed concern with justice shows that not just any harmonization, nor just any power imposition, will provide the framework for an agreement, but rather a determination of an applicable principle of justice, taking into account the nature of the conflict, the ideas and interests of the parties, and their ability to present appealing terms of trade.

Previous explanations of negotiated outcomes have come from political science, economics, mathematics, and philosophy. Political science explanations use power as their explanatory variable. The structural power model explains the distribution of shares in negotiated outcomes as the result of the distribution of power among the parties (Habeeb 1988; Rubin and Zartman 1995). But in reality, power differences have more to do with sabotaging than explaining agreement. Variance between the most defensible principles of justice and the distribution of power is a frequent and basic cause for breakdown in negotiations, as examples from Ethiopia. Panama and experimentation (Rubin and Brown 1975; Hammer and Baird 1978; Lamm and Kayser 1978) show. Negotiation in these cases is the process of coming to a distribution rule of justice from different starting points. Contrary to some claims (Stolte 1967), this is not a matter simply of power but of each side's calculations of acceptability.

The countervailing power model typically focuses on stalemate, a situation that is part of the Toughness or Negotiators' Dilemma: the tougher I am, the more likely I am to get a favorable agreement but the less likely to get an agreement at all; the softer I am, the more likely to get an agreement but the less likely to get a favorable one (Bartos 1987; Zartman and Berman 1982; Lax and Sebenius 1986). In fact, the central problem for negotiators is not to get most for themselves but to find a beneficial solution that the other(s) will accept. This is where the notion of fairness comes in: it helps coordinate the negotiators' expectations throughout the process of moving from stalemate to agreement (Schelling 1960; Young 1994).

Classical economic models of bargaining in bilateral monopoly (Edgeworth 1881; Zeuthen 1930; Hicks 1932; for a convenient collection of important passages from economic and related works, see Young 1975) refer to the convergence process along a single parameter and ultimately refer to bases of contending power as the determinant of the point of convergence. Outcomes are explained as a product of the conflict, based on criteria of efficiency, not of the process of cooperation, based on criteria of equity (justice); and when that process is taken into account, it is based on an assumed rather than a negotiated criterion for agreement (Bartos

1978). Typically, economic analysis identifies a number of possible outcomes that leave parties better off, whereas justice resolves that indeterminacy.

Game theoretic approaches, including those based on repeated plays as a basis for cooperation (Axelrod 1984; Axelrod and Dion 1988), are able to analyze decisions on the basis of predefined outcomes, but not the process of defining or shaping them. The parties, assumed to understand fully the consequences of their own and the other's actions, seek to maximize their payoffs by playing the cost of giving in to the other against the cost of deadlock (Harsanyi 1977; Rubenstein 1982; Brams 1990). Their criterion for acceptability is rational choice, but they cannot analyze the basis of preferences or the process by which interparty preferences are combined, both crucial matters in obtaining decisions by negotiation. Such analysis needs to take into account, or be supplemented by, explanations of the way in which criteria for the acceptability or justice of outcomes are coordinated.

Recent efforts in philosophy have turned to a discussion of some of these questions, centered around an attempt to devise a definition of justice that provides an overarching criteria for all actions. Economic and game theoretic reasoning plays an important part in this effort which, departing from the basic work of Rawls (1971), seeks to devise an outcome that is just because parties would arrive at it by a negotiation that takes into account each party's security (non-agreement) point and all parties' interests in equal treatment. Whether as contractualists (Gauthier 1986) or as idealists (Barry 1989), the various strains of this philosophical approach consider a standard to be just because it is negotiated, on the basis of some external criterion. At the very least, this approach makes it difficult then to use justice as an external criterion for evaluating negotiations; the pluralism that characterizes the debates in the disciplines also makes it difficult to accept any of the competing claims that there is one meaning of justice that can be claimed as that criterion. (The argument here is closer to Elster 1992, which in addition seeks out empirical cases and data for his investigation, as is done here.) The search for meaning and the discovery of many meanings of justice, however, is an important endeavor and one that is useful for the proposed line of argument

These various approaches and models are not irrelevant but incomplete. They do not capture the essence of the negotiation process; they assume away the most important dynamic, the determination of the basis on which an agreement will be reached, and they do not explain significant differences that make for success and breakdown.

In the rest of this chapter, we analyze the concept of justice and its role in negotiations, illustrating that role with an example from the ozone negotiations. We also examine the notion of process justice. We then turn to experimental evidence for the basis of choice among the various principles of justice, and show the position of justice in salient arms control and regional security negotiations. The chapter ends with some implications for further research.

Justice in negotiation

The notion of justice can be usefully categorized into subtypes (for related attempts, see Aristotle 1911; Deutsch 1975; Eckhoff 1974; Pruitt 1981; Cook and Hegtvedt 1983; Zartman 1987, pp. 20–4 [Chapter 2, above]; Albin 1992; Young 1994).[18] The first distinction is between distributive justice governing outcomes and procedural justice governing the conduct of the process (Lind and Taylor 1988). There are three broad subtypes or principles of outcome justice: (1) priority justice in which some external nonquantitative rule or precedent indicates a winner, (2) equal (or parity) justice in which all parties have an equal share, or equal access to or chances at a share, and (3) unequal (or proportional) justice in which outcomes are allocated unequally in proportion to some criterion, generally either by equity (or merit), according to which they who have or contribute most get most, or by compensation (or need) in which they who have least get the most.

These principles are simple and unambiguous, more so than most reality, and that is one of the problems with the philosophical and mathematical debates over the concept of justice. Allocations in the real world usually deal with matters complex enough to elude coverage by a simple principle, even though sometimes one principle may indeed underlay an ostensibly complicated deal. When a simple principle is inadequate, negotiators may seek compound justice, by matching principles so that one party is allowed equity to govern one issue if the other party gets compensation in another. But the basic notion of establishing agreement on principles of justice before being able to move further still obtains.

Thus negotiating parties have two questions to decide: which principle of justice – priority, equality or inequality – shall govern the negotiations, and why? How shall that principle be interpreted – priority, equality or inequality of what, and why? These are known as the "principle question" and the "referent question".

Unless only a single principle or set of principles is clearly applicable, each party tends to prefer the principle that favors its own cause (Hamner and Baid 1978). Unless these initial positions are overcome, it will be difficult to move ahead toward resolution and the negotiation is likely to fail.

There are two ways to establish the common principle of justice that will serve as the basis for continuing negotiation. One involves falling back, essentially without discussion, on some time-honored procedure of justice. Thus, two children arguing over candy could quickly agree on the familiar procedure whereby one cuts and the other chooses – both a procedural realization and a substantive guarantee of the equality principle (Young 1994; Hopmann 1993). Or two diplomats, unable to convince each other of the rightness of their position by priority principles, may fall into a pattern of exchanging roughly equal concessions, reciprocating until they reach a midpoint – another double realization of equality, procedural and substantive (Bartos 1978; Larson 1988; Kolm 1992). Or two countries, having arrived at a stalemate in the pursuit of their conflict, may agree to third-party arbitration or to submission of the dispute to the International Court of Justice. Arbitration and adjudication should in no way be confused with negotiation (including mediated negotiation), since the former shift the decision to a procedure of third-party justice and out of the hands of the parties. These shifts from conflicting openers to shared procedures convert the substance of the dispute to recognisedly just procedures, such as cut-and-choose, reciprocating concessions and arbitration or adjudication.

That negotiators tend to reciprocate each other's concessions, responding to softness with softness and to toughness with toughness, has been well established in laboratory experiments (Kelley *et al.* 1967; Benton *et al.* 1972; Bartos 1974; Smith *et al.* 1962) and also found in international practice (Jensen 1987; Hopmann and Smith 1978; Winham 1986; Bunn 1992), along with a similar time-lagged phenomenon in which the party which conceded less in the last round concedes more in the next (Druckman 1990; Stoll and McAndrew 1986). A more complex variation, referred to as "threshold adjustment," has been observed in international negotiations, where bargainers increasingly harden or soften their positions to the point of either deadlock or agreement (Druckman 1986; Druckman and Harris 1990).

The other way to establish a principle of justice is by negotiating a preliminary agreement about a formula to provide a roadmap for subsequent negotiations (Zartman 1978; Zartman and Berman 1982). Evidence shows that parties negotiate to establish a common principle or combination of principles of fairness drawn from the above list before or as they negotiate the specific outcome, and that the acceptability of the specific outcome is dependent on prior agreement on a shared sense of the criterion of acceptability, or justice. Preliminary understandings of this kind are an essential part of the formula that is necessary before the details of a negotiated agreement can be filled in. Negotiation being a sloppy matter of human interaction, there may be no sharp line dividing the disposal of the justice questions from more detailed bargaining; yet the distinction exists, is recognized by practitioners, and is necessary for analysis.

Beyond the principle question is the referent question, which is open to even greater ambiguities. Agreement on equality or inequality depends on coming to an agreement over equality or inequality of or based on what? The US and the Soviet Union, as the two leading superpowers at the time, could agree on equality as the reigning principle of justice in disarmament negotiations but took a much longer time deciding the "equality of what" when it came to translating that principle into throw-weight, missile numbers; missile types, and defense sites.

To illustrate the role of justice in negotiation in a concrete case, consider the negotiations for the Montreal Protocol of 1987 and the London Revisions of 1990 to limit emissions of ozone-depleting substances to the atmosphere (Benedick 1991; Chasek 1995). One way of formulating the problem is to say that the atmosphere is the common heritage of mankind and that all living persons have an equal right to its use. This suggests that each person (or state) should have a right to emit (only) an equal amount of ozone-depleting chemicals (CFCs, etc.) into the atmosphere. A rather different way of framing the issue is to start from the status quo with its larger emissions from the industrialized world, the result of actions before anyone knew of potential harm, and have everyone give up the same amount of emissions subtracted from their present baseline. Yet a third point of view is that the status quo is a measure of the relative claims that everyone has on the common resource, and so everyone should give up the same percentage of their present baseline. Each is an example of the equality principle applied to a different referent by a different rationale, although the third also represents an inequality principle as well in an exercise of compound justice.

The search for an acceptable justice principle or combination of principles makes the ensuing negotiation more focused and manageable. In reality, the ozone negotiations began in Geneva in December 1986 with a tacit agreement on equality as a preliminary answer to the principle question, followed by a debate between caps (favored by the European Community) and cuts (favored by the US, Canada, and Scandinavia) in production. By the third session five months later, cuts were generally accepted as the beginning of the answer to the referent question; in the last sessions, negotiation turned to the details of figures, dates and exceptions. The final agreement on the ozone called for a fixed percentage cut in CFCs for industrialized countries, a ten-year moratorium on compliance combined with financial and technical aid for developing countries, and an ultimate ban (cut plus cap) on all CFC production by a target year. It can therefore be described as compound justice – a negotiated compromise between inequality principles of equity for industrialized countries and compensation for developing countries, working to an equality principle for all.

Process justice

Process fairness is always important, but particularly so when parties cannot agree on outcome fairness. Unlike outcome fairness, process fairness has not been subdivided into a finite number of subtypes but is rather composed of maxims which, at most, fall under the heading of "full and equal opportunity" (Albin 1997; Young 1989). While process fairness is a substitute for outcome fairness in some social encounters, these tend to be limited to situations (such as "having one's day in court") where justice is guaranteed by authority and inherent in the process, and where winning rather than reconciling is the outcome, as in adjudication rather than negotiation (Raiffa 1982; Brams 1990; Prasniker and Roth 1992; Albin 1997).

In negotiation, however, there is a norm of process justice that is predominant and that is the reciprocity of equal or matching concessions (Gouldner 1960; Ikle 1964; Walton and McKersie 1965; Bartos 1978; Cross 1978; Pruitt 1981). Although the underlying rationale may be that reciprocity leads to equality, as noted, reciprocity has come to stand on its own as the expected norm of negotiation, a dynamic equal justice. Requitement, or the understanding that concessions will be reciprocated, is a basic element in the prenegotiation process of coordinating expectations and establishing rules (Zartman 1989b). Like outcome equality, reciprocity is a principle that can be applied to many different referents – not only numerically equal concessions but concessions of equal cost, concessions of equal proportion, among others (Kelley *et al.* 1967; Pruitt 1972; Pruitt 1981; HP Young 1991; R Young 1992; Young and Wolf 1992). Despite the prominence of equal concessions, unequal concessions or mismatching are an equally common, acceptable and often necessary occurrence if agreement is to be reached (Bartos 1987; Pruitt 1981; Cross 1969). As a result, unequal concessions are not considered unfair; reciprocity seems to mean merely repaid concessions, without a requirement that the repayment be equal in value to be just.

This is obviously a highly fluid situation characteristic of negotiation, and negotiators have often responded to "too little" or no concession as unfair. Part of the reason, particularly important in reciprocal concessions, is "partisan bias" or "reactive devaluation," the tendency to view the other's concession as smaller than one's own (Ross and Stillinger 1991). Procedures to help reduce these biases have been tested in experiments and in practice (Benedick 1991), including group sessions to allay the "enemy image" during negotiations and agreed definitions of reciprocity during the process. The problem is easily overcome only when the available options can be quantified in such a way that a palpably equal-split outcome is apparent (Benton and Druckman 1973), although in real-life settings this still leaves the referent question open. A number of strategies are potentially available for reframing the issues and thus reaching agreement among competing notions of justice: negotiating application, interpretation, circumvention, alternatives, and conciliation among principles, or use of group sessions to ‹explore value orientations and positive emotions (Druckman *et al.* 1988; Pruitt 1981; Rubin *et al.* 1994; Spector 1994).

Preferences among principles

Experimental research has identified a number of factors that influence preferences among principles and their interpretation, including group, culture, and age. Much experimental research assumes a pre-existing principle of justice as a distribution rule, usually citing the universal status of equality as a norm of justice (Cook 1975; Bartos 1978; Jasso 1980; Markovsky 1986; Alwin 1987; Stolte 1987). Cohesive social groups tend to emphasize equality, whereas economically-oriented groups emphasize inequality (equity) but with greater disagreement on its implementation (Deutsch 1975). Cultural determinants also have a role: American, Argentine, Russian and Egyptian students studied tended to be more egalitarian, whereas Indian students favored compensatory inequality, due apparently to a view of the world based on scarcity of limited resources; justice as equality was for them a goal rather than a operative norm (Druckman *et al.* 1976; Faure and Rubin 1993). The extent to which these differences operate among seasoned diplomats is still untested.

Age also influences notions of justice in bargaining. Piaget has posited, and some experiments have demonstrated, that fairness evolves through a sequence of stages from early input-based "mechanistic balancing" or formalistic reciprocity (ages 6–9), through strict equality (ages 10–12), to "mature equity" which takes into account individual circumstances (ages 13–14) (Piaget 1948; Solomon and Druckman 1972). Whether these findings hold across cultures, or, in other words, which determinant is dominant, is not yet tested. Furthermore, since most international negotiators come to their jobs well over these ages, available generalized knowledge is not particularly relevant to their situation.

However, when parties come to negotiate (that is, to decide outcomes jointly), they need to reconcile their differing notions and arrive at a common sense of justice, one that is both favorable to each and applicable to both. The problem for negotiation analysis is not one of finding out what determines each party's notions of justice but rather that of finding how they reconcile their different notions of just interests, as François de Callières (1963[1716]) pointed out long ago. Equality and its variants present the most obvious solution (Pruitt and Carnevale 1993; see also the philosophical literature on justice, and notably Barry 1989 on impartial justice) in part because of its prominence as a unilateral value, in part because of its utility as a "fair" meeting point or compromise solution between the parties' positions, and in part because the referent question is most easily answered with respect to this principle. Experimental studies indicate that shared notions of justice as equality have a higher and faster chance of producing agreements than different or divergent notions (Siegel and Fouraker 1963; Joseph and Wills 1963; Benton and Druckman 1973; Lamm and Rosch 1972).

The equality principle is particularly likely to be acceptable to the parties when they feel that they are similar or have equal standing or when they differ but their difference cannot be measured in any objective way (Rubin and Brown 1975; Druckman and Bonoma 1976). When the parties perceive themselves to be equal but challenge that perception or feel that it is in question, however, they spend more effort in defending their status in symmetry than in reaching an equal distribution of outcomes (Zartman and Rubin 2000). By contrast, inequality is most likely to be mutually acceptable when the parties differ according to some objective measure or contribution, such as number of hours worked on a common project (Messe 1971).

Yet equality is not always applicable and not always satisfying as a principle for an agreement. The next way of bridging the conflict is by joining together different principles of justice. Compound justice can be achieved where the simple application of a single principle is not possible, through a pairing of principles or an exchange of concessions. For example, if the two parties claim different interpretations of inequality (equity vs compensation) for different aspects of an issue (or different issues), an equality principle can be produced by offsetting one with the other. For such an exchange of concessions to appear just, it is necessary for each party to believe that it has given up roughly as much as the other party or that the other party had gained roughly no more than the first party; in other words, that the two parties are roughly equal in what they have lost or won, or at least not demonstrably unequal.

Finally, if the parties cannot agree on a simple principle of equality or on an equalizing formula of compound justice, they must work out an agreement on an inequality principle or a prior principle of justice. It is hard to devise experiments reflecting such situations nor has experimental thinking developed in this direction, so that there are few experimental conclusions to provide hypotheses for testing in reality

In summary, experimental works shows:

1   Parties tend to focus on a justice principle before agreeing on distributive details and such focus facilitates agreement.
2   The equality principle is an especially strong basis for negotiation. It is viewed as a fair and just basis for trades (fair process) leading to agreement (fair outcomes).
3   Where simple equality is not applicable, compound justice often underlies agreement.
4   The equality principle is not universal, however. Determinants external to the issue (group, culture, age, etc.) may affect preferences for principles and pose obstacles to agreement on equal treatment.
5   The devil is in the interpretation more than in the principle. It is usually the referent question rather than the principle question that takes the time to negotiate.
6   There are no experimental guidelines to understanding the process of devising formulas based on inequality or prior principles of justice, which are nonetheless a common occurrence in reality.

Distributive justice in arms control

Negotiation around a determining principle of justice is a predominant aspect of arms limitation bargaining. A principle of inequality (equity) was assumed from the beginning to govern the pre-World War I and II arms limitation negotiations, permitting the bargaining to shift to the task of translating that principle into detailed figures. After World War II, the bipolar and nuclear nature of the antagonists allowed equity and equality to mean the same thing – equal treatment for the superpowers, unequal treatment for the rest, and lengthy negotiations were devoted to finding precise translations of justice as equality, or in other words of answering the referent question. Justice as equity would have implied disarmament through percentage reductions that maintained the force structure imbalance, which would in turn place a premium on building capacity prior to negotiations, a policy which also characterized earlier experiences with nuclear testing.

It was agreement on justice as equality which ultimately permitted the conduct of serious arms control negotiations. But this did not occur until the 1970s after the Soviet Union had gained rough parity with the US in strategic systems. The process was complicated by the fact that equality in one set of terms (units, warheads, throw-weight, speed, vulnerability, weapons systems, etc.) necessarily meant inequality in others. Each party then tried to impose the referent of equality that favored its position, stalling negotiations on the level of the referent question. Different strategic, geographic, technological and political requirements meant that each superpower developed its own force structures, making determination of equality difficult.

The problem of defining equality in terms of specific weapons systems soon became apparent in the SALT I negotiations (Newhouse 1974; Jensen 1988; Whelan 1979). The process of arriving at "the parameters of May 20" was one of answering the referent question by limiting the weapons systems covered by the treaty to those which could be contained in a formula of equality; much of the rest of the negotiation was dominated by efforts to defend the equality principle against attempts to substitute others that were unacceptable because unequal. Equal numbers in a single weapons system can often be unequal in reality; such was the case in regard to submarine-launched ballistic missiles (SBLMs), since the Soviet Union was able to keep only 11 percent of its SLBMs at sea (and thereby useable) in contrast to 50 percent for the US. It was also discovered that restricted ceilings or reductions to select weapons systems can provide an appearance of inequality that is difficult to explain to the public. This was the case in the Interim Offensive Weapons Agreement of 1972 which made it appear that the Soviet Union would be allowed to have far more strategic weapons than the US.

In SALT II, justice as equality took the form of equal aggregates that provided the basis of the treaty (Talbott 1979; Wolfe 1979). By counting each part of the defense triad as one unit, this formula allowed the US and the Soviet Union to continue their asymmetrical force structure under the notion of equality, with the US emphasizing bombers and SLBMs and the Soviet Union relying more on ICBMs. In both and other disarmament cases, frequent reference was made to the principle during the detailed phase of establishing numbers and referents (Goodby 1988; Borawski 1993).

The effort to maintain equality with unequal force structures led to attempts to find a formula based on compensatory (unequal) justice, but the power of the equality notion worked to limit the notion of inequality. Prior to the significant Gorbatchev concessions on intermediate range nuclear forces (INF), the Soviet Union demanded compensation for the imbalance which British and French nuclear forces, not part of the bilateral negotiations, gave to the West and which threatened Soviet security as much as American nuclear forces. The US, for its part, often asked for compensation for certain Soviet military advantages such as superiority in conventional forces or Soviet presence on the European continent

Since the collapse of the Soviet Union, disarmament negotiations have reverted to the inequality principle of equity. In both the Conventional Forces in Europe (CFE) Treaty of 1991 and the START II Treaty of 1992, the former Soviet republics agreed to substantially greater reductions than the US and other Western powers, possibly in expectation of compensating economic aid and possibly because of decreased need or decreased ability to handle the financial burdens of armament.

In summary, arms control negotiations show:

1   Arms negotiations start from an established principle of justice as a time-honored formula and revise it only when the context undergoes a major change. Negotiators refer back to the principle for justification during the detailed phase of negotiations.
2   The strength of the principle is shown by the lengthy debate over its referents and implementation.
3   Inability to agree on the principle or the referent question blocks further negotiation.

Justice in regional security negotiations

Evidence for the need for prior agreement on a principle of justice also appears in negotiations over regional conflicts, although on a less systematic, case-by-case basis. Case evidence shows that the governing principle tends to be equality, but that the referent question then opened to negotiation requires a lot of attention before the detailed issues can be settled. Analysis of twelve years of the Namibian negotiations, beginning in 1977 and leading to the Washington Treaty of 1988, shows the necessity of a balanced formula expressing compound equality as a precondition to both sides' engagement to reach agreement on details (Crocker 1992; Zartman 1989a, Chapter 5). As long as the formula was merely the priority justice expression, "One person one vote in Namibia" (1977–84), no conclusive progress was possible because there were not sufficiently balanced payoffs for both sides in the unilateral withdrawal of South Africa from Namibia (all the more so because the US government during the Carter period made it plain that it would not reward apartheid South Africa with any kinder treatment for its withdrawal from South West Africa).

But when the formula, based on the equality principle, became "linked withdrawal of Cuban troops from Angola and of South African troops from Namibia," both sides had a stake in the outcome, and productive negotiation became possible. As long as the formula was one-sided, the other side could object to its lack of fairness as a basis for a settlement and block negotiations; when it was revised to express justice as a rough equality or equivalence (tailored in detail to the different conditions on either side of the Cunene River boundary), each element was seen as the fair and necessary price to be paid for the corresponding element on the other side. Angolan president Eduardo Dos Santos as he bought on to the formula of equivalence, on 24 July 1986 said, "We believe the time is right for negotiation of a just political solution."[19]

Another body of evidence appears in the prolonged negotiations over the Israeli–Palestinian problem. For 20 years, each side insisted on a priority principle of justice, one party calling for the return of all conquered territory, the other for absolute security. In 1967, the formula of equivalent justice, "Territory for security," was adopted in United Nations Security Council resolution 242, thereafter identified as the epitome of a principle of justice used as a basis for negotiation (Carrington 1980; Rubin 1981; Zartman *et al.* 1987; Ben-Dor and Dewitt 1987; Touval 1990). Recognizing the legitimacy of both claims, it declared that neither was obtainable without the other, and that justice was to be found in both elements and in the reciprocity of their exchange, a clear case of compound equality. Without such a formula, negotiations after 1967 would have been merely over a unilateral withdrawal or a zero-sum conflict over a single disputed good. The equality formula answered both the principle and the referent questions. It established the terms of trade for a fair exchange, leaving the determination of the quantities to be exchanged in the hands of the negotiating parties.

The establishment of the principle enabled the parties to arrive at a series of mediated agreements for partial Israeli withdrawal from occupied territories in Sinai and the Golan Heights in 1974–5 and then for full withdrawal from Sinai and a peace treaty with Egypt in 1979, in both cases based on the negotiated translation of the formula, "Territory for security," into specific implementing details. The process bogged down thereafter because the framing principle of justice was not adequate to the remaining situation in the eyes of either party; for the Likud government of Israel, security was already in hand and so was not a fair price for the territory of the West Bank, and for the Arab side, the question of a Palestinian entity was not addressed by the terms of trade. The engagement of the Likud and then the Labor governments, on one hand, and the Palestine Liberation Organization (PLO), on the other, in the Madrid peace process after 1990 and then its Oslo extension after 1993, brought the formula of equivalent justice back on the table. But it posed the next question of implementing details with a vengeance: how much security is bought with how much (extent, status, evolution) territory, in order that equivalence remain true to its nature of rough equality? On the other hand, in the post-Madrid peace process, bilateral negotiations between Israel and Syria have become intense over the question, how much territory for how much normalized relations (security)? Again showing the acceptance of the compound equality principle as a time honored formula and the shift of negotiations to the phase of implementing details.

In many other regional conflicts – in Eritrea, Ogaden, Sri Lanka, Western Sahara, Cyprus, Irian Barat, Kurdistan, Bosnia, among others – inability to agree on a governing sense of justice and insistence on principled negotiations based on conflicting notions of priority justice have long prevented negotiations from advancing to any agreement on details. In the dispute between Turkey, Syria and Iraq over the Euphrates waters, where the parties hold to different notions of priority justice, "it would be hard to resolve th[e] dispute unless a universal standard of fairness is established regarding the allocation of resources, one that could satisfy the minimum rights of owner and user" (Faure and Rubin 1993, p. 18), Even a quick review of these cases shows that power structures, rational choice, or alternative outcomes do not alone explain the absence of progress toward agreement in these case, which are blocked essentially because one side or both consider current terms under discussion to be unjust. Unable to harmonize their separate notions of justice or to agree on a combined notion, and unable to oblige the other party to agree to their sense of justice, they have been unable find a solution to their conflict

In Eritrea, the solution was found by the total defeat of one side, as the Eritrean People's Liberation Front (EPLF) not only defeated the Ethiopian army and government but actually replaced it with a coalition of its own, the Ethiopian People's Revolutionary Democratic Front (EPRDF) (Ottaway 1995). In Sri Lanka, and perhaps elsewhere in due course, the effects of continuing conflict wore down the commitment of both sides to their opposing priority notions of justice and negotiations became possible, in early 1995 in Sri Lanka; (see Wriggins 1995).

In summary, the historical record of regional conflict negotiations shows:

1   Parties interact to establish the principle of justice as the basis for their negotiations, and when they do not, further negotiations fail.
2   Compound justice as a principle is a common answer in complex regional security negotiations, in preference to the oversimplicity of simple equality and the zero-sum nature of priority principles of justice.
3   Countervailing, structural or skill power is inadequate to explain either the success, the failure or the nature of the outcome of security negotiations, yielding at best a tautology.

Further research agenda

It is important to restore justice to the position it deserves as part of human efforts to resolve disputes and solve problems. There are too many successes and failures in negotiation that simply cannot be explained through power alone and which become intelligible only when justice is included as an explanatory consideration. There is too much in the practice of negotiation that is doomed to failure if power is the only guideline for action and that becomes possible when negotiators are sensitized to considerations of justice. This analysis suggests much further research. While the predominance of justice principles as the basis of successful negotiations is well established, the incidence of equality vs inequality as the form of justice is unresolved. Even inequalities seem to be reduceable to some form of equal trade-offs, leading to the hypothesis that all negotiation is based on equal justice through interactional trade-offs. The question of why a particular principle is accepted is still largely unresearched and requires getting inside the negotiation process more than is often possible. The referent question is the subject of much innovative work in negotiation analysis which looks for new items for trade-offs (Young 1994; Raiffa 1982; Albin 1992) but needs to be placed more explicitly into the larger context of justice (Lax and Sebenius 1986, pp. 150–2; Raiffa 1982, pp. 235–55). Negotiation is a human activity and so will not show the same regularities found in physical sciences. However, if the form justice takes most of the time in negotiation and when it is done best can be better understood, then more successful and more satisfying negotiations can be produced.

5 Justice in negotiation[20]

Conflict between positions is the basis of democratic debate and the open society holds that truth appears only when conflicting positions are fully confronted publicly. When this debate is not allowed, stronger forms of conflict appear within states, but directed against their government, which in turn harnesses conflict to repress citizens and impose order. The management of conflict, or the process of turning conflict into order can follow a number of different forms. Institutionalized conflict is the nature of elections, legislation, and judicial proceedings, and other forms of government involve conflict less orderly. When institutions are not present to establish decision rules and hierarchies of authority, a looser form is required, known as negotiation. Negotiation is the mode of decision-making where the default decision rule is unanimity and therefore the parties are equal, that is, each has a veto. In negotiation, conflict between positions is overcome in a joint decision, without benefit of votes, institutions, or authorities. A minimum of order is a prerequisite, enough for the parties to communicate, but no more; even the decision rule itself is established only by unanimous agreement and is broken when there is no agreement. This amount of order is based on the characteristic mixed-motive situation, which requires both conflicting and common interests for the negotiation to take place – common interest in reaching agreement, which holds the process together, and conflicting interests to reconcile, which make the process necessary (Ikle 1964). All other processes to overcome conflict except force have already a higher prerequisite of order.

Epistemologically, these other processes are easier to analyze and their results easier to explain, in the sense that the explanatory variables are more evident in the process. Thus, voting can be measured (Rae and Taylor 1970), coalitions can be the subject of theory (Riker 1992), hierarchy can be conceptualized (Mosca 1939; Putnam 1976), institutions can be categorized (North 1991). The analytical approach to negotiation is less obvious. The predominant school, which takes many forms, explains negotiated outcomes through the use of power (Edgeworth 1881; Zeuthen 1930; Hicks 1932; Schelling 1960; Ikle 1964; Walton and McKersie 1965; Zartman 1974; Harsanyi 1977; Bartos 1987; Brams 1985), defined as actions taken with the intent of inflecting the other party's behavior in an intended direction (Zartman and Rubin 2000).

Power and justice

Power is not all, however (Zartman *et al.* 1996). If it were, the structural dilemma – whereby weak negotiate with strong and gain favorable (even asymmetrically favorable) outcomes – would not exist. Yet the structural dilemma is an interesting analytical problem, since many negotiations involve asymmetries that require explanation (Wriggins 1987; Zartman and Rubin 2000; Habeeb 1988). Some of these can be artificially elimi- nated by manipulating definitions of power. Thus, the standard behavioral definition of power as the ability to move a party in an intended direction (Tawney 1931; Simon 1953; Dahl 1957; Thibaut and Kelley 1959) brooks no dilemma, since it is conclusionary or outcome-directed; the existence of power is proved by the outcome and therefore the most powerful must always win, because the winner is always most powerful, that is, most able to move the other party.

The other common definition of power, which identifies it with resources, poses the structural dilemma most clearly. Actors with an over- whelming imbalance of resources frequently do well (Morgan 1994, p. 141) but also frequently do poorly in negotiation, and indeed, contrary to common wisdom, negotiations among unequals tend to be more efficient and satisfying than negotiations among equals (Pruitt and Carnevale 1993; Rubin and Zartman 1995). A more behavioral basis or source of power that is common to many approaches is the value of alternatives, variously termed security points (Zartman 1987, pp. 12–13), damage (Harsanyi 1977, pp. 179), reservation prices (Lax and Sebenius 1986, p. 51), threat potentials (Rapoport 1966, p. 97), security levels (Rapoport 1966, p. 101), resistance points (Walton and McKersie 1965, p. 41), best alternative to a negotiated agreement or BATNA (Fisher and Ury 1981), among others. Here too, however, the power of alternatives leaves many negotiated out- comes unexplained (Hopkins 1987). Power alone, by any but a tautologi- cal definition, does not always account for the maintenance of a veto over conflict resolving proposals; conflict is often preferred over a negotiated order by weaker parties under great pressure.

An alternative explanation revives the element of justice as a basis for acceptable orders or as a criterion for conflict termination. In the process of negotiating the exchange of division of items contested between them, the parties come to an agreement on the notion of justice that will govern this disposition; if they do not, the negotiations will not be able to proceed to a conclusion. Individual notions of justice act as a substantive veto on agreement, and must be coordinated an accepted as the first stage of negotiation. This notion of justice constitutes a formula on the basis of which parties then proceed to the disposition of details. The formula can be a procedural rule for establishing terms of trade, or one or more principles of justice on which such terms can be based (Zartman 1978; Zartman and Berman 1982). Inherent in this argument is the recognition that power alone cannot either produce or explain agreement and cannot substitute for justice determination in the process of negotiation (HP Young 1994; Zartman 1995; Zartman *et al.* 1996 [Chapter 4]). The analytical questions then become: what is the meaning of justice in negotiation and how is it determined? What alternative outcomes and explanations of outcomes are provided by power and by justice?

The most prominent notion of justice is that of equality or impartiality. Equal treatment is seen as fair treatment and equal outcomes are just deserts. Equality in its many forms is a common point of agreement for combining competing claims, forming a floor (and hence, bilaterally, a ceiling) on relative gains and providing an acceptable formula for agreement as split-the-difference in the end when other criteria have run out. It is also the basic element in the entire procedural ethos under which negotiation takes place, that of reciprocity or the equal exchange of equal concessions (Keohane 1986; Larson 1988). Where equality is desired but cannot or need not be determined, a looser form known as equivalent justice is often used. The basis of justice in these cases is simply an exchange deemed appropriate or roughly similar, and justice is to be found not in the relative size of the shares but in the mere fact of the exchange, as opposed to receiving the first item as a gift.

Yet there are also well-established principles of inequality that serve notions of justice in particular circumstances – equity (or merit or investment), in which the party who has or contributes the most receives the most, and compensation (or need or redistribution), in which the party that has the least receives the most. Even inequalities are equalizing measures, however, exchanged for some past or future equalizer, in the case of equity or compensation, respectively. Compensation is based on equalizing payments to one side, and "entitlement" and "deserving" are brought about through exchange for some external or non-tangible good from the receiving side, or for a good somewhere else on the time dimension (past or future). Thus, permanent seats on the UN Security Council were given to the Five Great Powers as a down-payment on future security, not because the Powers had nuclear weapons; merit scholarships are not given because of entitlement for intelligence but as a trade-off for future contribution to society (or to alumni funds); and developing countries receive compensation for reduction of ozone-depleting substances in exchange for future development (or for past mistreatment.

Without recognition of such exchanges, unequal divisions are unacceptable and negotiations stalemate. Thus, unequal justice norms can also be interpreted as a different kind of equality, not in exchange for the other party's contribution but in exchange for one's own contribution.

The justifying criterion shifted from an interactional (between-party) to an internal (within-party) exchange. Such equalizing is the meaning and purpose of equity in the legal sense, where various instances of compensatory justice are invoked to temper the severity of partial justice principles (Deutsch 1985; Homans 1961; Adams 1965; Messe 1971). Furthermore, starting positions of unequal as well as equal justice may yield equality as the distribution rule through a negotiating process.

A third type of justice principle is equal only in that it is to be equally applied ("equality before the law") but it designates a winner, according to an established rule or generalized formula. Priority (partial) justice refers to principles from external sources that decree a particular outcome – "first come first served," "finders keepers," "winner take all," "polluter pays," "riparian rights," "noblesse oblige," "primogeniture," and many others. These principles are usually absolute, incontrovertible; and indicate total allocation, not sharing. Since they are principles that favor one side, they are usually adopted to justify opening positions or the wants, needs and interests of each side, but they may also be used as the basis of agreement under the equal application principle …

The process of arriving at an agreed principle of justice in negotiation can be seen as evolving through three stages: absolute, comparative, and jointly determined. Different parties may initially have different notions of justice (often priority justice) that favor their positions (were they to decide the outcome unilaterally). However, they must place their own position ("Justice for me") within a social context ("Justice for me compared to you") relating to relative gains and losses. While a party acting alone would most likely adopt a self-serving notion of justice ("I deserve the goods"), the fact that it has to negotiate means that winning outright is not an option and a different notion of justice is needed; all things being equal, equality is the most frequently-held norm ("I deserve to do at least as much as you"). When the two comparative or social evaluations of justice are combined, a jointly-determined outcome is (or is not) produced, and the negotiation can go on to apply it. It should be remembered that these are analytical stages and their neat, discrete quality is not always reflected in the messy world of reality.

Determining the agreeable, applicable among the three principles of justice is only one step in establishing the negotiation in justice; the other step concerns the referent or application of the principle: equality or inequality or priority of what? If parties want to maintain their parity or equality in arms, they must decide which of many parts or measures of armaments they will use. When the UN Security Council enunciated the equivalence formula of "territory for security" for the Middle East in resolution 242 in 1967 they only started the process of determining what was territory and what was security in each of the occupied territories along the Israeli border, which was in turn the necessary prelude to the detailed question of how much territory for how much security. When the Serbs,

Croats and Bosnians came to an understanding about the semi-federative relation within Bosnia at Wright Patterson Air Base in late 1995 (the referent question first), they then had to decide the type of justice that would govern relations within and between the parts (the principle question). When legislators on a tax reform bill establish the new code on the basis of equality (flat rate), equity (regressive), compensation (progressive) or some priority principle, it still has to decide what is to be the referent of the principle (income, sales, head or other).

The propositions, or hypotheses, to be tested, then, can be stated in the form of a necessary proposition, "If there is a final agreement, then there was a prior agreement on justice"; the stronger necessary and sufficient form, "If there is an agreement on justice, then there will be a final agreement"; and its converse, "If no agreement on justice, no final agreement." As in many hypotheses, it is important that the two variables be kept separate and that separate evidence be found for each, lest the statement become an identity and agreement itself be taken as evidence for the existence of a shared sense of justice. Like war and peace, justice does not always wear a badge and is not present only when declared. Thus evidence in this inquiry may require interpretation, without thereby diluting its strength. Evidence may come in one of three forms. There may be explicit statements, either invoking justice itself or referring to its principles, such as equality or need or equity. There may be statements of position or policy which refer to principles of justice without explicitly naming them, and yet using them as justifications. And there may be policy or position statements which contain principles presented as self-justifying, where the analyst may be required to point out the justice principle. Thus, like M Jourdain, negotiators may be "speaking justice" without knowing it, although like any good diplomats they may also speak justice implicitly and indirectly but perfectly consciously. Like any good diplomats, negotiators may also speak justice explicitly but perfectly insincerely, using the term to cover its opposite. Such subtleties are no less present here than in any other research on power, interest, or preferences, which is the more common language of negotiations analysis.

The following analysis will examine the role of justice and fairness in the negotiation process. The first task is to seek to establish the proposition by looking for the separate, coincident and causal existence of the two variables, by examining a number of cases of negotiations that are relatively diverse and important and are deemed successful because they have achieved a final agreement. Was that agreement preceded by a joint agreement on the sense of justice that would govern the outcome? Was there an absence of agreement until that common principle of justice was established? Would power alone have produced different outcomes and different explanations? Once the proposition is established, it would be interesting to examine apparently disconfirming cases where there is a final agreement but no inter-party consensus on the governing principle of justice. Social interaction and social science being what they are, such cases would not necessarily be disconfirming unless they came in over-whelming numbers and in addition produced better results than the cases governed by prior agreement on justice. In these cases, the proposition could help provide guidelines to better agreements.

Cases

It would be impossible to make a quantitative test of these questions, since the evidence is in the idiosyncratic differences in each case. A number of important diplomatic cases will be used to illustrate and support the propositions and serve as a guide for further testing and refinement. These cases include the negotiations over southwestern Africa (Namibia and Angola) between 1977 and 1988; over disarmament in Europe between 1984 and 1986; the 1962 Cuban Missile Crisis; and two economic negotiations, the 1983–4 contract renegotiations between Ghana and its aluminum consortium and the 1977–9 trade negotiations over gas between Mexico and the US. These cases are chosen because they provide interesting and diverse illustrations of the propositions; once those propo-sitions are established, other, apparently more ambiguous cases can be analyzed in the same way.

Negotiations over Namibian independence pitted South Africa against the Namibian national liberation movement, the South West African Peoples Organization (SWAPO) but also against an array of other adversaries from the more moderate nationalist movements such as the Democratic Turn-halle Alliance (DTA) to the sovereign states of Angola and Cuba, in the presence of a number of mediators, including the Front Line States, the Western Contact group, the US and the Soviet Union (Crocker 1992; 1989a, Chapter 5). Faced toward the end of the 1970s with the inability of incorporating its South West African mandated territory within its own political system, South Africa turned to create an independent state in its own image by arranging an "internal solution." When it became apparent that this too was not susceptible of attracting international approval, and thus of solving the problem, South Africa, in 1978, agreed to the terms for a UN-supervised election for a constituent assembly that had been worked out through Contact Group mediation. When SWAPO then also agreed, and the UN Secretary General Kurt Waldheim added some new details of his own, South Africa found that the formula was no longer acceptable and withdrew its agreement. South Africa consistently proclaimed that a just solution was to be found in procedural terms, through a general elec-tion, although it attached a number of conditions – no external pressure, no violence – that would insure that a friendly neighbor could be assured. This was stated as a self-justifying principle of priority justice on many occasions. Prime Minister BJ Vorster said to the South Africa Senate in 1967, "There is only one solution ..., namely, that the people of South

West Africa should be allowed to decide their own future unhindered and without interference" (UNSC/PV 2082). Foreign Minister RF Botha echoed before the UN Security Council more than a decade later, on 27 July 1978, "It is for the people of the territory themselves to decide their own political and constitutional future. Their wishes in this regard are the paramount consideration. As was said in 1967, 'The people themselves will ultimately decide.'"

As South Africa began to lose control of who "the people" were (the referent question), however, its spokesmen began to add the second priority principle of friendliness, stability or peacefulness, also presented as a self-evident value. Prime Minister PW Botha declared on 18 October 1978:

> Any political party that takes part in a constitutional, peaceful way will be allowed to go to the polling booth ... and ... have the right and the possibility of winning ... But I am not going to allow foreign interests to force a minority government with guns on the majority of the people of South West Africa.
>
> (James Haagland, *Washington Post*, October 1978)

A year later, on 5 August 1979, he said: "The South African government, as well as the leaders of South West Africa, attach great value to an internationally acceptable solution ... however, ... if an eventual choice should be between stability or [*sic*] chaos, we shall choose stability" (*New York Times*, 11 August 1979). At the Geneva Pre-implementation Meeting on 13 January 1981, DTA leader Dirk Mudge declared,

> We accepted resolution 435 [and] ... we look forward to elections which would be truly free and fair. But we insist that the elections be conducted in an atmosphere of peace and security, and we insist that there should be reasonable and credible assurances that after the elections the democratic system and basic political, civil and economic right would continue to be respected. Mr Chairman, the concerns which I have expressed are valid; by all standards of equity; the questions which I have asked are reasonable.
>
> (*New York Times*, 14 January 1981)

The South African position was to trade in its rule of Namibia (South West Africa) for independence in such a way as to install a minimally friendly government, but it was couched in terms of priority principles of justice – free and fair elections under conditions of peace and stability.

SWAPO's position was simpler but also presented in terms of priority justice: it's ours, we fought for it, repeated SWAPO leader Sam Nujoma on many occasions. FLS (Front Line State) allies finally brought SWAPO around to agreeing to UNSCr 435 providing for one-person-one-vote elections under paired UN and South African auspices that SWAPO, which had already been declared "the sole legitimate representative of the Namibian people," felt were unnecessary. "South Africa's only role," said SWAPO's UN observer Theo Ben Gurirab (*New York Times*, 12 June 1977), "is to announce publicly that it accepts all UN resolutions on South West Africa and that means withdrawing from the territory, agreeing to UN-controlled elections, and releasing political prisoners."

The priority justice positions of each side did little to satisfy the other, and it is little wonder that the negotiations deadlocked. The two sides dickered over details, SWAPO continued to wage its guerrilla warfare ineffectually, and South Africa continued to hold elections for an internal solution that the international community refused to grant legitimacy. Even more striking was the fact that the mediators also clung to a principle of priority justice, rejecting any notion of division, exchange or sharing. UN Ambassador "Andrew Young and Vice President [Walter] Mondale have said that the US is no longer committed to linkage policy with South Africa, as pursued by [former Secretary of State] Henry Kissinger. 'Under his approach, the US agreed in effect to limit its pressure on South Africa to largely philosophical criticisms in exchange for Mr Vorster's cooperation with regard to Rhodesia and South West Africa.' Officials now explain that 'the State Department is no longer willing to hold back on South Africa in the hope of obtaining action on majority rule in Rhodesia and a new status for South West Africa.'" (*New York Times*, 18 May 1977) The US supported the UN position that the answer to the conflict lay in the priority principle of one-person-one-vote under UN auspices. Although this position was softened slightly a year later to allow paired UN–South African auspices in hope of extracting a South African agreement to UNR 435, it remained the essential basis of US policy, "the Carter Administration in effect [taking] the position that South Africa should cooperate on South West Africa and Rhodesia for its own good ..." (*New York Times*, 3 December 1978). While a single, well-chosen principle of priority justice may well attract the adherence of both sides in some cases, in others such as the Namibian instance it is not seen as just by both parties and so raises unreal hopes on one side while alienating the other.

It was a new linkage by the succeeding mediator who provided a principle of equivalence if not of equality. The objections of each side to the other's principle were to be met by a paired withdrawal of Cuban troops from Angola and of South African troops from Namibia, after which the free and fair elections could be held. As Assistant Secretary of State Chester Crocker explained in a "Voice of America" interview on 23 June 1982,

> The relationship that exists between these two issues was not invented by the Reagan Administration or by the United States – it's a fact, it's a fact of history, of geography, of logic. It's also a fact that no party can lay down prior conditions or preconditions to any other party. That's

not going to produce progress. The South Africans cannot be threatened into leaving Namibia – excepting on terms that are in some minimal sense acceptable to them ... The same applies the other way. And given the history, and the lack of confidence that exists on both sides of that border, we believe that it's unrealistic for any side to say to the other, 'You go first.' What we're seeking is parallel movement on the two questions – South African withdrawal from Namibia as provided under the UN plan, Resolution 435, and Cuban withdrawal from Angola.

The new formula was facilitated by a change in parties, the state of Angola replacing the movement of SWAPO in dealing with South Africa. The confrontation of two sovereign states with their own national interests helped the applicability of an equality principle of justice, with the referent question still to be specified.

Enunciation of a principle of justice, however balanced, does not assure automatic acceptance by all parties, and other conditions than simply its innate attractiveness are required for that acceptance. However, the equality (or equivalence) principle of a paired withdrawal formed the basis of the eventual solution in 1988 and, perhaps as important, guided in its spirit the search for just and equivalent implementing details for the final agreement – "a reasonable and balanced" set of conditions in the words of one side's spokesman and "a just and fair settlement" in the words of another's (*New York Times*, 31 August 1988; *Washington Post*, 12 August 1988). Angolan president Eduardo dos Santos finally indicated on 24 July 1986 that "We believe the time is right for negotiation of a just political solution" (FBIS Africa, 24 July 1986, SADCC meeting), and Cuban President Fidel Castro stated in the midst of the final negotiations, "If the agreement is completed and respected, Angola and Cuba will carry out a gradual and total withdrawal of all the [Cuban] internationalist contingent in Angola. There is a real possibility of a just and honorable solution to the war." (*New York Times*, 27 July 1988). The formula was specific enough to be considered an instance of equality, rather than simply equivalence, since the items exchanged – the withdrawal of foreign troops – were the same and even the number of troops – 90,000 South Africans and 80,000 Cubans – was nearly identical, even if their distance and their timetable for withdrawal was not fully coincident; most importantly, of course, South African gave up colonial sovereignty with its withdrawal, whereas Cuba gave up contracted assistance. The formula was not merely based on "getting something" in exchange for independence but rather a matched and balance trade-off that provided the guide for further details. It is noteworthy that the one missing element in the application of equal justice to both areas was the holding of elections in Angola, parallel to those in Namibia; this item, not part of the Washington Agreement of December 1988, was the basis of the complementary Estoril and Lusaka

Agreements of May 1990 and November 1994, respectively, which provided for the settlement of the internal Angolan conflict. The shift from priority to equality principles of justice that both sides could subscribe to provided the basis for the negotiated agreement in South West Africa.

The Stockholm Conference on Disarmament in Europe (CDE) represents a very different test for the notions of justice in negotiation. It shows that a common notion of justice (the principle question) can be identified early on but can run up against the referent question, that additional principles of justice may be required to keep negotiations moving, that that internal changes in the parties and in their relations with each other may be required in order to be able to complete the principle and resolve the referent questions, so as finally to arrive at an agreement. CDE grew out of the Helsinki Conference on Security and Cooperation in Europe (CSCE) in 1975. The Helsinki Final Act contained, among other things, both a no use of force (NUF) declaration and a few limited but instructive confidence-building measures (CBMs). In 1978 France proposed a European disarmament conference "from the Atlantic to the Urals" (in a Gaullist phrase), initially focusing exclusively on CBMs. The relationship between the conference and the measures was debated at the Madrid meeting of CSCE in 1983, resulting in the Madrid Mandate for the Stockholm Conference to "begin a process of which the first stage will be devoted to the negotiation and adoption of a set of mutually complementary [confidence and security building] measures ... [over] the entire continent of Europe" (CSCE Madrid Document, 1983). The conference began in Stockholm on 17 January 1984.

The careful wording of the mandate represented both a clear agreement on the principles of justice and a troublesome ambiguity on its application. The "mutually complementary measures" were to be an exercise in equal justice, since they were to be equally applied to all parties within the area and this equality of treatment was a crucial rule of standing and treatment for the CSCE members, but most particularly for the NATO and Warsaw Pact partners. Yet the referent question recognized that equality was hard to find in reality, for several reasons. CPSU General Secretary Leonid Brezhnev expressed the clash between principle and referent quite succinctly in an interview with *Der Spiegel* on 2 November 1981: "We naturally expect reciprocal [i.e. equal] steps from the West. Military preparations in the European zone of NATO do not start from the continental edge of Europe" (Borawski 1992, p. 28). The same problem was analyzed in careful detail by US Ambassador James Goodby (1988, pp. 154, 164).

The value of confidence-building measures is greater for the US than for the Soviet Union ... because greater openness in military activities should better serve the interests of the US ... In addition to this well-known problem, the Soviet Union faced another dilemma peculiar to the Stockholm Conference – how to reconcile their interest in a European security conference with their instinct that any agreement emerging from it should apply to US forces and territory with no less rigor than to Soviet Union forces and territory ... The asymmetrical geographical coverage probably caused real concerns in some quarters in Moscow, however, and the Soviet Union delegate sought to compensate for this by making proposals that affected the West to a greater extent than the East (... ceiling on exercises, ... high threshold on notification, ... naval activities on the high seas, [and] ... air activities.) ... Thus they sought to achieve not only a geographic offset to the unequal treatment they tried to portray in the outcome of the Madrid mandate, but also to provide for coverage of those US forces that they perceived to be a special threat to themselves. ... A third category of obstacles common to many of the issues already stated stemmed from the asymmetries in the way US and Soviet Union forces are structured and trained.

The negotiations faced a dilemma: how to implement the agreed principle of equality when its implementation could not be accomplished with equal interest and equal effect? Either the principle had to be changed, from equal to unequal justice, as the Soviet Union tried by seeking compensation for the asymmetries, or ways had to be found the apply the mandated principle of equality. As Soviet Ambassador Grinevsky said (or was instructed to say) as late as 22 March 1985 in round V, "most of the proposals ... [in NATO's SC.1 Amplified] continue to be aimed at laying bare the military activities of the Warsaw Treaty countries, at securing unilateral military advantages. As before, they do not meet the requirements of equality of rights, balance and reciprocity, equal respect for the security interests of all participating states" [Borawski 1992, p. 65], and again on 8 October at the end of round VII, "instead of confidence-building, they palm off its opposite – measures designed to expose the location and structures of the armed forces of the European states and to secure unilateral advantages" (Borawski 1992, p. 77). Until the referent question could be answered satisfactorily, the principle question remained abstract and negotiations were stuck.

The negotiators were working on the problem, however. A little publicized *walk on the wharf* in Stockholm by Ambassadors Goodby and Grinevsky produced the suggestion of a new and complementary principle of equivalenceSoviet agreement to CSBMs in exchange for US agreement to a renewed NUF (non-use of force) declaration. The suggestion was conveyed to President Reagan who included it as an apparent "precipitating act" (Saunders 1988, p. 437) in his speech to the Irish parliament on 4 June 1984:

> If discussions on reaffirming the principle not to use force, a principle in which we believe so deeply, will bring the Soviet Union to negotiate agreements which will give concrete, new meaning to that principle, we will gladly enter into such discussions.
>
> (Cited in Goodby 1988, p. 151)

The suggestion of equivalence came too quickly even to inform the NATO allies, who grumbled at the shift, and too early to affect the negotiations immediately. Equivalence of issues did not replace equality of application as the governing principle of justice; it only facilitated it, and other changes were needed to make the latter acceptable

These changes came with the leadership succession in the Soviet Union, not as a matter of personality or idiosyncrasy, but as a matter of the redefinition of Soviet Union interests that made the application of the equality principle possible. Confidence-building leading to arms reduction in Europe became a prime Soviet Union interest, therefore allowing a focus on "the whole of Europe" without implying asymmetry. The Europeanness of the Soviet Union was a historic Russian theme of importance to Gorbachev, overriding perceptions of geographical imbalance. In the midst of round VIII, the first summit meeting between Reagan and Gorbachev, in Geneva produced a final statement that "reaffirmed the need for a document which would include mutually acceptable confidence- and security-building measures and give concrete expression and effect to the principle of non-use of force" [Borawski 1992, p. 77].

Acceptance of the two principles of justice – equality and equivalence – allowed the negotiators to move ahead to the details of the agreement, translating the principled formula into specific measures, for the first time. The informal structure which took over by round VII and characterized proceedings through 1986 testified to the effect of agreement on the formula, allowing parties to work together in search of agreeable provisions. Concessions began to appear at the beginning of 1986, starting with Gorbachev's address on disarmament on 15 January and continuing in the IX, X and XI rounds between January and July. In the end, Ambassador Barry, Goodby's successor, judged, "We gave away more than we wanted, but we got ... a fair bargain, ..." (*Washington Post*, 22 September 1986). Power alone could not have produced and could not explain the agreement. Even though the agreement on terms close to the American position came after the weakening (as prelude to the eventual collapse) of the Soviet Union, it was not the pressure of that asymmetry that caused the Soviet Union to agree. The key to that agreement was its formulation in acceptable terms of justice, and until that was accomplished, the negotiations were stuck.

The third case is the well-known *Cuban missile crisis* of October 1962, on which much has been written, particularly as a case of national security and of Cold War confrontation. It was also an almost-textbook case of negotiation, involving a few simple moves. Countervailing power was used to carry the crisis into stalemate, from which war, capitulation, and a negotiated deal were the only ways out. Insistence on capitulation, which was within the grasp of US power, would have produced war; negotiation was necessary to produce a way out that avoided war or what Khrushchev termed "untying the knot" (Khrushchev 1962, p. 642). Even though the result reflected the unbalanced distribution of resource power, it became possible only when a notion of justice was addressed and resolved, and the process of resolving involved a number of attempts to create the appropriate balance by criteria of justice.

The installation of Soviet missiles in Cuba was decided in June 1962 (Khrushchev 1970, 493–4) and discovered by the US on 16 October (Kennedy 1969, p. 1). The Soviet Union action was later justified as a deterrent against the US invasion of Cuba, based on an absolute priority principle of collective defense, equally applied: "We had the same rights and opportunities as the Americans ... governed by the same rules and limits ..." (Khrushchev 1970, pp. 496, 493–5; Khrushchev 1974, p. 511). For the US, the right of self-defense against an aggressive move received very little mention in the Executive Committee and was assumed as the legitimate expression of an absolute priority principle of justice (Rusk in Trachtenberg 1985, p. 171; Kennedy 1969). Discussions centered on the choice of an appropriate US response between air strike and blockade, neither of which would have resolved the issue and removed the missiles (Kennedy and Dillon in Trachtenberg 1985, p. 195). The quarantine was chosen as the first response to force withdrawal from the Soviet Union; air strikes were left as the second, in a threat position (Kennedy 1969, pp. 32–3; Rusk and McNamara in Trachtenberg 1985, pp. 173, 182; Kennedy in Trachtenberg 1985, p. 200). It was earlier decided that the quarantine around Cuba would not be traded against a Soviet blockade of Berlin (Trachtenberg 1985, pp. 178–9). The purpose of the quarantine was to impose a stalemate that would force a decision and would provide an item for trade against the removal of the missiles, as the expression of a priority justice principle but one that was uninteresting to the Soviet Union.

In the search for a joint notion of justice, Ambassador Adlai Stevenson proposed another trade, that of missiles in Turkey and Italy plus the Guantanamo Bay naval base in exchange for missiles in Cuba, an offer of equivalence that was immediately rejected by the ExCom (Kennedy 1969, p. 27). Similarly, the proposal of Acting Secretary General, U Thant, for a temporary lifting of the quarantine in exchange for a temporary suspension of missile deliveries (which would leave some missiles in Cuba still approaching operational status) was rejected by the US (after acceptance by the Soviet Union).

The appropriate referents for equivalent justice contained within the Cuban area were offered by Khrushchev in his letter of 26 October: US promise not to invade Cuba in exchange for missile "demobilization" (Khrushchev 1962, pp. 642, 645). The second Khrushchev letter of the following day repeated equivalence but in more nearly equal terms but no longer limited to the Cuban area: Soviet missiles out of Cuba in exchange for US missiles out of Turkey (Khrushchev 1962, p. 648); the president considered that it might "make a good trade" whereas the State Department, in rejecting it, proposed the rejection of any equivalence ("no trade could be made" [Kennedy in Trachtenberg 1985, pp. 199, 201; Kennedy 1969, p. 79]). The Executive Committee instead opted to take up the previous offer: Soviet offensive weapons out of Cuba in exchange for US removal of quarantine and assurances against invasion.

Justice is never mentioned in the Kennedy–Khrushchev exchanges. There was much discussion of terms of trade, the ingredients of equivalent justice, however, and in the debate over the two Khrushchev letters, President Kennedy clearly indicated that " we have to face up to the possibility of some kind of trade over missiles" (Kennedy in Trachtenberg 1985, p. 199). Grudgingly, Khrushchev – who having less to crow about, crowed more – indicated that by agreeing even to symbolic measures, Kennedy was creating the impression of mutual concessions (Khrushchev 1974, p. 512). Before his assassination, Robert Kennedy was to conclude his book with a chapter on justification. Despite a lack of explicit references to please the researchers, there is no doubt that the last days of the crisis and the bulk of the bargaining were spent in an intense search for terms of trade that would justify the withdrawal of the missiles, the lifting of the quarantine, and the negotiation of an agreement.

Two economic cases are interesting because they show that justice is applicable beyond the realm of security, and because they both hinge on priority notions of justice that operated in opposite ways in the two cases. In Ghana, despite equal vulnerabilities of the parties creating power symmetry, they formed a salient point on which a sense of justice could be crystalized (Schelling 1960), whereas in Mexico, despite power asymmetry that actually favored a mutually beneficial solution, they formed an obstacle to agreement on an acceptable notion of justice and hence to any agreement at all.

In 1983–4, the new government of Flt Lt Jerry Rawlings renegotiated its 1962 *power supply agreement* with a consortium of US aluminum transnational corporations known as VALCO. The 35-year agreement granted "one of the lowest arms-length power prices paid by any aluminium smelter in the world" (Sawyerr 2000, p. 100) to VALCO, originally in the hopes that the Volta River dam project would accelerate Ghanaian industrialization and development. Twenty years later, the investment returns to VALCO had become considerable while the development returns to Ghana had fallen below expectations.

Three rounds of confrontational talks were held on Ghana's invitation between February and May 1983. Ghana proposed that the relationship be "normalized" according to some well-anchored principles of priority justice. The protected treatment accorded VALCO should be lifted, specifically focusing its demand on the price of electricity that the company should now pay at a rate based on the weighted average price paid by aluminium smelters around the world, later calculated at 22 mills/kwH; quantity of electricity and tax rates were also to be renegotiated. Two years earlier, the 1962 electricity rate of 2.625 mills had been increased to five mills, and in round one VALCO proposed a further increase to eight mills, but without providing any supporting justification. Its goal was "an overall formula whereby the profit of the operations of VALCO are computed and shared in a manner that results in a fair and reasonable return to VALCO, the Volta River Authority and the people of Ghana," but its position was rooted in a competing priority principle, the assertion of its contracted rights and the maximization of its profitability. In round two, VALCO contested Ghana's method of calculation but not its principle, and offered its own calculations for rates ranging from 8.1 to 15.5 mills (Tsikata 1990).

Before the next round, Ghana devalued its currency drastically to almost a tenth of the prior value, thus reducing VALCO's local costs and raising its profitability. In the negotiations, it then moved beyond the indexing principle for the base power rate to introduce certain considerations favorable to VALCO in calculating an operational power rate, but VALCO backtracked completely and repudiated the indexing principle. When Ghanaian negotiators tried a " walk in the woods" and hinted at flexibility on tax proposals, VALCO did not respond; instead it offered a much-qualified rate of 12.5 mills, again without justification. Ghana broke off talks and, citing the drop in the water level of the lake as a result of the sahel drought, cut off the supply of electricity until the water level would return to normal.

A month later, VALCO acknowledged that the current price paid was unfair, in September it put forward new proposals roughly based on an indexing principle and translating into 15 mills, and in January 1984 talks resumed. Agreement was reached in July on a base power rate of 17 mills indexed to the London price of aluminum, with adjustments, a l5 percent reduction in available electricity, a 15 percent rise in the income tax rate to 46 percent, and a number of other provisions, some of which favored Ghana and some VALCO. Six more months of contentious drafting sessions were required to produce a final agreement, in January 1985 (Faber 1990).

The VALCO negotiations foundered over the search for an appropriate principle of justice and could not move until one was found. Each party confronted the other over its absolute priority principle. Ghana appeared to be the more powerful party, in that it could close down VALCO's operations (and cite a valid external excuse); apparently it could take shutdown more readily than could VALCO. But that indication of power was based on a decision about the justice of its position, not on its objective alternatives; the revenues from VALCO for electricity were the main source of income for the Volta River Authority and its only source of hard currency for debt servicing, just as the income from the operations was the source of revenue for VALCO. Ghana could not impose its price, only its principle, leaving its translation into details expressed in mills to a year of further negotiations. That principle in comparative terms was one of compensation as unequal justice, heading toward an outcome of equality. VALCO's opening position was one of priority justice, holding on to its contractual rights. "By not taking into adequate account the desperate economic situation of Ghana, the grave discontent over the one-sidedness of the agreement as it operated at the time, and any sense of 'objective' justice other than that of acquired rights, VALCO was unable to maintain a credible negotiating position, "records the principal Ghanaian negotiator" (Sawyerr 2000, p. 12).

In 1977, Mexico planned to sell its *natural gas*, a free byproduct of its oil extraction, to the US, and in August Petróleos Méxicos (PEMEX) signed a letter of intent with a consortium of six companies serving two-thirds of the American states (Odell 2000, pp. 94–102). Among other details, the initial price of $2.60 per thousand cubic feet (Mcf), revisable every six months, was indexed to the OPEC price of high-quality No. 2 fuel oil FOB New York, a current practice of pricing gas by its energy equivalent (Zartman and Bassani 1987). At the same time, PEMEX decided to build a $1 billion pipeline to link up with the US grid at the Texas border, for which international financing immediately became available; transport costs via the *gasoducto* were estimated at 40 cents/MCF compared with $2.34/Mcf for liquification and shipping abroad. The entire construction could be paid off with 200 days of full exports at the contracted price or a year of full exports at about $2. The US had just gone through its worst natural gas shortage in history, and had a secure market in Mexico. The media on both sides of the border welcomed the agreement as "an absolutely golden deal" (Fagen and Nau 1979, p. 400). Yet the agreement collapsed: by the end of the year, Mexico announced that it would sell the gas domestically, at a price capped at 26 cents. " By paying for [the] pipeline and then using it only to ship gas internally, PEMEX probably *lost* money" (Odell 2000, p. 100).

Throughout a complex set of rapidly evolving events the main obstacle appears to have been a feeling in Mexico that the indexed price was unshakably just by an absolute priority principle. Gas was part of the national patrimony of Mexico and the OPEC referent was the gauge of fairness; any questioning of that price and its justifying referent was seen as evidence of renewed American exploitation of Mexico, and therefore actually hardened the absolute and reinforced the notion of justice. Yet the US could obtain gas from Canada at $2.16/MCF, its justifying referent and security point, and Mexico could not sell its gas to anyone but the US at anywhere near that price. Equality would have provided a salient principle of justice and there were plenty of referents to which that principle could have been attached – from equality to the North American price to equality as split-the-difference between that price and some lower Mexican return all the way down to the Mexican domestic price or the *gasoducto* transportation cost. In any case, power in no way explains the outcome; the US was clearly more powerful in resources terms, in alternative terms,

Table 5.1 Principles of justice

Case	Initial principles	Referents	Principle of agreement
Namibia	SA: priority (conditional elections) SA: priority (friendly relations) SWAPO: priority (liberation) US: priority (one person one vote)	who votes?	US: equality (equivalence) (paired with withdrawal from Namibia and Angola
CDE	CSCE: equality (CBMs by all of Europe)	what is Europe	US–SU: equivalence (CSBMs for NUF
Cuba	SU: priority (collective defense) US: priority (self defense, remove missiles) SUL equality/equivalence (remove missiles – Cuba for Turkey)		SU: equivalence (remove missiles for no invasion of Cuba)
VALCO	Ghana: priority (world) Ghana: inequality (index/ price index) Valco: priority (contract price)	what price?	
PEMEX	Mexico: priority (national price) US: equality (relative price)	what price?	

and potentially in actional terms. Instead, the negotiations snagged in a priority principle of justice that worked against Mexican (and US) interests, and so never reached the point of constructing an agreement.

Conclusions

Negotiation analysis has been presented here in order to show the interaction of conflict and order. Conflict occurs when interest-based positions rooted in absolute priority (or other) principles of justice are incompatible with similarly based and rooted positions held by other parties. Order through conflict resolution is provided when the incompatibility is overcome, either by the mutual acceptance of a priority principle and its referents or by the joint determination of a principle or equality or inequality and its referents. It is not yet clear what governs the choice of original principles nor the acceptance or determination of mutually agreeable principles, beyond the obvious (but basic) notion that original notions of absolute justice are chosen to favor the interests of the holder and mutual positions are chosen to preserve those interests in combination with the best way perceived. It is clear, however, that power alone, in any non-tautological definition, does not explain why a particular notion of justice is adopted or why a particular outcome is reached independent of justice considerations. The selection of an agreed sense of justice, however, does allow the parties to move on to a more detailed settlement of their conflict, and in its absence no such settlement is possible.

Political practitioners, including negotiators, are neither philosophers nor theorists. They therefore do not observe the niceties of analytical sequencing nor the neatnesses of analytical concepts. Identifying such concepts and sequences is therefore a matter of interpretation, as always. But the evidence of the role and importance of justice in conflict and order is clear, in both the decisions and words of the actors. Political analysis has long compartmentalized its treatment of political phenomena according to discrete variables, so that discussions of power, order, and institutions rarely meet discussions of justice, principles, and motivations, or meet only in glancing encounters. Without more sustained meetings, the analysis of conflict and order is incomplete. A new type of analysis of negotiation has been presented here that brings normative considerations back in and puts them in their place.

6 The Structuralists' Paradox in negotiation[21]

Negotiation takes place when neither party in a conflict is strong enough to impose its will or to resolve the conflict unilaterally. In such negotiations, the parties are formally equal, since each has a veto over an acceptable outcome. Yet two-party equality produces deadlock. Obviously there are power differences between the parties, however, asymmetries that can be used to break the deadlock. But these asymmetries then raise the Structuralists' Paradox: how come weaker parties negotiate with stronger parties and still get something? Expecting to lose, a weaker party should want to avoid negotiation with a stronger party at all costs, but it cannot; and, expecting to win, a stronger party should have no need to negotiate to get what it wants, but it must. Yet weak parties not only engage stronger ones in negotiation, they usually emerge with payoffs – and often with bigger payoffs – in the end. How does one account for the Structuralists' Paradox, and what is the effect of power symmetry or asymmetry on negotiation.

The dominant school – including the author of this work (Zartman and Berman 1982; Young 1967; Deutsch, 1973; Rubin and Brown 1975; Raiffa, 1982; Morgan 1994, p. 141; Mitchell 1995, p. 36) – has long maintained that power symmetry is the condition most propitious for mutually satisfying negotiations and efficient attainment of optimal results; if asymmetry favors the more powerful, it indisposes the less powerful and delays joint agreement. An opposing argument that, to the contrary, it is asymmetry that is productive of faster, better agreements has rarely been made and the reasoning behind it is not intuitively obvious. This question is examined here, with some surprising results.

The many concepts of power

Much of the answer hangs on the notion of power itself. The traditional definition equates power with force, as in the "realist" school in international politics (Waltz 1954; cf. Dahl 1976, pp. 47–8). The equation of power with force (in the social, not natural, science sense) is so pervasive that any discussion of power is "forced" to first clear the air by pointing out that force is a narrow and selective aspect of power that changes the other party's positions by eliminating or threatening to eliminate the other party. It is thus distinct from the larger exercise of power involving persuasion, influence, leverage, and pressure (see Swingle 1970, especially chapters 3 and 4).

Power as force alone is a definition that is ideological, reductionist inaccurate, and narrowing, and has done much to weaken a sound, thorough discussion of power. Conceiving of power as force alone is ideological because it becomes a justification for violence and a devaluation of non-violent means of causation. It is reductionist because it equates cause with its ultimate expression alone. Even force may not be as ultimate a cause as claimed, since it too can be refuted as a cause, even if not as an effect: countermeasures can be taken, at least before the final outcome of the use of force has taken effect, but of course not afterward. It is inaccurate since it denies the power of other causes. And it is narrowing in that it divides political science from its own subject, since force as power is of no help in analyzing intrastate as opposed to interstate politics. Force is indeed an element of power, a factor of importance, but it stands with others in producing the same effect. Power as force does not fit with the Structuralist Paradox, neither resolving nor relating to it.

Another standard way of defining power is to relate it to resources, leading to the "neo-realist" view of *power as a possession* (Organski 1968; Knorr 1970). The definition is logical and specific, since it gives a precise and direct, even quantifiable, measure. It also lends itself to comparative analysis, since both sides can have power through the resources they control, and the more powerful can easily be calculated in these terms. Unfortunately, resources come in many shapes and sizes, destroying the ability to aggregate them in a single measure. Resources also come shapelessly, in such items as leadership or moral sources of power, which cannot be measured at all (except tautologically, by their effects).

Power as possession or resources has its place in the concept of aggregate power or position power, referring to the total resources held by an agent, as contrasted with relevant power or issue power, which refers to those resources that can be directed toward a particular conflict or concern in the exercise that produces movement (Habeeb 1988; Lockhart 1979). The problem behind power as a possession is that it fails to take into account the use of the resources through will and skill. It takes more than brushes and paints to paint a picture, a point that seems curiously lost on the neo-realists. For size or possession alone is not ability; indeed, the two may be inversely related, as noted in the Structuralists' Paradox. In fact, if size were power, parties could calculate ahead of time and decide (like dogs or baboons (deWaal 1992; Dugatkin 1997)) to avoid certain social encounters, notably negotiation, because they could figure out who would lose.

A problem present in more sophisticated analyses of structural power, based on costs or alternatives, as well. For example, Kennan and Wilson (1990, p.1125), in a game theoretic analysis with the stronger party defined as the one with the smaller cost, write, " the waste of battle was avoidable if the stronger party had been identified initially; but tragically, battle may be the only credible test of strength," missing the point that prior measures of power all omit the ability to use the measured quality in a particular encounter. Yet the small and weak often do very well in negotiation, and the explanation of why is one of the tasks of this study.

Power can also be defined in such a way as to eliminate the Structuralists' Paradox completely, by making power synonymous with or measured by payoffs, so that the strongest always wins. Indeed, the common social science or behavioral definition of power embodies such a tautology. Since the early l930s (and possibly before), social scientists have had at their disposal a good working definition of *power as the ability of one party to move another in an intended direction*. As formulated by RH Tawney (1931, p. 159), it was related to, but significantly different from, Weber's definition in *Economy and Society* as the probability or chance of an actor realizing their own will even against resistance, regardless of the basis on which this probability rests (Gerth and Mills 1946, p.180). The definition was adopted by spokespersons for a number of disciplines in the 1950s – decision theorists such as Herbert Simon (1953), political scientists such as Robert Dahl (1957), and social psychologists such as John Thibaut and Harold Kelley (1959) – who sought a definition identifying power with its effects and separating it from its sources, as in earlier definitions.

This definition contains a number of important elements. First, it focuses on social power, the relation between parties abstracted from other causes of movement. Second, by extension, it implies the notion of applied and net power, recognizing that although both parties may apply pressure or power on each other, net power in the relation is registered by the resultant movement. Third, by further extension, power is conceptualized conclusionarily, that is, in terms of its results, that is, the movement of the target. It is not measured in terms of output, and so or because there is as yet no standard concept – let alone measurement – of effort or "force" (in the physics sense). Indeed, even movement is not standardized, since there is no single measure of "weight" and "speed" in social science.

It is this third implication that creates conceptual problems. For example, if one party (the agent) prevails over another (the target), does that mean that the target had no power? The concept as stated is unable to distinguish between an agent that prevails against no resistance (power) and one that prevails by a hair with tremendous effort; Weber at least recognized resistance. Or if it can make that distinction, as between net and applied power, it has no criterion by which to evaluate – let alone measure – the competing applications. It tells who wins but does not tell the score! Or again, if the target decides to give in, for its own moral or tactical reasons (such as to buy a counterconcession from the agent), does that mean that the agent has power, whereas it has none if the target is willing or able to hold that same amount of effort in check?

Or even more problematically, consider the assertion of Crozier (1964, p. 55), "If the two parties are completely free and the exchange is equal, neither party would be said to be in a position of power vis-à-vis the other. But if the terms of trade are definitely biased in favor of one or the other and if that inequality corresponds to the respective situation of the two parties and not to chance or to error, then one can speak of a power relation." This view would exclude consideration of situations where parties have the power to hold each other in check or to obtain equal value from each other, that is, in relations where the parties or their outcomes are symmetrical. In sum, the definition is weakened by an inability to handle notions of competing power(s), resistance as well as pressure as power, and applied as distinct from net power. Tawney (1931, p. 159) recognized these problems, and then passed on, because their solution was not his concern. His words, however, are incisive: "Power may be defined as the capacity of an individual, or group of individuals. To modify the conduct of other individuals or groups in the manner which he desires, and to prevent his own conduct being modified in the manner in which he does not. Everyone, therefore, possesses some measure of power, and no one possesses more than a measure of it. Men exercise only the power that they are allowed to by other men ... so that the strong are rarely as powerful as they are thought by the weak, or the weak as powerless as they are thought by themselves."

The element of intention raises additional questions. Movement produced in a direction intended by the agent defines power, but movement somewhere else is evasion or blunder. Yet it is common sense that unintended side effects of power (that is, of the production of results) are secondary consequences but not a primary exercise. Similarly, movement that was unintended by the target indicates power, but movement intended anyhow annuls it. In the end, the target is at least partly in control of the definition of the agent's power when power is defined as results. The target can deny, refuse, or co-opt the power as well as resist it. More troublesome yet, this social science definition has serious tautological difficulties, in that the operative element of the defining phrase is the very term being defined (Zartman 1974, pp. 394–7). Power is defined as the ability to move another, but power and ability are synonyms, and power becomes the "power to ..."[22]

Rather than serving as a definition that helps researchers to analyze and explain, the phrase returns to its social setting and becomes merely a qualifier, specifying social power rather than all sources of movement. In otherwords, to look for power is merely – but importantly – to pose the causal question (Dahl 1976, pp. 29–30, 37–9; Simon 1957, p. 5; Zartman 1974, pp. 396–7.

New concepts of power

To avoid this problem and to provide a usable definition of the concept, power here is define as *an action by one party intended to produce movement by another*. Thus power is defined neither as a component (resources) nor as a result (cause) but, in between the two, as a purposeful action, leaving the analysts' hands free to study the relationship of power with both its components and its results. This definition includes but rearranges elements in the Tawney concept interpersonal relation, intention, movement – while taking care of many of the above noted deficiencies. It is closer to (but more succinct and less conclusionary than) Habeeb's definition of power as "the way in which actor A uses its resources in a process with actor B so as to bring about changes that cause preferred outcomes." (Habeeb 1988, p. 15). Separating power as an action from both its source and its result opens the way to useful sub-categorizations, analysis and causal distinctions.

One way of categorizing the actions intended to produce movement is as pressure (negative), inducement (positive), and resistance (negative or positive response). Pressure and inducement generally comes in contingent terms, that is, "if you do something, I will [or not] do something else"; contingent moves can be further divided into threats and warnings (negative) and promises and predictions (positive), depending on whether the source of the move is the agent or an external force (Schelling 1960; Zartman 1987). In Habeeb's definition (1988, p. 21 ff.), the "way" resources are used to bring about changes and cause preferred outcomes relates to three variables: alternatives, commitment, and control. Raven and Kuglanski (1970), as well as Raven and Rubin (1983), provide a different categorization of the way resources are used, referring to informational, referent, expert, legitimate, reward, and coercive power.

Conceptualizations such as these have the strength of breaking down the exercise of power (a single concept, not two) into a number of alternatives, closer to the notion of different types of energy used in the physical sciences. They have the weakness of not constituting different points along a single dimension, so that it becomes impossible to identify missing forms or to establish whether the components comprise a universe or not. The fact that the components do not lend themselves to quantification is probably less important than the fact that they differ among themselves in nature, that fruit is defined as apples plus oranges plus … rather than as different forms of a single characteristic (such as flesh-covered seeds, for example).

A variant conceptualization, stemming from a rational choice approach, considers *power as the value added to a particular outcome* (Schelling 1960; Zartman 1974). One agent exercises power in its relations with another when its moves can negatively or positively alter the value of a particular action's outcome for the target. This approach retains the bilateral relational notion of power, and provides a common dimension along which to compare and aggregate different exercises of power. A stronger party is one who can add (or subtract) more value to the other's outcome. Although the concept is quantitative in nature, it is obviously not easily quantifiable, neither in the base value of outcomes nor in the increments related to power. It does not per se indicate the sources of the ability to move the target in an intended direction – the "how" of the "what" – but it does provide a comprehensive identification of cause and effect. It also allows for further research and conceptualization on those sources, providing the link between the previous conceptualization and the central concept. It translates both the simplicity and the difficulties of a real situation for the target, who must aggregate all the relevant apples and oranges, including the dissuasions and inducements provided by the agent and the counters to them, into a single decision.

Power as ways of using resources and power as added value are two complementary conceptualizations that permit theoretical generalizations and propositions about power as an exercise in negotiation. Habeeb's (1988) and Raven and Kruglanski's (1970) elaboration of ways in which the agent can move the target can be used as a basis for testing and further generation of types, in the search for a prominent, unifying, and comprehensive dimension. Using decision analytic techniques, concepts and measures of value can be developed for use in a modification of Schelling's (1960) diagram as a simple portrayal of improved and weakened outcomes.

For example, if A has the ability to reduce the value – or its perception of the value – of option Ä for B (from r to r'), and to increase the value of option Ä for B (from s to s'), then A has the power to obtain a more favorable outcome for itself.

Thus, comparative effects of power can be measured. Such attempts open up the reality of power and causality in social encounters, and allow a more useful statement of the analytical question, as follows: what types

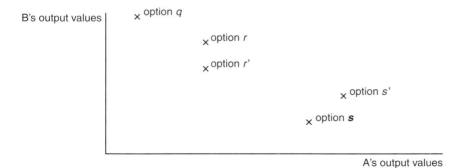

Figure 6.1 Power as an added value (based on Schelling 1960, pp. 47–51).

of actions are deployed by an agent to cause the target to move in the direction the agent intends in a social encounter, on the basis of what resources, and with what success? This becomes the basic question to pose in the analysis of the specific social encounters known as negotiation.

Power and negotiation

Negotiation is joint decision-making under conditions of conflict and uncertainty, combining divergent positions into a single outcome. Each of two or more sides attempts to obtain what it wants through the exchange of information, typically in the form of offers and counteroffers. As conflict theorists have observed, negotiation is only one of a family of approaches to the settlement of conflict; the others are domination, capitulation, inaction, withdrawal, and the intervention of third parties (Pruitt and Kim 2004). As decision theorists have noted, negotiation constitutes one of three modes of social decision-making, where the others are adjudication and coalition formation (Zartman 1974). A vast literature on negotiation has emerged over the last several decades (see, for example, from different disciplines, Pruitt and Carnevale 1993; Bazerman and Neale 1992; Brams 1990; Kremenyuk 2002; Young 1991; Lewicki *et al.* 2003; Lewicki *et al.* 1986–97; Raiffa 1982; Raiffa *et al.* 2002; Zartman and Berman, 1982; Zartman 1978; Schneider and Honeyman 2006, among others), and the present work builds on this substantial foundation to look more closely at the meaning of power in the context of international negotiation

Refinements in the conceptualization of power, as discussed above, are necessary if the concept is to be useful in the analysis of negotiation as a social encounter. Power as force and power as a possession provide little insight and slim basis for analysis of negotiation. Instead they set up the Structuralists' Paradox, that the most powerful party in terms of force or resources does not always win at negotiation. But when power is conceptualized as an ability, it is hard to define the most powerful party other than in tautological or conclusionary terms as the one who wins. Since winning is rejected as a component of many definitions of negotiation – as a win-win rather than a win-lose proposition, or as an encounter in which both parties are better off or they would not agree – the tautological definition is misleading as well as inadequate. The definition adopted here, of power as an action, allows conclusions on the effectiveness of different types of power (actions) over a number of cases, but does not permit a conclusive judgment as to the most powerful party in an individual case until the contest is over. It does allow a better formulation of the specific question of this inquiry. Do unequal power sources (as an estimate or as resources) produce dissimilar behaviors (as action) yielding unequal results?

This formulation relates questions of power structures to power behaviors (action). But in reality, it is not the fact of structural symmetry or asymmetry that can be related to behaviors but its perception, or *power as a perceived relation.* Part of any social interaction is a matter of perception, a problem that natural scientists need not worry about – when one object acts upon another, neither has any perception to distract it. Much of power is a matter of perception, which may help the party produce its intended results or may stymie it. Perception mediates objective reality, although of course reality imposes certain limits on the implications of perception; if one party perceives itself to be better armed, richer, or more skilled – that is, more powerful – than the other, when in fact it is not, that party may act on the basis of its perception but most likely will fail, tripped up by reality. Of course, perception is not immutable either: the target may have the ability to change the agent's perception. Therefore, the symmetry or asymmetry of a perception is related to such elements as force and resources, as well as to the reputation and prospects of a party to produce past and future movements on the part of its targets (Roth 1985, Chapter 3; Feiwel 1989, Chapter 8; Stern *et al.* 1989, Chapter 8.)

Investigating asymmetry through perceptions of power rather than seeking an objective reality has several advantages. It approaches power as the parties do, through their own eyes, instead of relying upon some apparently scientific standard that they might not use. It registers the element that governs behavior the parties' perception of their own power, the other's power, and the relative standing of self and other – whether these are "objectively correct" or not. And it focuses on motivating perceptions. It is to perceptions of power, therefore, that this inquiry turns.

Negotiating perceptions of asymmetry

Common wisdom holds that perceptions of equal power among negotiators tend to result in more effective negotiation and more satisfactory outcomes than perceptions of unequal power (Rubin and Brown 1975, p. 199). Effectiveness refers to the frequency of mutually cooperative behavior and positive-sum outcomes, and satisfaction refers to parties' judgments about the results. We know that satisfaction is notoriously fickle because of the phenomenon of post-partem blues and also because of the need to inflate results when reporting to home audiences and superiors. Nonetheless, the notion is meaningful and can be researched.

The basis for this hypothesis stretches from the Melian Dialogue between Athena and Sparta as recorded by Thucydides to recent experiments (see Rubin and Brown 1975.) Its logic comes from two basic principles of negotiation, the ethical norm of reciprocation, suggestion equality, and the structural position of the parties as veto holders, also implying equality. It also comes from the inherent notion of respect in social dealings, where the maximum amount of deference each can give to the other and still not be caught in an Alphonse-Gaston dilemma or in a loss of face and status is equality. Furthermore, common wisdom also holds that in situations of perceived asymmetry, the stronger party tends to act exploitatively while the weaker acts submissively, an unpropitious situation for effective and satisfying negotiations.

When the weaker do overcome their submissiveness, their behavior is no more productive of good procedures (effectiveness) and results (satisfaction). They resort to organization or ideology, the weapons of the weak (Michels 1962). When enough weak parties are present, they will organize a union to provide them with strength, particularly if it produces a winning coalition. Ideology as well as organization can be the basis of a coalition and lead to assertiveness, rather than submissiveness, even (or maybe especially) if the coalition of the weak is not winning. The Third World Group of 77 (G-77), the Neutral and Non-Aligned Movement (NNAM), and the Alliance of Small Island States (AOSIS), among others, are examples. Under these circumstances, coalitions are likely to form in an effort to offset the initial power disadvantage and transform submission into resistance. There is no common knowledge as to when the weaker will act submissively and when they will be ideologically or organizationally insubmissive.

Ten case studies from recent history permit an examination of the common knowledge that (in)equality equals (in)efficiency (Zartman and Rubin 2000). Seven cases are asymmetrical, in that one side unambiguous regarded the other as more powerful, a judgment that was reciprocated by the other. US–Canada negotiations of 1986–7 negotiated the terms of a free trade area between the two countries, in which Canada was not only the weaker in that a larger percentage of its trade was with the US than vice versa and it would suffer more from a failure in negotiations, but it was also the demandeur. US–Indonesia diplomatic exchanges over aid conditions in the early 1950s pitted a stronger, developed economy against a weaker, developing economy, but in a situation where the stronger country also had a political goal of reducing Indonesian ties with Communist China. Similarly, US–Egyptian aid and reform discussions of the 1980s and early 1990s brought together an acknowledged strong, developed country and its weaker aid recipient to determine aid amounts and the recipient's fulfillment of conditions of economic reform and restructuring. European-Andorran negotiations between 1979 and 1990 between the conglomerate giant and one of the smallest countries on the continent took over a decade to establish free trade relations. India–Nepal negotiations on water resources between the 1960s and the 1990s confronted a large state with a range of means and resources against a much smaller and weaker state even though it held some important headwaters. Finally, the North–South negotiations at the UN Conference on Environment and Development (UNCED) in 1990–2 brought a powerful, developed coalition against a weaker, underdeveloped group where both were demandeurs on different aspects of the first issue but only the South was a demandeur (and the North uninterested and uncompelled) on the second.

Three other cases were symmetrical: the Mali–Burkinabe negotiations in 1986 over disputed territory and the termination of a series of border wars between two of the least developed states in a poor savannah region of West Africa constitute a low perceived-power case (Pondi 2000). The US–Chinese negotiations to end the Korean War in 1952–4 (Hao and Zhai 1990; Vatcher 1958; Fan 2000) and the US–Japanese negotiations over cooperation in the construction of the FSX fighter in 1985–9 (Spar 1993) constitute high cases. Finally, the Arab–Israeli negotiations over peace and territory in 1949 after Israeli independence, in 1974 after the October War, and in 1977–9 after Sadat's visit to Jerusalem (Touval 1982, 1997; Quandt 1977, 1988, 1993) have further implications as an ambiguous case in which the relative power level of the parties varies according to perceptions, expectations, resources, and dynamics. A disproportionately large number of asymmetrical cases was chosen for analysis, for two reasons: first, because in international relations the number of asymmetrical encounters vastly exceeds more symmetrical relations; and second, because these are the most theoretically interesting cases.

The effectiveness of asymmetry

Contrary to received knowledge and experimentation, it appears that perceived asymmetry is the more productive condition for negotiation, whereas perceptions of equality actually interfere with efficient processes and satisfying results. Asymmetrical negotiations in the cases studied often went more smoothly than their symmetrical counterparts and produced more mutually satisfactory outcomes. Symmetry produces deadlock because the behaviors associated with the particular power status produce impasse rather than an effective process to satisfying results. In this, the negotiation findings are similar to results of studies of the balance of power, which indicate that equality is the most unstable condition.

High-power symmetry brings together two parties experienced in dominating behavior; it allows each party to hold the other in check; and therefore it makes them primarily concerned with maintaining their status – locking in their side of the symmetry – rather than reaching an agreement. Low power symmetry brings together two parties that act in the reverse way – symmetrically – to produce the same result. They deadlock because they do not have the power to make the other move, and this therefore makes them primarily concerned with defending whatever little status they have – locking in their side of the symmetry – rather than reaching an agreement.

Symmetry in conflict situations tends to produce and reinforce hostility and prolong negotiations. As a result, it calls for a mediator, a role that is possible among Low-power parties but much less so between High-power opponents. Faced with each other, Mali and Burkina Faso acted not like two weak states but like apprentice strong powers, trying by all their meager available means to dominate each other. Unlike typical self-perceived strong or weak parties, they did not even care about their relationship as neighbors or as members of several regional communities; the only relationship that was an effective concern – and that finally brought the negotiations to a conclusion – was with the foreign, formal colonial patron.

This finding should not be overextended. One of the implications of the original notion of symmetry was that, therefore, parties should try to convey to each other a sense of equality, to facilitate effective negotiations, and this implication still holds. The point of the new finding is that precisely because parties in the symmetrical relation were more or less equal, they were afraid of losing that equality to any small edge of advantage that the other might produce. In this delicate situation, it would have been useful for the parties to spend some energy – in fact, probably a lot, in the atmosphere of suspicion which reigned – to assuring the other that it was indeed an equal.

All this is not to say that asymmetric negotiations were always easy. Perceptions of inequality delayed negotiations, either by causing their breakdown as in the US–Canada case, or by inserting considerations of feelings, face, and status that required extra time to handle, as in the UNCED negotiations or the US negotiations with Indonesia and with Egypt, where status became one of the principal issues. Furthermore, equalizing actions, rather than simple status equality, were often required before the parties could get on with their business. The Canadian walkout, the Chinese and American meticulous (sometimes ridiculous) concerns for equal treatment, and various incidents in the Arab–Israeli negotiations are cases in point. In a dynamic rather than a static sense, the sense of the hypothesis about power symmetry finds support in the need for an enabling atmosphere of equality, even if that atmosphere or its detailed translation into action is not sufficient alone to assure efficiency.

Perceived asymmetries – based on such things as gross national product, military strength, physical size, and other objective indices – do indeed produce different attitudes and actions in the exercise of power. The more powerful do indeed attempt to dominate in their exchanges with less powerful counterparts. The North imposed its concerns over environment on the South at UNCED and largely ignored the South's concerns for development. The US opened prenegotiations with Canada with antidumping and countervailing duties measures as pressure and it imposed its notion of a free trade agreement to resolve a series of irritants rather than a set of fundamentally changed set of trading rules between the two countries. The US brought significant pressures on Indonesia and on Egypt to impose its conditions for aid, on Indonesia's foreign trade policy with China and on Egypt's domestic economic practices. France and Spain turned their attentions to Andorra's trade and labor practices with heavy handed domineering. India continues to treat Nepal with dominance and disdain, as it did throughout the extended negotiations. Only in the UNCED negotiations did the North allow the South to set the agenda, in order to draw it into the process that the North considered important, but then dominated the remainder of that process as it produced agreement on items and in terms the North considered important. (As a result, less than half a decade later, the South was making plans to scuttle the deal because its part of the tradeoff was not being honored).

It is unclear whether the strong act high-handedly because of their self-perception (their sense of their own strength) or their relative perception (their feelings of bilateral asymmetry). The one case that would test the hypothesis, the high–high case of negotiations between the US and China, does suggest that the parties acted on their self-perception and that they locked themselves so obstinately into their impasse because both acted "highly" toward the other. This incompatibility was couched and justified in Cold War terms but was caused by each party's sense of its high-ness. The Japanese–American case did not provide the same proof because the parties were held together by their cooperative relationship, whereas the US–China relationship was a hostile one.

The party perceived as the stronger on the basis of undeniable power possessions – the US, the European Community, India, and the entire developed "North" – adopted forms of a take-it-or-leave-it strategy toward its negotiating partner located along a spectrum of weakness – Canada, Egypt, Indonesia, Andorra, Nepal, and the G-77 South. On first encounter (except in the UNCED case), these dominating strategies were dominant. The weaker party was interested enough in a positive outcome to the negotiations not to want to "leave it" because its security point (the outcome attainable without an agreement) was uncomfortable, and so it felt obliged to take it. If the weaker party hesitated, the stronger added a second strategy of pressure: take-it-or-suffer, in effect, worsening the target's security point even further. The stronger parties regarded themselves as having more important things to do, since they were strong, and although they valued the bilateral relationship, they often found their weak partners annoying with their lesser concerns and narrow interests. In no case did the weaker states act submissively.

Incidentally, Andorra and perhaps Nepal may be weak in any company, and act accordingly, but Canada, Egypt, and Indonesia are high-power parties compared with a number of their other usual partners. Egypt especially is a dominant power among Arab states and acts it, and Indonesia is a leading power in South East Asia. Their behaviors were a combination of ingratiatingly cooperative and knavishly clever, sometimes even ideologically aggressive, but in no case submissive. Rather than remaining in their submissive role, as the asymmetry (and buttressing data from laboratory experiments) would have predicted, the weaker pulled a number of tricks out of their bag. Contrary to their structural position of powerlessness, they took actions appropriate to that position and so gained power over their opponents and the outcome. They blustered, dawdled, cajoled, borrowed power, vetoed temporarily (by walking out) or longer (by at least threatening withdrawal), and generally made a nuisance of themselves over an issue that mattered much more to them than to the distracted strong partner busy with other problems. In this way, they increased their (effective) power far more than initial asymmetry would have predicted. While the dominant party was standing tall, the smaller party was dodging between his legs. Often the big party set the framework or the principles for the agreement, and the little party gnawed away at the details.

The weaker parties' diverse efforts to level the playing field were ways of borrowing sources of power, enabling actions intended to move the stronger party in a desired direction and countering the actions of the stronger party. Power, says Foucault (1984, p. 311), "... is a collection of actions on possible actions ... An action on actions." For every action taken by the stronger in the case studies, the weaker develops an action of its own – an action on an action. And there were many such actions to be taken. The feisty Canadians, the ideological Indonesians, the bureaucratic Egyptians, the intriguing Andorrans, and the clever Nepalese all find their own ways to challenge, circumvent, upstage, or outmaneuver their supposedly stronger negotiating partners. Most if not all of these sources of power were available only to the perceived-weaker party and not its target, for the very reason that it was weaker. These sources can be categorized into target, context, and others:

1   Weaker parties try to *borrow power from the stronger target itself*, by seizing on aspects of the target's nature of position that can support their own demands, or, in another wording, can add value to their own positions, making them more attractive to the target itself. These aspects include common interests in a position, common interests in solving a problem, pairing of two positions, and common interest in the joint relationship.

1a *Appeals to common interests*: both Canada and Andorra's evocation of common interests with adversaries in features of a free trade arrangement.

1b *Solutions to common problems*: Egypt's indication of both parties' interest in overcoming the problem of its underdevelopment; Nepal's reminder of both parties' need to resolve the water problem.

1c *Pairing positions*: South's agreement to support environment in exchange for the North's support for development as goals; Canada's demand for a dispute resolution procedure in exchange for an agreement that removed minor irritants for the US.

1d *Appeals to relationships*: Nepal arguing that, as India's long-standing neighbor, it deserves special consideration; Canada's admonition to the US to preserve the special North American relationship; Indonesia insistence on the American position of world leadership and its own position of neutrality to create a delicate relationship that tied the US hands; Indonesia's appeal to the US interest in having a strong political ally and warning against pushing the Indonesians so hard that they regard the US as an enemy; Japan's concern for the US alliance.

2   Weaker parties try to *borrow power from various third parties* and sources, existing or created. These sources either directly provide added (including negatively, i.e. subtracted) value for positions or indirectly provide alternative sources of support that add or subtract value from positions to make them more attractive or more costly. Such external sources include other parties to the issue, internal segments of target, other opponents of target, external sources of gratifications and deprivations, and public opinion.

2a *Coalitions with other parties*: attempts to maintain G-77 solidarity at UNCED; Indonesia's repeated attempts to rally neutralist support.

2b *Links to internal factions*: Andorra's efforts in the EU to play off France against Spain; Southern use of green and development lobbies in the US and other Northern countries to weigh in on Northern government positions.

2c *Joining one's enemy's enemy*: Mali's efforts to ally with France (traditionally an adversary of Burkina Faso); Indonesia's very act of cooperating with China.

2d *Co-opting external forces* through warnings and predictions rather than threats and promises: Canadian arguments to show that value to the US of a free trade agreement; Indonesian and Egyptian warnings of unavoidable internal reactions if the US pushed reforms too far; G-77 predictions during the UNCED negotiations that resources will be distributed in the former's favor in the future.

2e *Use of public opinion*: South's use of the media in the press-covered and NGO-attended UNCED sessions; Syngman Rhee's attempt to take the prisoners issue to public opinion.

3   Weaker parties try to *borrow power from the context*. Many contextual features are intentionally designed to level the playing field, or to give it the appearance of levelness. These sources of power do not provided added value to positions, but rather give equal access to proceedings. These features and elements include procedural rules, agents, norms and principles.

3a *Use of rules*: Canada's effort to set up dispute settlement procedures as the price of its agreement; G77 insistence on using UN procedures that allowed it to comment on secretariat proposals.

3b *Appeals to higher authority*: Mali's and Burkina Faso's efforts to draw in the Organization of African Unity; Andorra's appeals to the EC over the heads of France and Spain.

3c *Use of intermediaries*: the South's use of the secretariat and the conference chair to provide a procedural buffer in dealing with the North; Egypt's efforts to bring in the US as "biased mediator" to deliver an Israeli agreement.

3d *Appeals to principle*: Egypt arguing with the US for increases in annual economic assistance on the grounds that their counterpart, Israel, is receiving more aid than Egypt, or the South arguing justice for the underdeveloped at UNCED,

4 Finally, weaker states gained sources for power by *using the negotiation process itself* and its evolution to make their moves at appropriate times. These times are at the beginning, in snagging the attention of the stronger party, and then further down the line, after the stronger party has played its dominant role in setting the agenda, leaving the details open to shaping by the weaker party.

4a Efforts to seize opportune moments: Canadian use of anti-GATT feeling to create bilateral trade agreements and creation of fast track procedures to give specific deadlines and a window of opportunity.

4b Attention to details: Egypt's assertion that it is requesting a temporary increase in US economic aid – not an indefinite commitment; Canadian focus on dispute management procedures.

Through such actions, constituting power, most of the weaker partners in the case studies – with the exception of the South at UNCED – were able to work out results that were not to their disadvantage, and often in their favor. The initial asymmetry was not played out to the end but was righted in the course of the exercise. It is this righting action that overcomes the structural dilemma and allows perceived weaker parties to engage in negotiations to obtain a fair outcome. Rarely if ever does the weaker turn the tables totally and emerge the winner; it would not be in its capability or interest to do so, lest the stronger power refuse the unexpectedly asymmetrical outcome. The stronger party's agreement must be bought by some part of the outcome just as must the weaker party's agreement.

Often it is through the invocation of contextual benefits for the stronger that the weaker can make off with incidental benefits of its own. Such benefits may be found in the relationship itself, which the stronger wants to preserve (Stein and Pauly 1993). This relationship – a geographic imposition of neighborliness (US–Canada, EC–Andorra, India–Nepal) or a geopolitical imposition of dependency (US–Egypt, US–Indonesia, North–South, even in the otherwise symmetrical US–Japan case) – is something precious enough to the stronger power that it does not want to lose it. Dependency is not one-sided in such cases, if ever (Bacharach and Lawler, 1980); instead, there are interdependencies at different levels, serving as the basis for the exercise of power in both directions (Elias 1970, pp. 93–4, 107–9). Relations of interdependence at different levels, giving rise to power exercise through different tactics, serve to equalize initial asymmetries in the exercise and the resource structure of power.

In coda, it should be noted that when these interdependencies no longer obtain, the equilibrating structure falls apart. The Cold War gone, if the US no longer were to care about maintaining good relations with Egypt or Indonesia, the latters' tactics or counterpower would be likely to be met with increasing impatience and decreasing effect. Thus, the blandishments of the South at UNCED, designed to press the North into giving equal attention to development as much as to environment, fell on the same deaf ears as did even sharper blandishments by the same weaker side two decades earlier in the negotiations on the New International Economic Order (Rothstein 1979; Zartman 1987); indeed, the softening of Southern tactics in the 1990s was a harbinger of the melting importance of the relationship between the First and the Third Worlds. The symmetrical cases reinforce this finding: China and the US had no positive relationship to restrain them, and Mali and Burkina Faso, despite their common membership in West African organizations of "cooperation," cared more about their relationship with France than with each other.

Geographic impositions are less vulnerable; the US and the European Community continued to care about maintaining good relations with their weaker neighbors, Canada and Andorra, respectively, although India sometimes did take its neighbor, Nepal, for granted, knowing that Nepal had its back against the mountain and was unlikely to borrow power from China on the other side.

Another major source of power – seen as means of controlling – was the ability to bring in support from external actors. This calculation was not a constant element in the initial preparations for the negotiations, and even when it was it was a very subjective estimate. For the most part, parties engaged in negotiations on the basis of positive estimates of their capabilities and then, as the negotiations proceeded, worked to overcame their difficulties through the acquisition or materialization of external support.

Conclusions to power and equality

In sum, targets that appeared to be comparable in power to oneself occasioned symmetrical negotiations that were painful and inefficient because all the parties' efforts went into assuring that the playing field keep the appearance of being level. It is this analysis that contains the key to the apparent disparity between experiment and reality. In experiments, conditions were so controlled as to isolate and focus on a single variable, whereas in the real world reality is more complex and ambiguous. In fact, experiments have been conducted which specify that near-equality is the most unstable condition of all, and that equality combined with a competitive Motivational Orientation and a sensitive Interactive Orientation is explosive (Rubin and Brown 1975, pp. 246, 256). Those are exactly the conditions filled by reality in international (and other) politics.

On the other hand, targets that appeared less powerful than oneself occasioned exploitative behavior – whether from high power or low power agents with the targets, as we have seen, responding rather creatively and effectively, in an effort to level the playing field. In negotiations, particularly within a relationship established over time, the parties know their role and play them complementarily. High-power parties may try to dominate initially, but they are restrained by three factors. One is the clever tactics of the weak who know how to handle their bigger partner, like the mice and the elephants, the children and their parents, the workers and their employers, and so on. Second is the distraction of the powerful by many other issues, faced with the concentration and commitment of the less powerful on the issues that matter to them. And third is the constraining effect of the relationship itself, which limits the crushing effects of high-sided dominance and gives the low-side a threat, an appeal, and a chance. Asymmetry, the most common structural setting for international negotiation, brings better results more efficiently than we tend to think possible.

It is interesting that this element of asymmetry, which proved critical in negotiations, is the one carryover from the elements identified in the study of asymmetry in the initiation of war (Paul 1994, pp. 31–3), and it relates directly to an established understanding of the process of escalation (Pruitt and Kim 2004). Parties run through their estimates of domestic sources of power, both material and intangible, making necessarily subjective evaluations. They enter into negotiations when they feel that they have a favorable edge in some relevant aspects of issue power, whatever the larger aggregate power position may be. In the military context, Paul (1994, p. 35) writes:

> the weaker challenger can initiate war against the relatively stronger adversary if its key decision-makers believe that they can achieve their political and military objectives through the employment of a limited aims/*faits accomplis* strategy … Superior aggregate military and economic power of the defender need not deter a challenger … The support of a great power ally and the possession of short-term offensive capabilities can increase the probability of such war initiation.

Negotiation has no equivalent to short-term offensive capabilities, but differences can straighten out faulty perceptions of relative power. However, in negotiation, external involvement is called mediation, and the crucial conclusion about biased mediators is that they can be effective in assisting negotiations only if they deliver the party toward whom they are biased (Touval and Zartman 1985). In negotiation, external intervention rides the diplomatic equivalent of a Trojan horse.

7   Prenegotiation
Phases and functions

After all these years, we still have trouble living with concepts. Unlike tangible realities, such as a dog, concepts have no clear beginnings and ends, no unambiguous middles, and not even a usefulness that is beyond debate. A dog – that does not exist to the left of its nose or the right of its tail, is clearly distinguishable from a car or even a cat, and would require a name if it did not have one – offers none of these problems. We may try to dodge the boundary problem and focus on the essential or functional nature of the concept, but that will only satisfy philosophers, who have less trouble with concepts than most of us anyhow, and not practitioners. A phase is a particularly troublesome form of concept because a time dimension is added to its other elusive qualities and because other relational questions are raised. Is a phase part of subsequent phases, for example, and is the sequence of phases a one-way street or can there be backtracking and even leapfrogging? None of these questions ever arises about the good old dog!

   Prenegotiation is such a troublesome phase concept. There is no doubt that there is something before negotiation, but it is less clear whether it is a prelude to or a part of negotiation, whether there is a difference in nature between these two, how sharp the boundaries are and how reversible the flows, or what the relation is to other contextual events such as crises and regimes. These are questions that this volume seeks to confront and elucidate. This attention to prenegotiation is timely and appropriate, for while a number of writers have identified it as an important element of the overall process of negotiation, few have developed the concept. Practitioners, in particular, emphasize that the usual academic treatment of negotiation as beginning when the parties sit down at the table in fact takes no account of the most challenging phase of preparations and therefore misses an important aspect of the process of narrowing disagreement between parties.

Phases

Saunders (1985a, p. 25; 1985b, 22 passim) has most eloquently drawn attention to the need to "reach back and more extensively into the period before the decision to negotiate is made, and analyze what can be done to help parties reach that decision." His starting point, however, is the decision of third parties to pursue negotiation, and his prenegotiation period covers two functional needs, "defining the problem" and "developing a commitment to negotiation on the part of the parties," which are followed by a third phase, "arranging the negotiations." The first two phases centre around the creation of a political commitment to solve a problem that has been defined in such a way as to be susceptible to mutually satisfactory management. The fourth phase, negotiation itself, involves efforts to come to closure or to crystallize the previous intent or search in a concrete agreement. However, even then, "it is apparent that, in many ways, negotiation has already begun in the earlier stages of the process" (Saunders 1985a, p. 35). Hence, the word "negotiation" is being used, as it often is, in two ways, referring both to the whole process, including the preliminaries to itself, and to the ultimate face-to-face diplomatic encounters.

Zartman and Berman (1982, pp. 42, 82, passim) identify the first of the three phases of negotiation as the "diagnostic stage," the phase of "bringing about negotiations ... long before the first formal session opens." Admitting that the beginning moment of the phase is usually not clear-cut, they see it going on until the "turning point of seriousness," when each party has perceived the other to be serious about finding a negotiated solution and the second or "formula phase" begins. However, they warn that phases tend to be grey around the edges, that in fact the work of each phase continues underneath its successor, and that backtracking is possible, indeed desirable, when the succeeding phase finds itself ill prepared by its predecessor. Zartman (1985, 1989) later focused exclusively on the diagnosis phase and its appropriate contextual conditions. Similarly, Haass (1990) has adopted the notion of the ripe moment (Zartman 1989; Touval and Zartman 1985) and has written insightfully about measures to be taken when the moment is not yet ripe.

Recently, a group has begun to look at the specific problem of initiating negotiations in relation to the notion of de-escalation. For the most part, Kriesberg and Thorson (1991) and his colleagues consider prenegotiation (without using the name) as the phase in which conflict is transformed into a search for a cooperative agreement by measures inducing a lowering of conflict (deescalation), a redefinition of relationships, a re-evaluation of the appropriate means or of the effectiveness of alternative means to an end, and a consideration of potential third-party roles. All of these are useful and even necessary components of the preparation for negotiation, and they suggest defining components of the phase although they do not identify it or define it per se (Gulliver 1979; Lockhart 1979).

Out of all these elements, it is important to focus on some basic items if one is to understand the concept of prenegotiation: a definition of the phenomenon, an identification of its component characteristics, and an indication of its function (usefulness) in the process through which parties achieve conflicting goals. Prenegotiation begins when one or more parties considers negotiation as a policy option and communicates this intention to other parties. It ends when the parties agree to formal negotiations (an exchange of proposals designed to arrive at a mutually acceptable outcome in a situation of interdependent interests) or when one party abandons the consideration of negotiation as an option. This definition leaves the essential characteristics of prenegotiation implicit, however, because it concentrates on the limiting characteristics. In essential terms, prenegotiation is the span of time and activity in which the parties move from conflicting unilateral solutions for a mutual problem to a joint search for cooperative multilateral or joint solutions. From both definitions, it is clear that the nature of the activity lies not in conducting the combined search for *a* or *the* solution but in arriving at and in convincing the other party to arrive at, the conclusion that *some* joint solution is possible. If that appreciation creates a better understanding of prenegotiation, however, its sharpness should not be overdrawn, tempting though sharpness may be. It is impossible to perceive a potentiality for a joint solution without considering potential joint solutions and discarding some of them. This is the importance of Saunders' first stage, summarized in his good phrase, "getting one's mind around the problem."

At the same time, it should be clear that whatever parties do differently during prenegotiation, that activity is part of the general process of coming to agreement out of conflict and hence of negotiation itself. Once again, sharpness should not be exaggerated. Ultimately, life is a seamless web, and analysis, indeed knowledge, is basically a matter of making order and distinctions out of it. Indeed, what happens prior to prenegotiation is related to negotiation too. But the initiation of the prenegotiation process, by definition and by nature, begins when one side considers the multilateral track as a possible alternative to the unilateral track to a solution in a conflict, and it continues into the next phase when both parties reach this conclusion. (Saunders' opening moment which focuses on third-party perceptions and behaviors extends the period a bit but does not affect either the essential nature of the activity or its position as part of the larger negotiation process.)

The question then is not the absolute distinction between two parts of the same and evolving process, but how to get to negotiation. The definitions we have already examined make some assumptions about elements in the answer. They hypothesize that parties arrive at the decision to negotiate separately, differently, and not concomitantly; that they shift from, or at least add a multilateral track to, their previously exclusively unilateral strategy; and that there is an identifiable decision for which a cause may be sought, explained, and, indeed, eventually produced.

Partial answers and further hypotheses are also available from the early literature on prenegotiation. The decision to negotiate is found to be associated with "a plateau and a precipice" – a mutually hurting stalemate combined with a recent or impending catastrophe (see Chapter 14). The nature and perception of the stalemate, the role of escalation, and the positioning of the catastrophe or crisis are all matters to be pursued. Parties shift from unilateral solutions towards multilateral or negotiated ones when the unilateral track is blocked or overly costly or when the alternative track is more promising or comparatively cheaper. The comparative effectiveness of negative and positive sanctions and inducements has been investigated only preliminarily and needs more work. Parties often decide to negotiate when they perceive the distribution of power between them moving towards equality (Zartman and Berman 1982, pp. 48 ff., 54 ff.; Saunders 1985b, pp. 3 f.). Relations between perception and reality and increases in the efficiency of perception are yet further issues to be developed

Functions

All these questions and hypotheses, and others that flow from them, have both an explanatory and a practical value. All are causative questions, susceptible of comparative investigation so that causal sequences and correlations as well as intervening variables can be identified. But, by the same token, all are important questions for practitioners, providing general guidelines for the improved conduct of negotiations. Furthermore, both policy-makers and academics benefit from the same syllogisms and causative statements, a point often missed on both sides but most frequently by practitioners delighting in the use of "academic" in its derivative and disparaging meaning. The academics' question "What causes A?" is the mirror image of the policy-makers' question "what will happen if I do B?" and the same as the latter's question "How can I help bring about A?" An answer to any of them is a step to answering the others. The search for answers in this volume is useful to both audiences.

The first and clear answer is that prenegotiation is necessary. In each of the case studies, prenegotiation is not just a definitional construct but a preparatory phase without which the negotiation would not have taken place. But there are other uses in the identification of prenegotiation and an understanding of its characteristics. If one turns the definition into an attempted explanation and asks *how* does prenegotiation lead to negotiation, one can discover both ramifications of a process and prescriptions for behavior. Prenegotiation is a purposive period of transition that enables parties to move from conflicting perceptions and behaviors (unilateral attempts at solutions) to cooperative perceptions and behaviors. Where they once saw only an enemy, bound on undoing its opponent and untrustworthy in any joint efforts (and behaved accordingly themselves, thus justifying a similar perception on the part of the opponent), by the end of the period they have to be able to see an adversary who is nonetheless capable of cooperative behaviour and of some trust (and to reflect such characteristics themselves). Where each party regarded the problem with a winning mentality, seeking only ways to overcome and get what it wanted, by the end of the transition they must shift to a conciliatory mentality, believing the solution is to be found with, not against, the adversary and preparing to give a little to get something, to settle for an attainable second best rather than hold out for an unattainable victory. These are significant shifts, often greater than anything involved in finding the final agreed outcome, but necessary preconditions to that search. These shifts are not unshakable, it must be emphasized; they are continually being tested in the actual negotiation and from time to time may need explicit reaffirmation.

But they are the necessary substance of the prenegotiation period. How are they brought about? There are at least seven functions of prenegotiation, to be performed in no special order.

Risks

Because negotiation, as an exercise in mutual power, involves an exchange of contingent gratifications and deprivations ("I will do this, if you will do that"), it is a very risky undertaking. Before prenegotiation, the risk is too high to be affordable. Prenegotiation may lower the risks associated with cooperation and may prepare escape hatches in case things go wrong. But, above all, it makes the extent of the risk clearer. Because exit costs are lower in prenegotiation, where no engagements have actually been made as yet, parties can be freer about stating maximum terms and real interests clearly. The exchange of information reduces the unknown and hence the risks of eventual concessions. The parties come to know what to expect.

Costs

Prenegotiation allows the parties to assess and come to terms with the costs of concessions and agreement, and also with the costs of failure, before firm commitments are made. One major element of power in negotiation and also a reference point that helps establish the value of the final agreement is the security point – the value of what is obtained by each party without an agreement. Outcomes must be better than security points to be worthwhile, but both outcomes and security points have costs. The costs and benefits of various agreements as well as of no agreement must be estimated by the parties. Like risk and reciprocity, costs can be estimated without ever meeting the adversary but those estimates will be based on poorer information than what a party could obtain by meeting in prenegotiation. A clearer idea of costs works back to lower risks, because the risk and cost of the unknown can be reduced. As Griffiths makes clear in his article, prenegotiation is necessary to enable or oblige the parties to sort out their *own* motives for negotiating in the given context.

Requitement

Studies have shown that beyond hurting stalemate, requitement or a belief in reciprocity is the second most important element in beginning negotiations. It does no good to see one's unilateral path to a solution blocked, if one is sure that the other side will not repay concessions with concessions (Larson 1988). But fear of reciprocity is its own undoing: one does not make concessions because one is sure the other side will not repay, and the other does not repay concessions because it is sure that the other will not either. Prenegotiation is the time to convince the other party that concessions will be requited, not banked and run away with. Such exchanges and assurances are less risky during this phase because they are indicative of future behaviour rather than commitments. They are taken to be credibly indicative, however, because a promise of requitement that was not honored in the negotiation period itself would be considered a strong case of bad faith, harmful to the party's reputation. The chance to explore requitement not only allows parties to see if concessions are possible but also allows responding conceders to see what would happen and where they would be if counterconcessions were offered. All this information is necessary to the decision to negotiate. Requitement is basic to both of Tomlin's (1989) procedural phases – commitment to negotiate and decision to negotiate.

Support

Prenegotiation allows each party to estimate and consolidate its own internal support for an accommodative policy, to prepare the home front for a shift from a winning to a conciliatory mentality. This involves not only changing the public image of the adversary but also putting together a domestic coalition of interests to support termination rather than conduct of conflict. As elsewhere, the first step is to prepare for change in the conflict policy, a step related, but prior to, a determination of the new outcome. Like the other aspects of prenegotiation, the construction of domestic support should not be merely the affair of each side. Each party has a role to play in the other's politics, and that party which has first concluded that negotiation is a conceivable outcome has an especial challenge to reach into the domestic political processes of the other and help build a supportive coalition for accommodation. Griffiths (1989) characterizes this activity as informal coalition-building with counterparts on the other side, and Stein (1989) and Hampson (1989) show the importance of heading off, or building on, domestic opposition as a key activity in determining the course of prenegotiation.

Alternatives

The core function of prenegotiation involves turning the problem into a manageable issue susceptible of a negotiated outcome. Three of Tomlin's (1989) prenegotiation phases break down the agenda-setting functions. Identifying the problem, searching for options, and setting the parameters and steps along the path to finding a formula. The process involves inventing and choosing among alternative definitions of the problem, inventing and choosing among alternative ways of handling the problem so defined, and setting the themes and limits – parameters and perimeters – that are necessary to guide a solution. Indeed, the whole process of multilateral conflict resolution can be considered as one of eliminating alternatives, until only one solution remains. (This is in itself a useful approach to the analysis of the situation and diametrically different from the usual one which consists in studying negotiation as a process of selection.) Even though selection and elimination go hand in hand in reality, formal negotiation can be considered to be more the selection phase and prenegotiation the elimination phase. It is in the latter phase that parties put aside some of the salient possibilities for agreement, avoid worst alternatives, and begin to focus on a few that appear most promising.

Any conflict can be defined in several ways, some of them more susceptible of resolution than others. One part of the shift from a winning to a conciliatory mentality consists in coming together on more resolvable definitions of the problem and eliminating competing zero-sum definitions and their inherently one-sided solutions. But even among the other variable sum solutions, there are some which imply greater difficulties, complex ramifications, and more costs than others, and successful prenegotiation works to eliminate these, leaving only a few definitions and alternatives in place to deal with in depth in the formal negotiation.

Thus, there are two possible patterns of formal negotiation: one in which the parties work out the diagnosis and formulas of successive alternatives, as shown by Stein (1989) on the Middle East, and one in which the dynamic is centered on a competition between a few salient alternatives; both are identified by Griffiths (1989) and Hampson (1989) on arms control. In either case, prenegotiation is concerned with the setting of the agenda, the elimination of some issues, and the selection of those encompassed by the mutually acceptable definition of the problem, as Winham's (1989) discussion of the General Agreement on Tariffs and Trade (GATT) shows. But these same studies also show that agenda formation is determined not just by its own substantive concerns but also by its links with the previous function, that of gathering support – shaping an agenda that brings internal forces on board (Putnam 1988). Prenegotiation is as much a process of finding a solution that is supportable as of finding support for an ideal solution.

However the process of selecting and discarding alternatives is conducted, it is a process of establishing boundaries to the issues to be considered and of setting agendas, or, in a less two dimensional image, of "getting one's mind around the problem." If it is not clear how the problem is defined, what the limits to the negotiable issues are, and what the agenda for the negotiation is, prenegotiation has not done its job and, indeed, is not over.

Participants

Just as a certain amount of selection needs to be done among the alternative definitions of and solutions to the conflict during prenegotiation, so it may also be necessary to select those who are susceptible of coming to agreement from among the participants to the conflict. Just as all aspects of the conflict are not likely to be solved, so it may not be possible to include all parties in an agreement. As parties crystallize their positions, they may find themselves confronting a choice about whether to join the growing coalition or not, just as the coalition will face the choice of whether to stretch its own boundaries to include a particular party or not. Like the range of alternatives, the number of participants to an agreement has to be judged carefully, lest there not be enough of them to create a lasting settlement. Leaving out either the major contender or the major issue may produce an agreement but not a solution.

In between the dilemma of comprehensiveness versus compatibility is the tactic of building a coalition large enough to make a stable agreement no broader than necessary to cover the bases, a tactic of participant incrementalism (Zartman 1987a, pp. 292–4). A core group of agreers can come together and gradually expand its membership, coordinating its selection of participants with its selection of issues and definitions of the conflict. Although this may sound like a multilateral process not relevant to bilateral conflicts, its logic can also be extended to the multiple components that usually make up any party. In the building of domestic support both by the negotiating party and by its adversary, a party must choose those to include in its participating coalition and those to accept in the other party's coalition as well (Putnam 1988). Thus, as much as setting the agenda, prenegotiation selects the participants at the table (and perhaps even begins to look to their seating arrangements). These considerations are crucial in multilateral prenegotiation, as Winham and Stein's articles (1989) on the GATT and on the Middle East (and interested outside powers) show. They are much less of a factor in bilateral prenegotiation, as Tomlin, Griffiths and Hampson show, but that is only because the two participants have already decided to leave out other parties whose claim on the action is based on different criteria.

Bridges

The principal function of prenegotiation is to build bridges from conflict to conciliation, with the changes in perception, mentality, tactics, definitions; acceptability levels and partners, that have already been discussed. While these other measures all cover important aspects of that shift, prenegotiation also sets up temporary mechanisms that provide for the change itself on a transitional and provisional basis. One is a temporary suspension of conflict activities. Although the cease fire is the bestknown form of this change, its functional equivalent can also be found in trade disputes where conflicting practices would be suspended, as Winham (1990) discusses, or in arms control situations where moratoriums on testing or on production would be introduced, as Griffiths (1989) and Hampson (1989) discuss. Ceasefires and moratoriums are down payments on confidence; temporary, vulnerable, provisional concessions that at the same time form the basis of potential threats. They remove the danger of misinterpretation of intentions, but they also remove the possibility of unilateral acts either to effect or to affect a solution. As such, they are more likely to conclude than to open prenegotiation. The resolution process must be brought to the point where the power structure is no longer in doubt and unilateral efforts to gain advantage are no longer permissible for a ceasefire to receive the parties' support. Beyond that point, a refusal of a ceasefire is a sign of bad faith, and before that point it is not.

A second measure is the building of trust. Before prenegotiation, parties in general can be expected (and can expect) not to trust each other, because each is looking for unilateral advantage; by the end of a negotiation they must have established some mutual trust to be able to make an agreement. The initial steps of the shift are made in prenegotiation, as parties conduct small tests of trust and construct mechanisms by which trust can be shown and monitored (Zartman and Berman 1982, pp. 27–41). It is wrong to expect that trust will or must be firmly in place for formal negotiation to begin. Parties will and should be wary of each other from the beginning to the very end, because we know that it is rational to defect or cheat at the last moment (in the phenomenon of crest or end game), and in any case, neither cheating nor agreement would be possible if trust were not the norm (Bartos 1974).

An understanding of the nature and components of prenegotiation is a worthwhile objective in itself. Because there is a need for a preparatory transition between the conflict and conciliation processes, there is a need to analyze it and to test the structures and functions involved. Once they are established and their workings better understood, such knowledge becomes useful to those who, practise negotiation as well as to those seeking to explain how and why specific cases worked out the way they did.

Frameworks

A better understanding of the functions of prenegotiation can also throw light on other – sometimes competing – concepts that inform current studies of cooperation and conflict. Much of the contemporary analysis of cooperation among selfish states takes place within the concept of regimes, the minimal and often implicit rules and routines governing interaction. Prenegotiation performs many of the same functions as a regime, or vice versa. On issues covered by regimes, therefore, one might expect that prenegotiation would be less necessary, shorter, or different in nature; even conflict regimes, which provide rules of the game for the conduct and limitation of hostilities, would offer a framework for building and assessing many of the prenegotiation functions. Yet regimes cover large areas of interaction, whereas the success of negotiation depends on the identification of specific definitions of problems, the selection of participants and alternatives, and the establishment of parameters and agendas. Each of these activities involves at least potential conflict, not of the armed type, of course, but of the basic type related to incompatibilities of interests. Thus, even within regimes, prenegotiation is necessary to focus the ensuing process of agreement on appropriate items, but this process should benefit from some of the work already being done through the regime. One would want to avoid the illusion that prenegotiation would therefore be "easier" on issues covered by regimes; it is hard to use a comparative because there are no control cases for the comparison, and the prenegotiation may be difficult nonetheless. Indeed, prenegotiation within regimes may well be "easier" only in the sense that it would not have been possible at all if the terrain had not been prepared by the regime. That indeed is the purpose of regimes, as Winham's study of the GATT and Fisher's of the Commonwealth show. Proof of such statements would have to lie in logic rather than in empirical testing, because of the difficulties of comparison, but even on that basis a case could be made for the usefulness of regimes to the negotiation process (Krasner 1983; Axelrod 1984).

The value of such questions lies in the linkage they establish between two major fields of inquiry that have communicated too little – the search for broad frameworks of analysis such as regimes, and the study of processes and activities of interaction such as negotiation. Such works as do exist are for the most part in the field of North–South economic negotiations (Mahler 1984; Crawford 1984; Aggerwal 1983; Zartman 1987a; Rothstein 1979) but the interpenetration of the two fields of inquiry should be much broader. Prenegotiation provides the link. As Winham's study of pre negotiation within the GATT shows, prenegotiation within explicit regimes can subsume certain functions such as those dealing with risk, cost, and requitement and focus within already established routines and rules on those dealing with alternatives, participants, support, and bridges. Without the functional economies that the GATT provided, it might not have been possible to get through the prenegotiation of a Uruguay Round.

The other field of inquiry into types of events similar to those covered by prenegotiation is centred on crises. The study of crises has provided a focal point for much otherwise disparate material involved in international relations; in a crisis-ridden world, the management of crises when they occur and the prevention of crises before they do occur are realistic concerns and conceptual challenges. Prenegotiation comes to the rescue. Not only is it necessary to the management and prevention of crises, so that negotiations themselves may be more effective and efficient, but it also stands in a creative, if uncertain, relationship to crisis.

Prenegotiation is crisis avoidance. While at first glance it may appear unclear whether crisis precedes prenegotiation or whether prenegotiation staves off crisis, it soon becomes apparent that the only reason why negotiation should follow crisis is that human beings tend to disagree on the reality of an impending crisis and only lock the stable door after the horse has bolted. But they do lock it, and negotiate under the shock of a crisis, only because they fear another one. The last crisis has brought us to our senses and made us negotiate (and hence prenegotiate) because we fear the next one. The study of Middle East prenegotiation, as in Stein's chapter, shows the effect of a recent and again looming crisis, as does Hampson's study of American arms control negotiations. More striking is the role of crisis avoidance even within a regime such as the GATT, in Winham's analysis of prenegotiation.

Other fields of study in international relations can benefit from the attention given here to prenegotiation. Regimes and crises are only two important examples of concepts that stand in some relationship to prenegotiation and suggest useful questions about its role and functions. The following studies on a wide range of cases address these questions, explore these functions, and investigate the nature of prenegotiation. The reasons parties turn to negotiation, the stages of the prenegotiation process, the functions of prenegotiation, the explanation of outcomes of prenegotiation – these are the general questions that each case examines, with results that are gathered together in the conclusion to the book. The concept may not emerge as concrete as a canine, but this work brings out the inherent reality and importance of prenegotiation.

8   In search of common elements in the analysis of the negotiation process[23]

Like the famous wise men who blindly confronted the elephant and brought back conflicting accounts based on its salient characteristics, contemporary analysts of negotiation appear to be talking about different things under the name of the same phenomenon. Some have even called for a search for a common understanding of the subject so that analysis can proceed on the same epistemological track.

This review, however, suggests that a common understanding the of negotiation process has already developed and analysts are using it. The diversity which can be found in a number of approaches – five of which are identified[24] – is merely different ways of talking about the same phenomenon, and in fact even involves the same questions and parameters presented from different angles and under different names. There is more unity than some have suspected, and different approaches reinforce and complement each other's analysis. However there still remain many aspects of the process which elude this common, but multifaceted, analysis. The common notion of the process has led analysts to confront these continuing problems, but there is of course no certainty that further answers to obdurate problems will not produce new terms of analysis and even new notions of the whole process.

It is paradoxical and perhaps confusing that there is no single dominant analytical approach to negotiation. The confusion arises from the presence of many different attempts at analysis, sometimes inventing their own wheels to carry forward their insights and sometimes crossreferencing from a number of different analytical approaches (see cases in Zartman 1987a, 1987b; Davidow 1984). The fact that all of these are studies of great value only confirms the analytical confusion. The paradox, however, arises because behind this analytical diversity there lies a single phenomenon to be analyzed. Although some authors have a hard time seeing the essential identity of the negotiation process (Young 1975), most others, including those who then focus on different subtypes for analytical purposes, start with a common definition of the phenomenon (Pruitt 1981; Raiffa 1982; Walton and McKersie 1965; Ikle 1964).

Negotiation is a process of combining conflicting positions into a common position, under a decision rule of unanimity, a phenomenon in which the outcome is determined by the process (Kissinger 1969, p. 212). The essential element of process is important because it posits a determining dynamic, not just an assortment of scattered actions or tactics. The challenge then becomes one of finding the nature of that dynamic and its parameters. It is because this challenge has not been met to universal satisfaction that there are still a number of contending approaches to the study of the process. The same reason also explains, in part, why there is such resistance among practitioners of the process toward adopting and applying the work of analysts to their own practice.

The question still remains, if there is a single recognized phenomenon, and if the various approaches that are employed to analyze that phenomenon are all insightful, why is there not greater consensus on how to explain negotiation. This study will propose some answers to that question, but in the process it will heighten – but also seek to remove – the paradox. The answer proposed is that each of the analytical approaches puts forward a deterministic analysis in its most rigorous form but useful insights can be obtained when the unreal conditions of determinism are dropped: it is the clash between deterministic integrity and realistic looseness that keeps each of them separate from the others, trying to overcome its internal problems of analysis rather than facing external problems of coordination. The fact that many of the separate approaches are supported by a disciplinary basis also keeps them locked in their internal analytical problems.

However, the underlying paradox is that the approaches are really more similar than has been recognized, not only studying the same phenomenon but also answering the same or similar questions in the same, or similar ways but under different disciplinary labels. Exorcising these differences may permit an economy of side movement and an increase of forward movement in the analysis of the negotiation process.

The basic analytical question for all approaches to answer is, how are negotiated outcomes explained? To find generalized answers and to get away from the idiosyncrasies of history, the analyst must find dominant operationalizable variables that provide terms in which the answer can be given. These in turn should be able to provide useful insights – indeed, even strategies or behavioral rules – for practitioners seeking to obtain the best possible outcomes for themselves. Thus, practical forms of the same question are, how can each party deploy its own efforts to obtain an outcome favorable enough to be acceptable to itself but attractive enough to the other party to draw it away from its own attempts at a unilateral solution and win its acceptance of an agreement? Or, in the terms of the classical Toughness Dilemma, when should a party be tough and when should it be soft, knowing that conceding little will mean holding to its position but decrease the chances of an agreement whereas conceding a lot will increase the chances of an agreement but move it away from the positions it values? Five different "families" of analysis will be examined to see how these questions are handled and where the differences and similarities of the approaches lie (for other attempts to show the differences in some or all of these schools, see Walton and McKersie 1965; Young 1975; Hopmann 1996).

Structural analysis is based on a distribution of elements, in this case of instrumental elements or power, defined either as parties' relative positions (resource possessions) or as their relative ability to make their options prevail (or to counter the other's efforts to make its options prevail). (See Schelling 1960; Wriggins 1987; Bacharach and Lawler 1980; Habeeb 1988). Structural analysis is the most commonplace, even journalistic, approach and its deterministic statement that "the strongest side wins" is, usually tautological and post-hoc. To avoid the tautology, the deterministic identity between power structure and winning has to be broken, by using an independent measure of power and by focusing on the way in which sides of different relative strengths achieve their outcomes. The latter has received some attention in the analysis of situations of asymmetry, where the better performance of the weaker of the two sides makes for an interesting challenge for explanation. While the general category of explanation given can be called "tactics," those tactics generally serve to restore the structural equality of power between the two parties (Snyder and Diesing 1977, pp. 118–244; Hopmann 1978; Deutsch 1973; Zartman 1985b; Wriggins 1987). Various tactics provide various prescriptions for overcoming asymmetry.

By these paths, by the time that structural analysis has moved away from its initial post-hoc formulation that outcomes are determined by the power positions of the parties, it has shifted toward simply tactical analysis based on a different definition of power. Power becomes no longer a position or a possession (something a party "has") but a way of exercising a casual relation (something one "does" to bring about an outcome, and not just the potential ability to do so) (Habeeb 1987; cf. Lasswell and Kaplan 1951, p. 75; Simon 1957, p. 5).

While such studies may be termed structural because they deal with power, that element is treated as a responsive, incidental and situational characteristic rather than as an element in a theory or conceptualization of the negotiation process. This is a common problem with studies of power, and in the case of negotiations it has produced an array of insightful if idiosyncratic books of proverbs on how parties can be brought to agreement (Karass 1970; Nierenberg 1973; Fisher and Ury 1981). Their emphasis is on various angles of insight into the negotiation process.

Yet despite a lack of theoretical focus or coherence, these studies do propose ways to make a given offer appear more attractive, to induce the other party to accept the first party's current offer or to induce it to improve its own offer. Whether or not these tactics operate on either current offers, expectations, or outcomes obtainable without negotiation (security points), they do so in one of only two ways – either by altering the contingent value of current offers relative to the other two points of comparison (expectations and security points) or by identifying certain procedures ("fractionate" or "trade off ") or atmospherics ("trust" or "confidence") that facilitate the basic process. All these tactics are acts of (attempted) power and all of them are ways to bring about acceptance of a given offer. Furthermore, they all focus on a part of a common and general process of replacing unilateral and conflicting positions with a common position or outcome, whether that process is explicitly stated as such or not. Explicit statements about the nature of the process would be useful and would facilitate links between approaches, but even in their absence it is clear that the process is the same.

Strategic analysis is also based on an array of elements but its structure is one of ends, not of means. Strategic analysis, as portrayed in game theoretic matrices, begins with the assumption that outcomes are determined by the relative array of their values to the parties, under conditions of rational (i.e. preferred) choice. The standard strategic models – Prisoners' Dilemma Game (PDG) and Chicken Dilemma Game (CDG) – are symmetrical and therefore incorporate the same assumption of equality as found in structural analysis. It has frequently been noted that game theory excludes any use of power as a result of its rigorous analytical forms and its clear logic of determinism; it records values as given and shows the strategies that will be chosen and the consequences of doing so (Young 1975; Axelrod 1984).

As a result, it had been observed that strategic analysis is of real value only in comparing the decision to negotiate with the decision to hold out, again like the insights gained from an analysis of symmetrical structures. Since game theory values are given (and indeed, at worst, sometimes inferred from the strategies adopted), there is no way to fractionate or trade off, only to enter the value of any such external operations into the appropriate box in the matrix, and there is no way to change any of those values within the matrix, only to record any changes from one matrix to another.

Yet when the rigorous assumptions that provide the basis for its determinism are relaxed and game theory presentations are used heuristically as the starting point for analysis, a number of the associated limitations fall away and new possibilities appear. Strategic analysis shows that the only way to break out of deadlock is through asymmetry and that therefore instead of working to improve offers or cooperation (absolutely or in relation to expectations, which cannot be shown on a matrix), parties are best advised to alter the payoffs or perception of payoffs associated with nonnegotiated or unilateral outcomes. This in turn brings in new understandings of power, seen as the use of security points to induce or resist changes in bargaining positions. (Snyder and Diesing 1977; Zagare 1978; Brams 1985).

Movement is the essence of the negotiation process and movement cannot be shown on a matrix. But the conditions which produce movement – again, power – can be shown on a matrix and analyzed from it, just as movies result from a succession of stills. The result is the same process as indicated in the relaxation and refinement of structural analysis, in which parties move from their unilateral options to a common cooperative decision so shaped as to be more attractive than their security points. The problem with strategic analysis at present is not its rigidity but its limited scope. Many of the important and more detailed questions on how to move parties toward a common solution lie outside the analysis; even such important insights as the ways to reinforce commitment (Schelling 1960; Baldwin 1987) are triggered by a need to consider security points but are outside game theory analysis. An effort to render more precise the importance of the security point in comparison to unilateral demands and multilateral compromise is an important new advance of the strategic approach, although the calculation of Critical Risk depends on a shift from ordinal to cardinal values in the matrix (Ellsberg 1975; Snyder and Diesing 1977).

On the other hand, strategic categories of encounters can help answer some of the puzzling analytical questions of negotiations. For example, the Toughness Dilemma may be resolved by use of the two game theory dilemmas: whereas parties who see their situation as a PDG may do best by playing soft to open and tough to punish (Axelrod 1984), parties who see themselves in a CDG do better by playing tough to demand and soft to reward. But this, in turn, confirms an answer from structured analysis to the Toughness Dilemma, based on appropriate tactics for strong and weak powers, respectively. Further examples could be produced where strategic analysis, despite apparent limitations, ends up discussing elements of the same process, and often the same process problems, as other approaches but in different terms.

Process analysis has the common feature of explaining outcomes through a series of concessions determined by some element inherent in each party's position. The particular element varies slightly according to the particular version of the theory; most process analysis is based on a security point theory in some form although there are also few other variations used. Process analysis indicates that the party will concede on the basis of a comparative calculation of its own vs. its opponent's costs, or of its own costs vs. some acceptability level (Zeuthen 1930; Cross 1969; Pen 1975[1952]; Hicks 1932; Snyder and Diesing 1977), and on this basis it can determine which will concede how much until the final point of convergence is reached. This is of course a way of diagramming a negotiation process that is the same as that discussed by other approaches.

Other variations are end-point theories and concession-rate theories, the first determining the parties' movement so as to maintain a fair and maximizing outcome and the second determining the parties' movement on the basis of reactions to each other's degree of concession, the two being two parts of the same process (Bartos 1978; Zeuthen 1930; Nash 1950: Cross 1969, 1978; cf. Pruitt 1981). These latter variations (endpoint and concession-rate theories of process) are only prescriptively deterministic, that is, they indicate how parties will act and where they will end up if they want to reach a mutually fair and maximizing outcome, and thus they are not good descriptors of the process. But they do serve the useful function of providing a baseline against which unfairness and power can be measured, and hence they are relevant to some understanding of the process (Pillar 1983).

But it can be seen that process theories, which originate in economics, are in fact structural theories which indicates that the weaker party will concede until the tables are turned, at which point the other party will concede in its turn, and so on to agreement. Hence, they are theories of power, with power measured in terms of a comparison between offers and security points, or in other words, in terms of critical risk factors. Although this is never done in these theories, to the extent that parties can alter each other's or their own security points, they exercise power as well as simply possessing it; that reduces the deterministic possibilities of the theory but increases its reality. The similarity between process and strategic theories has long been recognized (Harsanyi 1975[1956]; Wagner 1975[1957]), although their mechanisms are indeed different. The similarity with structural theories should also be registered; although many structuralists would probably not "read" game theory or "talk" bilateral monopoly, their analyses are complementary, covering the same phenomena within the same process.

The neatness of the theoretical processes only works in idealized situations and then only with idiosyncrasies (Khury 1968; Bartos 1974, 1987; Hamermesch 1987). Concession behavior does not always match; often it mismatches or nonmatches (tracks) (Pruitt 1981), and parties do not even concede responsively but rather try to teach and learn, respond and elicit responses, at the same time, combining several types of behavior that makes theoretically neat patterns unrealistic (Coddington 1968; Cross 1969; Bartos 1987). But the point is that in the process, analysts are discerning both involuntary and voluntary, mechanical and manipulative, process and power elements that make up negotiation, all of them clustered about a similarly understood effort to combine conflicting positions into a common one. As the references in this review are beginning to show, analysts do not even belong exclusively to one school or another but sometimes borrow naturally from different approaches. Yet the fact that the field is seen as pluralistic as it is, or that bibliographies remain largely in the author's discipline, means that there is not enough natural borrowing and cross-referencing.

Behavioral analysis provides an obviously different explanation of negotiated outcomes by using the negotiators themselves as the focus of analysis.

The terms of analysis used are the personalities of the negotiators, either directly or in interaction. Personality in social psychology can be used to refer to personal predispositions that exist at a number of different levels, from biologically-ingrained needs to more influenceable attitudes. At whatever level, this school of analysis responds to a common belief about negotiation, that "it all depends on the personalities of the negotiators"; the challenge then becomes to translate that popular perception into identifiable and nontautological variables that can be used for analysis.

A more literary and intuitive basis for behavioral analysis began with Nicolson's (1939) distinction between Shopkeepers and Warriors. It had been extended and developed through a number of forms into Snyder and Diesing's (1977) Softliners and Hardliners. There are many character-izations possible for these basic types, but some can be given in terms already used by other school: the Hardline Warrior sees situations as a Prisoner's Dilemma Game and acts as a mismatcher, expecting toughness to lead to softness and softness to lead to toughness, whereas the Softline Shopkeeper sees situations as a Chicken Dilemma Game and follow matching behavior, expecting toughness to lead to toughness (and dead-lock) and softness to lead to softness. Thus behavioral analyses take up the same parameters as elements in the same process as other approaches, combining them into typologies equated with the behavior rather than leaving them independent as behaviors.

A more developed approach involves categorizing personality types according to their Interpersonal Orientation, an approach that is both more insightful and more complex because it is not merely dichotomous and because its effects depend on interaction rather than on simple or direct taxonomic associations. Opposed to a Low IO type are two types of high IOs – Cooperators and Competitors; either produces a positive result when negotiating with the same type of personality but when cross-paired the match is unproductive because the two types grate on each other. Rather than explaining an outcome in its own terms, as the previous typologies tend to do, IO analysis operates on the basis of a casual inter-action (Rubin and Brown 1975). It also identifies different types of out-comes, depending on joint or comparative maximization, a point also developed in studies of Motivational Orientations (MO) (Rubin and Brown 1975; Filley 1975). But this approach too deals with such elements as the propensity to compromise, to construct positive- (or divide zero-) sum outcomes, or to adopt a tough or soft line (i.e. a flatter or a steeper concession rate) during the process of combining conflicting positions into joining decision. In a desire to escape the limitations of a behavioral dichotomy, a greater refinement of these typologies has been used by Shell (1999) on the basis of the Thomas–Kilmann (1977) Conflict 'Mode' Instrument identifying five bargaining types or strategies (accomodating, problem-solving (collaborating), compromising, competing, avoiding) and relating them to four different situations (balanced concerns, relationships, transactions, tacit bargaining) depending on the relation between the importance of relationships and the conflict over stakes. It is not clear whether these categories are innate personality types (as the "modes" imply) or selectable strategies, nor how specifically they fit different situations.

Integrative analysis, like behavioral analysis, would seem to constitute an exception to the general understanding of a negotiation process. Although it too conceives of negotiation as a process, its process runs through stages, in which the outcome is explained by the performance of behaviors identified as specifically appropriate to each successive stage (Gulliver 1979; Saunders 1985; Zartman and Berman 1982; Zartman 1978).

Rather than seeing a process that works from fixed points of discord to a common point of convergence, integrative analysis emphasized the disarray of parties' interests in their own minds and the need to manipulate conceptualizations of the problem into mutually satisfying positive-sum outcomes before proceeding to an elaboration of a detailed division of the spoils. By extending its concept of the negotiation process back before the time when positions appear as fixed points, integrative analysis not only allows for greater and more positive manipulation of those positions (Fisher and Ury 1982) but also meets practitioners' understanding of negotiation by drawing attention to the pre-negotiation part of the process (Bendahmane and McDonald 1984, 1986; Zartman 1985b).

But again, these positive aspects of the approach should not obscure the fact that the subject is the same process as analyzed elsewhere. Its emphasis on opening options is preliminary to a focus on closure, using expanded possibilities of mutual benefit to buy agreement to an outcome that is less – or at least different – than original demands: the same process can be described as giving something to get something, a process of establishing terns of trade for an exchange of items in the absence of fixed prices but also of fixed monetary units. In previous terms, integrative analysis explores the mechanics of the Shopkeeper but also, more realistically, of the Shopkeeper confronted with Warrior aspects of the problem and with the need to get around them. Negotiators – at least diplomatic negotiators but probably most others – are not merely Shopkeepers, who can make a deal on any issue; there are items better postponed and interest that are properly nonnegotiable, and there are limits to acceptable deals that are imposed by security points. If finding a common agreement through this maze is more than a matter of convergence, it is a matter of convergence as well.

A growing branch of this analysis, based on the initial introduction of the term "integrative" by Walton and McKersie (1965), focuses on precise mechanisms for identifying the best possible deal that can be gotten by both sides given the differences in the nature of their interests. While this is a complex extension of the Nash (1950) point that occupies a basic position in the strategic and process approach, the complexity of stakes makes a simple positive-sum outcome too schematic to be useful (Valavanis 1958; Ikle and Leites 1962; Barclay and Peterson 1976; Raiffa 1982; Sebenius 1984). The process involves finding as many dimensions of components to the parties' interests as possible in order to provide the best trade-offs and thereby insure the greatest durability to the outcome. In addition to finding how much of a conflicting position a party must give up to gain assent, the process also involves finding how much of a non- (or less-) valued position a party can trade to gain a more valued position (Homans 1961, p. 62). But the element of conflict is never absent, and the process of shaping a single multilateral decision out of conflicting unilateral claims remains. It should be clear that the study of negotiation has come a considerable way in the past two decades in building and expanding on a common concept of a process, sharpening the much looser characterization given in the *International Encyclopedia of the Social Science* (Ikle 1968) as "A form of interaction through which [parties] ... try to arrange . .. a new combination of some of their common and conflicting interests." The "form of interaction" has taken shape as a process of combining conflicting positions into a common outcome by joint decision, allowing more specific focus of attention on how this is done, whether by power, by patterns of movement, by restructuring stakes and values, by interacting personality types, or by a series of steps. Yet just as clearly there is much more to do to know the process, although many of those further directions are indicated by using the common concept of process as a starting point.

One problem raised by the notion of negotiation as a process is that of measuring success, an answer to which is necessary to an evaluation of behavior and prescriptions for its improvement. The question of success is more complex than it may appear (Zartman 1987a). The nature of negotiation is to arrive at a mutually satisfactory agreement, with any one (and therefore, each) side getting the best deal possible and the other (and therefore, each) getting at least enough to make it want to keep the agreement. By that very nature, negotiation is not a process of winning and losing, so that success must be evaluated against the problem, not against the adversary. (In addition, there is a subcategory of negotiations in which one party's aims are to deny the adversary a particular payoff rather than to get as much as possible for itself, making positive-sum evaluations more complex). Thus, a number of criteria are potentially relevant for the evaluation of success, none of them giving a completely satisfactory answer.

First, *signature* of an agreement is a prima facie or nominal sign of success because it indicates a judgment by the parties that they expect to be better off with the agreement than without and that they can do not better by either continuing negotiations or choosing an alternative outcome. Second, this perception can be verified empirically to see if the parties are indeed *better off* either by comparing their condition before and after the agreement or by comparing their position after the agreement with their presumed position at the same time in the absence of an agreement (a more relevant comparison but a counterfactual one that involves some judgment). While nothing says that the parties must be equally well off or even equally better of, further evaluations could also investigate how unequally better off the agreement made them and also whether they were pareto-optimally better off, that is, whether they had missed opportunities to improve the condition of either of them without making the other less well off. Since some negotiations may be designed to redress power inequities while others may reflect power inequities, the criteria of success based on the relative improvement of the parties' positions will vary. Third, the results can be evaluated against the parties' *opening positions,* with all the caveats about initial inflation of demands that is inherent in the process. Nash points and Bartos solutions – discussed previously under end-point determinism (see pp. 132–3) – are a function of opening positions and can serve as a baseline to evaluate actual outcomes. But all three of these criteria for evaluation have flaws and complexities that call for further work – there is presently very little – on systems of evaluation.

Another topic of concern is the analysis of negotiations in the case of the two very different types of stakes – those solvable by division and those by exchange. Although much of the earlier literature on negotiation focused on the more obvious topic of division through *concessions* (Schopenhauer 1896; Nicolson 1964; Schelling 1960) with its notion of negotiation as winning or losing, much more attention lately has been drawn to the improvement of exchanges (Homans 1961; Axelrod 1970; Nash 1950; Sebenius 1984; Zartman 1987a) with its notion of mutual satisfactions or *compensations.*

The importance of resolving problems by exchange bears much emphasis, for in their conflicts parties often forget that resolution by multilateral decisions means "buying" the other party's agreement through inducements in terms of items which they value in order to make agreement attractive to them (Homans 1961; Nash 1950). At the same time, such emphasis carries a different image of negotiation from an encounter of conceding and winning, portraying instead a positive-sum process where "everyone wins (something)." Unfortunately, this is not the whole picture. Just as there must be a little Warrior in every successful Shopkeeper, so there is inevitably some zero-sum aspect to every positive-sum. Once parties have created a greater good, there is some need to decide how to divide and share it. Furthermore, there are some stakes that are indivisible and there are others that are unexchangeable and therefore necessarily divisible. These aspects of negotiation are still not the subject of exhaustive or definitive treatment, and they are somewhat different from the earlier, insightful analysis of redistributive bargaining (Walton and McKersie 1965).

Beyond *concession* and *compensation* is the notion of *construction* the third means of bringing divergent positions into a common accord. *Construction* means reframing perceptions of the stakes so that things are seen differently and the zero-sum nature of the outcomes is removed. Again, some stakes escape such creative reformulation, or even when subject of an attractive formula they prove intractable in detail.

A third topic of continuing inquiry highlighted by the generally accepted notion of the negotiation process is the Toughness Dilemma (see Zartman 2005d). The question of when to be tough and when to be soft, and the paradox on which is it based, has already been identified as the major tactical question for analysis and practitioners alike. By now, it is plain that there is no way out of the dilemma as presented, and that correct and insightful answers depend on some intermediate variable, such as personality, timing, phase, power, etc. But there is still no sense of any hierarchy among these intermediate variables – other than the eternal debates among disciplines as to which gives the best analysis – and no notions as to which are trumps. Somewhere between the anecdotal proverbs and the unoperationalizable theory lies a not yet fully mined terrain of inquiry that may require new parameters.

Finally, an area of negotiation that falls outside the current paradigm is multilateral bargaining (Zartman 1994; Crump and Zartman 2003; Crump 2003). The current process notion has thus far worked to exclude effective consideration of multilateral negotiation and those that have been treated well tend to be reduced to bilateral analysis (Lipson 1985, p. 220). When not reduced to dyads, multilateral negotiation tends to be treated merely descriptively even if insightfully, a problem that has posed particular challenges in regard to the successive GATT rounds (Preeg 1970; Evans 1971; Cline *et al.* 1978; however cf. Winham 1987). There have been a number of excellent attempts to devise an approach to multilateral negotiations (that is, large number of participants, not merely a few more than two, as in Raiffa 1982; Zagare 1978) that indicate some promising directions (Zartman 1994).

One set of approaches treats multilateral negotiations as a problem in *coalition*-formation (Rubin and Brown 1975, pp. 64ff.; Snyder and Diesing 1977, pp. 349ff.; Raiffa 1982; Dupont 1994; Hampson 1994). However, coalition is a very different process from negotiation, and to the extent that it covers the shaping of outcomes to be decided up or down by some sort of weighted decision rule, it hides a separate negotiation process. There is something going in the interstices of coalition that needs a separate analysis that is not yet available. Like the strategic approach to bilateral negotiations, to which it is related, coalition analyzes what happens between negotiations and impinges on them but does not capture them.

In a second approach, *preferences and scaling* have been used in some different and imaginative ways (Sebenius 1984; Friedheim 1987; Hipel and Fraser 1984). But they too indicate ingredients to an agreement rather than the process by which it is obtained; as in coalition, negotiation becomes voting or at least approaches it. Other approaches are conceivable but have not been used – small group dynamics might provide a new analytical context, as might a conceptual examination of the construction of an agreement out of individual pieces.

In multilateral negotiation as in the predominant bilateral mode, the two categories of ingredients are parties and stakes. Negotiated agreements are made out of stakes by parties. Bilateral negotiation has its general process model as a basis for analysis, which permits many approaches to coexist and reinforce each other. Multilateral negotiations need either to fit into that concept of process or invent its own basic model to enjoy the same benefits. In any case, in regard to bilateral negotiations, there are many wise men but only one elephant, and the two should not be confused with each other.

9   Order as a political concept[25]

Order and chaos (or conflict) constitute the poles of politics and their study is the essence of political science. The build-up and breakdown of order are the basic subjects of political analysis, but they are particularly topical at the beginning of the third millennium. The old millennium has crashed in disorder. The search for order is the sign of our times. Both in the world system and in the sovereign systems of states order has broken down, raising challenges to analysis and action. The earlier systems of world order in this century – the colonial order and the bipolar order – were structured on conquest and conflict, but these orders have changed, yielding place to uncertainty. The successor system is not yet evident, and attempts to order interstate relations through such diverse and conflicting concepts as international organization, uni- or multi-polarity, transnational regimes, competing culture blocs, or a North–South divide remain inconclusive (Zartman 2007).

Similarly, the nature of the state as the highest form of political organization is undergoing tremendous changes, proving permeable to transnational penetration, undermined by interlinking domestic forces, and overridden by international regimes and organizations. The concept of sovereignty has been called into question by the Secretaries-General of the United Nations himself (Boutros Ghali 1995, Annan 1996). But at the same time the riddled state is expected to regulate more aspects of human activity than ever before in the history of humanity. Extreme forms of authoritarian order, as in apartheid systems in the Third World and totalitarian systems in the Second, give way to institutionalized participation that is unable to preserve order (Huntington 1969; Huntington and Nelson 1976). Some end up with such a high degree of concentrated power that they implode, consuming the collapsed state and its fragments in their disorder.

Conflict is not necessarily chaos, any more than the opposite of any particular form of order is not disorder. Order appears in many, often ostensibly opposite forms: conflict and cooperation, war and peace, liberty and security, oppression and justice, and indeed in many of the concepts and values found in the other chapters in this collection. Moreover, order is what permits inquiry and analysis in any discipline, as it turns data into knowledge; science looks for regularities or orders in events, so that theory serves "to bring order and meaning to a mass of phenomena which without it would remain disconnected and unintelligible" (Morgenthau 1960, 3). Thus, inquiry into the concept of order needs to begin with a search for taxonomies of order, in order to address both analytical questions of cause and relationship, and normative questions of purpose and preference. It is useful, therefore, to turn to the concept of order itself, its meaning and its types, in order then to proceed with an analysis of current issues involving order at the edge of the millennium, and finally to address the question of universality within the concept and its issue applications.

The concept as defined and applied

Unlike many other concepts of political (and other social) science, the concept of "order" and its meaning do not divide the discipline into great definitional debates. Krasner apparently initially justified his inquiry into regimes as "related to the most fundamental concern of social theory: how is order established, maintained and destroyed," but the most fundamental concern disappeared in the final version, except in Susan Strange's (1983, p. 345) recounting to question it. Order implies a relationship among items based on some principle (Bull 1995, p. 3; Hoffman 1965, p. 2). It often carries a suggestion of, or is even used synonymously with, harmony or stability, "a good disposition of discrepant parts, each in its fittest place," according to Augustine (1950, XIX, xii, 249), or as a mother might say, "Johnny, go put some order in your room," according to a common family injunction. There is therefore, almost unavoidably, a value attached to order, as something the study of politics seeks to discern and the practice of politics seeks to achieve. Ivorian President Felix Houphouet-Boigny quoted Goethe to say, "I prefer injustice to disorder: one can die of disorder, one does not die of injustice" (Zolberg 1966, p. 42), and after his death his country proved the point. An association is political, according to Weber (1947, p. 145), if "the enforcement of its order is carried out ... by ... force"; whereas to Aristotle (1950, II 1, 1) an association is political if it is sovereign and inclusive, all associations being "instituted for the purpose of attaining some good."

In its broadest sense, then, order is all understanding, or at least all political understanding, and politics is the search for order. For all its precision, that is too broad a notion to handle, but it at least indicates that the interesting question is less "whether order?" than "what/which order?" "whence order?" and "what is the relation between order and other concepts or values that are equally crucial, universal and timely to our age?" It also indicates that the great debate in political science over order is more nearly normative, over the appropriate order and the appropriate tools and approaches to study order (and therefore to debate the prior question).

A determination of what orders are currently available and salient leads to two interlocking categorizations, based on principles of process and structure (Aristotle 1948; Goodin 1993; O Young 1983, pp. 98–101; Lewin *et al.* 1939). One typology of political orders is based on the type of decision-making processes, which are limited in number:

1   Authoritarian, commanded from the top of a hierarchical structure, whether executive or judicial (Linz 1975).
2   Coalitional, composed of subgroups of shifting size in which the part decides for the whole, the most common form of which is democratic (O'Donnell and Schmitter 1986).
3   Negotiated, composed of formally equal subgroups operating under the unanimity or unit veto rule.
4   Inherent or spontaneous (Hayek 1984, pp. 307–9), run by the hidden hand of some external agency or inner force such as the market.

The other typology draws on the structural relation among the component units, depending whether they are equals or unequals, and whether their relationship is therefore symmetrical or asymmetrical. There is some overlap between these two categorizations; authoritarian orders are necessarily composed of unequals but the other three process orders can operate with either type with different consequences (Aristotle 1948; Aron 1965, pp. 44–5).

The orders of the day

Scholarship paces events, as it should (despite the claims of external interference through this phenomenon): there is more interest and scholarship these days on state collapse or democratization than on revolution or monarchy. "Transformations of political discourse in the West have been a function of changing conceptualizations of threat to the existence of political order ..." (Pasquino 1993, p. 19). Thus, following the collapse of communism, authoritarian order is not at the top of the current agenda for research and debate, whereas the other three forms of order – democratic coalitions, oligarchic negotiation, and inherent, automatic orders – have produced new analysis and concerns. *Order through coalition* has received new emphasis in current concerns about the process of democratization (Huntington 1991) and the evidence that previously non-democratic orders of governance lack the coalition fluidity necessary for their immediate transformation into democratic orders (O'Donnell and Schmitter 1986). Balance becomes the source of order; a statesman "must perpetuate order, which he can do by keeping the multitudinous aggressions of men in balance against each other," indicates Barzun (1946,

p. 208). Yet even in established democratic orders, ascriptive components such as ethnicity and gender pose similar problems of voter rigidity (deTocqueville 1850; Mill 1847). The result is that democracy is no longer analyzed with the primary focus on the individual voter, as in earlier studies (Adorno *et al.* 1950; Lipset 1980) but on aggregated votes. Analysts have repeatedly and variously noted that the presumed egalitarian status necessary for free choice by individual voters is negated by the inegalitarian status of the ascriptive blocs to which they belong and also by achievemental effects on attitudes, participation and choice, bringing a reexamination of the new relevance of classical solutions to both aspects of the rigidity problem, ranging from proportional representation to gerrymandering (Dahl 1993; Guinier 1994).

The rigidity problem has led to other avenues of analysis. The issue of preconditions to democracy (Lipset 1998) is being reexamined. Either socio-economic development to higher levels of literacy and productivity or economic reform to pluralist economic competition is claimed by some to be necessary antecedents to competitive political pluralism. Passage from an authoritarian to a democratic order is found to require a negotiated transition of elite pacts if it is to avoid a replication of the authoritarian bloc in new conditions (Linz and Stepan 1996; Rose *et al.* 1998; O'Donnell and Schmitter 1986; Zartman 1991). Ethnic voting blocs must be broken by crosscutting, interest-aggregating parties if they are to avoid becoming permanent ethnic majorities, yet political parties tend to become vehicles for ethnic voting blocs. As scholars come to the conclusion that there is no best form of democratic constitution (Dahl 1993; Kumar 1998, 54), research on democratization devolves into the "puzzle phase" (Kuhn 1962) as its focus is drawn to transitional institutional structures, voting regulations and practices, transparency guarantees, and post-electoral implementation. The flaws of simple majoritarian systems are receiving greater emphasis as democracy at its best comes to be seen as a coalition process in which all have a share in power (Lijphart 1977). In the legislative area, coalition voting has been subject to sophisticated statistical and game-theoretical analysis carrying coalition theory to its most developed point, although circumscribed by the conditions of the legislative arena (Brams 1994, etc.).

In international politics, order based on the coalition process has a more established position. The basic mechanism comprising a flexible coalition of status quo states against a rising hegemon, known as the balance of power, is still central to international relations theory. If half a century of bipolarism took some of the flexibility out of the coalition behavior, the decade of post-bipolar uncertainties has not produced the anti-hegemonic coalition against the remaining superpower that the theory might have predicted, probably because its political yoke is easy, its economic burden is lightened by a lot of free riding, and its values are widely shared. In the process, the opposite coalition behavior of bandwagoning has also come to light as an alternative, particularly for small states (Walt 1987). Another new extension has been the analysis of regime building and multilateral diplomacy, theoretically quite different than the generally assumed bilateral character of negotiation, as a matter of managing complexity through coalition (Hampson 1995; Zartman 1994; Young 1989). Although basic coalition theory dates from an earlier era (Riker 1962), these new uses of the concept have broken out from the simpler assumptions of that theory and require further theoretical expansion and then testing.

Negotiated orders have been the subject of an enormous burst of attention and analysis in the last decades of the millennium. Negotiation has been characterized as involving "an initial disorder – the dispute – and an endeavor to reach an order – the settlement" (Gulliver 1977, p. 21). It has long been thought that negotiation is applicable only to the uninstitutionalized order of international relations, leaving coalition and authority and their variants as the contending systems of order for domestic systems. If there are signal dates in the real world for a new focus on negotiation, they bracket the Sixties – 1962 in international relations when the Cuban Missile Crisis turned superpower military confrontation to diplomatic bargaining and 1968 when youth around the world, refusing authority, sought to negotiate new realities. It was also the time of seminal works (Schelling 1960; Ikle 1964; Walton and McKersie 1965) that launched the analysis of a form of order different from the others – neither commanded nor divided but based on unanimity between or among formally equal parties about a constructed outcome. The new attention has opened an entirely new area of analysis untouched in previous accounts which only dealt with outcomes – bills, treaties, institutions, constitutions – while ignoring the way in which they were achieved (Strauss 1987; O Young 1983).

Negotiated orders have a participatory legitimacy shared with a voted order but without the necessary losers, and their threefold choice (accept, reject, continue) allows for a positive-sum creativity that the twofold choice of voting and the one-fold choice of authority do not provide (Ikle 1964). On the other hand, negotiations require a recognition of the parties' legitimacy, an ability to accept half a loaf, and a tolerance of ambiguity in decisions that some situations do not permit. Without the tools of negotiation analysis, it would not be possible to investigate many areas of political activity such as international regimes, labor-management relations, conflict management, business deals, and preparation of legislation; yet it is significant that these very issue areas are the ones where much remains to be done and learned about negotiation (Smith 1996; Moravcsik 1994).

Thus negotiation can be treated as both a dependent and an independent variable. Two questions dominate: what is the order inherent in or producing negotiation? Also, what are the implications of negotiation for the order it produces? Negotiation processes follow one of two patterns (or a mix of them) –either concession/convergence distributive bargaining producing zero-sum ("win/lose") outcomes, or paired concessions in compensation bargaining, or formula/detail constructive bargaining producing positive-sum ("win/win") outcomes; there is a high process-outcome correlation, but the determinants of the initial choice between the two are not yet clear (Walton and McKersie 1965; Axelrod 1970, 1984; Zartman 1978; Hopmann 1996). Among them, constructive bargaining produces more stable outcomes since distributive bargaining contains an incentive for later rejection by the losing party. Compared to other types of order, institutionalized negotiation orders such as consensus legislation, international regimes, civil society groups, pacted transitions, and institutional amendments, among others, tend to be more creative, more flexible, and more able to handle change (Keohane and Nye 1989; O Young 1983; Strauss 1980; O'Donnell and Schmitter 1986; Vandewalle 1996). Recent work has reinforced the conclusion that elected orders confirm legitimacy but only as a prerequisite, and that the real work of satisfying crosscutting majorities and minorities through effective governance is produced by negotiations among the elected parties and their appointed agents (Kumar 1998, pp. 28, 59, 68, 128, 137–40, 145, 164, 169, 192, 231, 236).

Most recently, spurred by approaches in other sciences, a new type of order has begun to receive attention, the *spontaneous or inherent order* or the political equivalent of the market (Schelling 1960, Chapter 4, 1960; Hayek 1973). International politics has long focused attention on the balance of power mechanism as an automatic pattern into which states' actions fall, although uncertainty remains as to whether balance of power is indeed an automatic effect or a voluntary coalition (including balancer) policy. A more recent modification of a different type is the long-cycle theory (Modelski and Thompson 1996) and the power-cycle theory (Doran 2000) that treat world order in dynamic terms but in very different ways. Social scientists and philosophers have long sought a natural order of things, a self-maintaining equilibrium, and in the postwar era have asserted but then disclaimed the homeostatic tendencies of social systems.

Rational choice analysis carries something of an inherent order mechanism under its innocent assumption of rationality, not surprising since rational choice is putatively the political equivalent of market economics (realist theory is less convincing in the same role in international politics (Waltz 1979, pp. 88–93; Olson 1965; Bates 1986). However, the proposal of the political system (state or international system) as the equivalent of the market, larger than the sum of the parts of rational political actors, does not provide the same convincing insights (Green and Schapiro 1994) and has already been co-opted and worn out (if not discredited) by last century's emphasis on raison d'état, Staatsmacht, and eventually the totalitarian state. The millennial search continues for a political order that has its own regularities and mechanisms and can be subjected to scientific theory and analysis, independent of the vagaries of human choice.

Contemporary concerns

In the absence of riving debates about the concept itself, many related issues remain to be worked out. Some of these issues have to do with putative opposites, such as the relation between order and change, order and justice, or order and process; whereas others deal with supposed synonyms, such as order and legitimacy, or order and law, or order and power. None is new (what is, in political theory?) but all are of particular concern for political relations at the turn of the millennium.

The relation between *order and change* is a continuing concern thrown into new prominence at the end of the Cold War. In the late 1960s, "law and order" became the designation of the right, the forces against change; the slogan of the XVIII World Congress of Political Science focusing on the "Corporate Millennium" emphasized an order of change. The juxtaposition of the two themes recalls that order is not the opposite of change: there is orderly change and the change of orders, as in patterns (or anatomies) of revolution, development, transitional measures, and constitutional amendment (Apter 1971, pp. 19–21). Thus, the eternal question regarding the relationship between order and change takes on two meanings: the scientist looks for regularities in new clusters of events, the practitioner (including the victim) looks for orderly – i.e. if not non-violent, at least predictable – change.

New subjects of attention for interpretative scholarship on change and order at the end of the millennium include state collapse (Eisenstadt 1966; Huntington 1969; Zartman 1995); interstate systemic transformation (Doran 1991; Knutsen 1997; Gilpin 1981) and transitions from one type of order to another (Huntington 1991; Dahl 1971; O'Donnell and Schmitter 1986; Casper and Taylor 1996). In international politics, the inability of realistic theory to explain, let alone predict, the collapse of the bipolar system and the avenues of its succession has raised questions about its theoretical power and defensive answers about its constrained applicability. In the now merging areas of interstate and intrastate conflict, the search for non-violent change has led to the new field of conflict management and transformation, to investigate patterns of conflict and ways of channelling violent conflicts into political interaction (Pillar 1983; Zartman 2007). Indeed, to some, government itself is conflict management, providing an orderly process and mechanism for handling conflict among legitimate demands (and resources) and controlling its escalation into violence (Przeworski 1970; Zartman 1996).

Like peace and mercy, *order* is not necessarily *justice*. In some extensive run, orders are likely to be overtaken by the struggle for justice if they do not already achieve it (Goethe and Houphouet-Boigny notwithstanding), but since the bases of justice themselves change over time, today's just order may be tomorrow's cause for revolt (Bull 1977). Justice is the subject of a discussion of its own in this volume, analyzing the most recent periodic burst of scholarship devoted to the definition of a just order that can stand up to the inevitable changes in criteria (Barry 1989; Rawls 1971). For all the travesties that it perpetrated on humanity, communism began as a search for a just order, but order soon became its own criterion, overriding justice, both in its domestic polities and in its regional system. Since the defeat of world communism, research on order has been less focused on the achievement of justice than on other, more inherent criteria. Only in the case of fundamentalist religious – most strongly Islamist – orders is justice cited as the motivating factor in the imposition of an authoritarian system, with the same inherent deformation as already seen under communism (Moussalli 1998). Similarly, in international politics, after the Cold War the strongest authoritarian order is a weak hegemonic order, criticised more for its ineptitude in the pursuit of justice than in the injustice of the order itself.

Order and legitimacy are distinct terms, so that "legitimate order" is not a redundancy, any more than the might that makes order makes that order right. Legitimacy, defined as "the right to rule" (Lasswell and Kaplan 1951), can only refer to domestic political orders, where rule occurs, but it raises the question whether the reigning order is indeed legitimate and how legitimacy is determined (Beetham 1991). There is still no answer to that question, despite some sophisticated polling techniques and rational choice analyses, usually only practicable in more or less legitimate orders (Rogowski 1974). Nor are the two elements independent of each other: order contributes to its own legitimacy, as legitimacy contributes to order. In the anarchical international order, legitimacy needs a new definition to be researchable, perhaps referring instead to the right to exist, if not directly to the concept of justice itself. In the absence of a direct determination, more applicable in domestic polities, investigations relating to legitimacy in an international order necessarily involve questions about the process of its establishment, about the allocation of its benefits, and about the balance of benefits and responsibilities (von Haldenwang 1999).

The relation between *order and process* has been central to the analysis, emphasizing the fact that order is by no means to be considered static. Order is both process and outcome, and the processes of current import – coalition, negotiation, the political equivalent of the market – are open to wide exploration. In all three areas, the potential is still underdeveloped. Coalition theory (Riker 1992) has not kept up with its application; negotiation theory is still a matter of many different views of the elephant; and theorists are still searching for the political equivalent of the market. Whether in domestic or diplomatic legislation, coalitions are best subject to theoretical analysis when they qualify as constituted units with well-determined interests and positions. But when their interests are inchoate and their existence itself the subject of political action, as is most usually the case, even the best analysis becomes inductive or ad hoc. Similarly, negotiation analysis has long been based on an assumption of established positions, bottomlines, and concession/convergence behavior, conditions which allow neat theory but which omit most of the negotiation process and conceive it in unrealistic terms. The political "market" too can only be a process. Important conceptualization of a political system as a mechanism with explicable and foreseeable consequences, developed in the 1950s and 1960s, has been put on the shelf for the moment, ready for retrieval in response to new questions and new bursts of inspiration.

The relation between *order and law* is also a subject of current debate. In domestic relations, law is roughly synonymous with order, despite the ideological appropriations of the phrase, but the heated debate is over how much of public and private life needs to be ordered by law. While the provision of private socio-economic security from the cradle to the grave has been somewhat reduced in many countries, legal regulation of everything from abortion to zebra fish is viewed by many as overly intrusive and sparks a conservative call for "less government." The answer for many is found in Locke's assertion of civil society as an order without authority among players, capable of regulating its own affairs without invoking Hobbes' Leviathan, but the relation between the two – the subsidiarity question – is unclear: is law needed to regulate what civil society does not, or is civil society needed to regulate what law does not? Yet civil society is an increasingly important subject of inquiry particularly in regard to the developing countries (Norton 1995, 1996, 2005), where the problem is an alternative not to intrusive government but to lame or privatized government (Callaghy 1984). The need for law to provide order in a polity is still under debate.

In international politics, where there is practically no government at all, the same question is the basis of the dispute between the realists and the liberals over whether the international order is anarchic and to which state "behaviors" are constrained by regimes, that is, by soft law, institutions or "principles, norms, rules and procedures" (Waltz 1979, p. 89; Keohane and Nye 1989; Krasner 1983); the debate remains unresolved, although the liberal school is better equipped to explain cooperation than its opponent, which is more attuned to conflict.

The relationship between *order and power* also raises important boundary questions, some of which are evoked in the chapters on power in this collection. For all its definitional uncertainties, power is the central concept of political science and also the cause of order, whether acting in coalition, negotiation or more automatic dynamics, and whether distributed or structured equally (symmetrically) and unequally (asymmetrically). So analytical relationships divide into power for creating order and power as an order for doing something else. The first question concerns the way one arrives at a particular order, a matter of particular importance under system or regime change, whether in domestic polities in transition (from authoritarian order presumably to democracy) or in the international system mutating from bipolar coalitions to unipolar hegemony or multipolar pluralism. The domestic question has occasioned a vigorous literature (O'Donnell and Schmitter 1986; Bunce 1989) pointing to the importance of powerholders negotiating to retain protection if not position in the transition; analysis of the evolution of the international system is limited by the uniqueness of the most recent case.

The second question concerns the implications of various orders as power structures. The ongoing debates over bipolar vs multipolar stability in international politics and over the importance of a hegemony vs a middle power coalition for regional integration are concerns of this type. While the verdict seems to have tilted in favor of bipolarity (or now even unipolarity) over multipolarity as the key to stability, there is a tinge of argument to please the court or acquiescence to the current order of things in the analysis. Unfortunately, a deeper, but less satisfying conclusion is, arguably, that any of the three orders is stable if it is played "right," that is, each order contains stability mechanisms of mutual restraint whose use depends on the dominant parties' sense of responsibility (to maintain stability!) and not on any inherent homeostasis. To identify royal philosophers, bilateral regimes (Kanet and Kolodziej 1991), and balance of power as such mechanisms confirms the need for a place for will and skill in political analysis, along with more objective mechanisms and regularities.

While developed polities in general have worked out their institutional structures, developing countries continue to debate the effects of a centralized, if not authoritarian, power structure vs a pluralistic – either parliamentarian or dual executive – system. The most notable enactment of this debate occurred in the early 1990s in the twelve countries of Africa where civil society made the extraordinary move of seizing sovereignty from the authoritarian incumbent and drawing up a new social contract. The same question faces others on the continent and elsewhere in the Mideast, Asia and Latin America facing the same desire for transition from authoritarian rule, even without a sovereign national conference. An authoritarian order faces the challenge of keeping the father of the nation dynamic and honest, whereas, as noted, the coalesced order faces the challenges of coalition instability or of keeping the Great Coalition honest and dynamic, and the negotiated order faces the challenge of participation, recognizing both those who are part of the problem and those who are not part of the problem, as a legitimate part of the solution. While democracy is without exception the favored solution to the power-and-order problem, it is used to justify both truly democratic, democratizing and non-democratic orders, and its inevitable abuses and inefficiencies return the analysis to focus on problems of effectiveness and responsibility.

The millennium brings a startling – or refreshing – new angle to the problem of power orders by introducing the prospects of a weaker state facing an increasing number of challenges. International politics has already begun to grapple, albeit inconclusively, with the problem of permeable and circumvented sovereignty weakening the fiber of its state system (Lyons and Mastanduno 1995; Deng *et al.* 1996). In internal politics, the need for the state, whatever its power structure, to rely increasingly on cooperation with other non-state actors, returning to prominence the concept of civil society as a crucial element in the internal order and an answer to the problems of effectiveness and responsibility. The concomitant result is an increasing need to recognize the importance of negotiation – rather than authority or coalition democracy – as the decision-making order within the networks, dialogues, regimes, outsourcing, etc that are needed to tie the pieces together. The state has come back as the heart of political analysis just in time to be subject to deep surgery and bypasses to overcome its weak and blocked circulation.

The universality of order

It is hard to imagine that any of these concerns could be limited to a particular cultural area of the world or would be a worry of only a Western mind. Order itself is universal and its forms are several. Each has its advantages and disadvantages, and none is the cultural property of any particular country or region. There may be (or have been) a Confucian order in China, an Islamic order in Iran, an Enarquic order in France, or a monarchial order in Morocco, but the concept of order is common to them all and their peculiar characteristics can also be found here and there around the globe. It is hard to compare, analyze or even talk of them without using common concepts of order.

Nonetheless, the point of view of political culture would aver that particular conceptions of order dominate the ethos and practice of large world areas, based on current political systems, historical traditions, predominant religions, and regional configurations. From this point of view, admittedly generalized and perhaps caricatural (i.e. exaggerating known features), Asia – both East or Confucian and Western or Arabo-Muslim – can be said to favor a centralized hierarchical political order, as contrasted with the Judeo-Christian Atlantic West which is characterized by a pluralized competitive order. China and Egypt would be typical of the first, the US and Europe of the second.[26] The Confucian system dominant in China (and reinforced by the Marxist–Leninist–Maoist ideology) regards hierarchy as superior to competition as an ordering principle, and enlightened authoritarian command is its form of decision-making. A deeply inbred fear of social chaos (*luan*) preconditions the Chinese preference for a strong central authority. A strong government is also perceived to be better able to deliver social goods. Its political geography has long been seen in terms of concentric circles, based on the pivotal Middle Kingdom, and indeed the vast country of China has one time zone. Values are in service of the collective and emphasize communal harmony. Foreigners are held separate, socialization into dominant cultural patterns is the main function of education, and political participation is through the single party (Dreyer 1999; Pye 1978, 1988; Lieberthal 1995; Johnston 1996; Pomeranz 2000). Negotiation becomes difficult to practice, and instructive discourse is preferred.

Despite very different sources, Arabo-Muslim political culture has remarkably similar characteristics, as seen in Egypt and most other Arab countries. The authoritarian system center about the leader (*za'im*) is predominant, the single party or at least the dominant party runs the political system, and democracy has a hard time taking hold. If the Arab world is broken up into separate states, the Arab nation and the single Islamic community (umma) are idealized and mythologized, and the classical language of the Qoran is the standard of civilization and the word of the God (*al-Lah*). Egypt is the Mother of the Earth (*masr umm al-duniya*), even if some other Arab states would claim at least paternity. Although in both East and West Asia pluralism is bound to exist, it is conditioned and contained with the centralized authoritarian order.

In contrast, the Atlantic West is characterized by competitive pluralism, multiparty democracy, a multicultural stew in the melting pot, and many time zones (Jones 1987; Pomeranz 2000). The US is no more united than its federalism will allow, and European unity takes place only by preserving its multistate system (cf. Walker). Where pluralism has to be contained, it is through binary logic, manichean conceptualization between good and bad, black and white, and legal confrontation. France invented, and the US applied, the separation of powers within government, and this pluralism has been paralleled historically by the richness of American associative life in civil society (deTocqueville 1850). Even where the European monarchial tradition has left a shadow of centralism, it has been eaten away at the edges throughout history by the English barons, the German states, Italian (even including papal) tolerance for ambiguity, and French democracy. This is a negotiatory polity par excellence, combined with the elections and coalitions of democracy.

These vignettes can be either dismissed as *images d'Epinal* or endlessly debated and diagnosed as clashing civilizations, as can no doubt the whole area of political (or any other) culture (Huntington 1996). Yet there is a lot of literature and discussion behind the general picture of the three cultures that the vignettes present, and they represent a certain consensus about different notions of order in different parts of the world, even in their abbreviated form.

But the overriding point is that these images reflect a common notion of the meaning of order and of the forms which it can take, even if elements in that universal typology find different supporting examples from different regions. In response to the original questions, different regions may answer differently over which order is preferable but they enter into the debate on the basis of a common understanding of the orders possible and practiced among political beings on this earth. And the sources of these different orders, as well as their consequences, are also part of the common heritage of humankind. To rephrase the nineteenth-century doggerel,

> Of forms of government may fools contest:
> Whate'er is best administered is best,

we may conclude.

> On forms of order let the wise contest
> And from universal types debate the best.

This contemporary debate between centralized, authoritarian and pluralist, competitive political orders is too eternal and too important to be assigned geographic or cultural roots and preferences, when its ingredients and stakes are universal. Political concepts are the common heritage of humankind, not the pep songs of local teams playing turf games under the name of civilisational clashes. On the edge of the millennium, it is hard to imagine a centralized authoritarian order capable of the Confucian wisdom and the freedom from computer glitches necessary to handle a globalized world, and by the same token it is exciting for the discipline to take on the conceptual and analytical challenges that that world poses to an order where competition, negotiation and coalition constitute the necessary and dominant sources or order.

Part II

Negotiation to manage conflict

10 International mediation[27]

International conflicts are frequently the subject of third-party mediation. We do not know how common mediation was in earlier history (the earliest recorded occurrence comes from some 3,500 years ago), but it was practiced in *Romeo and Juliet* with catastrophic effects, and has been a frequent occurrence for at least 400 years. Although the end of the Cold War has brought about many changes in international politics, it has neither reduced the incidence of international conflicts nor the tendency of third-parties to mediate those conflicts that they find especially troublesome.

"Conflict" here refers to politico-security issues. Typically, in international economic or environmental disputes, rival parties are not as forcefully competitive, nor are the means of conducting the dispute as violent as in politico-security conflicts. Conflicts over politico-security issues take place within a context of power politics, which has a major effect on international mediation. This premise provides the conceptual underpinning of our analysis of the participants' motives in mediation, the conditions that affect the performance and roles of mediators, and the keys to effective mediation of international conflicts. The term "international conflict" refers here both to interstate conflicts and to domestic ones that are affected by the involvement of external parties. When external parties provide political, economic, or military assistance or asylum and bases for actors involved in domestic struggles, domestic conflicts inevitably assume an international dimension.

Mediation is a form of third-party intervention in a conflict. It differs from other forms of third-party intervention in conflicts in that it is not based on the direct use of force and it is not aimed at helping one of the participants to win. Its purpose is to bring the conflict to a settlement that is acceptable to both sides and consistent with the third-party's interests. Mediation is a political process with no advance commitment from the parties to accept the mediator's ideas. In this respect, it differs from arbitration, which employs judicial procedure and issues a verdict that the parties have committed themselves beforehand to accept. Mediation is best thought of as a mode of negotiation in which a third party helps the parties find a solution which they cannot find by themselves. To accomplish its purposes, mediation must be made acceptable to the adversaries in the conflict, who must in turn cooperate diplomatically with the intervenor. But mediators often meet initial rejection from the conflicting parties; thus their first diplomatic effort must be to convince the parties of the value of their services before the mediation process can get started.

The mediator's motives

States use mediation as a foreign policy instrument. Their intervention as mediators is legitimized by the goal of conflict reduction, which they typically proclaim. The desire to make peace, however, is intertwined with other motives best described within the context of power politics. To understand these motives it is most helpful to employ a rational-actor approach, using cost-benefit considerations. Mediators are players in the plot of relations surrounding a conflict, and so they have an interest in its outcome; otherwise, they would not mediate. In view of the considerable investment of political, moral, and material resources that mediation requires and the risks to which mediators expose themselves, motives for mediation must be found as much in domestic and international self-interest as in humanitarian impulses. Mediators are seldom indifferent to the terms being negotiated. Not surprisingly, they try to avoid terms not in accord with their own interests, even though mediators' interests usually allow for a wider range of acceptable outcomes than the interests of the parties. Self-interested motivation holds for superpowers, medium-sized powers, and international organizations.

Mediation by states

Mediating states are likely to seek terms that will increase the prospects of stability, deny their rivals opportunities for intervention, earn them the gratitude of one or both parties, or enable them to continue to have a role in future relations in the region. Both defensive and offensive goals can be promoted through mediation, and they often blend together. (For a further discussion of states' interest in managing conflict, see Udalov 1995 and Zartman 1995) Mediators act defensively when a continuing conflict between others threatens the mediator's interests. An end to the conflict is therefore important to the mediator because of the conflict's effects on the mediator's relations with the disputing parties. For example, if two of the mediator's allies engage in a conflict, it can disrupt and weaken the alliance or strain the parties' relations with the third-party mediator. A conflict between two states may also upset a regional balance or provide opportunities for a rival power to increase its influence by intervening on one side of the conflict.

In some situations, a conflict may threaten to escalate and draw in additional parties. Actors who fear such escalation and expansion may seek to reduce the conflict to avoid becoming involved in hostilities. Mediation in such cases may involve one intervenor or it may be a collective endeavor by two or more states acting within or outside the framework of an international organization. For example, the efforts to mediate the various conflicts arising out of the dissolution of Yugoslavia involved the European Union, the Organization for Security and Cooperation in Europe, NATO, the United Nations, the informal "Contact Group," Russia, and the US. Even rival powers, protecting their turf, are known to have cooperated and engaged in joint mediation when they feared that continuation of a particular conflict might endanger their security (for example, US–Soviet cooperation on Laos in 1961–2, the Arab–Israeli war in 1973, and finally, on Kosovo in 1999).

The second self-interested motive for mediation is offensive: the desire to extend and increase influence. In this case, the solution of the conflict has no direct importance for the mediator and is only a vehicle for improving relations with one or both parties. A third party may hope to win the gratitude of one or both parties in a conflict, either by helping them out of the conflict or by aiding one of them to achieve better terms in a solution than would otherwise be obtainable. Although the mediator cannot throw its full weight behind one party, it can increase its influence by making the success of the negotiations depend on its involvement and by making each party depend on it to garner concessions from the other party. Mediators can also increase their presence and influence by becoming guarantors of any agreement, which necessarily includes risks and responsibilities.

A number of historical examples illustrate these interests. US mediation in the Rhodesia/Zimbabwe conflict in 1976–9 and the Soviet mediation between India and Pakistan in 1966 were inspired by a mixture of defensive and offensive motives. From a defensive vantage, the US feared the Rhodesian conflict would provide opportunities for the Soviet Union to gain influence by supporting the African nationalists. But because the African groups concerned were already politically close to the Soviet Union and China, the US mediation was also an attempt to improve relations with these groups and thus extend American influence.

Soviet mediation between India and Pakistan was partly inspired by its desire to improve relations with Pakistan, a country that had hitherto been on better terms with the US and China than with the Soviet Union. It also sought to build its prestige and establish a precedent that would justify future involvement in the affairs of the region. At the same time, there were important defensive motives for its intervention. The Indo-Pakistan conflict provided China an opportunity to extend its influence into Pakistan and thus establish a presence close to the southern borders of the Soviet Union. By reducing the conflict, this expansion would become more difficult for China.

The US has been the most active mediator of international conflicts since 1945 (Touval 1992). This involvement is consistent with an interest-based explanation of mediators' motives. Because the US feared that conflicts would provide the Soviet Union with opportunities to intervene and expand its influence, the US often sought to dampen conflict, and mediation was an appropriate instrument to that end. In addition, without reference to the Soviet Union, US help was sometimes solicited by smaller states engaged in conflict because of the US' power and prestige. Pressed by its friends for support, and always fearful that support for one side in a local conflict would throw the other side into the Soviet embrace, the US often found that the least risky course in such situations was to mediate between the disputants.

That Americans were involved in mediation more often than the Soviet Union during the Cold War can easily be understood if we remember the preeminent status that the US has enjoyed in international politics for many years, and the unequal extent of the two powers' spheres of influence. The Soviet sphere was at first limited to Eastern Europe and China. Starting in the mid-1950s, it expanded to include a few additional countries that became dependent on Soviet military aid (at the same time, however, China broke away from the Soviet sphere). The remainder of the world, sometimes called the *Free World*, was considered by the US as part of its own sphere (notwithstanding that some states in this group proclaimed themselves to be nonaligned). Although actual American influence varied among these *Free World* states, what they had in common was that the Soviet Union carried less influence there than did the US. Thus, the wider sphere of American influence explains why the US mediated so many more conflicts than did the Soviet Union.

Since the end of the Cold War, humanitarian concerns of public opinion have come to play a more important role in shaping foreign policies than in the past. The need to respond to domestic public opinion has sometimes led a government to intervene in foreign conflicts, including civil wars, even when they are not perceived as impinging on its security interests. Since mediation carries fewer costs for intervenors than military action, especially if pursued through international organizations, collective mediation seems to be on the increase. Examples of such mediation include the mediations in Afghanistan, Angola, Burundi, Haiti, Liberia, Mozambique, Rwanda, Sierra Leone, Somalia, Sudan, and the former Yugoslavia.

Mediation by small- and medium-sized powers

Mediation by small- and medium-sized powers is also motivated by self-interest, some of which is related to domestic concerns. Such interests include the possibility that a conflict may spill over into the mediator's territory; the fear that the local conflict may expand and draw in powerful external actors (India's mediation in Sri Lanka prior to its military intervention is an example of both these concerns); the reluctance to take sides in a conflict between other nations (Saudi Arabia in many inter-Arab conflicts); and the attempt to promote norms that tend to enhance the mediator's own security (the 1963 Ethiopian mediation between Algeria and Morocco concerning the validity of borders inherited from the colonial period).

Small- and medium-sized powers may also wish to enhance their influence and prestige through mediation. Egypt's and Algeria's mediation between Iran and Iraq in 1975 was motivated by the desire to prove their usefulness to both belligerents, as well as to reduce intra-Islamic conflict. Algerian mediation between the US and Iran on the issue of American hostages seems to have been inspired by the hope that mediation would generate goodwill from the US public toward Algeria and thus help improve relations between Algeria and the US. This hope was related to US support for Algeria's adversary, Morocco, in the Western Sahara war against the Algerian-supported Polisario movement. Other cases in which states sought to enhance their international standing through mediation include India's attempt to mediate between the US and the Soviet Union and China in the 1950s; Ghana's effort to mediate in the Vietnam war in 1965–6; and Romania's try at an intermediary role in that same conflict, in US–Soviet relations, and in Arab–Israeli relations (notably in helping to arrange Egyptian President Anwar Sadat's visit to Jerusalem in 1977).

Small and medium states have few alternative foreign policy instruments at their disposal, and mediation increases their usefulness and independence in relation to their stronger allies. Moreover, when pressed to take sides in a conflict, they may seek to escape their predicament by assuming the role of a mediator in the conflict. In the post-Cold War era, small and medium states continue to have a role as mediator. Kenya and Zimbabwe attempted to mediate the Mozambique conflict, Zaire the Angolan conflict, South Africa the conflicts in Nigeria and Swaziland, the Association of South East Asian Nations (ASEAN) the conflict in Cambodia, Norway the Palestinian–Israeli conflict, and Saudi Arabia the conflicts in Yemen and Lebanon. Many states – including South Africa, Togo, Tunisia, Algeria, Saudi Arabia, Costa Rica, and Colombia – consider mediation of the conflicts in their regions to be a major element of their foreign policy.

Mediation by international organizations and NGOs

The motives of international organizations are somewhat more complex than those of states. Peacemaking is the r*aison d'etre* of several international organizations and is thus enshrined in their charters. Yet intergovernmental organizations are also subject to the particular policies and interests of their member-states. The end of the Cold War freed international organizations from their bipolar constraints, and they rushed into mediation and conflict management. As a result, their reputations and resources became overextended and their efforts were not rewarded with the expected quick success. In as short a time, member-states pulled back, blamed the organizations (which they ran), and greatly reduced their mediation activities. On his own, UN Secretary General Boutros Boutros-Ghali sent special representatives to conflict areas; the Organization of African Unity (OAU) added a section on conflict prevention, management, and resolution to the Secretariat; ASEAN took on new mediation roles; and the Economic Community of West African States (ECOWAS) and the West African Economic Community (CEAO) mediated conflicts in their midst. Thus the post–Cold War era has seen new regional organization activity to fill the slack left by the United Nations, plus a gradual reevaluation of UN potential. The UN experiences in Somalia, Rwanda, and Cambodia have shown both the great possibilities for mediation by the world organization and the difficulty in separating its role from the specific – indeed, narrow – interests and concerns of leading member-states in the Security Council.

Non-state mediators, whose interests are not as apparent or suspect as the primary players of power politics, nevertheless share motives of self-interest. At the very least nonstate mediators have a role and a reputation to establish or defend and thus an interest in appearing as good and successful mediators. (The concerns of the World Council of Churches and the All-African Council of Churches in launching their mediation of the Sudanese civil war in 1971 is an interesting example (Assefa 1987), as is the highly motivated work of the Vatican in 1978–84 in mediating the Beagle Channel dispute (Princen 1992) and of the Sant'Egidio community in mediating in Mozambique and Algeria (Johnston and Sampson 1994; Zartman, ed. 1995)). Often this role extends beyond mediation to become an organizational interest in establishing a presence and in keeping the organization clean and ready for other functions. In this regard, non-state mediators come very close to state mediators in the nature of their interests.

Concern for peace as a value in and of itself, suspicion of interested mediators' motives, and perception of the inherent limitations on states' mediating roles have led a variety of nonstate actors to propose themselves as international mediators. Many of these are interested in a particular outcome, not because it affects them directly, but because they believe in its inherent desirability. Thus, the several private agencies striving for usefulness in the Rhodesian and Liberian civil wars were working to find an acceptable path to Zimbabwean independence and to a new political system in Liberia, respectively, not some other outcome. All nonstate actors have an interest in enhancing their positions as useful third parties, not out of any venal egotism but because they believe they have something to offer; furthermore, a reinforcement of their standing and reputation helps them do their job.

The parties' motives in accepting mediation

Opponents in a conflict face two interrelated questions: whether to accept mediation and, if so, whose offer of mediation to accept (Maundi *et al.* 2006). Parties accept intervention because they, like mediators, expect it to work in favor of their interests. The most obvious motive is the expectation that mediation will gain an outcome more favorable than the outcome gained by continued conflict – that is, a way out. The parties also hope that mediation will produce a settlement when direct negotiation is not possible or will provide a more favorable settlement than can be achieved by direct negotiation. Although the adversary may not have a similar assessment, it may accept and cooperate with the mediator if it feels that rejection might cause even greater harm – for example, damaging relations with the would-be mediator, decreasing the chances for an acceptable negotiated outcome, or prolonging a costly conflict. Such considerations sometimes help to induce states to accept intervention even in domestic conflicts (for example, Sri Lanka's acceptance of India's mediation, and Angola's acceptance of US mediation). The parties may also accept mediation in the hope that the intermediary will reduce some of the risks entailed in making concessions and the costs incurred in conflict, protecting their image and reputation as they move toward a compromise. They may also believe a mediator's involvement implies a guarantee for the final agreement, thus reducing the danger of violation by the adversary.

The acceptance of mediation by international organizations can also be premised on the ability of these organizations to bestow normative approval, rather than on their capacity to influence the adversary or arrange for a satisfactory compromise. This factor is applies tothe United Nations but is perhaps clearest in the case of the International Committee of the Red Cross (ICRC). The ICRC's ability to offer an improved image to a fighting or detaining authority can be a powerful incentive for the parties to accept its services and to accede to its proposals.

Partiality and acceptability

If the acceptance of mediation is based on a cost-benefit calculation, then the assumption that mediators must be perceived as impartial needs to be revised (Touval 1982). The mediator's impartiality is not as important to the adversaries' decision to accept mediation as is their consideration of the consequences of accepting or rejecting mediation: how will their decision affect the prospects of achieving a favorable outcome? Also, how will it affect their future relations with the would-be mediator?

Initially, third parties are accepted as mediators only to the extent that they are seen as capable of bringing about acceptable outcomes; then, their subsequent meddling is tolerated because they are already part of the relationship. Although there is no necessary relationship between a mediator's past partiality and its future usefulness, good relations between it and one of the adversaries may in fact be an aid to communicating, to developing creative proposals, and to converging the two parties' positions. Closeness to one party implies the possibility of "delivering" it, thereby stimulating the other party's cooperation. Indeed, the implications of closeness can be carried one step further: since mediators are not likely to be successful (that is, attractive to the other party) if they are perceived as preferring a solution favoring the party to which they are close, a biased mediator's acceptability and success lies in the likelihood of its delivering the party toward which it is biased into an agreement.

Several examples illustrate these points. In the Rhodesia/Zimbabwe mediation, the Africans' belief that British and US sympathies were with the white Rhodesians rendered British and US mediation promising and stimulated African cooperation. In several mediations between Arab parties and Israel, the Arabs' belief that the close American–Israeli ties would enable the US to deliver Israeli concessions made American mediation attractive to them. In the Tashkent mediation, the Soviet Union was accepted as a mediator by Pakistan, despite its close relationship with India. Pakistan perceived the Soviet Union as concerned enough about Pakistan's growing cooperation with China to want to improve its own relationship with Pakistan and as close enough to India to bring it into an agreement. Algeria was accepted by the US as a mediator with Iran not because it considered impartial, but because its ability to gain access to and facilitate the agreement of people close to Khomeini held promise that it might help to release the hostages.

Although they cannot fully side with one party, mediators can allow themselves some latitude in their degree of partiality. This latitude may allow them to express their preference regarding the outcome of the negotiation. In the Zimbabwe and Namibia negotiations, the US was not indifferent to the nature of the settlement: the outcome had to open the way for majority rule. Although this meant that the US supported the essence of the African position and, by implication, sought to eliminate the white settlers as a sovereign political actor, the white settlers nevertheless accepted US mediation as a means to get them out of a no-win situation.

An interest in specific outcomes is quite common in the mediations of international organizations. The United Nations, the OAU, the ICRC, and the Organization of American States (OAS) all have some general norms that they wish to uphold beyond the principle of peaceful settlement. They try to promote solutions that can be interpreted as compatible with the standards of the Geneva conventions and of their charters and that protect their image as guardians of these standards. Indeed, they can formally condemn parties for deviating from these standards as a means to enforce them. The European Community, trying to mediate a settlement of the disputes arising out of the dissolution of Yugoslavia in 1991, and concerned about the impending dissolution of the Soviet Union, enunciated the principle of the inviolability of internal borders within states, equating their status to that of international borders. On the other hand, the OAU was so strongly attached to the principle of successor state integrity that it was incapable of mediating the Biafran or Namibian conflict, so strongly attached to the principle of *uti possidetis* (legitimacy of inherited boundaries) that it was unable to mediate the Ogaden war, and so strongly attached to the principle of noninterference in internal affairs that it was unable even to constitute a commission to mediate the Sudanese and Rwandan civil wars.

Acceptance of mediation, whether the mediator is a state or an international organization, is not automatic. It depends on the promise of attractive outcomes for the parties. When the OAU establishes an ad hoc commission to mediate a dispute, consultation procedures give the parties an implicit say in the composition of the commission. The result is often a balanced slate rather than an impartial commission, because members are likely to seek to protect the interests of their friends and not to form their views solely on the basis of abstract principles.

Independent non-state agencies, such as the ICRC or the Sant'Egidio community, do not have partiality or composition problems. Nevertheless, their acceptance as a mediator is still not automatic. Conflicting parties are not concerned whether the ICRC or Sant'Egidio will perform humanitarian functions objectively, but whether the framework of its involvement will further their interests. Thus, states may deny that an armed conflict that would justify an ICRC intervention is occurring or has occurred or that a Sant'Egidio venue for dialogue is appropriate. Yet, the legal framework is sometimes subject to negotiation, and the terms of involvement can be influenced by their perceived effect on the interests of the parties, rather than by the latter's perception of the mediator's impartiality.

Mediators must be perceived as having an interest in achieving an outcome acceptable to both sides and as being not so partial as to preclude such an achievement. Again, the question for the parties is not whether the mediator is objective, but whether it can provide an acceptable outcome.

Timing of mediation

Since mediators are motivated by self-interest, they will not intervene automatically, but only when they believe a conflict threatens their interests or when they perceive an opportunity to advance their interests. Such threats and opportunities are unlikely to be noticed when there is a mild disagreement between parties. Usually it is only after the conflict escalates that its implications are perceived. By then, the parties are likely to have become committed to their positions and to a confrontational policy, ever reducing the common grounds on which mediation must proceed. For that to succeed, the parties must be disposed to reevaluate their policies.

Two conditions are especially conducive to such reevaluation: mutually hurting stalemates and crises bounded by a deadline or, to use a metaphor, plateaus and precipices (1989a). A mutually hurting stalemate begins when one side realizes that it is unable to achieve its aims, resolve the problem, or win the conflict by itself; it is completed when the other side reaches a similar conclusion. Each party must begin to feel uncomfortable in the costly dead end that it has reached. Both sides must see this plateau not as a momentary resting ground, but as a flat, unpleasant terrain stretching into the future, providing no later possibilities for decisive escalation or graceful escape.

Mediation plays upon the parties' perceptions of having reached an intolerable situation. Without this perception, the mediator must depend on persuading the parties that breaking out of their deadlock is impossible. Indeed, the mediator may even be required to make it impossible. Thus, deadlock cannot be seen as a temporary stalemate, to be easily resolved in one's favor by a little effort, a big offensive, a gamble, or foreign assistance. Rather, each party must recognize its opponent's strength and its own inability to overcome that strength, as well as the cost of staying in the stalemate.

For the mediator, this means cultivating each side's perception that its unilateral policy option – to take action without negotiation – is a more expensive, less likely way of achieving an acceptable outcome than the policy of negotiation. A plateau is therefore as much a matter of perception as of reality for the parties and as much a subject of persuasion as of timing for the mediator. Successful exploitation of a plateau shifts both sides from a combative mentality to a conciliatory mentality.

A crisis, or precipice, represents the realization that matters are swiftly becoming worse. It implies impending catastrophe, such as probable military defeat or economic collapse. It may be accompanied by a policy dilemma that involves engaging in a major escalation, the outcome of which is unpredictable, or seeking a desperate compromise that threatens one side as much as the other. It may also be a catastrophe that has already taken place or has been narrowly avoided. Whatever its tense (because parties are bound to disagree about the inevitability of an impending event), it marks a time limit to the judgment that "things can't go on like this" (Zartman 1987, pp. 285 ff.).

For the mediator, the crisis as precipice should reinforce the dangers of the plateau, lest the parties become accustomed to their uncomfortable deadlock. Mediators can manipulate stalemates and crises: they can use them and they can make them. If there is a recognized impending danger, mediators can use it as a warning and as an unpleasant alternative to a negotiated settlement. And if they do not agree that a crisis exists, mediators can work to implant a common perception that it, or a mutually hurting stalemate, does exist. In its most manipulative role, a mediator may have to create a plateau or a precipice, usually citing pressure from a fourth party. That is what the US did in 1977 to get the Namibia negotiations started, citing irresistible pressure for sanctions if the sides did not start talking. Plateau and precipice are precise but perceptional conditions, and they have governed the timing of successful mediation in most cases. They are not self-implementing: they must be seen and seized. Unfortunately, they depend on conflict and its escalation. It would be preferable if the need for a ripe moment could be combined with the desirability of treating conflict early, as sought in preventive diplomacy. To do this, mediators need to develop a perception of stalemate at a low level of conflict, or to develop a sense of responsibility on the part of a government to head off an impending conflict, or to develop an awareness of an opportunity for a better outcome made available through mediation. Kissinger worked powerfully on the Israelis' peception of ripeness in the disengagement negotiations.

Modes of mediators

Mediators use three mode – communication, formulation, and manipulation, in that order – to marshal the interests of all the involved parties toward a mutually acceptable solution to the conflict. Since mediation is helping the parties to do what they cannot do by themselves, each of these three modes refers to a different level of obstacle to direct negotiations.

When conflict has made direct contact between parties impossible, thereby preventing the parties from talking to each other and from making concessions without appearing weak or losing face, the mediator can serve as communicator. In this situation, mediators simply act as a conduit, opening contacts and carrying messages. They may be required to help the parties understand the meaning of messages through the distorting dust thrown up by the conflict or to gather the parties' concessions together into a package, without adding to the content. This role is completely procedural, with no substantive contribution by the mediator, and in its simplest form it is completely passive, only carrying out the parties' orders for the delivery of messages. Tact, wording, and sympathy, mixed in equal doses with accuracy and confidentiality, are necessary character traits of the mediator as communicator.

The second mode of mediation requires the mediator to enter into the substance of the negotiation. Since a conflict may not only impede communications between parties, but be so encompassing that it prevents them from conceiving ways out of the dispute, the parties need a mediator as formulator. Formulas are the key to a negotiated solution to a conflict; they provide a common understanding of the problem and its solution or a shared notion of justice to govern an outcome. Just as the conflict often prevents the parties from finding imaginative ways out, it may also prevent them from seeing the value of the mediator's suggestions at first hearing. Therefore, the mediator as a formulator often needs to persuade the parties, as well as to suggest solutions to their disputes. Persuasion involves power and therefore requires greater involvement than mere communication. Not only does the mediator get involved in the substance of the issue, but it must also lean on the parties – albeit in the subtlest ways – to adopt its perceptions of a way out. Mediators as successful formulators must be capable of thinking of ways to unblock the thinking of the conflicting parties and to work out imaginative ways to skirt the constraints on the parties.

The third mode requires the mediator to act as a manipulator. Here the mediator assumes the maximum degree of involvement, becoming a party to the solution if not to the dispute. As a manipulator, the mediator uses its power to bring the parties to an agreement, pushing and pulling them away from conflict and into resolution. When the obstacle to agreement is the seemingly paltry size of the outcome, the mediator must persuade the parties of its vision of a solution; it must then take measures to make that solution attractive, enhancing its value by adding benefits to its outcome and presenting it in such a way as to overcome imbalances that may have prevented one of the parties from subscribing to it. The mediator may have to go so far as to improve the absolute attractiveness of the resolution by increasing the unattractiveness of continued conflict, which may mean shoring up one side or condemning another, either of which actions strains the appearance of its own neutrality. This is the role of the "full participant" that American diplomats played in the 1970s Middle East peace process and in the 1980s Namibian–Angolan negotiations.

Mediation is a triangular relationship. When the mediator operates as a communicator, it operates as a bridge between two contestants, or as a pump on the conduit between them. As a formulator, the mediator assumes a position of greater activity, one from which pressures and messages emanate as well as pass through. As a manipulator, the mediator becomes so active that it calls into question the triangular relationship. It may even unite the two adversaries in opposition to the mediator; for example, in the Yemen civil war (1962–70) the two sides resolved their differences in order to oppose Egyptian interference, when Egypt was acting more as an intervenor than as a mediator. But the mediator, by throwing its weight around, threatens and is threatened by the possibility of turning the triangle into a dyad. The mediator's threat to side with one party may bring the other party around, for fear that mediation might end and with it any possibilities for a solution. As a threat to the mediator, each party may try to win the mediator over to its own side to increase its chances of winning rather than of having to come to terms. At the same time, of course, each party may regard the mediator with high suspicion as a potential ally of the other side. Although it makes the mediator's job more difficult, suspicion is functional because it keeps the mediator honest.

Power in mediation

Power – the ability to move a party in an intended direction – is often referred to in mediation as "leverage." Although leverage is the ticket to mediation, mediators tend to remain relatively powerless throughout the exercise. The extent of the mediator's power depends entirely on the parties, whose acceptance of a mediator depends on its likelihood (potential power) of producing an outcome agreeable to both sides. This circular relationship plagues every mediation exercise. Contrary to a common misperception, mediators are rarely "hired" by the parties; instead, they have to sell their services, based on the prospect of their usefulness and success. From the beginning, the mediator's leverage is at the mercy of the contestants. The parties, whose interest is in winning, view mediation as meddling, unless it produces a favorable outcome. They welcome mediation only to the extent that the mediator has leverage over the other party, and they berate the mediator for trying to exert leverage over them.

A mediator has six sources of leverage: first, persuasion, the ability to portray an alternative future as more favorable than the continuing conflict; second, extraction, the ability to produce an attractive position from each party; third, termination, the ability to withdraw from the mediation; fourth, limitation, the ability to block other alternatives; fifth, deprivation, the ability to withhold resources from one side or to shift them to the other; and sixth, gratification, the ability to add resources to the outcome. In every case the effectiveness of the mediator's leverage lies with the parties themselves, a characteristic that makes leverage in mediation difficult to achieve.

The first source of leverage is persuasion. The mediator in any mode must be able to point out the attractiveness of conciliation on available terms and the unattractiveness of continued conflict, a purely communicative exercise independent of any resources. Secretary of State Henry Kissinger, whose country was not devoid of resources or the willingness to use them, nevertheless spent long hours painting verbal pictures of the future with and without an agreement for Egyptian, Syrian, and Israeli audiences. His actions may not have been sufficient in the last rounds of the withdrawal negotiations, but they certainly were necessary. President Jimmy Carter's mediation at Camp David in September 1978 and in Cairo and Jerusalem in March 1979 bear the same characteristics of the power and limitations of persuasion.

Mediation is unwelcome until it can extract a proposal from one party that is viewed as favorable by the other. This second source of leverage is the most problematic, yet it is the basis of all mediation. The crucial moment in mediation comes when the mediator asks a party's permission to try for the other's agreement to a proposal; this exchange is the heart of the formulation mode. But its success depends on the parties' need for a way out of the impasse of conflict – demonstrating the importance of the mutually "hurting stalemate" as an element of the ripe moment. Assistant Secretary of State Crocker and his team shuttled back and forth between Angola and South Africa in search of attractive proposals to carry to each side, but that exchange was not forthcoming until the conditions of 1988 made the stalemate intolerable to both sides.

The third source of leverage, termination, lies in the mediator's ability to withdraw and leave the parties to their own devices and their continuing conflict. Again, the impact of withdrawal is entirely in the hands of the disputing parties; they may be happy to see the mediator leave, but if the mutually hurting stalemate is present, they will be sensitive to the threat of leaving. However, if the mediator needs a solution more than the parties, it will be unable to threaten termination credibly. Secretary Kissinger brandished the threat in mediating the Golan Heights withdrawal in 1974 and activated it at the second Sinai withdrawal the following year. Another example comes from the 1995 Bosnia Peace Conference at Dayton. It was only after Secretary of State Christopher told the delegations on 20 November, the twentieth day of the conference, that in a few hours he would announce that the Conference had failed, that the parties finally resolved their remaining differences, bringing the conference to agreement.

Limitation is the fourth spurce of leverage, ivolvingthe meditor's ability to block off any other venues for mediation or any other alternaives to mediation in general. The mediator must be able to convince the parties that its mediation is "the only game in town," as Crocker used to say about his mediation in the Angolan–South African conflict in the 1980s, and to make sure the parties do not see renewed war as a better alternative than mediation, as the Eritreans and Ethiopians did in the midst of mediations in 1999. Multiple mediators bring outbidding and ineffectiveness, unless firmly coordinated.

The remaining sources of leverage use the conflict and the proposed solution as their fulcrums, thus making manipulation their primary mode of mediation. Leverage derives from the mediator's ability to tilt toward (gratification) or away from (deprivation) a party and thereby to affect the conditions of a stalemate or of movement out of it. The activity may be verbal, such as a vote of condemnation, or more tangible, such as visits, food aid, or arms shipments. The point is to worsen the dilemma of parties rejecting mediation and to keep them in search of a solution.

The mediator might shift weight in order to prevent one party from losing the conflict because the other's victory would produce a less stable and hence less desirable situation. Such activity clearly brings the mediator very close to being a party in the conflict. Arms to Israel and Morocco, down payments on better relations with South Africa, and abstentions on UN votes are examples of US shifts – in-weight during various mediation processes. The Soviet Union threatened to shift weight away from India in the Security Council debate on the Indo-Pakistan war, and Britain threatened to shift weight against the Patriotic Front in Rhodesia. Threats of this kind are effective only to the degree that they are believed.

The last source of the mediator's leverage is the side payment, the subject to which the term "leverage" is usually applied. As weight shifts affect the continuing conflict, side payments may be needed to augment or enhance the outcome to one or more parties. Side payments require considerable resources and engagement from the mediators, thus they are rarely made and certainly not the key to successful mediation. Yet when the outcome is not large enough to provide sufficient benefits for both parties or to outweigh the present or anticipated advantages of continued conflict, some source of additional benefits is needed. Side payments may be attached to the outcomes themselves, such as third-party guarantees of financial aid for accomplishing changes required by the agreement, or they may be unrelated to the outcome itself, simply additional benefits that make agreement more attractive. The graduated aid package attached to the Israeli and Egyptian agreement to disengage in the Sinai and then to sign a peace treaty is an example. Sometimes the demand for side payments by the parties may be as extraneous to agreement as is their supply.

Of all these, the principal element of leverage is persuasion – the ability of the mediator to reorient the parties' perceptions. Like any kind of persuasion, the mediator's ability depends on many different referents that are skillfully employed to make conciliation more attractive and continuing conflict less so. These referents may include matters of domestic welfare and political fortunes, risks and costs, prospects of continuing conflict and of moving out of it, reputations, solidity of allies' support, world opinion, and the verdict of history.

The other basic element in leverage is need – the parties' need – for a solution that they cannot achieve by themselves, for additional support in regional or global relations, and for a larger package of payoffs to make a conciliatory outcome more attractive. Perception of this need can be enhanced by the mediator, but it cannot be created out of nothing. Side payments with no relation to the outcome of the conflict are effective only insofar as they respond to an overriding need that outweighs the deprivation of concessions on the issues of the conflict itself. Parties can be made aware of needs that they did not recognize before, particularly when the chances of assuaging them seem out of reach. The provision of Cuban troop withdrawal from Angola, which met South Africa's need for a countervailing reward, led to the South African troop and administration withdrawal from Namibia, yet this need was not formulated during the 1970s rounds of the mediation. Persuasion often depends on need, but then need often depends on persuasion.

What do these characteristics say about "powerful" and "powerless" mediators? The common distinction between "interested" and "disinterested" mediators is less solid than might appear. All mediators have interests, most mediators are interested in the conflict situation in some way, and "biased" mediators may even have an advantage in access to one or both of the parties. If mediation were only persuasion, or "pure" persuasion, it would not matter who practiced it, and entry into the practice would be equally open to any silver-tongued orator. But mediation is more than simple persuasion, and the basis of effective persuasion is the ability to fulfill both tangible and intangible needs of the parties. The mediator's leverage is based therefore on the parties' need for the solution it is able to produce and on its ability to produce attractive solutions from each party.

Although official mediators are usually needed to help conclude agreements between disputing parties, unofficial (that is, nonstate) mediators may be effective persuaders and may be useful in helping to reorient the perceptions of the parties' values and opportunities. If the required mode of mediation is low – limited to communication – and the felt need for a solution is high in both parties, informal mediation may be all that is necessary to bring the parties to negotiation. However, the higher the required mode, the lower the felt needs, the more structural interests involving a third party, and the more the conflict involves states rather than nonstate actors, the less likely informal mediation can be an effective substitute for the official attention of states. Statesmen are not necessarily better mediators, but they can provide interest- and need-related services that informal mediators cannot handle.

Unofficial mediation in Africa provides a good illustration. Textbook cases of mediation were effected by the World Council of Churches and the All-African Conference of Churches in the southern Sudanese civil war in 1972, and the Sant'Egidio community in Mozambique in 1990–2 and Algeria after 1994. The church bodies widened the perceptions of opportunity among the parties and persuaded them to move to resolution. The mediators were not unbiased, having closer ties with the southern Sudanese and Mozambican rebels than with the government, and they were not without means of leverage, being able to threaten a resumption of supplies if the government broke off talks; in Algeria, all they could offer was a venue and encouragement. The stalemates that had been building over the years were reinforced by a mediator-induced perception of an attractive way out for the parties. The nonstate mediator played a major role and deserves credit for the operations; the subsequent collapse of the Sudanese agreement a decade later and the incompleteness of the Algerian démarche were due to other causes, not to a failed mediation. But behind the nonstate mediator in the Sudan stood an international organization – the assistant secretary general of the OAU, Mohamed Sahnoun – and behind him stood a mediator of last resort – the emperor of Ethiopia, Haile Selassie; and around the non-state mediator in Mozambique stood an array of interested states – the US, Russia, Italy, Portugal, Kenya, Zimbabwe, and South Africa. At a number of telling points in the operation, state actors were needed because guarantees that only a state could provide were required. The loneliness of the non-state mediator in Algeria in 1995 goes far to explain its limited success.

An example of a private mediation backed by a state was Carter's intervention in Haiti in 1994. When the ruling junta refused to give up power and transfer it to the elected president Aristide as demanded by the United Nations. Carter went to Haiti, persuaded the junta leaders to withdraw, and negotiated the terms of their withdrawal. Carter succeeded this time mainly because his mediation took place hours before the scheduled launch of an American military invasion intended to remove the junta by force and because political credibility was added by the participation of Senator Sam Nunn, chairman of the Senate Armed Services Committee, and General Colin Powell, former chairman of the Joint Chiefs of Staff.

Many other mediations have benefited from informal support and assistance in a mediation performed by a state actor. Although any efforts to improve premediation conditions make a contribution, private efforts actually to mediate in the Northern Irish, Falklands, Cyprus, and current Arab–Israeli conflicts have been notorious failures. Ripe moments and leveraged buy-offs by state mediators are the necessary ingredients, and even they may not be sufficient.

Ethical dilemmas

Mediators often pursue the double goal of stopping a war and settling the issues in dispute. They will pursue both, trying to end the bloodshed and to devise a settlement that is perceived to be fair by the parties involved, and thus be acceptable and durable.

However, in trying to achieve these goals, mediators are often confronted with the realization that settling the conflict in a manner that is considered fair by the disputants is likely to take a long time. Mediators may therefore face a dilemma of whether or not to give priority to a cease-fire and postpone the settlement of the conflict for later. Viewed somewhat differently, the choice may be seen as one between order and justice; to be sure, the two objectives are closely related. A durable cessation of hostilities requires a peace settlement. Justice requires order, and order, to endure, must be just (Zartman and Kremenyuk 2005). But these are long-term historical perspectives. For mediators, the choice is immediate: what should they do next? Should they pursue both objectives simultaneously, or should they give priority to a cease-fire?

The ethical dilemma arises because the issue is not merely one of sequencing. The sequencing has consequences. As we have seen, warring parties are more likely to settle when the continuing confrontation hurts badly and produces grave risks. A cease-fire, ending the bloodshed, is likely to ease the pain and reduce the risks. It will create a tolerable stalemate, a situation that the disputants might find preferable to the alternative of granting the concessions necessary for a compromise settlement. But cease-fires tend to be unstable and are often punctuated by wars and additional bloodshed: for example, the cease-fires between Israel and various Arab parties, between India and Pakistan, between Greeks and Turks in Cyprus, and between the warring parties in the former Yugoslavia.

Unfortunately, it is impossible to predict reliably which course of action will ultimately cost more – an early cease-fire that may collapse and be followed by more fighting because the conflict remains unresolved, or a continuation of a war while the search goes on for a definitive settlement of the conflict. An argument for giving priority to a cease-fire is that predictions of the near term are generally more reliable than those of the more distant future. The mediator can be certain that an ongoing war will produce casualties. The proposition that cease-fires break down, leading to the renewal of war and producing higher casualties over the long-term, is far less certain. Nevertheless, the dilemma exists.

Another dilemma is whether to facilitate an attainable settlement that violates international norms or to hold out for one that is consistent with principles of justice adopted by the international community. One might argue that mediators of international conflicts should pursue terms that are attainable, even if they are attainable mainly because they reflect the balance of power between the adversaries, rather than jointly held notions of justice. There are two important arguments against such a course of action. One is that such a settlement is unlikely to endure. One of the parties (sometimes both) will resent terms that it considers unjust and will seek to overturn them at the earliest opportunity. The other argument concerns the wider ramifications of such settlements for world order. A settlement that is inconsistent with international principles may tend to undermine their validity, creating uncertainties about the norms and thus weakening constraints upon international conduct. In other words, such settlements, while appearing to settle a particular conflict, may cause wider long-term damage by undermining the foundations of international peace and security.

The dilemma facing mediators in such situations is stark. What comes first – striving to protect the norm of respect for the integrity of states, trying to teach members of warring ethnic groups (Serbs, Croats, and Bosnian Muslims; Greeks and Turks in Cyprus; southern and northern Sudanese; Armenians and Azeris in Afghanistan) to coexist in peace, or saving lives by separating the groups and postponing the search for justice until later?

A good answer would require prescience. It is possible that promoting a settlement that is perhaps attainable, but inconsistent with international norms, might cause serious long-term injury to international peace and security. Should mediators work for terms that seem attainable, provided they promise to stabilize a cease-fire, despite their corrosive long-term effects? Viewing norms as merely tentative and conditional propositions is destructive to order. But eschewing settlements that do not conform to established norms, even if doing so allows mutual slaughter to continue, is also destructive to peace and order. Such dilemmas are not new. But these and other ethical issues have become pressing for international mediators in recent years.

Conclusion

More interest and less leverage is involved in third-party mediation than is commonly assumed. Adversarial parties and potential mediators each make an interest calculation that involves much more than the simple set-tlement of the dispute. Their calculations include relations among the conflicting parties and third parties and the costs and benefits of all of them in both conflict and conciliation. Leverage comes from harnessing those interests and from the third party's ability to play on perceptions of needs, above all on needs for a solution.

Mediation acts as a catalyst to negotiation. It facilitates the settlement of disputes that parties ought to be able to accomplish on their own, if they were not so absorbed in their conflict. Mediation becomes necessary when the conflict is twice dominant: providing the elements of the dispute and preventing parties from seeking and finding a way out. Even when it is suc-cessful, mediation can only cut through some of those layers, providing a means for the parties to live together despite their dispute – it does not provide deep reconciliation or cancel the causes of the conflict. Left again to their own instincts, the parties may well fall out of their mediated settle-ment, and there are plenty of cases (often unstudied by analysts and prac-titioners focusing on the moment of mediation) in which the hard-bargained agreement has subsequently fallen apart under changed conditions or revived enmities. For this reason, although the mediator is often tempted to start a process and then slip away as it develops its own momentum, it may in fact be required to be more involved in the regional structure of relations after its mediation than before. Yet it must not be a crutch forever, lest it become a party to the conflict. This is the final chal-lenge and dilemma for mediators: how to disengage from a mediating role without endangering the carefully brokered settlement.

11 Negotiations and prenegotiations in ethnic conflict

The beginning, the middle, and the ends[28]

Some basic elements – when, what, who, and how – are involved in strategies of negotiation and prenegotiation. As a result, it is impossible to lay out a single linear strategy for negotiations, or even for mediation. Instead, the effects of each of these elements must be examined to make available the full richness and creativity that is needed to prepare bilateral solutions when a government can no longer handle the problem by itself.

When to begin negotiation

The determination of when to negotiate is related to the life cycle of the ethnic conflict. It is usually impossible to tell when a conflict begins, and frequently, the conflict involves the resurgence of latent feelings or dormant grievances when a group perceives itself as deprived of some social benefits because of its ethnic identity. The sense of deprivation may be direct, as in South Africa or southern Sudan, or it may be relative to others in society or even to expectations, as in Biafra, Northern Ireland, or the Kabyle region of Algeria (Gurr 1970). But for deprivation to turn into ethnic conflict, it must be seen as arising from discrimination against the deprived as an ethnic group. There are also situations in which two minority groups of the periphery carry on a feud between themselves, like the Hatfields and McCoys, but usually the Hatfields are in charge of the government and the McCoys carry on the feud from the deprived periphery – as the Shona and Ndebele in Zimbabwe, or the Kikuyu and Luo in Kenya. The appropriate response to groups that feel deprived – in a responsive and responsible political system, whether democratic or not – is a process of petition and remedy. The problem is brought to the attention of the authorities, and benefits and opportunities are distributed better. That action in itself often involves some exercise of negotiation and lies in the gray area between unilateral and bilateral solutions to grievances.

But if, at any point, the "change-absorbing institutions" of government do not or cannot handle the grievances (Eisenstadt 1966, p.10), ethnic groups find themselves in need of new strategies. They face three imperatives: they must attract government attention, constrain negative responses, and mobilize and consolidate their own support. Blocking one government measure may be a good way to get attention and at the same time to mobilize support, but things may not fall into place in order, and it may be necessary to mobilize support under unfavorable conditions of repression in a way that means passing up chances for positive attention. Frequently, once the political system has had a chance to respond and there are no satisfactory results, the dissatisfied group must go through a period of "solidarity-making" before it can begin the problem-solving process (Feith 1962).

Needs

One element of the conflict life cycle has to do with the needs of the protest movement. In the first phase, the movement is a petitioner, seeking to bring its grievances to the attention of government, but as a subordinate. Negotiations among unequals are possible in this phase as part of the *petition-and-response* process. But if this phase fails, the second phase is one that requires the dissidents to oppose the government more fiercely, attracting its displeasure and even inviting repression. This is a phase of *consolidation*, in which the dissidents need to focus on strengthening their ranks and representativeness, assert their legitimacy, and back up their claim to be an equal negotiating partner with the government. Only when this consolidating phase is over can the dissidents move on to phase three, which takes them back to problem solving and *negotiation* again, but on a new footing.

Obviously, there is a lot of movement back and forth between the second and third phases, as the government tries to weaken the dissidents' cohesion and support and contest their legitimacy so as to get an upper hand in the negotiations. However, if the government is too successful in its efforts, it can push the conflict back into phase two, where neither side is willing to negotiate and where the conflict is further from any resolution. From the consolidation phase, where the government will try to break up the protest into manageable splinter groups, the government will try to push the protest further back into phase one, where it can handle the petitions of the tractable splinters and isolate the intractable ones. Thus, government and protesting groups try to push the protest back and forth across the successive phases, with the middle, or consolidation, phase being the main battlefield across which the protest ebbs and flows.

Unity

The question of the dissidents' unity is another element of the conflict life cycle. In the early, petition phase of the ethnic conflict, there are likely to be several organizations representing different aspects of ethnic activity and, therefore, various parts of the ethnic group. As the dissidence enters into the *consolidation* phase, the group is under pressure to bring this diversity under one roof so that it can exert maximum pressure on the government and assert its legitimacy and representativeness on behalf of the protest. But as the conflict bogs down in phase two, this unity is likely to come under severe strains and eventually fall apart. Parts of the group will challenge its leaders for their inadequate policies and offer their own prescriptions as a better way out of the impasse. Failure also encourages dreamers and, therefore, more pluralism. Only when one of the new groups starts making progress again in furthering its cause does it have a claim on the exclusive allegiance of the dissidents. Yet, as already seen, this moment is ambiguous, in that the movement needs solidarity in order to compel the government to provide it with some success, and it needs success to attract solidarity. These conflicting needs and pressures tend to keep the conflict in phase two, where it is not ready for resolution.

Paradoxically, there is another moment when the dissidents' unity is threatened – at the end of the process. The closer the ethnic protest moves toward success, the greater its need and efforts to maintain unity and the greater the temptation for rivals and splinter groups to cut loose and try to make deals on their own. Such splinter groups seek to turn the group effort to their own advantage by offering a slightly better deal to the government. If they succeed (and the arrangement holds), they have provided a better, mutually satisfactory outcome for the two sides. If they fail and are swept aside, they may well have helped clear the way for a more lasting solution by eliminating an option that at least seemed attractive to some. This was the case of Abel Muzorewa in Zimbabwe in 1979 and Tahar ben Ammar in Tunisia in 1955, both cases of the "disposable moderate" on the road to independence. Of course, all is not positive: splinter groups may also so shatter and enfeeble the protest in the process that the conflict is again thrown back into the second, or consolidation, phase, with the loss of a potentially appropriate moment for resolution.

Goals

A third element in the life cycle of a conflict has to do with its goals. Ethnic protests are a search for appropriate outcomes, so that "resolution" also depends very much on when the solution is negotiated. Much literature points to the fact that initially, members of a protest seek to attract the attention of the government to their existence and their insufficient share in the benefits of society. They want more, not less, government attention – but attention of a positive, not an intrusive, nature. During this phase, the government's role and primacy are not contested but, rather, are appealed to. This is the usual condition of North African Berbers and Native Americans. If the period of *petition* is prolonged, the protesters eventually realize that they cannot depend on the goodwill of others and must make procedural as well as substantive demands. The protesters demand greater participation in the distribution of benefits. At this stage, protesters are calling for *collaborative* control of their own destiny. This is the stage that Tamils and southern, eastern and western Sudanese are in today.

But if participation is not enough to assure satisfaction, the protest moves on to the third phase, *secession*. At this point, the protesters have reached the conviction that they cannot get redress of grievances from collaboration with the government but must take their entire destiny into their own hands, despite the cost or danger of reduced resources. This was the story in Biafra. "More of less" is calculated to be greater than "less of more," although the logic of the phase may even carry further, to indicate that self-determination is better in and of itself, even if the material benefits are not greater. Both "greater" and "better" give different insights into the famous statement by Sékou Touré, Guinea's first president: "It is better to have poverty in freedom than richness in slavery."

Of course, these phases do not describe neat and clear divisions. Not all protesters reach the same conclusion at the same time, and the conservative, non-risk-taking tendency in human nature indicates that many will not dare petition when the leaders are in the petitioning stage, many will want to petition and will not dare to collaborate when the leaders are in the *collaborating* stage, and many will not dare to secede but will be willing only to petition and collaborate when the leaders have reached the stage when they see secession as the sole solution. Similarly, not all leaders will reach the same conclusions at the same time. Furthermore, governments, too, have a conservative, status quo tendency, responding to considerable pressure only by finally adopting the option that would have satisfied the previous stage. That is why "too little, too late" is frequently the judgment on government responses to ethnic protest (Favret 1973). As the government finally comes to the reluctant conclusion that a given outcome is necessary, the protesters have similarly learned that it is not enough and have moved on to the next outcome stage. Because this learning process often involves not only the conversion of some leaders but also the replacement of others, backtracking becomes difficult.

Means

Finally, the conflict life cycle can be thought of in terms of means. The protest begins with the normal activity of *articulation* of demands, in which individuals bring requests and grievances to the attention of the authorities on behalf of their constituents. This is a totally political phase, calling, above all, for skills of expression and persuasion. If it fails, there is pressure to move to a *mobilization* phase. Mobilization is still a political exercise, but it calls for actions that provide a visible backup to the demands.

The people are used in marches, campaigns, and demonstrations, but in an expressive rather than an instrumental role: they are seeking not to tear down the walls of government but merely to impress those inside. There is, however, an element of threat in this exercise, in that the mass could turn into a mob if not heeded. In the third phase, it does so, and the means become those of violence, exercised as a guerrilla movement. At that point, the mobilization and articulation leaders become less necessary and are pushed aside in favor of confrontation leaders, who can mobilize small groups.

Often, class as well as ethnic values are thrown into the protest at this stage, accentuating the shift from the previous leadership. If this phase fails – or curiously, if it moves toward success – a fourth phase may be necessary – that of conventional military violence. This, too, requires different tactics and different leadership.

Each of the four ways of carrying out the protest – artculation, mobilization, confrontation, and war – involves different persons to lead and different relations between leaders and their followers. The passage from one phase to another is often accomplished, therefore, by changes in leadership and by internal political conflict. Yet contrary to the opinions of those involved and also to the judgments of some analysts, negotiators are needed at each phase. Even in the last phases, it is rare that a military victory is so complete that some negotiation is not necessary. But it is at the middle two elements of mobilization and guerrilla activity that it is hardest to combine the requirements of the means of protest with those of negotiation.

Stalemate

It would be analytically neat if these various elements in the conflict life cycle had nicely synchronized phases; unfortunately, the fact that each runs on its own time and logic makes for the richness of opportunities and the elusiveness of possibilities in conflict resolution.

These life cycles have one thing in common, however. Even though the passage from one phase to another is never crystal clear, it is generally triggered by a stalemate in the current phase. As long as there is hope in the present course, there is no need to change. But when a given goal or means is blocked, it causes people to rethink what they are doing and reevaluate the situation. This is true internally, within the protest movement, and externally, between the movement and its opponent, the government. Stalemate is the key to both the escalation process and the shift of ends, means, tactics, and leadership (Zartman and Faure 2005). The internal and external elements are intimately related. When a movement sees itself blocked in its achievement of an important goal, it is faced with the decision either to raise or to call, to change and intensify its attack or to seek accommodation at the present level. (It can also fold, of course, either retreating to the previous level or giving up entirely. That decision is often likely to lead simply to a takeover of the protest in different forms by others – that is, to the same escalate-or-accommodate decision as was previously posed.) Thus, stalemate marks a particularly important moment for negotiation.

Testing the patterns

It would take a large number of cases to test these patterns. Unfortunately, not only do cases of ethnic protest vary widely, but cases of negotiated settlements are few indeed. Indeed, one may well ask what happens to ethnic protests. Except for anticolonial protests – which in the post-World War II era have generally been resolved through the independence of the territory as colonially constituted – ethnic protest generally appears to rise and fall, in most cases, without any attempt or success at resolution. Its declines and revivals are marked by incidents, often accidental or circumstantial in nature, that have more to do with a learning or socialization process, opportunity-cost calculations, and arousal and fatigue than with a conscious attempt to analyze and resolve. Indeed, even scholarship follows these waves, turning attention to the phenomenon when it forces itself on public attention; but content to let well enough alone, as if ethnic conflicts will never return, in times in between.

The anticolonial movement illustrates again and again the notions of blockage and relative deprivation as the sources of ethnic protest. The contribution of World War II, with both its evidence of the weakness of colonial powers and its proclamation of the goals of anticolonial liberation, has frequently been noted (Emerson 1960; Wallerstein 1966). What has been less noted has been the economic element. The Korean war boom in demand for raw materials meant a sudden increase in the economic fortunes of colonial economies, contrasted with an exclusion of colonial populations from benefiting from that boom for ascriptive reasons. Economically, the anticolonial movement was a redistributive movement of ethnic protest.

Other cases can help identify specific triggers of the same nature. The southern Sudanese revolt began in 1955 as a protest against the prospects of continuing discrimination under the impending new circumstances of independence. The Tamil protest in Sri Lanka began with the Standardization of Marks measure in 1972, which discriminated against the educational achievements of Tamils. The Kabyle rebellion of 1980 in Algeria occurred because Kabyles took the new liberalization spirit of President Chadli Ben Jedid literally and thought it applied to them. In all of these cases, ethnic awareness was present for a long time and conflict was latent, but it took a specific incident – often not directly related to ethnicity, as in Sudan – to start the protest. In terms of conflict resolution and negotiation, it would have been best to recognize the problem immediately and deal with its current manifestation. That was a small order in Algeria and a tall order in Sudan, and in Sri Lanka it touched on intentional measures that were the source of the problem.

Many conflicts, including those in Northern Ireland and revolutionary Algeria, illustrate the conflict between the need for solidarity and the need for resolution, with the former preventing the latter from being pursued. South Africa also provides an example of a situation in which the weaker side had to build up its organization and mobilization before it could allow its representatives to talk with the government. Of course, in all these cases, the governments have helped the consolidation process either by refusing negotiations or by offering to negotiate only under unacceptable conditions. Agreeing to negotiate without conditions, this analysis suggests, would have been wiser from the governments' point of view and would have been no worse from the dissidents' point of view. French and British decolonization experiences elsewhere show the wisdom of negotiating early, when some consolidation has been accomplished and the identification of an *interlocuteur valable* serves to legitimize an appropriate negotiating partner.

An equally eloquent reason for negotiating early in the course of an ethnic protest is found in the escalation of goals. Ethnic rebellion to attract greater positive (and less intrusive) attention from the government was the characteristic of the post-independence rebellion of the Berbers in Morocco, where the phenomenon was identified, and also of the Berber (Kabyle) rebellion in Algeria. The rebellions died in 1959 and 1963, respectively (after being put down militarily), when the Berbers achieved representation of their own interests in politics. Similarly, Tamils and Eritreans, having seen the government backtrack on their previously acquired status, came to feel that only by taking their destiny into their own hands through self-determination of independence or something close to it could they be guaranteed a fair result.

Southern Sudan offers an interesting case in the evolution of goals. Originally calling for greater benefits, the southern Sudanese turned to a call for participation and then, when that proved illusory, finally called for independence. When a federal solution collapsed in 1978 after having been negotiated to mutual satisfaction in 1972, the new ethnic movement in 1983 called not for secession but for a revolution of the whole Sudanese polity, including the north. The example shows that it takes more and more to satisfy the movement as each phase ends in disillusionment over the limitations on current goals (not the reverse, as some might suspect and as governments often hope).

The effect of pluralistic tendencies on the course of negotiation is more problematic. In the beginning, pluralism does not appear to be an obstacle, as long as the government negotiates with a group that is large enough to claim some representativeness. Perhaps radical splinters can puncture a potential agreement; they seem to have done so in regard to the Palestine Liberation Organization (PLO), but they failed in Tunisia and Morocco in 1955. Indeed, such splinter groups are useful as bargaining ploys for more moderate majorities seeking to get the best early deal from a government, although they are not without counters.

Stalemate-induced pluralism is a trap rather than an opportunity. Competing groups render potential negotiating partners vulnerable to criticism and one-upmanship from their rivals, as the PLO case demonstrates. Because splits in an ethnic movement tempt the government to make a lesser deal with weaker parties, the dynamic does not favor the elaboration of a resolving agreement. If the government has no incentive to deal with a united movement that can speak for its constituency, splits do not give it an incentive to resolve the problem with partial groups.

The history of the Rhodesian negotiations for the first twelve years after the 1965 unilateral declaration of independence provides eloquent examples. By 1977, after the attempt by Secretary of State Henry A. Kissinger and the joint initiative of US Representative to the United Nations Andrew Young and British Foreign Secretary David Owen, the end was in sight, although it was not clear when or where it was (Low 1985). The internal settlement marked the attempt of some nationalist leaders to take advantage of the moment to grab the benefits of a solution for themselves or, in other words, to split. They failed not so much because the internal agreement was intrinsically unworkable but because the regime of Rhodesian Prime Minister Ian Smith could not bring itself to implement it wholeheartedly. In the process, too, the government had shown itself to be ready for a deal and thus was weakened for its final encounter with the real nationalists at Lancaster House.

The effect of the escalation of means on negotiations is also ambiguous. The guerrilla and perhaps mobilization phases are less conducive to negotiation than are the articulation phase or the last phase, out-and-out war, as studies of succeeding political generations in Algeria have shown (Quandt 1970) and contrasting studies of Tunisia have supported (Micaud *et al.* 1964). Yet, as noted, at some point even warriors must negotiate, as they did in Zimbabwe and the south Philippines (the Moro rebellion in 1976), even though it splits their ranks, as it did in Sri Lanka and Sudan. Once violence has been tried, it probably must be played out to a stalemate for the ripe moment for negotiations to appear. Warriors have to carry their investment in violence to the point at which major escalation is needed to get out of the deadlock and they cannot make it, before they can try the other track. It is interesting that they are often willing to try negotiations at that point because it enables them to stay in control, whereas major escalation poses the danger of a new leadership, as all four of the aforementioned examples indicate.

With whom to negotiate

After the first question, when to begin negotiations?, comes a more unsuspected query, with whom to negotiate? Usually, and certainly at the beginning of the ethnic protest, the protesters are citizens – albeit deprived citizens – of their country. At this point, negotiations are only internal and bilateral, but as the conflict goes on, the dissidents need to seek and gain outside supporters, sources of power, and sanctuary. Once the insurgency establishes a physical presence in a neighboring country, the nature and particularly the structure of the negotiations change. Negotiations become trilateral, goals and dynamics become more complex, and results become more difficult to achieve.

From bilateral to trilateral

It is in the interest of both the government and the dissidents to keep negotiations bilateral, if negotiations are indeed taking place. A complication arises, however, if negotiations are not taking place. In that case, it is in the interest of the dissidents to bring in a third party as a source of power, but such an intrusion is definitely not at all in the interest of the government (Zartman 1992). Nevertheless, governments often push dissidents to seek external support and sanctuary, because the governments think that they can and should win rather than talk; and by trying so hard to win, they make things worse for themselves.

In such a situation, the insurgents are presumed to be in a coalition with the third party (which will be called the *host* in the following discussion), whereas negotiation implies that a coalition will be built between the insurgents and the government. Behind this tug-of-war over the alliance possibilities of the insurgency lies the possibility of an alliance between the two states – the government and the host – on the backs of the insurgents; this occurred between Iran and Iraq against the Kurds in 1975 and between India and Sri Lanka about the Tamils in 1987. But even if a coalition is not envisaged on that side of the triangle, the interstate relations will be the dominant influence on the relations between the government and its ethnic opposition.

Each of the three parties has its own interests within this triangle. The government has a choice between winning the insurgency away from its host or using the host to influence the insurgency. Also, the government has a wider choice of seeking an accommodation with the neighbor-host on a broad range of issues that concern neighboring states or of seeking accommodation with its ethnic insurgents, often against the advice and interests of the host. To make these choices, the government will have to decide whether the neighbor–host state is interested in improving bilateral relations or is just using the insurgency as a cause and excuse for bad relations, just as it will have to judge whether the insurgency is interested in a settlement or is still focusing on the needs of consolidation.

Similarly, the host–neighbor will have to choose between good or bad relations with its neighbor, a question that may override the earlier, independent matter of whether or not to offer support and sympathy to the ethnic issue. If the host wants good neighborly relations, it is in the perfect position to act as mediator; with potentially good ties with both sides and a motive for mediation, it can deliver the side it is closest to – the insurgents. If it wants bad relations, it can support the insurgents as a surrogate, either to keep neighborly relations bad or to use as a bargaining chip when the time comes. The host–neighbor must decide how hard it can press the government, because it can conceivably draw the government into an agreement that will cause its overthrow at the hands of domestic hard-liners, thus giving the host a worse government as a neighbor. It must also decide how attractive it would find an agreement between the government and the ethnic opposition that would provide precedents for the host–neighbor's own ethnic problems.

Finally, the insurgency has its own choices and strategies to decide. Although it is the ally-presumptive of the host state, it must face the problem of closeness in that relationship. Specifically, is it an autonomous actor – even though it is a prisoner of the host state in its sanctuaries – or is it only a puppet of the host? At the same time, it must decide whether it is ready for accommodation or only for consolidation. The fact that it has fewer choices open to it shows its greater vulnerability and the consequent vulnerability of negotiations.

These multiple questions clearly show the crucial importance of the change from bilateral to trilateral relations and its effect on the possibilities of negotiation. In general, it is in the interest of the government and the insurgency to negotiate, assuming that they want a solution to the mutual problem. And in the same general-interest sense, it is not in the interest of the host-neighbor to see negotiations between the government and the insurgency, as such negotiation would remove its own bargaining chip. Thus, the trilateralization of relations worsens the situation for negotiations, requiring new efforts to reverse the balance of interests. To negotiate successfully in a trilateral situation, the government has to pay a higher price, in that it has to satisfy two parties, with divergent interests, instead of just one.

There is one salient way to change the host–neighbor's calculation of what is in its interests: to render the hosting of the insurgency costly and offensive to the host-neighbor. Only then does it develop a direct interest in resolving the problem with which it otherwise is not directly concerned. Once this shift in interest has occurred, another latent role can come into action. The host-neighbor is the party best placed to act as a mediator in the conflict. Mediation is difficult when the conflict is only internal and when no party has any direct leverage over the two opponents. But when the conflict has been externalized, the host–neighbor can legitimately take on the role of mediator. It has leverage over the insurgency, by virtue of its sanctuary, and over the government, by virtue of its ability to produce a solution. But the road to this impasse is long and hard, and subjective animosity and historic feuding may block progress. The host–neighbor may just not want to play its natural role, whatever its objective interest.

Examples of trilateral ethnic disputes

The record is full of illustrations of these dynamics. In the southern Sudanese rebellion, as the continued warfare threatened to embroil neighboring Ethiopia, it was brought in as a backup mediator. Once the insurgency actually moved to Ethiopian territory as its sanctuary – after the 1972 Addis Ababa Agreement had collapsed (and once the imperial regime had been replaced by the Communist regime of Mengistu Haile Mariam) – Ethiopia became a restraining force rather than a mediator, and relations between the Sudanese People's Liberation Army/Movement and Ethiopia tightened considerably. Efforts by the new Sudanese government – first of General Abdel Rahman Siwar al-Dahab of the Transitional Military Council and then of Sayed Sadiq al-Mahdi of the civilian government – to reopen negotiations stumbled not only against the substantive obstacle of the Islamic legislation in Sudan but also against the procedural obstacle of Ethiopia's greater interest in keeping the sore open than in reviving the mediatory possibilities.

In the Algerian nationalist challenges to colonialist France, Tunisia – considerably inconvenienced by the occupation of a part of its territory by the National Liberation Army – tried to mediate with the French. But it was in no position to deliver the agreement of the Algerian National Liberation Front, and French attacks against Tunisian territory serving as sanctuary weakened its mediatory role. Nonetheless, Tunisia played an important part in softening Algerian opposition to negotiation and in facilitating contacts. More recently, Algeria has resisted entering negotiations over the western Sahara even as a negotiator, claiming, instead – at most – a role as a disinterested friend, while Morocco has shunned negotiations with the Sahrawi dissidents and, instead, has insisted on negotiations with the host-neighbor.

In southern Africa, both Angola and Mozambique were brought into direct negotiations with South Africa over the fate of the dissidents in neighboring territories, defined as ethnic rebels by South African law. In Namibia, Angola moved from a mediator to an active party in the negotiations, ending up with the Lusaka Agreement for the control of the ethnic rebellions of both parties and with direct negotiations with South Africa over implementation of UN Resolution 435. At the other end of the battle line, Mozambique negotiated a similar accord with South Africa at Nkomati, providing for control of the ethnic rebels of both parties, in order to avoid direct negotiations of their own with their own respective dissidents, the National Resistance Movement (RENAMO) and the African National Congress. Obviously, none of these arrangements solves the issues behind the rebellion.

In Sri Lanka, trilateralization of the conflict has led to different possibilities. Because the Tamil population is a minority on an island, the case of sanctuary is not posed as acutely as it would be in the absence of a water boundary. Nonetheless, Sri Lanka Tamils enjoy the full range of support both from Tamils in southern India and from the Indian government. As the conflict continued, in the mid-1980s, India moved in as a mediator and failed. It then took a more active role, moving militarily to force the ethnic rebels to acquiesce in a solution close to the Tamils' own demands. In the terms used in the previous discussions, India delivered the agreement of the ethnic rebels to their own, not to the government's, solution. However, because the agreement was not a total victory for the rebels, their acceptance – even enforced – was not total either. Yet without Indian participation, neither side could have reached even the imperfect agreement at hand, because neither side was strong enough to make or to hold an agreement against its own internal critics. By escalating the conflict and thereby putting pressure on the neighbor, India was able to play a positive role that then turned against it.

Lessons learned

Despite the wide variety of cases, some broad conclusions for negotiation are clear. First, entrance of a third party – especially a sovereign-state third party – into a conflict between a government and its ethnic dissidents complicates relations mightily. It brings in a whole new gamut of issues and interests, in that it places the hitherto internal conflict within the new context of neighbor-state relations; and it places the conflict on a new level, because it involves sovereign states.

Second, this complication hinders negotiations. The dyadic interests of the parties line up in such a way as to work against negotiations rather than for them and, more specifically, to reduce the interest of the rebels in solving the conflict by accommodation rather than by continued conflict.

Third, like any escalation, trilateralization can act as a threat – a riser in the stairway of escalation. As trilateralization is in no party's intermediate interest – that is, it may serve a very short-term purpose and a long-term purpose, but it makes things worse all around in the middle run – it is something that everyone can agree to avoid if they think carefully and rationally. That is, of course, a major and perhaps even unreal condition.

Fourth, for the trilateralization to turn from a negative to a positive effect, the entire conflict must escalate beyond the initial trilateralization itself to the point at which it is no longer useful but, to the contrary, begins to hurt the host-neighbor. Only then can the host envisage a helpful role in negotiations.

Fifth, the potentially useful role that the host-neighbor can play is that of a mediator, whereby the host-neighbor helps find a solution and then delivers the agreement of the ethnic rebellion to which it has given support and sanctuary. Alternatively, the host-neighbor can join the rebellion to topple the government, directly or indirectly. Although it may take a new government to make an agreement with the insurgency, that is usually a poor bet. As opposed to governments overthrown by the pressures of an internal conflict, governments overthrown by the pressures of external conflict tend to dig in their heels and harden their line against the foreign enemy, unless the latter has actually imposed its own candidate.

The ends: what to negotiate

The third question about negotiations with ethnic rebellions concerns what to negotiate or how to end negotiations. The options are undoubtedly limitless. Categorization has to be conducted along a number of crosscutting dimensions, because a spectrum of outcomes along a single variable does not cover all of the useful and creative typologies that are needed for imaginative negotiations and formulas for solutions.

Assimilation, integration and compensation

At one end of a multiple-dimension spectrum are outcomes that solve ethnic problems by denying ethnicity, as opposed to those at the other end, which rely on ethnic compensation. Nonethnic solutions include assimilation and integration. Assimilation refers to the incorporation of ethnic minorities into a dominant national ethnicity. Amharization in Ethiopia, Wolofization in Senegal, Gallicization in France, and Anglicization in the US have been tried as ways of creating a single nation – although when the solution does not work, by definition, it becomes the cause for the very ethnic problems that it seeks to cure. Yet this is probably the most successful approach. It involves equal opportunity for all under a dominant culture, regardless of race, creed, or color. It is particularly effective at the outset of ethnic protest, when its promise has credibility behind it and when the enforcing government or change-absorbing institution is in a dominant position. This type of solution can be obtained by negotiation combined with petition or by political pressure and threats of greater protest.

In integration, minorities are brought together into a new, rather than an old, dominant culture. Assimilation and integration are often hard to separate. For example, it is difficult to tell whether the resolution of ethnic problems in the US involves assimilation into an Anglicized culture or integration into an American culture, or whether the solution in Ivory Coast involves assimilation into a Baoulé culture rather than integration of all groups into a Franco-African Ivorian culture. Integration has also been claimed as the operative solution in India, in Israel, and in other countries where modernization and the leftovers of colonial culture are ingredients in a new national culture. Minorities are asked not to become like someone else but, rather, to contribute to a new identity to be taken on by all. The outcome is hard to negotiate, because it does not exist until integration has devised the new culture; and when the new culture is in place and other groups seek to join, the result is harder to distinguish from assimilation.

Compensation, or affirmative action, is a third outcome for deprived minorities. When, as a result, minorities become no longer deprived but pampered (in the eyes of the majority – like the pre-Nasserite Copts in Egypt, the Tamils in Sri Lanka, or the Asians in Kenya – then the old solution becomes a new problem. But until that occurs, compensation is an enlightened solution, imposed by a minority in revolt on a majority with a conscience. Compensation can be negotiated, as it has been in the US, but the necessary conditions of conflict and conscience do not make it a very common solution. Moreover, compensation must be seen as a way for a minority to catch up with the majority, not as a way to overtake it. Therefore, it must be a temporary measure, to be discarded when quotas can be filled naturally. It would seem that compensation can no longer be considered as a solution once the possibility of secession has been raised, as it depends on an inextricable sense of community and obligation.

Separate collective status

In addition to the denial-compensation spectrum, there is a whole range of solutions of separate collective status, based on different ways of combining communal participation in central power with some degree of self-management. One such solution, known as power-sharing, refers to a central governmental coalition of ethnic (or other) group representatives, in which decisions are collective (hence, each group has a veto) and ties are tight between the representatives and their constituencies (Lijphart 1985; Laitin 1987). Such a solution depends on specific and sometimes elaborate rules and, hence must be preceded by negotiations. The Netherlands and Switzerland are often cited as examples, but there are also looser cases. The Berber "seat" in the Algerian council of ministers, the southern Sudanese vice-president in the 1972 Addis Ababa Agreement (while it lasted), and the proportional representation system in the executive according to the Lebanese National Pact are also approximations of power-sharing. Only the Algerian example was the result of explicit negotiations. Yet the conditions for power-sharing are also precise and limiting. The ethnic group must be cohesive, and it must be a solid supporter of its representatives. Because, as seen in the discussion of the conflict life cycles, consolidation is a passing phase that requires much effort, the conditions of power-sharing are likely to be fulfilled only temporarily. Negotiations, therefore, must not only put a solution in place but must also cover the ongoing mechanisms of maintaining it. Lack of consolidation dogged the Addis Ababa Agreement. It eventually fell apart because there were ethnic subdivisions within the southern Sudanese minority on which the politics of the north could play. It would have taken even greater statesmanship on the part of President Nimeiri to maintain the agreement than to negotiate it.

Competition, or regional bargaining, is another solution, but competitive relationships are subtle and are more difficult to negotiate explicitly. Competition is the local version of power-sharing. Instead of being based on collective decisions among ethnic leaders at the top, it is based on competition among ethnic regions at the bottom, before arbitration by national (presumably, nonethnic) leaders at the top. Dependence on the top is maintained; as in power-sharing, there is a high degree of local group and leader-follower cohesion, and allocations are made by the top according to some fair and independent criterion. Ivory Coast practiced such a system, although it was never set up explicitly or by negotiation. The system worked as long as there was no constant winner and as long as local groups (such as the Bété) could get some extra attention and extra benefits when they feel that they are being discriminated against. However, because of its serious preconditions, competition can only evolve rather than be created; and often, the breakdown of competition – for reasons of perceived unfairness – causes ethnic conflicts, as Ivory Coast also shows.

An alternative outcome that is at the same time more standard and more suspect is that of regional autonomy. Self-government for minority areas has been the path to successful solutions in Italy, where the five regions that enjoy a special status – Sicily, Sardinia, Val d'Aosta, Alto Adige, and Venezia Giulia – all suffered ethnic unrest until they were granted cultural and administrative autonomy. The fact that ethnic unrest has not been completely abolished in Italy does not diminish the effectiveness of regional autonomy. It should be compared not with an ideal situation, such as assimilation or integration, but with alternative possibilities of ethnic conflict. Negotiations over regional autonomy in Italy have been long and recurrent, to the point at which negotiation itself appears to be part of the solution, as autonomous arrangements and relations are repeatedly readjusted. A comparable situation, in which autonomy was part of the solution and its abolition part of the problem, was the Ethiopian "federation" – in reality, a decade of autonomous status for Eritrea. Over a quarter of a century of Eritrean rebellion began when plans became known for abolishing regional (federal) autonomy.

Yet state leaders fear autonomy, anticipating that the region will break off along the dotted lines if a separate territory is defined and given self-rule. In fact, history shows the reverse: with home rule, the population becomes preoccupied with its own issues; as in many other instances, responsibility tempers demands. Yet home rule is not enough, as can be seen in the initial analysis of ethnic demands: ethnic rebellions arise only secondarily because minorities want to be left alone but primarily because they have not been accorded their fair share of national benefits. Therefore, regional autonomy must involve not merely setting minorities adrift in their own boat but also providing for their regular and equitable supply from the central storehouse. Central allocation and regional suballocation are the two components of regional autonomy, under conditions that involve intensive and continuous negotiations. Regional autonomy differs from power-sharing in that it does not require a specific coalition of group representatives at the center but leaves local allocation in the hands of the local group.

Another creative use of regionalism is regional fracture – that is, the use of regional organization to include several ethnic groups, or to break up a single ethnic area into several regions, or to mix and cut up ethnic areas into regions that bear no relation to any ethnic criteria. The first is hallowed in political annals as gerrymandering, which can serve either to drown one ethnic group in a multiethnic (or nonethnic) seat or to give an ethnic group a larger population to dominate. The second was the solution in Nigeria in preparation for the Second Republic, although it allows larger ethnic groups to be seen through the smaller provincial boundaries. The third was the basis of the Kendall–Louw (1987) proposal for a South African government based on 301 judicial districts.

For these solutions to work, there must be enough attraction in the new units to reorient attention away from ethnic solidarities; more specifically, goods for allocation must be made available exclusively within the new units to an extent that overcomes the benefits, psychic as well as material, of pursuing ethnic exclusiveness. Such measures may not solve the ethnic problem, but they are likely to have an effect – usually of reducing the scope of ethnic dissidence by fracturing it, so that the new groups either have a new focus or become submerged in the conglomerate. These measures may be too clever to work; they may well spur the pressure for unity, as occurred in the Tamil regions of Sri Lanka, or they may increase resentment with the submerged minority. Again, the result depends on the combination of positive and negative measures – the government's willingness and ability to co-opt or buyout the components of the fractionated ethnic group.

It is not always possible to negotiate such solutions because of the very ambiguity in their nature. Most frequently, measures of regional breakup are adopted and imposed by a government to deal with its ethnic groups and then are enforced as a less direct use of power than simple ethnic suppression. Yet negotiation can be used, probably under one of two conditions: either in hierarchical bargaining, whereby – as often occurs – the government decides but nonetheless has to bring its constituent groups along by horse-trading and consultation, or in a "national convention," whereby parties see the need for a common solution to defend the higher order in the last throes of disruption. Providing a sudden awareness of an overarching common good where it has been previously challenged by local (ethnic) nationalisms is difficult and is rarer than providing an over arching common authority.

Classical solutions

The last three solutions are classical forms that lie beyond the possibilities already mentioned – federation, confederation, and secession. Federations have existed historically, but always as a devolution of power. The Central African, Cameroonian, Malaysian, Tanzanian and American federations all brought their components together into a conglomerate in which the parties jealously combined the maintenance of their own home rule with the added benefits of a larger sovereignty. Even in the case of the Nigerian and Libyan federations, existing divisions were maintained within the larger framework, rather than handing down new powers from on high. Federation is an act of coming or staying together, not a way of handling ethnic fissiparous tendencies. Leaders tend to fear federation as much as they fear regional autonomy, and for the same reasons. Yet there is not a federation in the newly independent Third World that has not evolved into a more centralized government within a short time, rather than the reverse, and almost all of the federations (except Nigeria) have simply been abolished in the process. Federation then becomes part of the process of constitution-making – the setting up of the compromise rules by which the body politic pledges to govern itself; it is therefore always the result of negotiation at some level.

Confederations, on the other hand, are the figment of a legal imagination, found nowhere in contemporary reality, except perhaps Switzerland. The stark necessity of locating sovereignty somewhere and respecting its overwhelming exercise means that a confederation is really a federation, as in Switzerland, or else it is only an alliance of sovereign states, as in Senegambia (Welch 1966). Confederations have never been successful in providing solutions for ethnic problems, probably because ethnic disputes that arrive at the point of contesting sovereignty require a clearer outcome than confederation can present.

The final solution is provided by secession, when ethnic groups feel that the only way to obtain their just deserts is through their own control of their destiny. Colonial situations – in which the conflict is defined in ethnic terms, whatever the ideological overtones that may accompany it – are an example of this phenomenon; and subsequent rebellions – such as the Eritrean, the Bengali, the Katangan, the southern Sudanese, the western Saharan, the western Somali, the Assam, the Tamil, the Pashtun, Baluch, and Sindhi, and many other minority disputes – all are cases in which the formerly colonized is then accused of attempting to colonize its own component ethnic groups to the point at which secession seems to be the only answer. By the time secession is called for, the protest movement is so desperate that it ignores the fact that the seceding unit would have real problems with its viability. The form, transition, and conditions of secession and independence are all subjects necessarily subject to negotiation; and if they are not, the aftermath of a unilateral declaration leaves many unresolved questions that need to be negotiated.

In reality, secession has succeeded in only a few cases in modern times. Bangladesh, with its unusual noncontiguous relation to the mother country, Singapore, seceding from its federation, and Eritrea, recovering its separate colonial status rom Ethiopia, are unique postwar examples. A few other cases, such as the breakup of the Mali Federation or that of the United Arab Republic, concerned unions too short-lived to be significant. There are, of course, plenty of other cases in which secession has been posited by ethnic minorities as a solution, but they have not yet got their rebellion to the point of strength at which negotiations are imposed. Beyond the decolonization, therefore, experience tells very little about how to negotiate secession. One element is sure and important, however: dissident minorities that are bound on secession refuse to enter negotiations until the goal of independence is admitted by the other side, rather than letting it emerge from the negotiations. Negotiations then turn to the ways of defining and implementing secession – although, in the process, the type of secession and the nature of post-secession relations are still important aspects of the formula phase of negotiations.

The range of outcomes

Outcomes translate power relations and the evolution of the conflict. Some outcomes – such as regional breakup, assimilation, and integration – depend on a strong government position vis-à-vis the ethnic groups. Others – such as affirmative action, power-sharing, regional autonomy, and federation – presuppose a strong ethnic commitment to the higher unity and identity of the state, alongside a concern for management of their own affairs. Outcomes may evolve from negotiations themselves, although they are best prepared by a crystallizing consensus before negotiations actually begin. Some radical outcomes – notably secession – can only be settled before negotiations open.

Conflict is a process of eliminating possible outcomes until the salient and agreed solution stands out amid the conflict. If that outcome proves unworkable, however, the search goes back to the battlefield, and the attempt at a solution can be considered merely a way of testing and rejecting an ostensibly prominent alternative. Negotiated outcomes can prove unworkable if they are not applied, if they do not function when applied, or if they leave out of their ambit some opposing groups that are powerful enough to disrupt them. These potential problems should be considered carefully during the negotiation process. If the conflict is costly enough and the negotiated outcome attractive enough to the parties, it will be implemented; but the threat of renewed conflict must be sufficiently perceived that the implementor (the government) does not simply bank the end of the conflict and throw away the agreement. Concerning leaving out a powerful player, it is never clear whether it is better to negotiate with the moderates, isolating the extremes, or to negotiate with the extremes, jumping and "enclosing" the moderates. The obvious key to the choice is the strength of the moderates versus the radicals, but other elements enter as well: the vulnerability of the radicals to co-optation even if they are strong, the distance that separates the radicals from the moderates, and the elements available for exchange and side payments to sweeten the argument, among others.

12 Structures of escalation and negotiation[29]

Escalation is an augmented effort to prevail. It can be either unilateral or bilateral but in either case, it is a responsive action. Unilaterally, a party escalates on its own, in response to its previous action or to that action's insufficiency. Bilaterally, the more common understanding of the term, each party responds to the other's increasing effort to prevail. Thus conceived, escalation is an expression of power, a rational approach to conflict, as parties take increasing actions to change the other party's behavior.[30] Escalation is the pursuit of conflict designed to end conflict. But the designed end can be either on the escalator's own terms, as in victory, or on jointly decided terms, as in negotiation. Escalation ends when the parties can or will escalate no more, that is, when one or both run out of resources, when one prevails, or when both come to an agreement that removes the incompatibility of positions.

Escalation and negotiation are opposite actions, one to increase conflict and the other to decrease it. Not only are they headed in different directions, but they demand different attitudes and convictions, one to beat the enemies and the other to come to terms with them, sometimes referred to as a winning vs a composing mentality. They thus seem to be mutually incompatible. On closer look, this absolute incompatibility does seem to be conditional, since some escalations appear to be designed to bring the other party to negotiation while other appear designed to prevail, but this differentiation does not entirely erase the difference in attitudes and convictions required for the two actions. The need then remains to find out the relation between escalation and negotiation. The present interest is to place conflict resolution within the context of conflict dynamics.

The many faces of escalation

When a party takes an escalatory action in transitive escalation, it does so to achieve a purpose, notably to produce an outcome to the conflict either by prevailing over the other side or by bringing it to settlement (Schelling 1960, 1966; Kahn 1965; Young 1968; Cross 1969; Snyder 1972;

Pillar 1983; Morgan 1990, 1994). In so doing, it seeks to exercise power over the other party. Power is an action by one party intended to produce a change in another party's behavior. It can be exercised either by a direct (fait accompli) or by a contingent action, that is, by an action done ("I have closed the Panama Canal; that will change your mind about our trade agreement.") or an action to be done ("If you persist in your behavior, I will close the Panama Canal; that will change your mind."). As such, it can be reckoned as an added value, a cost/benefit increment that can be combined negatively, as a deprivation, or positively, as a gratification, with the current value of a given or demanded position in order to change a party's evaluation of a particular course. For example, the cost imposed by closing the Panama Canal, added to the value of a previous course of action, diminishes that value and makes the posited course of action worth less, motivating the party to reconsider its action compared to alternatives previously valued less. (An example of a gratification would be an action, done or contingent, to decrease Canal transit fees.) The value of the second party's position on the trade agreement is now lowered by the cost of the Canal closing or raised by the benefit of decreased Canal fees.

Such added values can be the result of a volitional action by a party, positively as a promise or negatively as a threat, as indicated in the example. Or they can be the result of an involuntary effect, negatively as a warning or positively as a prediction. The warning might be, "If you maintain your position on the trade agreement, our mutual trade will dry up and your farmers will suffer"; the prediction might be, "If you accept my position of the trade agreement, our trade will blossom and your farmers will grow rich." These two aspects of power – voluntary and involuntary – correspond to transitive and intransitive escalation, respectively. Threats and promises, and *faits accomplis*, are the ingredients of transitive escalation, decisions that are taken to increase or decrease the conflict, whereas warnings and predictions are references to intransitive escalation, negative and positive, the inherent intensification and relaxation spiral of conflict. They show that even intransitive escalation can be used by conflicting and bargaining parties to try to alter each other's behavior. Escalation commonly refers to rising deprivations – threats and warnings – that parties impose on each other. The question then remains, how can this escalation be used to bring itself and the conflict to an end?

Escalation may indeed be related to ripeness but it is not the whole subject, and the two topics are not identical. The focus here is on the dynamics of escalation, or the pursuit of conflict, to determine where conflict can and does contribute to its own resolution. Although the subject of the present inquiry is the relation between conflict (escalation) and negotiation, its purpose is not to establish whether escalation is a precondition, necessary even if not sufficient, to negotiation, as in the case of mutually hurting stalemate (Zartman 2000), but to the contrary, whether negotiation is the possible sequel to escalation, that is, not whether stalemate must take place before negotiation but whether negotiation can take place after escalation.

Probably the most important characteristic of escalation for its use in negotiation is its distinction from mere intensification. Conceptually the difference is clear, even if reality does its usual job of treating conceptual distinctions sloppily. Intensification refers to a gradual increase without a change in nature, whereas escalation – as its etymology indicates – refers to a step-like increase in the nature of conflict, a change in saliency (Schelling 1960; Smoke 1977). Against "more and more," escalation is "something else." These new measures form risers for the steps of escalation, rather than constituting the famous "slippery slope" (reinforcing the distinction between intensification and escalation, since the image of the slope runs down and the stairs run up). Thus, the escalation here considered is a noticeable (even if not unambiguously) and conscious or at least identifiable action, and as such a use of power.[31]

In sum, escalation is a monumental staircase, with the stairways heading in all directions, but with clear treads (the horizontal "steps") and risers (the vertical "lifters"). Or rather, it is an assemblage of two (or more)-sided stepladders, where each party tries to mount higher than the other in a strenuous climb. It should be emphasized that this competitive climb is perfectly rational, at least to a point (Patchen 1988, pp. 241–60). Something worth wanting is worth escalating for. Much folk wisdom testifies to this fact: "if at first you don't succeed, try try again"; "in for a penny, in for a pound"; "put your money where your mouth is." But at the same time, somewhere there is a limit, where the cost of escalation outweighs the benefits of prevailing; This is the emphasis of the business discussions of escalation, referring to an unproductive unilateral extension or entrapment (Meerts 2005). Unfortunately, this limit is not a line but a zone. Unfortunately too, it depends on the action of the other. If one more increment will win the prize, then it may be worth it, but if it only invites a counter-increment from the other party, it is not. (Unless, of course, the *next* increment ...) And then, if the parties could see ahead how many increments each was willing to invest, they could calculate at the bottom of the ladder their relative strengths and interests, and decide whether to win, lose, or bargain.[32] (Except, of course, each party would then be rational to bluff about strengths and interests ...) So how and where does the process of escalation relate to the process of negotiation?

Escalation and negotiation

The relation is in the treads and risers. Escalation is a succession of risers, and between the risers is a tread, the status quo after one escalation and before the next one. The risers continue until one party outrises the other, or until they match each other and can go no further; in either case, each must decide whether to hold out wherever they are (on the tread), escalate again, or negotiate their way out of the conflict. Two of these situations constitute dynamic conflict: escalation (risers) and outcome (treads). The analytical question of interest here is, where in the tread-and-riser process is the third outcome, negotiation, proposed, and when does it occur? It needs to be emphasized that the question here concerns the inauguration of negotiations, not their successful conclusion, since the latter depends on other factors, notably the ability of the parties to create an enticing opportunity in the course of their negotiations.

Hypothetically, there are many possible answers. The decision to negotiate can come from the escalator itself, in relation to its own escalation, at one of four points: either during one's own riser (1a), or right after one's own escalation (1b), or once the effect of one's escalation has passed (1c), or just before one's planned escalation (1d). In other words, is negotiation initiated during escalation, under the memory of a recent escalation, when that memory has faded and new prospects are not yet looming, or under the threat or warning of a new escalation. The first, second and third actions are exercises of power undertaken to produce negotiations, whereas the fourth appears to be independent of the exercise of power.

The decision can also come from the target party, at one of three points: just after the other's riser (corresponding to the first two moments of the escalator, since the first moment needs a little time to sink in) (2a), in the middle of the tread with no relation to risers (2b), or just before the other's threatened riser (2c). All three of these points refer to the other party's escalation. In terms of power, the target party is responding with an offer to negotiate to the efforts of the escalator to prevail or to open negotiations in the first and third cases, whereas the second does not appear to have any relation to the other party's exercise of power.

It should be noted that in both series, "after" refers to a short period following the latest escalation, not just subsequent to it at any distance, which would be meaningless. "Long after" is the second option in both cases, after the effect of the escalation is passed. The short period is necessarily a bit soft and difficult to define within specific limits. It is not clear whether it should be calculated from the beginning of the escalation or from some point during its course, and whether it should be calculated to the first mention of negotiations by one side or their opening by both sides or some intermediate point. The period itself may vary for many reasons, including the length of the preceding conflict. The difficulty of precise calculation, however, should not invalidate an important measure and the concept behind it. When the case examples of this effect (assuming that it exists) have been collected, it may be possible inductively to assign a time limit.

Finally, negotiation can take place in relation to the two escalation processes by combining the first two effects, that is, when one party's escalation has outrisen the other (escalation to raise) (3a), when it has met the other (escalation to call) (3b), or when it has returned to the other's position unilaterally (shortfall) (3c), or bilaterally (stalemate) (3d) (Zartman and Aurik 1991). In other words, the result of the first raise is to produce an imbalance that forces the target to negotiate while leaving the initiator in a strong position; whereas the latter three – call, raise and shortfall, and stalemate – all contain the result of a deadlock or stalemate in which neither side sees the desirability or possibility of further escalation, as a result of one side's policy success (3b), or failure (3c), or both sides' inability. In any of these instances, however, the threat of further escalation by one party, especially if it sees that escalation as possible but not desirable, can be instrumental in reinforcing the effects of the stalemate. These instances require further exploration into the intent of the exercise of power: in the case of escalation to call, the intent to produce negotiations is clear, whereas in the case of shortfall the intent to produce victory is clear and it has failed, and the case of escalation to raise can be either.

Instances of escalation

Ten studies have been undertaken to throw some light on the relation between escalation and negotiation. The cases were chosen as major instances of conflict escalation; ten others could have been used, and scholars are invited to test the preliminary conclusions presented here using other instances. The cases do come from around the world, and involve various levels of state power. The dynamics they show are similar whether the case took place during the Cold War or after. A detailed history or careful analysis in each case would be longer than the space available here, so the dynamics are briefly summarized below and the type of relation identified. The escalator is marked (E) and the target (T) for identification purposes only; designations do not preclude prior or counter-escalations by the target. References are given for fuller case analyses. This type of concise summary does not permit causal inferences beyond a sequential correlation; in all cases, however, fuller accounts show the causal link inferred here.

The Cuban Missile Crisis in 1962 came to a quick end after one escalation, followed by some minor relaxation, and before a threat of a second major escalation. The US (E) established a naval quarantine around Cuba on 22 October after discovering Soviet missile construction a week earlier; it reduced the perimeter from 800 to 500 kms two days later when Soviet ships turned around but boarded a (non-Soviet) ship the next days as construction continued. Faced with urgent threats and warnings of airstrikes (transitive) and nuclear war (intransitive), the Soviet Union (T) proposed an agreeable compromise on 26 October, four days after the previous major escalation and two days after escalation in its procedural expression (1b, 1d)

The Kutch and Kashmir crisis in 1965 followed a series of ratcheted escalations until both sides were exhausted but the initial attacker more so, and a peace agreement was mediated. Before the completion of an Indian military modernization program and after the death of Nehru, Pakistan opened a series of skirmishes in the Rann of Kutch, forcing the territorial dispute to an ad hoc international tribunal, and then began guerrilla attacks on Indian Kashmir in August. The Indians escalated with an attack with conventional forces and seized territory on the Pakistani side of the de facto border, whereupon Pakistan responded with a drive into southern Kashmir. India (E) then escalated again in early September with a attack across the de jure frontier well south of Kashmir and took and held territory near Lahore. With India in the more favorable position, having proven that Kashmir could not be taken from it by force, and Pakistan (T) out of spare parts, both parties agreed to a UN-demanded cease-fire on 22 September and to a Soviet Union-mediated truce on 10 January of the following year. The time between the latest in a series of transitive escalations into a full war across the recognized international – i.e. not Kashmiri – frontier and the ceasefire was three weeks (1b, 2a, 3a) (Thornton 1985).

A series of escalations to call in the early 1970s after inconclusive rounds of escalations to raise brought a negotiated settlement to the Vietnamese war. The war in the 1960s was an escalating stalemate, as symbolized by the Pyrrhic repulsion of the North Vietnamese Tet offensive at the end of January 1968; the US continued heavy airraids through the following nine months, while combat continued inconclusively on the ground. The Paris peace talks began at the end of the following January, but a month after their opening, a major North Vietnamese offensive took heavy American casualties. An American peace proposal was offered in October 1970. The Paris and back channel negotiations were punctuated by US (E) escalations into Cambodia in April–June 1970 and Laos in February 1971, and by the North Vietnamese (T) conventional army spring offensive of March 1972 and the US and South Vietnamese counteroffensive to retake Binh Dinh province in July.

The US bombing and mining of Hanoi–Haiphong began in early May 1972, a move heavy with risks for further intransitive escalation, if Russian ships were to hit a mine or if Soviet–US summit communications were to hit a snag. Instead, the escalating costline for non-agreement crossed the declining benefit-line for further US concessions and the Vietcong Politburo decided to table significant proposals in early September and October 1972, producing progress and then deadlock in mid-December. After a negative deadline constituted by the Christmas bombing of North Vietnam, the parties resumed negotiations on 9 January 1973 and an agreement within weeks thereafter. After the initial North Vietnamese effort in the early and mid-1960s in continuation of the previous war in Indochina, the war was a repeated set of US escalations matched by North

Vietnamese responses. The time between the escalation and the opening of serious negotiations in mid-1972 was about four months, and between the last escalation and the reopening of the final negotiations was three weeks (1b, 2a, 3d).

The third round of the border crisis between Iran and Iraq in 1974 took a specific turn with the involvement of Iranian support for the Iraqi Kurds and the limited escalation of the previous rounds of 1959 and 1969 took a much more serious form, leading to stalemate and negotiation of a mediated agreement in Algiers in March 1975 (Leib 1985; Ghareeb 1981). After 1972, the central undemarcated portion of the Iran–Iraq boundary became the scene of increasing incidents, compounded by Iranian support of the restive Kurds on the other side of the border. A UN Special Representative mediated a ceasefire and border demarcation agreement between the two neighbors in March 1974.

However, Iraqi vice-president Saddam Hussein decided that the usual past sequence of a limited spring–summer offensive, Iranian–Kurd-induced winter stalemate, and Iraqi late winter negotiations was undesirable for his regime and so he staked his career on a full-scale military offensive. Every Iraqi advance against its Kurds brought increased Iranian involvement on their behalf across the border, violating the ceasefire. By September, the Iraqi spring–summer offensive had captured almost every Kurdish town, provoking a large Kurdish refugee flow across the border, and most of the Iranian supply routes had been closed. Iran (E) then produced an important escalation by introducing sophisticated weaponry (radar-guided antiaircraft missiles and antitank batteries) that slowed the Iraqi offensive as the winter snows arrived. However, the Iraqis (T) maintained their pressure on the Kurds throughout the winter and prepared for a final decisive escalation when spring thaws appeared. At the beginning of March, both parties came to Algiers for the first OPEC Summit, during which they came to an agreement on their common border and on the Kurdish question. The Iranian escalation had fallen short of its intended decisive impact and faced with an impending counterescalation by Iraq, Iran agreed to negotiate (1b, 2c, 3c).

In the conflict between South Africa and Angola in late 1983 centered on Namibia, a South African military escalation was countered by an Angolan diplomatic escalation, leading to a brokered truce. After the South African invasion of Angola failed to bring the National Union for the Total Independence of Angola (UNITA) to power in 1975–6, it withdraw to fight the rebellion of the South West African Peoples Organization (SWAPO) in Namibia and to launch raids across the border against SWAPO and Angolan army camps. Increasingly deep and frequent raids in May 1978, March and October 1979, June 1981 and June 1982, reached the level and the length of the previous decade's invasion, without reducing SWAPO's attacks on Namibia. UNITA's advances also increased during the period, moving into northern Angola at the beginning of 1983 and within 100 miles of Luanda in September, but its lines were stretched and it could not hold its advances.

At the beginning of December, UNITA and the South African Defense Force (E) launched their twelfth annual campaign into, a more intense escalation than previous efforts. Operation Askari's deep penetration into northern Angola led only to increased Angolan (T) dependency on augmented Cuban forces and in January 1984 to a large arms deal with the Soviet Union. The day Operation Askari began, Assistant Secretary of State Chester Crocker met South African Foreign Minister RF Botha to urge some unilateral confidence-building gesture; ten days later, South Africa proposed a ceasefire for the end of January, just before the rains. At the same time as Operation Askari was going on, amid much diplomatic activity, South Africa responded to US pressure by proposing a ceasefire and then withdrawing much of its military force a week before the ceasefire date, upon receiving assurances that Angola would not fill the gap, and negotiated a disengagement from southern Angola in Lusaka in mid-February (1a, 3c).

In the same Namibian conflict, a military escalation and counter-escalation in 1987 left the parties locked in a stalemate with the threat or danger of a massive escalation ahead, leading to a mediated conflict resolution. With the beginning of the dry season in July, both the Angolans with the Cubans (E) and South Africa with UNITA (T) launched major offensives in southern Angola, with heavy losses. The Angolan attack was halted and UNITA returned to the offensive against the Angolan base of Cuito Carnevale at the end of the year. Following a massive $1 billion Soviet arms buildup in May, the Cuban–Angolan side meeting in Moscow in early November decided to out-escalate South Africa, by doubling the number of Cuban troops, to a total higher than the 50,000 South African troops in the theatre of operations. The new Cuban troops immediately moved south, across the tacitly agreed southern border for their operations, engaged South Africans wherever they met them, caused significant white casualties among South African troops, and announced a new doctrine of hot pursuit which could carry them across the border for the first time into South African territory. By March 1988, the battle for Cuito Carnavale was bogged down in the rains.

At the same time, both Cuba and the Soviet Union let it be known that they were tired of the Angolan adventure and ready to negotiate an agreement, essentialy on the "linkage formula" of paired Cuban withdrawals from Angolan in exchange for South African withdrawal (i.e. independence) in Namibia. Diplomatic contacts had been going on under US persistence for a while, always to run up against the usual obduracy of both sides. However in mid-January 1988, as Cuba announced new troop levels after the Moscow agreement, Angolan president Eduardo Dos Santos proposed a meeting with the US, with Cubans present, which at the end of the month, broached new details of major importance. The US urged a precise timetable, which Angola produced in a first draft in mid-March, as the battle for Cuito Carnevale ended in a draw, leading to full exploratory talks among Angolan, Cuban, South African and American delegations in May. The November 1987 decision to escalate troop commitments by Cuba, Angola and the Soviet Union, while South Africa and Angola, with their UNITA and Cuban allies, respectively, were checking each other's offensives to an escalated draw around Cuito Carnevale, effectively brought Angola to offer three months later and South Africa to accept in another two months negotiations leading to the paired withdrawal agreements signed in Brazzaville in December (1b, 2a, 3b, 3c).

In the first Gulf War between Iran and Iraq, in 1987, after eight years of inconclusive escalation and counter-escalation, Iranian attempts at winning through escalation fell short with massive costs, and Iraqi counter-escalation "to call," backed by the threat of a much more horrendous escalation, brought an end to the fighting. In that year, the last Iranian human-wave offensive, Kerbala 5, in the Battle for Basra was repulsed by Iraq with 50,000 and 20,000 killed, respectively, and Iraq began to gain the upper hand, regain its territory, and press the Iranians beyond their ability to respond. UN Security Council resolution 598 of 20 July 1987 demanded a ceasefire, which Iraq accepted on condition of Iran's acceptance and safe in the belief that it would not be forthcoming; the rejection left Iran isolated diplomatically and hence short of military materiel, with its economic means and its cannon-fodder youth in ever shortening supply.

In a desperate response, Iran (E) re-escalated in February 1988 by reviving its missile "war of the cities" with raids on Baghdad, only to find that over the next six weeks every one of its SSMs was met by nearly three Iraqi missiles. Iraq (T) returned to the offensive in April with a succession of invasions into Iran, withdrawing back to its border each time it took some territory. At the same time, reports again arose about the Iraqi use of chemical weapons, as had been verified in previous years, and confirmed by Iraq in July. Added to the missile raids on urban civilian complexes, the use of poison gas raised the threat of a horrible escalation without its ever having to be mentioned explicitly. When Saddam Hussein called for negotiations and an "honorable peace" on 17 July, Iran accepted resolution 598 the next day. When nothing happened, Iraq resumed its pattern of invasion-and-withdrawal, driving up to 40 kms into Iranian territory. The ceasefire was finalized on 8 August, to go into effect on 20 August, and negotiations began in Geneva a week later. Iraq's escalation to call was accompanied by the threat of a huge escalation, following in two weeks by agreement to negotiate (1b, 2a, 2c, 3b).

A decade of civil war in El Salvador burst into a major offensive in 1989 by the Farabundo Marti National Liberation Front (FMLN) at the end of the year, which failed to hold conquered areas in the capital but could not be dislodged from its rural bases; four months later, UN mediation took hold, leading to eight agreements between April 1990 and January 1992, ending the civil war. After 1983 its leaders saw that even victory would be costly, and in the following year, the government and paramilitary forces increase in strength, with US support, and election of a moderate rightwing civilian president, Jose Napoleon Duarte, led to the opening of talks later in the year. The peace talks stalled and government military fortunes continued to improve over the following three years. The FMLN was able to mobilize public pressure in favor of peace talks, counterbalancing the government's military power, but rebel proposals for negotiations were repeatedly rejected until late 1987. Several months of contacts under an agreement mediated by Costa Rican President Oscar Arias also collapsed at the end of the year. Seeking to overcome the failing popularity of his predecessor over the rising death and destruction of the civil war, the newly elected president, Alfredo Cristiani, proposed dialogue in his inaugural speech in June 1989. But in November, the rebels (E) launched their maximum effort of the war, penetrating into Managua and other cities. The offensive was repulsed and was unable to spark a popular uprising in the cities, only an increase in popular support for an end to violence. But it also showed the government (T) that it could not overcome the rebellion. A month after the initiation of the offensive, the UN Special Representative, Alvaro de Soto, made contacts with FMLN leaders and with President Cristiani, opening UN mediation. Intensive shuttle diplomacy finally brought the parties together in March 1990 and produced the first of the eight agreements at the beginning of April (de Soto 1999; Byrne 1996) (1b, 2a, 3c).

After three years of steady conflict over the Armenian enclave of Karabagh within Azerbaijan, an escalation and repulsed counter-escalation in 1993 led to a ceasefire (Mooradian and Druckman 1999). After a period of Azeri dominance of hostilities over its Armenian enclave following the independence of Armenia and Azerbaijan in 1991, the Karabagh legislature declared its own independence in January 1992 and Armenian irregulars (E) broke the Azeri blockade of the area and established connection with Armenia through the Lachin Corridor. As fighting continued, ceasefires were signed in May, August and September. However, new Karabagh offensives in February, March and April 1993 widened the Corridor, and in June, August and October escalated operations beyond the Corridor to larger Azeri towns to the south, taking a fifth of the country's territory. Armed forces from Armenia and Mountainous Karabagh then defeated a December Azeri (T) counterattack by February 1994 but were overextended; neither side was able to move the battlelines. After Kazakh, Iranian, and international – Conference for Security and Cooperation in Europe (CSCE) – attempts at mediation failed or were blocked, Russia began mediation in November 1993, bringing the parties three months after the stalemate set in to negotiate a ceasefire in May that managed the conflict without resolving any of its basic issues (1b, 2a, 3a, 3d).

Table 12.1 The stairs of escalation

Case	1 Escalator	2 Target	3 Relation	Time: Esc. to negotiation
Cuba 1962	after, threat	after	call	4 days
Kashmir 1965	after	after	raise	3 weeks
Vietnam 1972	after, threat	after	stalemate	4 months, 3 weeks
Gulf 1974	after	threat	shortfall	6 months
Angola 1983	during/after	after	stalemate	10 days
Angola 1987	after, threat	after	shortfall	3 months
Gulf 1987	after	after, threat	call	2–4 weeks
Salvador 1989	after	after	shortfall	4 months
Karabagh 1994	after	after	raise-shortfall	2 months
Bosnia 1995	after	after, threat	stalemate	1 month

After three years of Serbian ethnic cleansing and military conquest of much of Bosnia, an escalation in 1995 by Croatian and Bosniac forces, combined in a Federation (E) since the previous March, followed by an escalated NATO intervention, brought all parties to a settlement. In the first half of the year, Bosnian Serb (T) tactics continued to seize territory, neutralizing the UN protection force (UNPROFOR), the UN peacekeepers, and avoiding NATO retaliation by tactical concessions. In July, this tactic culminated in the capture of Bosniac safe areas at Srebrenica and Zepa in the east and the massacre of their male populations. However, in the west, the Croatian forces successfully regained the offensive to retake Western Slavonia in May and Krajina in August, destroying the Serb objective of a single contiguous Serb Republic in Bosnia.

Two events at the end of August brought the conflict to a fragile stalemate. Serb mortar bombing of the Sarajevo market produced instant and continuous NATO bombing of Serb positions within two days, expanded ten days later to include the use of cruise missiles and "smart bombs." At the beginning of September, the Croatian and Bosniac forces joined to continue their drive from Serb-held territories in Croatia into Bosnia itself, regaining significant parts of the lost territory and bringing their holdings close to the diplomatic target of 49 percent of the Bosnian territory. By the end of the month, the drive was poised to enter traditionally Serb territories of Bosnia and take the Serb town of Banja Luka. Restrained by the US mediating team as Serb President Slobadan Milosevic called for a ceasefire at the end of the month, the Bosniacs delayed the ceasefire agreed on 5 October for an additional six days and took the Bosniac town of Sanski Most. As a result, the Serbs agreed to meet the Croats and Bosniacs to begin negotiations at Dayton on 1 November (1b, 3a, 3b).

Initial findings

Ten cases have been presented, in rather rough initial form, indicating nonetheless some rather clear results that invite some substantial refinement. First, the correlations indicate that decisions to negotiate follow a party's escalation of the conflict, and deeper analysis into the course of the conflict, only alluded to here, confirm that these correlations do indeed have a causal effect. Parties escalate their conflict behavior, and then, unable to win outright by that behavior, decide to explore coming to terms. Opposing parties feel the effects of the escalation and decide that the appropriate response is not a (further) counter-escalation but a matching exploration of negotiation. The beginnings of a major change in attitudes and commitment take place following the escalation that gives way to negotiation. It must be emphasized – because the discussions on ripeness have already indicated a huge propensity to misunderstanding – that what is caused is only the decision to explore negotiations, not the successful conclusion of a negotiated agreement, which depends in turn on lots of other things that the literature on negotiation itself explores. Escalation is – or at least can be – pre-negotiation behavior.

Second, the cases do indicate that escalation (as distinguished on occasion from renewed conflict at a non-escalatory level) usually did not take place while negotiations were going on. However, there were exceptions, which only reinforce the idea that escalation can be intended to produce negotiations, not victory, and are not incompatible with them.

Third, not all escalations produce a decision to negotiate (or else there would never be more than one escalation). The cases show three interrelated types of escalation – escalations to call, failed escalations to raise or shortfalls, and escalations that stalemate (whatever they were intended to do). The typology is partially overlapping: both calls and shortfalls stalemate, so that types one and two are subtypes of three, although they may not constitute the entirety of type three. Calls are intentional stalemates, shortfalls are failed raises that do not change the previous stalemate out of which they sought to break.

As in many other pieces of life, the distinction between escalations to call and to raise is not always as clear in reality as in concept. It often takes a while for the distinction to become clear to the receiving side, so escalations to call often have to be repeated many times, as Cuba, the first Gulf War, and perhaps other cases show, increasing the risk of their being misunderstood. The problem with the distinction is compounded by the fact that it may be used tactically, where an escalation to raise may be presented as only an escalation to call and therefore not justifying a response. In the midst of the second Intifada, and the debate over reopening Israeli–Palestinian negotiations over the extent of the withdrawal of the Israeli occupation, the Hezbollah killing of an Israeli soldier was labeled by the US as a "provocation" and responded to by an Israeli deep raid on a

Syrian radar station in Lebanon, "meant as a warning to Syria and not as an invitation to further conflict in the region." At the same time, Israel called Palestinian mortars firing across the Gaza border into Israel "really an escalation by Yasir Arafat himself." Edward Djeredjian commented, "I don't think that either Syria or Israel perceives any interest in a military escalation that can bring wider fighting. But the risks of miscalculation and escalation are always there, and that is the danger." (*New York Times*, 17 April 2001, pp. Al, A6). The next day the Israeli Defense Force occupied a portion of Gaza in retaliation, vowing to stay "days, weeks and months" but then withdrew under intense international criticism. (*New York Times*, 18 April 2001, p. A1) The nature and message of the escalations was unclear.

But some successful escalations to raise also produce negotiations, just as presumably some of the other types and results of escalations do not produce negotiations. This exercise has focused on the finding that escalation and negotiation are not incompatible and that the first can lead to the second, with some indication of subcategories of the first (escalation). But it has not established (or sought to establish) the other side of the picture, that is, which escalations lead to negotiation and which do not. The constant or unknown factor is human will and free choice: some decision-makers seize the opportunity (which they themselves may have created) and some do not. But beyond free choice there are patterns, which have only begun to be discovered here.

Fourth, one element of these patterns is time, about which the cases have shown a rather large range. Negotiations opened between six months (Gulf 1974) and four days (Cuba 1962) after the escalation. In the longer-range cases, the decision to negotiate was still clearly a result of the latest escalation, in most cases accompanied by the danger of worse to come, either transitively as a threat or intransitively as a warning. Threat was much less frequently necessary in the shorter-range cases. Length of time is determined by the amount of time it takes for the effect to sink in; escalations need time to be perceived by the other side and to show their limits to the using side. But the length of time is also affected by the nature of the intervening conflict; in some of the longer periods, the war continued in a winter or wet-season time of lowered activity while the parties honkered down and considered their options. In the very short periods of time, a threat deadline or a mediator's pressures focused the parties attention. The only clear evidence of the cases is that it is impossible to specify (and hence to predict) a lapse of time when the effect will be felt.

Fifth, the cases suggest at least that there is more to the decision to negotiate than simply stalemate. The preceding effort – that is, the escalation itself – is important too. The conflict is worth a try, a test, an investment. The escalation is a down-payment on commitment, a measure of importance, like any intensification (Patchen 1988). But by its stepped nature it is also an attempt to jolt the adversary into rethinking its own investment and commitment, raising the ante to provoke either withdrawal or negotiation by the other side. How many escalations it takes to accomplish this goal is still open to research – and maybe never to conclusive determination.

Sixth, by the same token, escalation is also a self-provocation for the escalator, one last try after which cost/benefits need reevaluation (at the same time as the adversary is doing the same thing). Escalation is therefore a catalyst to thinking negotiation. And it is a catalyst to thinking negotiation rather than withdrawal (by both sides) because it represents a major increment of sunk costs, both material and psychological, that prohibits out and out withdrawal and favors recuperating at least some benefits through negotiation. The cases, in their many varied ways, all support this complex calculation.

Seventh, even when it works, escalation is often not enough. Two additional measures are often necessary. One is the future shadow or more escalation, the reluctant threat. What clinched the target party's acceptance of the view that the time of counter-escalations was over was the danger of something worse on the horizon, something that the escalator was willing and able but not eager to do. Reluctance is a useful ingredient, inherent in many escalations, since escalation involves cost and the escalator is just as content to achieve the same results at lower cost. But it also removes – or at least reduces – the element of challenge in the threat and confirms the presence of a way out of the conflict. Threat or precipice, and way out or requitement, are also elements in classic ripeness. The other additional measure is mediation. As is often the case on conflict resolution, even the presence of all the elements of pre-negotiation, including ripeness, are not enough to get the parties to overcome their fixation on the pursuit of conflict settlement and reconciliation. They need help.

Eighth, the operational implication, therefore, is that adversaries and mediators should push for negotiations once an escalation has been attempted by the other side, as Druckman and Carlson have also found in their chapters. Such demarches are obviously best timed when the escalation fails, or arrives at either a call or a shortfall. But even if it succeeds, by the reasoning of the previous point, it may be what the escalator needed, for its own domestic or psychological reasons, to enable it to now undertake negotiations. Unless the escalation actually won the war, in which case negotiation is moot, the escalation is likely to have restored the escalator's ability to negotiate, winning the battle perhaps but still leaving the war tied. Escalations provide opportunities for negotiators to seize.

This is a very preliminary study, designed to document the importance of the topic and indicate research directions. A number of clear implications stand out for further research. First, studies of negotiation need to take into account the course of conflict. Few now do. Because of the newness of the study of negotiation, the attempt to explain outcomes out of the negotiation process, and the focus on understanding and improving the practice of negotiation itself, most accounts at best devote almost exclusive attention to "who said what to whom with what effect," and little to the ongoing conflict on the ground. The processes of conflict and conflict management, and their study, still tend to remain separate. Much of what happens in negotiation can be explained through an interactive process that still invites better understanding and conceptualization. But some or much of that process reflects the course of the conflict itself. Except in the cases of the Cuban Missile Crisis and the Vietnam War, where confrontation was the main element, there is little on escalation and its relation to the initiation and conduct of negotiation.

Second, studies on escalation and negotiation need to develop a higher degree of resolution, along many dimensions. A finer-tuned notion of correlation needs to be developed, with an appropriate explanation of lag times. Notions of "after," "between," and "before" are not sharply delimited. Correlation needs to be complemented by historical research on causality (see Mooradian and Druckman 1999 for a good example). More differentiation needs to be made in regard to the size of escalation and a non-tautological test of tolerance for pain (Carlson 1995). In dealing with size, proper attention must be paid to the problem of comparing different types of escalation. "The word escalation and all its synonyms are about to drop out of the lexicon as a result of overuse," it was noted on the Intifada II. "Over the last two weeks, the situation has been escalating, getting worse, intensifying and deteriorating almost daily [with no negotiation in prospect]." (Shalev 2001). As already indicated, if it has been established that escalation is (or can be) pre-negotiation behavior, research now needs to distinguish those escalations which lead to negotiations from those that do not, and why, and consider how many escalations are needed to produce a negotiation.

Third, different types of controls are necessary to improve the robustness of findings. Studies of decisions to negotiate which correlate causally with escalations need to be tested by studies of decisions to negotiate which do not relate to escalations, and of escalations which do not produce decisions to negotiate. Only by comparing what did not work with what worked can one understand the latter. This study (at this stage) has shown that escalations, and especially escalations that intentionally or unintentionally produce stalemates, produce a decision to negotiate. The next round of research should help answer that both calls and falls can lead to negotiations, so that conflict and management can be brought together in a single phrase.

13 Negotiating the rapids

The dynamics of regime formation[33]

International regimes are continuous two-dimensional negotiations for the purpose of resolving a problem of coordination under uncertainty among sovereign states. This characterization contains a number of important propositions, some pointing out new aspects of regimes and others taking a position in the ongoing debate on the subject, while at the same time building on many aspects of the work already done on regimes. The main thrust of this work is to correct the "one-time" image of regimes as something that is decided through a process but that then remains relatively fixed, inviting analysis of ratification, compliance, and effectiveness. It is a profound misunderstanding of the regime-building process to believe that it is merely a matter of legislation and compliance. Regime-building is ongoing negotiation.

Instead of the static picture, we propose to substitute an image continually in motion or evolution through negotiation, negotiations on an initial agreement followed by post-agreement negotiations (PAN), with parties sporadically negotiating both with other parties to the regime and within their own domestic and intraparty levels. In the process, we will explain, over the next three chapters, why the nature of regimes makes stable guidelines for agreement (formula) and implementation (details) difficult to attain, and what the effect that the dynamic nature of regimes is on analysis and practice.

This more dynamic image is expressed in a number of propositions, stated here, which will be developed in the course of the following analysis:

- Proposition 1: Regimes are recursive two-dimensional (vertical, horizontal, and sometimes diagonal) negotiations for the purpose of inter-state problem-solving, rather than two-level negotiations over a treaty ratification.
- Proposition 2: Regimes govern the behavior of parties (member states and their citizens) by imposing an agenda for combat as well as by providing justifying norms and limiting constraints.
- Proposition 3: Parties continually seek to adjust regime rules and

party behaviors to fit their approach to the problem rather than simply complying (or not complying) with regimes.

- Proposition 4: Disparities among parties in power, interest, costs and benefits perform the motor role in moving regime negotiations through their recursive iterations.
- Proposition 5: Recursive regime negotiations repeatedly pose the question of absolute costs under uncertainty ("Will we cost ourselves unnecessarily now and forever to forestall uncertain dangers of future costs?") rather than either on uncertainty of cooperation or on relative gains.
- Proposition 6: The stability of a regime is a function of the degree of certainty of information about the transaction problem, the degree of divergence of the participating states' interests, and the degree of harmony of current norms and expectations. The greater the capacity of a regime's negotiated formula to resolve the transaction problem, to meet participating states' interests, to fit current norms and establish coherent expectations, and so to overcome opposition to it, the more stable the regime. The inherently fluid nature of problems, power, interests, norms and expectations involved in international regimes makes such stability rare, necessitating repeated (recursive) negotiations to stabilize the formula that meets these criteria.

Despite the insightful work conducted over the past decade and a half on international regimes (Rittberger and Mayer 1993; Hasenclever *et al.* 1997), important aspects of the nature of regimes have been lost through the approaches used. Regime studies have spent much of their attention on the conditions of regime creation but little on its process.[34] Once the regime is created, it has generally been examined to determine its effectiveness in terms of the parties' compliance with its provisions rather than in terms of its evolution in dealing with the subject problem (Hasenclever *et al.* 1997, pp. 2, 42–3; Chayes and Chayes 1993; Underdal 1992; HP Young 1994; Victor *et al.* 1998). The regime is studied as essentially an intergovernmental compact, with little consideration of its effects on the ground and on its own evolving nature. By current criteria, it is hard to evaluate the success of regimes, since they are judged statically but in reality constitute a moving target, like checking the speed of a train by using a single snapshot.

These characteristics of the current study of regimes miss the basic nature of a regime as a living thing, established in answer to a problem of cooperation under uncertainty and evolving – indeed, expanding and contracting – as part of a continual re-creation process.[35] The dominant method in that repeated creation is negotiation, a process that is too little considered in the study of regimes. Most of the regime literature focuses on *why* states cooperate, and neglects *how* states cooperate in conceptual terms. The neglect of the regime-building process goes hand in hand with the general neglect of conceptual study of multilateral negotiation. While it is hard to understand why regime studies have paid so little attention to negotiations for regime creation, it is perhaps more understandable that they missed the creature's dynamic character once created, since much of this evolution has occurred in the past two decades since the original defining work on the subject (Krasner 1983).[36] Now, two decades later, it is possible to propose a different approach to the understanding of regimes because the moving picture of history has imposed a more dynamic subject than originally presented.

The following essay integrates the negotiation process into the study of regimes as the framework for a renewed attention to the subject, including an examination of cases of regimes in evolution. It will first examine the general nature of regimes in international relations, then lay out six analytical assumptions about the process of regime-building, then examine the four factors involved in regime evolutions that meet in the negotiation process, then explain the challenge of building a stable regime, and finally address the question of dynamic stability and evaluation.

Regimes in international relations

As a result of the inattention to the process of regime creation and evolution, uncertainty persists about the name and nature of international regimes. Regime is one of those concepts – from "power" all the way to "love" and including "integration," regimes' predecessor concept – where "we all know what they mean" but a solid working definition and a process understanding are still being sought. In the case of regimes, the confusion arises from unclarity over the relation between the object and the processes that maintain it.[37]

The study of regional integration, predecessor of regime studies, was plagued by ambiguities of a similar type. Integration as an outcome was continually confused with integration as a process. The process of integrating frequently led to results short of the outcome of integration and aroused concomitant counterpressures, pushing it away from an integrated outcome. Yet that process was assumed to be composed of steps toward a goal that, in specific realities, was never reached. The analytical power of the approach was bedeviled by its teleological assumption.

Regime-building, a looser reincarnation of integration, is endangered by similar debilities despite some inherent safeguards. Because of the syntax of the term, "regime" clearly defines an outcome and requires a distinct (if more cumbersome) modifier, such as "regime-building" or "regime formation," to indicate a process. Also, because of the looser nature of the subject, many regimes can be said to have actually come into being: there is a "there" there. Yet the problem is that there are many "theres" there, making it unclear what the empirical universe is from which one can draw generalities and regularities. The 1983 definition – "principles, norms, rules and decision-making procedures around which actor expectations converge in a given issue area" (Krasner 1983, p. 1) – is usually cited as the subject of consensus but the debate has moved to the particular empirical objects to which it properly applies. Regimes can cover many forms, scopes and degrees of formality, and regime-building may be a component of an evolving regime. It is hard to analyze the process of regime formation without a better idea of the point in the process that can be called a regime. And so scholarship has turned to other interesting topics, leaving the ongoing process of regime-building to fend for itself.

Partly to overcome these problems and partly out of the fad-value of a new term, recent discussion of the subject has moved from "regimes" to "governance." In the process, it has taken refuge in the wider spaces of imprecision. Governance, directly derived from the Greek term for "rudder," refers to a widespread process of political steering, and international governance can take place through many types of interaction – from war to America's Cup – that most people would agree to place outside of regimes. However, the shift to governance has one merit for present purposes: it draws attention to an ongoing process of steering rather than a one-time event. That aspect is the major focus of this study, for which the term "regimes" will be retained, if only for its inclusion of the notion of issue-areas.

A regime is a living organism par excellence and its stability is unlikely to be a steady state endpoint. Indeed, the concept of "regime" was devised to meet the need for something (even) looser and less rigid than international law or international organization. It would be a denial of the concept and a disservice to the idea of regime to analyze it as "arriving" when it achieved legal or organizational status. Instead, regimes persist as regimes by maintaining their flexibility, their ability to change in response to the same sorts of varying needs for coordination and problem-solving as gave them birth, and their adaptability to the shifting constellations of power and interest of their members.

Regimes are quite different from many other types of negotiated agreements in that they are not simply negotiation outcomes, processed and filed, but are ongoing agreements moving through time. Compliance is therefore an inappropriate or at least incomplete notion since regimes and their treaties evolve. Regimes cannot be understood as complying with their initial documents, any more than individuals "comply" with the conditions of their birth or nations "comply" with their constitutions. At the same time, regimes are not simply the international manifestation of an agreement, but must be understood to involve the actions of member states in interpreting, applying and avoiding, and responding to the initial agreement and its subsequent variations. Since regimes are behaviors as well as rules and regulations, they involve the actions of parties to stay within but also to get around the rules. All this involves negotiation.

In an image, regimes are watercourses flowing through time and space. Neither just the source nor the surface, they involve the entire body of water from its upper manifestations as international agreements to its benthic effects on local politics (and local and national politics' effects on the surface). What is going on in the water and how the water reacts with the bottom are important elements in understanding movement on the surface and in the flow over time. Similarly, to pursue the metaphor, obstacles to the course such as dams, shallows, and bends are important to an understanding of the flow. Too often, only their surface manifestations (the regime agreement) have been studied, and the slowly growing literature on local regime-related activities (the bottom) has not been related to the surface. The Brundtland Commission's exhortation to "think globally, act locally" has implications for analysis that have not been pursued. It takes an understanding of resistance along the bottom to understand why the forward flow of the regime is slowed, and without this, there is often an unwarranted optimism – seen also in the earlier analysis of integration – over the creation of the superficial agreement. Thus,

- Proposition 1: Regimes are recursive two-dimensional (vertical, horizontal, and sometimes diagonal) negotiations for the purpose of interstate problem-solving, rather than two-level negotiations over a treaty ratification.

Some of the ambiguity can be brought under control through some clearer specification of the concepts. Regimes are instruments of *inter*national cooperation that fall short of *supra*national organization, instruments of coordinated and collectively self-managed interdependence. Coordination and management is required to secure information, "organize negotiation processes, set standards, perform allocative functions, monitor compliance, reduce conflict and resolve disputes." (Eden and Hampson 1990, p. 6). Thus, the regime is more than simply "rules, norms, regulations and behaviors" (Krasner 1983); it is the institutionalized effort to shape, monitor and support these outputs, with the understanding that that institutionalization remains *inter*, and not *supra*national. Since specific encounters mark the formalization of the evolving regime, characteristics of the multilateral negotiation and domestic political processes govern the building of regimes.

More broadly, in regard to international relations theory, this analysis is placed squarely in the too-sparsely inhabited territory between neo-realism and neo-liberalism. In part this is because neither school is fully and exclusively adequate to the subject, since "realism" focuses on an explanation of conflict and cannot handle cooperation, whereas liberalism explains cooperation and cannot handle conflict. Yet regimes involve both, and so are the exclusive domain of neither approach. The original questions of regime analysis – basically empirical but with important theoretical implications – were: Do regimes shape state behavior, or do states simply do what they can and want (as the realist Athenians maintained (Thucydides 1960[–411], V 89/267))? Only when taken caricaturally are the answers mutually exclusive.

It is held here that regimes do matter and states (that is, decision-makers acting in the name of states) do modify their behavior in function of the engagements taken within regimes, including behavior designed to reduce the amount of behavior regimes modify. Regimes matter as opportunities, as constraints, and as a political arena or battlefield. Parties do try to do what they can, and will try hardest when perceived vital interests are involved, but what they can do is constrained by their relations with other states acting in their own interests in regimes (and elsewhere). The polar positions – that regimes do not exist or that they exist as corporate actors that actually do things – seem so far beyond simple common sense and empirical evidence as to be not worth the debate. What continues to be of concern is how states behave within and toward their collective conventions, whether tacit or explicit. And that question can only be answered by considering regimes as a two-dimensional dynamic process. Thus,

- Proposition 2: Regimes govern the behavior of parties (member states and their citizens) by imposing an agenda for combat as well as by providing justifying norms and limiting constraints.

It is important here to underscore – if only through repetition – what the approach does not imply. In stressing their evolutionary nature, the argument does not remove from regimes their institutional or constraining nature, any more than the frequent revision of a tax code deprives it of its authority at tax collection time, or the evolving and amended nature of a constitution removes its capacity to govern the political process. States behave within a regime as it stands between negotiations, although that behavior will include local negotiations (the second level of the two-dimensional negotiations) over implementation. In other words, there may be some fluidity and even contestation within the regime but there is no vacuum.

But by the same token, this view does not see a regime as a permanently fixed statute, the content of which no longer becomes the focus of politics once it is enacted and compliance with which is the only (or main) question left to be resolved. States – and other actors who constitute the "local" levels – continue to act on the basis of power, interest and values, and it is the very nature of the regime as soft law that allows for this continuing interaction of states over its shape and the regime's continuing evolutionary nature. Analysis that considers otherwise is trying to make the regime of soft law into something it is not, an understandable temptation to render it more studiable by making it more concrete and hence more compliable. But that is to miss its nature, to rush its evolution, and to fall into the teleological trap of integration studies.

Assumptions for analysis

Several assumptions are necessary to start the analysis. It must first be assumed (1) that regimes are a problem-solving effort, impelled by a felt need for some order – norms, rules, regulations and expectations – in existing interactions, because the cost of disorders and transaction inefficiencies impedes the achievement of the purposes for which the transactions were instituted. Regimes grow out of interdependencies and interactions; they do not initiate them but they do further and expand them. Recognizing the initiation of a regime as a problem-solving or problem-response effort addresses several questions in regime analysis. It facilitates analysis of the causal question: regime initiation is caused by states responding to conflicts in the conduct of transactions. In this, they are motivated by and use power, interests, norms and values. It also facilitates an evaluation of regimes and their stability, since they have a purpose to accomplish. This question will be addressed at the end of this chapter.

Furthermore, (2) formal cooperation comes when the interests of the cooperating parties are inchoate and need organized coordination (Morgenthau 1960, p.183; Lipson 1991). The formalizing event is often preceded by preparatory and partial negotiations, as well as by the triggering problems. Sometimes the incremental process begins bilaterally and even non-governmentally, and the main round serves to collect and coordinate these diverse efforts around a coherent formula. Formalization is not likely to be an imperceptible rise on a featureless trend toward a regime. It is a response to a problem, triggered by an exogenous challenge or an endogenous breakdown in current attempts at self-regulation – a relatively sharp escalation in the feeling of need. Such intensified feelings may be spontaneous or may be directed by particular parties whose power and/or interests were affected. The result of these activities is an explicit attempt at regime creation through multilateral negotiation. This step represents an important threshold in the formation of a regime and should be recognized as the point of formal regime creation, ending the informal phase. While some attempts at self-regulation may never leave the informal phase, they need to be analyzed as something else than a regime that has passed its formalizing threshold.

It can therefore be assumed (3) that the process of regime-building is, at least at the hands of some of the parties, a purposive exercise heading toward the establishment of rules, regulations, norms and expectations governing the given issue area. The formalized process starts with agreement negotiations and continues with recursive post-agreement negotiations. Regimes do not build themselves, although in seeking to build a regime, policy agents may start a process that takes on a dynamic of its own and is larger than their simple policy goals and efforts. The role of spontaneity in regime-building will be addressed in point (6).

As a result, (4) some of the parties are interested in preventing regime formation or at least limiting the attainment of the goal of others. Thus, concomitantly if not symmetrically, progress toward regime formation arouses a counterprocess of limiting regime effects. Indeed, it may be hypothesized that this opposition will grow with the evolution of the regime: the more the integration, the more the opposition, until a point in the regime-building process where stability is reached. A soft and loose regime does not provide much cause for opposition (except against the foreshadow of its expansion), but as it expands, constrains and formalizes, it arouses more status-quo-oriented opposition, even as it may attract more supporters. But the fluid nature of the type of problem international regimes handle and the high degree of uncertainty involved mean that even when apparent stability is reached, in terms of parties' power and interest, new information and new forms of the problem are likely to re-call that stability into question.

Therefore, it can be assumed (5) that any momentary process of regime building has its own interactional dynamic, in which the outcome will lie somewhere between the extreme positions, although not necessarily in the middle or on the side of progress (as sometimes assumed). Thus, regime-building is marked by periodic confrontations between proponents and opponents as the former seek to advance the process and the latter to retard, evade or undo it. These confrontations typically take the form of negotiations, and they result in a new status quo in the evolution of the regime. In this way, regime-building is neither a one-shot affair nor a smoothly flowing evolution, but a series of negotiations large and small taking place within an independently evolving context.

Finally, (6) the outcome of these negotiations is often built up inductively, cobbled together out of the most pressing pieces, or sectorially, addressing only the squeeky-wheel aspect of the problem rather than its whole structure. Some order may grow out of the transactions themselves, either as behavioral patterns or as implicit attempts at self-regulation (such as a social practice of traveling on one side of the road), but there are few if any known cases where such spontaneous order has met the felt needs (cf. Camazine *et al.* 2001). Not only is empirical evidence of spontaneous regimes lacking but there is a logical case to be made against their success. In fact, spontaneity is a less likely characteristic of regulation than of accentuated calls for greater, explicit efforts at regulation.

More likely than a single spontaneous pattern or regulation are multiple and hence competing attempts that undermine each other, creating worse needs for order (such as the right-siders' vs the left-siders' traffic patterns). Also more likely than collective self-regulation are individual units' attempts at regulating themselves and then perhaps others, again creating competitive patterns (such as the spreading local efforts to establish standardized time areas in the US before the national times zones were created). On the international level, such attempts often begin regionally before spreading around the globe; for that reason, regional attempts comprise half the cases examined below in this volume.

The process is an incremental one, in which parts are put together by trial and error into a momentary, unstable resting place preparatory to further movement. Definitions are often avoided in favor of lists of covered activities, which are only later joined under a definitional umbrella. Areas of attention are identified and combined to form the scope of the agreement. A package is constructed out of either a core coalition of key interests or a diverse coalition of disparate interests; then the agreement is expanded, to the extent possible, either to extend the coverage or fill in the holes. Commitments are outlined and then strengthened, against resistance to weaken them. Negotiations on environmental regimes have characteristically begun with statements of intent, codes of conduct, or differential obligations, exceptions and reservations, which are then gradually turned into binding obligations; private watch groups monitoring behavior replace signatories' engagements or international organizational constraints, until new norms have been introduced far enough to constitute comprehensive expectations, rules and regulations. The salient formulating – but not necessarily initial – negotiation lays out the basic formula and the subsequent post-agreement negotiations fill in and revise the details.

Attempts have been made to categorize the disorder of this incremental process into various models, so that alternative ways of forming regimes can be evaluated and utilized (Benedick *et al.* 1991). The models are scarcely watertight and tend to spill over into each other as the incremental process seeks its own path on each occasion. The taxonomic difficulty is not only posed by unruly reality; it also stems from the many dimensions along which models could be constructed. These include scope of coverage, stringency of obligation, inclusiveness of parties, degree of institutionalization, provisions for extension, quantity of resources, means of enforcement, among others.

Regimes begin in some specific form and evolve under the impact of various stimuli, according to a number of different patterns. They include:

1   A universal and comprehensive treaty, which is then subjected to overall review and revision from time to time, as in the Law of the Sea (Sebenius 1984; Friedheim 1993).
2   A framework agreement of general principles, followed by specific protocols applying the principles to narrower component issues, as in the Ozone Treaty sequence from Vienna to Montreal to London (Benedick 1991), analyzed by Chasek in a subsequent chapter in this book.
3   An action plan of loose goals, followed by the negotiation of implementing treaties gradually tightening the obligations, as in the

Mediterranean Action Plan and its children (Haas 1990; Chasek *et al.* 1996; Wagner 2003) (sometimes referred to, with 2), above, as the transformational approach (Lang 1989; Dunoff 1995; Young *et al.* 1996]).

4 A basic trade-off between two opposing blocs and principles which then turns into an organization for their pursuit. As in the Conference and then Organization for Security and Cooperation in Europe (CSCE/OSCE) (Leatherman 2003, 2004).

5 An agreement to hold a periodic review conference, intercalated with monitoring and specific regulatory sessions, as in the World Administrative Radio Conference (Fliess 1987).

6 A small core agreement, expanded gradually to include related issues in order to maintain its own coherence, as in the acid rain agreements.

7 A process-oriented convention on implementation measures tied to levels of scientific information and policy coordination but without commitments, followed by interim negotiations, like the Climate Change Convention (Patterson and Grubb 1992; Bodansky 1993; Barrett 2003).

8 A weak and ineffective attempt to handle a recognized problem whose initial inadequacies in turn becomes the goad to a tighter and more effective agreement, such as the Whaling Convention of 1946 or the 1954 Convention for the Prevention of Pollution of the Sea by Oil, which turned into a ban on whaling by the International Whaling Commission in 1985 and Maritime Pollution (MARPOL) Convention of 1973, respectively, or the evolution of the Helsinki Commission (HelCom) on the Environmental Protection of the Baltic Sea.

9 International standards with self-selected national exemptions (Korula 2003).

10 A cluster of small sectoral agreements, joined together in later negotiations to cover the entire issue area, also as in the acid rain agreements.

11 A growing network of bilateral agreements rationalized into a multilateral ensemble, as in the transboundary air pollution agreements among European countries giving rise to consolidated controls in 1979, 1984–5, 1988, and 1991 (Scapple 1996).

12 A limited-party agreement, expanded by new adherents to complete the coverage, as in the Chemical Weapons Agreement (Floweree and Aberle 1993) or the Uruguay Round process (Winham 1990) (sometimes called a strategic construction approach; see Barrett 1998; Zartman 1987, p. 292).

13 Statements of principles giving rise to a regional convention which then is extended globally while continuing to search for an effective formula, as in the African and then world ban on dumping toxic wastes in the Basel Convention; and possibly others.

In reality, these ideal types are softened, combined, or complemented by each other when regimes are established and as they evolve. Nonetheless, it is clear that each form in this latitudinal taxonomy opens up its own longitudinal taxonomy of evolutionary possibilities. There is not enough experience as yet to know which of these forms is best, what "best" means, or what their individual implications are. It does not seem that any particular type provide the best way to stability. Since different issues pose different problems for solving and challenges for cooperation, different types and patterns of regimes will be appropriate as paths for negotiations.

Factors in regime evolution

The process of regime formation does not stop with its initial act. Negotiation continues as regimes evolve, rather than ending with the signing of an instrument of agreement. Loopholes need to be tightened or loosened, new members bought in or old ones dropped, obligations strengthened or lifted, ambiguities removed or provided, coverage extended or reduced, and so on. Because of the change and uncertainty inherent in the subject, the initial form of the regime is simply unlikely to solve the problem. But even if it did, to the satisfaction of some of the parties at the moment, those parties, and other parties or potential parties would continue to return to the negotiating table to revise, reduce, expand, and/or correct the form of the regime in place. The effort is a learning process, and if some parties do not want to learn, the need to do so is forced on them by the learning of others. Negotiation continues in order to deal with the problem, both to shape the ongoing process of cooperation and to revisit and rectify engagements originally included or excluded. The idea of an ultimate instrument governed thereafter by *pacta servanda sunt* is a notion of a bygone era.

But negotiation is not only a multilateral exercise among the signatories; it is also an exercise in reentry, application, implementation, and response between the upper and the lower levels of the "watercourse." Negotiators or their domestic colleagues return home to sell, mend, and enforce the results of their negotiation, and they return to the next round of negotiations with the results of their implementation, including new instructions and inputs and new awareness of the regime's imperfections. This vertical contact with the "lower level" does not concern ratification alone (Putnam 1988; Evans *et al.* 1993). As the stream flows on, there is a rolling wave from the bottom that stirs up new material and carries it to the surface, affecting its force and flow.

There are four factors simultaneously involved in regime evolution, coming together from time to time in renegotiations.[38] One is the *system maintenance* or inertial tendency of a regime to persist as constructed at any moment. Parties become engaged and committed to a relationship and seek to maintain it, even incurring momentary losses as a result. Frequently they negotiate to maintain the relationship against threats of loss resulting from its discontinuance, even though its maintenance may have visible costs and the costs of discontinuance may be only hypothetical (Stein and Pauly 1993). Regime maintenance may be the consequence of sunk costs (Lynn-Jones 1988, pp. 498–9), with sunk costs interpreted in terms of non-material commitment as well as of finances.

Systems maintenance tendencies as commitments to past engagements or investments will find themselves confronted by new situations with their own costs and interests, and the continued operation of the relationship will enter as an element in the cost and interest calculations in responding to the new challenges. The inertia or system maintenance tendency behind an established regime can outweigh worsened relations between the parties resulting from conflicting interests in a new situation (Rittberger and Zürn 1990), although of course highly conflicting issues can destroy an established regime. The elephant issue in 1991 under CITES is an case of system maintenance in which the protection rules were reaffirmed above all for purposes of continuing the regime rather than for meeting the merits of the particular problem.

There is a danger in identifying this factor in such a way that it reifies the relationship itself as an actor. It is on the parties as actors that the exigencies of the system maintenance operate, pressing for sustained (although not necessarily increased) cooperation rather than working in both negative and positive directions as in the other factors discussed below. System maintenance is reflected in the fact that the regime continues between negotiations, whatever the pressures of the other factors. Again,

- Proposition 2: Regimes govern the behavior of parties (member states and their citizens) by imposing an agenda for combat as well as by providing justifying norms and limiting constraints.

The second factor is the *adjustment* of the basic formula and implementing details of the regime's initial instrument, with the parties' continually reviewing the effectiveness of problem-solving, coverage of issues, intensity of obligations, thoroughness of information, and degree of monitoring. Parties seek to maintain, gain or regain through negotiation what was gained, not gained or lost in past negotiations. Some try to close loopholes, while others seek to reopen them; some find the degree of commitment inadequate for the effective working of the system, while others find it constraining and onerous; and so on. States refuse, leave or limit their cooperation under the agreement if the loopholes provide unequal (relative) gains in favor of others or if obligations outweigh the perceived (absolute) gains for the cooperating parties (Greico 1990, p. 35; cf. Greico 1988). It is simply wrong and even ideological to claim that the comparison of gains is necessarily interparty or intraparty; it is either or both depending on the vagaries of the case, not even necessarily depending on some consistent intervening variable (although the search for such a variable would be enlightening). Thus, the successive Ozone Treaty negotiations involved a continual review of obligations and membership in order to recognize and reduce a common danger. In sum,

- Proposition 3: Parties continually seek to adjust regime rules and party behaviors to fit their approach to the problem rather than simply complying (or not complying) with regimes.

The third factor involves a *cybernetic* series of learning loops tying domestic governance to international governance (Kolb and Faure 1994). After negotiations, regimes return to the domestic scene of the participating states for the next round of action. Such action involves implementation by domestic agencies, including further debate and negotiation within governmental institutions, but it also involves further pressures by domestic non-governmental organizations for and against the newly established regime (Susskind 1995). Obviously, the two strands are joined, as NGOs pressure legislatures, lobby executives, and test the courts. In a broad sense, this interaction too is negotiation, with its associated pressures and security points. Its output is both a set of implementations of the previous international negotiation and also a set of inputs into the next round, where it rejoins the momentary results of the two previously discussed processes.

The ingredients of the domestic process are multiple and diverse, varying according to the individual states' agendas. They can include elections – critical or continuing; intergroup encounters among the crucial sectors of society, business, science and public interest groups; and the competing attempts of various sides in the debate over the regime to mobilize their followers. Ultimately, the nature of the domestic interaction is contained and shaped by the nature of the polity itself. Defensive participation in the Mediterranean Action Plan (MAP) led the Algerian government to create scientific positions in environmental science and maritime pollution, whose holders under the subsequent regime constituted a specialized interest group which enabled the country to play a more positive role in subsequent negotiations (Haas 1990; Chasek *et al.* 1996).

A particularly important aspect of the domestic bed for regime-building concerns the development of norms that underwrite the negotiation of rules (Sjöstedt 2003). It is importat to underscore the necessity for harmony between domestic norms and international negotiations, as well as the dismantling effect that the absence of such coincidence can have on regime implementation. The effect is two-directional, of course; consensual norms on the international level can affect domestic thinking and knowledge. There is no formula for calculating which causal arrow is stronger.

While the domestic dimension of regimes has been noted occasionally, and the two-level structure of regime negotiations has been subject to some analysis (Druckman 1978; Putnam 1988; Evans *et al.* 1993), the domestic dimension has not been brought in as a constituent part of the process of regime evolution. Specifically, two-level negotiations have been considered as necessary for ratification and therefore as ending with the initial agreement, whereas the present analysis sees the domestic reaction and interaction as an integral component of regime evolution as well as initiation. In sum,

• Proposition 1: Regimes are recursive two-dimensional (vertical, horizontal, and sometimes diagonal) negotiations for the purpose of interstate problem-solving, rather than two-level negotiations over a treaty ratification.

Finally, to all these endogenous factors must be added an *exogenous factor*, involving accidents, unforeseen challenges, new information, neighboring and competing regimes, and other external inputs and changes (Myers 1995). As noted, regime building begins with a problem or conflict, generally caused by exogenous factors, and the subsequent trajectory of the regime is deflected and accelerated by further events of the same nature. The ozone negotiations were impelled by periodic injections of new scientific information; the regional and global negotiations and declarations surrounding the Basel Convention on Hazardous Wastes were similarly driven in spurts by incidents in the very subject matter of the convention; the evolving European security regime was shaken and reshaped above all by the Bosnian crisis.

Exogenous challenges can also come from other regimes. Competing efforts to deal with aspects of the same problem in overlapping geographic or functional areas occur at the intersection of various regime systems as networks and systems of negotiated regulation come into shape (Kremenyuk 2002; Chasek 1994). European regimes to deal with acid rain and maritime pollution impinged on global acid rain negotiations and on the Mediterranean Action Plan, respectively; the UN, NATO, WEU (Western European Union) and OSCE (Organization for Security and Cooperation in Europe) all influenced each other's evolution in competing for the same functions. As regimes grow, they run up against other growing regimes and the two, like two meeting streams, become involved in the complex and contradictory processes of maintaining their own separate integrity and taking each other's jurisdiction into account. A current example of two regimes' meeting each other is found in the environmentalists' attacks on the North American Free Trade regime, where boundary or turf wars are taking place over the ownership of political or issue space not unlike the wars that have marked international relations over geographic boundaries.

At given points in the evolution of the regime, these four processes bring the parties back to multilateral negotiations again, to formalize the regime's evolution. Sometimes this formal encounter is mandated by the agreement, as a review process or periodic meeting of the contracting parties; sometimes it is necessitated by the second element, need for adjustment, or the third, domestic inputs, or the fourth, exogenous events, which require a return to the drawing board; sometimes it is unspecified and therefore needs a clarion call (as provided by Malta in the Law of the Sea) or a convenient anniversary (as seized upon 20 years after UNCHE (UN Conference on the Human Environment) in Stockholm to call to order UNCED in Rio). The ability of the regime to deal with change can be provided in the regime itself or invented as changes and challenges arise. Both impose strains on the regime: the first can be taxing beyond the regime's capability for response, while the second involves two actions (invention and then application of the response) and thus poses a greater challenge to negotiations, (Levy *et al.* 1994, p. 9).

The outcome of the negotiation is determined by the power and interests of the parties to the encounter at the time of the negotiations, within the context of the evolving regime. Since the encounter is one of problem-solving under uncertainty, power is conceived of in relation either to the problem or to the solution. Always a concept both crucial and elusive (Zartman 1997; Zartman and Rubin 2000), power can be characterized here as the actions taken to block or form a regime, based on the degree of necessity of a party to the regime or coalition in formation (veto power) (Porter and Brown 1995, especially p. 104). So conceived, power can be turned into measurable indices, based on parties' contribution either to the problem (e.g. as degree of consumption or of pollution) or to the solution (e.g. as contributor to a fund). Similarly, interest is best characterized in terms of the costs of the problem and its solution, tempered again by the element of uncertainty. This element too can be refined into a measurable index, calculating the ration of preventive cost to cost of danger, modified by their probabilities. Such a calculation would of course be heuristic at best, since the very nature of the problem is the uncertainty of the probabilities. These indices will not be calculated here, but their ingredients will be a qualitative part of the case analyses. In sum,

- Proposition 4: Disparities in power, interest, costs and benefits among parties perform the motor role in moving regime negotiations through recursive iterations.

The mixture of power and interests among the parties translates into different roles which they can play. Dynamic stability is achieved through an appropriate balance of roles. A limited list of role strategies from which parties can chose can be identified inductively, although there is not yet a clear conceptual dimension (other than metaphorical) to the list (Sjöstedt 1993; cf. Sprinz and Vaahtoranta 1994).[39] Parties can *drive, conduct, defend, brake, derail, ride,* or *leave. Drivers* (discussed as structural leaders in Young 1991, p. 288) try to organize participation to produce an agreement that is consonant with their interests. *Conductors* also seek to produce an agreement but from a neutral position, with no interest axe of their own to grind. *Defenders* (termed brokers or entrepreneurs in Young 1989, p. 373) are single-issue players, concerned with incorporating a particular measure or position in the agreement rather than with the overall success of the negotiations. *Brakers* are the opposing or modifying resistance, brought into action by the progress being made on either the broad regime or on specific issue items. *Derailers* are out to destroy the regime, not merely soften or slow it down. *Riders* are filler, with no strong interests of their own and so available to act as followers. *Leavers* pursue an exit policy, either partially through individual exceptions and derogations, or wholly through withdrawal from the negotiations and the regime.

Conducting and *driving* are the strategies which best fit regime formation. These strategies depend on a procedural or substantive leader who agglomerates parties into agreement. While pursuing its own interests, each party is brought to play its own score in the right way to bring a harmonious result. The *conductor* could be a sovereign with its own interest-related agenda subordinated to getting a generally satisfactory agreement. But the multilateral conference nature of negotiations weigh in favor of a more disinterested leader to provide order to the proceedings. Thus many environmental and other regime conferences give a prominent role to a secretary general, conference chair, secretariat, or other organizing agency, as a key to the effective creation of integrative outcomes (Boyer 1996). States more often choose a *driver*'s over a *conductor*'s strategy, for many reasons: often, no state is powerful enough to be hegemonic, interests are usually defensive and partial rather than global, potential leaders are above all regional and interest group players and so is tainted. In this situation, the procedural *conductor* is actually welcome, since it allows parties to pursue their interests more effectively, facilitating agreement. The impact of a procedural or *conductor* role is important to recognize, since it underscores an effective alternative to the allegedly necessary role of a hegemon. All of these roles are available, to be used by various parties at various times, although a party's adoption of one role – *driver* or *conductor*, for example – colors the ability to shift to another later on.

Thus, the evolutionary process of which the negotiation is a part has a synchronic and diachronic dimension. The particular outcome represents the results of the encounter of the moment, but it is also a stage in the battle over the evolution of the regime, as it moves from encounter to encounter of parties and from constellation to constellation of power and interests. Rather than being a tabula rasa, the agenda is set by the condition of the regime at the time of negotiations, whether this refers to the initial pressing problem (where the unmanaged problem is the tabula) or to the later reconsiderations (where the flawed regime and its difficulties are the tabula). Thus, "where you go depends on where you're coming from" (see Munton and Castle 1992, and Cutler and Zacher 1992 in general). Their evolving nature makes regimes temporary, contested, unstable, and continuously expandable and perfectable rather than being overarching and deductive as a optimal formula should be in a negotiated agreement (Zartman and Berman 1982).

For those trying to move the process forward, instability is a vulnerable but creative characteristic of negotiations for an environmental regime; the temporary formula should be so constructed that it calls for its own improvement and moves the process along – one which "falls forward" as a temporary solution that, constructively, cannot last in its momentary form (Scapple 1996). However, for opponents, that same instability is an opportunity to capitalize on and impede, to renegotiate later for a looser agreement, or to use to fall backward toward less or different regulation. Thus, the regime formation process is anything but linear. It goes up and down from negotiation to negotiation, constellation to constellation, the dynamics – perhaps better, the kinetics – of the synchronic encounter determining the points that mark the diachronic evolution.

Thus, the evolution of the regime at any given point is a function of the systems maintenance (M), adjustment (A), cybernetic (C), and exogenous (E) factors.[40] Symbolically,

$$R = f(+M \pm A \pm C \pm E)$$

While the first factor works to maintain the regime, the other three factors can work in either direction, to strengthen or weaken it or to alter its direction, according to the conjuncture of power, interests and values of the parties in their recursive negotiations.

Obstacles to stability

Within the standard definition of negotiation as the process by which conflicting positions are combined to form a common decision, the negotiators seek to produce a *formula for agreement on the resolution of the problem*, which is then translated into acceptable implementing details (Zartman and Berman 1982). Multilateral decision-making is an exercise in managing complexity, since it is characterized by such a large number of interacting variables that there is no dominant pattern or dimension (Klir 1985). Parties entering a multilateral negotiation situation give a conceptual scan of the complexity, and then refine it into a cognitive model constructed out of the interrelated elements of simplification, structuring, and direction (Zartman 1994). Simplification means reducing the number of elements to the most important (which will vary by party interests, costs and benefits, and by situation), structuring means giving them some priority and relation to each other, and direction means moving these components toward an intended policy goal, usually located along a spectrum depending on whether a particular issue outcome or a general agreement is more important to the interests of the party. When to this characteristic complexity the element of uncertainty is added, regime evolution takes on an additional dimension of complexity that provides it with identifiable features and implications.

A formula has particular importance in regime building, especially when understood as a shared sense of justice or terms of trade (Young 1994; Brams and Taylor 1996; Zartman *et al.* 1996). A sense of rules, regulations, expectations and behaviors must rest on agreement on broad principles of fair allocation in the given issue area. The uncertainty of the problem and its costs, as well as of the costs of managing it, means that that agreement on relevant principles of justice is likely to be loose, contentious, tentative, and fluctuating. Yet the nature of the principle of justice is the basic subject of the formula, which in turn allows Homans' Maxim to be played out to the fullest, and Homans' Maxim is the key to any negotiation.

It is the absence of such consensus on the basic trade-off, for example, that has kept the meta-regime on environmental matters advanced at Rio in 1992 from making clear and unambiguous progress: whether environmental matters to be governed by a principle of compensation (for delayed development) or equity (for incurred investments) or equality among all parties is still an unresolved question, in regard both to the general environmental debate and to the various subregimes in formation (global warming, ozone depletion, desertification, among others) that derive from it.

The basic reason why regimes are ongoing negotiations and cannot resolve their problem of coordination once and for all is that the problem is characterized by ignorance and uncertainty. While any negotiated outcome involves contingent agreements to handle future events, regimes characteristically confront high levels of uncertainty about the nature and magnitude of the problem itself with which they are concerned. More than other multilateral negotiations, negotiations over regimes are rule-making exercises rather than one-time redistributions of tangible goods. Their main goal is to harmonize national legislation and establish rules for the ongoing allocation of costs and benefits against changes and challenges of undetermined nature and magnitude (Scharpf 1989, p. 12; Zartman 1994, p. 6). The parameters of the problem become clearer or take on new forms as time goes on, necessitating meetings of the parties from time to time to reconsider their previous decisions.

This uncertainty is not the frequently discussed "veil" which is said to favor fairness as a fallback solution (Rawls 1971). Whereas the veil of ignorance obscures preferences equally for competing options, the ignorance in regime decisions obscures the uncertainties of future costs and gains, but not the reality of present costs of problem-solving. The parties have to calculate the likely cost of engagements that they make, against the uncertainty of the costs of the problem they are seeking to alleviate. Against these costs are also calculated benefits, both from the status quo and from the possibly impending changes, although costs weigh more heavily in their calculations; as indicated in prospect theory, parties tend to be more risk averse concerning gains than losses and therefore future opportunities need to be very sure if they are to outweigh investments in the status quo (Farnham 1994). The fall-back solution is this case is conservative inaction or lowest-common-denominator compromises, rather than liberal fairness, making regime adjustment negotiations a slow, careful process (Brams and Kilgour 1999). In sum,

- Proposition 5: Recursive regime negotiations repeatedly pose the question of absolute costs under uncertainty ("Will we cost ourselves unnecessarily now and forever to forestall the uncertain threat of future costs?") rather than either on uncertainty of cooperation or on relative gains.

In considering these calculations, debates over relative gains or relative compliance as the key issue, which have taken on such importance in international relations literature, are misplaced. Of course, every absolute loss or gain has its relative or externally comparative dimensions, just as every relative gain or loss starts as an absolute (that is, an internally relative) increment; the standard terms are misleading. But states establishing policy on global warming or deep sea mining or human rights or pollution are concerned first and foremost with the costs for them of abatement and prevention to meet dangers and opportunities whose very existence is unproven, not with the comparison of their costs against someone else's or the chances of someone else's noncompliance. These latter two elements are of course not irrelevant or unrelated, but they are not the primary focus of policy-making. The primary concern is over absolute costs, or over absolute costs relative to one's own uncertain gains.

As a result of uncertainty, the problem of finding agreeable solutions is exacerbated, reinforcing the change in the nature of the problem. The question is not so much one of fearing defection from a salient solution but rather one of multiple equilibria, a problem common to both Prisoners' Dilemma and Battle of the Sexes Games in the game theoretic terms in which the regime debate is often couched (Hasenclever *et al.* 1997, pp. 104–13). Often these equilibria are not polar opposites but matters of degree, as in differences in constraints, quotas or restrictions, for example (Wolf 1997). But they reflect tenaciously held positions since parties' uncertainty over the need for or benefit from constraints increases their reluctance to undertake the costs necessary to adopt them. Since know-

ledge and other givens affecting cost calculations are continually changing, multilateral policymaking through negotiation needs to reoccur from
time to time.

The final reason why regimes are recursive negotiations with great difficulties in achieving stable, longterm formulas relates to its nature as a
normative construct. Just as regime-building rests on the coordination of
many states' interests and power under uncertainty, so it also depends on
the presence of supportive norms and coordinated expectations around
the world. The task is sizeable and elusive for several reasons. On one
hand, its very magnitude is a challenge. Bilateral or even regional negotiations have their problems in finding a normative base for the international contracts they create but their terrain of action extends to only a
few states; the problems in developing a consensus simultaneously in the
US, Canada and Mexico on the benefits of free trade and circulation as
the basis for implementing the North American Free Trade Association
(NAFTA) stand as an example. But global regimes must rest on a much
broader consensus involving nearly two hundred countries. Obviously the
importance of each country's contribution to that consensus will vary, just
as the power and interest of the parties will vary in its contribution to the
negotiations. But the magnitude of the quantity is of a different order
from smaller contracts, nonetheless.

On the other hand, norms are a circular matter in regime-building.
Regimes themselves are norms, principles and expectations, as well as
rules and regulations, as developed by Sjöstedt (2003). But they also rest
on an existing normative and expectational structure, just as they affect
that structure by their negotiation and implementation. If the regime
brings in new norms in conflict with pre-existing values and expectations,
it will require some education, debate, and publicity before it can begin to
be accepted and then implemented domestically, whatever the diplomats
may decide among themselves. The most striking example, on the
regional level, is the enormous campaign that accompanied the conver-
sions from national currencies to euros in the participating European
Union member states. An equally telling case is the education and change
of mentalities required for the notion of global warming and associated
remedial measures to take hold in the public consciousness as a basis for
acceptance and implementation of the Climate Change Convention and
its protocols. One-time (or even several-time) negotiation of new regime
norms is not sufficient when these norms and expectations clash with
existing verities.

To put it positively, the challenge to regime builders is to devise a
formula that will resolve their problem of coordinating their efforts to
handle a threatening danger of uncertain costs and magnitude, in such a
way that possible (but unforeseeable) future changes in their interests and
relative power and in the nature of the danger remain satisfied by the
formula, and a concordance is established between ambient norms and

expectations and those contained in the regime. While flexibility would appear to be the answer, the appearance is deceiving. On one side, over-flexibility too frequently is the result of an inability to agree on effective precision, leaving a weak regime that does not solve the initial problem. On the other hand, while flexibility is appropriate, it has to be flexibility in the right direction, re-posing the problem of uncertainty and change. In other words, getting it done requires getting it right. Thus,

- Proposition 6: The stability of a regime is a function of the degree of certainty of information about the transaction problem, the degree of divergence of the participating states' interests, and the degree of harmony of current norms and expectations.

The greater the capacity of a regime's negotiated formula to resolve the transaction problem, to meet participating states' interests, to fit current norms and establish coherent expectations, and so to overcome opposition to it, the more stable the regime. The inherently fluid nature of problems, power, interests, norms and expectations involved in international regimes makes such stability rare, necessitating repeated (recursive) negotiations to stabilize the formula that meets these criteria.

Two types of processes are involved in the multilateral negotiation of regimes, *coalition* and *consensuation*. Coalition is the more usual way of thinking about multilateral negotiation, relating to both parties and to issues. Coalition among many parties is often used as the theme for analyzing multilateral negotiation (Olson 1965; Snidal 1985; Lax and Sebenius 1991; Dupont 1994; Hampson 1995) and gives rise to limited number of strategies. Parties seek either to aggregate other groups and parties into a growing winning coalition, or to divide opposing groups into smaller parts so as to absorb or merely to weaken them, or to confront other groups to defeat them or work out a deal with them. Although coalitions are usually conceived of as international groupings of states, trans-national cooperation across states is a growing characteristic of multilateral negotiation. Transnational coalitions of scientists, technologists, and business constitute one type of coalition who mobilize their pluralistic resources – knowledge, skill, and money – to either raise the consciousness or strike an interest deal with political leaders accountable to constituent groups.

But coalitions can be made among issues as well, in order to reduce their complexity and make them manageable for agreement. Issue coalitions have their own tactics. Fractioning, packaging, linkages and trade-offs – the basic devices of the negotiation process – are all ways of making coalitions among issues, interests and positions. Two categories of trade-offs are available. One is the standard notion of substantive exchanges, where one party's concession on one item is traded for another's concession on another item, including new items not previously on the agenda used as side-payments. The move from the Tokyo to the Uruguay round of negotiations within the General

Agreement on Tariffs and Trade (GATT) involved bringing into the GATT regime new issues that had previously been excluded and that allowed for the basic trade-off of the Uruguay Round (Winham 1986, 2002). Trade-offs can also be made within with same item, by trading breadth for depth in regulation. Many are the cases where a regime began with a relatively strict coverage of a relatively small number of items, often achieved through a small number of steep steps, and was later expanded to cover a larger number of items. The opposite approach is a relatively broad coverage through loose restrictions or gentle steps. Each has its problems that require recursive negotiations to deal with: the first can lead to incoherence and imperceptible results, whereas the second invites generalized resistance and tends to "fall backward," to less effectiveness.

Other trade-offs are procedural, buying agreement with special treatment, through such devices as exceptions and inducements. By providing exceptions to the agreement, a principle can be established but its effectiveness temporarily weakened. Later, the incipient regime can be consolidated by negotiating away the exceptions, possibly against other trade-offs in new circumstances. Or, as the reverse of the exception, restrictions can be traded for inducements, which are then tapered off as compliance proceeds on its own and becomes it own inducement. Many environmental negotiations have turned to compensation as a way of establishing trade-offs across the North–South divide. Indeed, the entire structure of UNCED is based on a massive trade-off designed to bridge the North–South gap between environment and development. Compensation can provide an immediate transfer of resources but has an air of bribery; it must be so structured that individual parties are not able to enjoy its benefits as a public good while opting out of it of its obligations.

The other type of negotiation process is consensuation, where the limits of the parties' positions is ascertained beforehand and then a proposal tabled which falls within those limits and achieves acceptance without bargaining. Consensus is the largest coalition, a coalition of the whole that is characteristic of multilateral negotiation, and it is based on a decision rule under which, essentially, abstention is an affirmative rather than a negative vote. (There may be some fora and occasions where votes can be taken and smaller coalitions win, but these are exceptional and generally operate within a broader context of consensus). Multilateral agreements are arrived at by consensus when a coalition formed by a significant but unspecified number of parties is in favor and the rest do not oppose. Parties not in agreement can abstain without blocking the outcome, and parties opposing can be left out as long as their number does not become significant. Strategies of incremental participation and agreement then become possible (Zartman 1987, chapter 10). At the same time, the significant number requirement means that lowest common denominator (LCD) agreements without teeth are common (cf. Brams 1999).

Dynamic stability and evaluation[41]

This chapter has yielded and developed a number of propositions, working hypothesis which should be useful in guiding research into new angles on regimes, leading to a better understanding of the phenomenon. These propositions are not causal hypotheses. In part, that development needs to follow from further research, but in part, the propositions indicate a process that does not lend itself easily to causal modeling. The evolution of regimes through multilateral negotiation will course along over time, stayed and deflected by the changing effects of surface, benthic and exogenous pressures and events. The effects that such influences will have on the basic uncertainty of the problem and on the cost calculations of the parties are unpredictable, but, more seriously, the parameters for analysis under varying situations remain to be identified.

But the discussions have shown that negotiations make a difference, and that regime analysis without taking that fact into account is at best incomplete and at most misoriented. How do they make a difference? In continually (or recursively) providing an alternative to compliance or withdrawal by giving an opportunity to adjust the course of the regime. It is in not taking account of the third alternative that analyses of compliance distort the reality of choices available to practitioners of regimes,[42] and they have done so by arguing only over whether regimes matter to states without asking whether states matter to regimes. Ikle's (1964) work at the foundation of negotiation analysis made the fundamental observation that negotiation is a threefold choice between acceptance, rejection, or improvement, equivalent in regard to regimes to compliance, withdrawal, and negotiation. Hirshman (1970) has shown that voice is one of the three situational responses of an actor along with exit (withdrawal) and loyalty (compliance). Negotiation matters because it enables the parties to avoid the stark choice between compliance and withdrawal by engaging in recursive negotiations to adjust the efforts to solve the initial or evolving problem and to enter into those problem-solving efforts the feedback from domestic reactions.

How then can regime-building be evaluated, if it is a fluid and ongoing process? And how can regimes stabilize expectations if they are constantly renegotiated (Hasenclever *et al.* 1997, p. 185)? In all the terms of this discussion there is a certain dynamic, a teleology, but less than that which infused the notion of integration. It assumes three dimensions, that regimes move back and forward according to the power and interest constellations of the moment, that they reverberate up and down in tying local to national and global effects, and that they spread "sideways" to meet to a felt need for order in a given issue area. Together, they produce the dynamic stability discussed previously, whereby a regime meets the needs for which it was created by growing to the maximum relevant membership and by eliminating the conflict and disharmony in the concerned issue area. Thus, it is not necessarily by greater and greater regulation, or more and more members, or even tighter and tighter regulations, or – above all – by more and more complex institutionalization, that the success or evolution of the regime can be judged, but by its coverage and harmonization of its chosen subject. Regime formation – as, in turn, the negotiations which punctuate it – is above all a conflict management device and, as such, a collective security engagement.

It is against these two components that its effectiveness and evolution must be judged. On one hand, the regime should aim to include all the parties to the conflict (as in a collective security agreement) rather than (as in a collective defense agreement) pitting itself against some relevant but excluded parties. At one stage, it could be judged positively if it included most of the relevant members, even at the cost of exceptions from the full coverage of the agreement; later, it would have to be judged according to its effective coverage and the removal of those exceptions. The same phased progress would have to be used to evaluate compensation and other inducements. On the other hand, it should aim to solving the initial problem, eliminating transactional conflict among the parties and between the parties and the regime goals. This includes providing ways of continuing to manage and eliminate new instances of conflict in the issue area that appear in the future and providing supports for the conflict management system – setting standards, monitoring practices, gathering information. It is the nature of the issue or regulated activity that is the measure of success, not some external criterion, and that measure may actually vary as time goes on, rather than requiring an ever more integrated response.

If this is close to notions of regime resiliency (Powell 1994), it steps back from that criterion by recognizing that robustness or staying power comes not from the reified regime itself but from the continuing efforts of committed parties to keep the regime resilient. Regimes are not quite in permanent flux (Kratochwil 1989; Neufeld 1993); they are in frequent challenge and periodic adjustment, like any other norms. They keep "strong" by their adherents' beating back challenges and they change when challenge becomes overwhelming. That change may come by their being discarded, in times of issue realignment, but it more frequently comes from regime readjustment. This is the process this study identifies.

14 Ripeness revisited

The push and pull of conflict management[43]

Ripeness theory is intended to explain why, and therefore when, parties to a conflict are susceptible to their own or others' efforts to turn the conflict toward resolution through negotiation. The concept of a ripe moment centers on the parties' perception of a Mutually Hurting Stalemate (MHS) and a Way Out. The MHS provides the push to begin negotiations; the Way Out provides the pull into a negotiated solution. Once negotiations have begun, the pressure of the MHS needs to be maintained and the Way Out transformed by the parties into a resolving formula that provides a Mutually Enticing Opportunity (MEO) for agreement.

The push and pull of ripeness

The MHS is optimally associated with an impending or recently avoided catastrophe as the necessary but insufficient condition for negotiation to begin (Zartman and Berman 1982, pp. 66–78; Touval 1982; Zartman 1983, 1989, 2000; Touval and Zartman 1989; Hopmann 1996). When the parties find themselves locked in a conflict from which they cannot escalate to victory and this deadlock is painful to both of them (although not necessarily in equal degree or for the same reasons), they tend to seek a Way Out. A recent or impending catastrophe can provide a deadline or sharply increased pain. In different images, the stalemate has been termed the Plateau, a flat and unending terrain without relief, and the catastrophe the Precipice, the point where things suddenly and predictably get worse. If the notion of mutual blockage is too static, the concept may be stated dynamically as a moment when the upper hand slips and the lower hand rises, both parties moving toward equality, with both movements resulting in pain for the parties.

The basic reasoning underlying the mutually hurting stalemate lies in cost-benefit analysis, based on the assumption that when parties find themselves on a pain-producing path, they prepare to look for an alternative that is more advantageous. This calculation is fully consistent with public choice notions of rationality (Arrow 1963, Olson 1965, Sen 1970) and public choice studies of negotiation (Brams 1990, 1994, Brams and

Taylor 1996) which assume that a party will pick the alternative which it prefers and that a decision to change is induced by making less preferential the present (conflictual) course. In game theoretical terms, it marks the transformation of the situation in the parties' perception from a Prisoners' Dilemma Game (PDG) into a Chicken Dilemma Game (CDG) (Brams 1985; Goldstein 2007). It is also consistent with prospect theory, currently in focus in international relations, which indicates that people tend to be more risk averse concerning gains than losses of equal magnitude and therefore that sunk costs or investments in conflict escalation tend to push parties into costly deadlocks or mutually hurting stalemates (Kahneman and Tversky 1979; Bazerman *et al.* 1985; Stein and Pauly 1993; Mitchell 1995; Farnham 1994; McDermott 2007).

The other element necessary for a ripe moment is the perception of a Way Out. Parties have to sense that a negotiated solution, but not necessarily a specific outcome, is possible for the searching and that the other party shares that sense and the willingness to search too. Without a sense of a Way Out, the push associated with the MHS would leave the parties with nowhere to go. Leaders often indicate whether they do or do not feel that a deal can be made with the other side, particularly when there is a change in that judgment. The sense that the other party is ready and willing to repay concessions with concessions is termed requitement (Zartman and Aurik 1991). This element is also necessary (but, alone, insufficient), since without a sense of the possibility of a negotiated exit from the MHS, fruitful negotiations cannot take off.

These components of the ripe moment contain both objective and subjective elements. The MHS and WO are both necessarily perceptual events, not ones that stand alone in objective reality; they can be created if outside parties can cultivate the perceptions of a painful present and a preferable alternative, and therefore can be resisted so long as the party in question refuses or is otherwise able to block out those perceptions. Natural resistant reactions, as well as cultural barriers, can inhibit autonomous subjective recognitions. As with any other subjective perception, there are likely to be objective referents or bases to be perceived. These too can be highlighted or created by a mediator or an opposing party when they do not yet exist or are not immediately recognized by the parties themselves. But it is the perception of the objective condition, not the condition itself, that makes for a MHS and a Way Out. If the parties do not recognize "clear evidence" (in someone else's view) that they are in an impasse, a MHS has not (yet) occurred, and if they do perceive themselves to be in such a situation, no matter how flimsy the "evidence," the MHS is present.

Like the MHS, the WO – and the MEO that it can turn into – is a figment of perception, a subjective appreciation of objective elements, but unlike the MHS, it is an invention of the parties (and their mediator) internal to the negotiation process, not a result of an objective external situation. It must be produced by the parties, using their analysis of the conflict and its causes, their appreciation of their interests and needs, and their creativity in crafting a mutually attractive solution. It resolves the conflict, but among the several formulas for agreement that may do so, it is perceived to contain elements that continue to carry the resolution process into the future. A negotiated end to a conflict contains forward-looking provisions to deal with the basic dispute, with unresolved leftovers of the conflict and its possible reemergence, and with new relations of interdependence between the conflicting parties.

Since the MHS and Way Out are subjective matters, they can be perceived at any point in the conflict, early or late. Nothing in their definition requires them to take place at the height of the conflict or at a high level of violence. The internal (and unmediated) negotiations in South Africa between 1990 and 1994 stand out as a striking case of negotiations opened (and pursued) on the basis of an MHS perceived by both sides on the basis of impending catastrophe, not of present casualties (Ohlson and Stedman 1994; Sisk 1995; Zartman 1995b; Lieberfield 1999a, 1999b). Nonetheless, the greater the objective evidence, the greater the subjective perception of the stalemate and its pain is likely to be, and this evidence is more likely to come late, when all other courses of action and possibilities of escalation have been exhausted. In notable cases, a long period of conflict is required before the MHS sinks in, whereas few if any studies have been made of early settlements and the role of long-range calculations. However, given the infinite number of potential conflicts which have not reached "the heights," evidence would suggest that perception of an MHS occurs either at a low level of conflict, where it is relatively easy to begin problem-solving in most cases, or, in salient cases, at rather high levels of conflict, a distinction that could be the subject of broad research (Zartman 2005). In any case, as suggested, conflicts not treated "early" appear to require a high level of intensity for an MHS perception to kick in and negotiations toward a solution to begin.

As the notion of ripeness implies, ripeness can be a very fleeting opportunity, a moment to be seized lest it pass, or it can be of a long duration, waiting to be noticed and acted upon by mediators. In fact, failure to seize the moment often hastens its passing, as parties lose faith in the possibility of a negotiated resolving formula or regain hope in the possibility of unilateral escalation. By the same token, the possibility of long duration often dulls the urgency of rapid seizure. Behind the duration of the ripe moment itself is the process of producing it through escalation and decision. The impact of incremental compared with massive escalation (Zartman and Aurik 1991; Mitchell 1995; Zartman and Faure 2005), and the internal process of converting members impervious to pain (hawks) into "pain perceivers" (doves) (Mitchell 1995; Stedman 2000) are further examples of research questions opened by the concept of ripeness.

It is useful to spell out the negotiation process before further developing the conceptual components. It is generally accepted that after their pre-negotiation or diagnosis phase, negotiations proceed to elaborate a formula and its details – a common understanding of the conflict/ problem and its solution, a common sense of justice, and/or a set of terms of trade (Zartman 1978; Zartman and Berman 1982; Hopmann 1998). The formula can take one of two forms: a minimal agreeing formula to end or lessen conflict violence, or a resolving formula to address the conflict itself (with much grey area in the real world between the two types). An agreeing formula is a conflict management measure, the minimum on which the parties can agree, a ceasefire to end or suspend the violence, but not a resolution of the conflict. A resolving formula is a conflict resolution agreement, dealing with the issues of the conflict, an enticing opportunity that the parties perceive as a way out of their problem. There can be several potentially resolving formulas (just as negotiation is made up of a number of competing formulas in general), each objectively identifiable as a fair solution; only one of them, at any moment, constitutes an MEO attractive enough to the parties interests to pull them into an ongoing process of eliminating the causes and resurgence of the conflict. Although MEO might be considered "just another name" for an adopted resolving formula, the name emphasizes the pull factor and its components so necessary to completing negotiations, in contrast to the push effect necessary to starting them.

The enticement and attraction of resolution

Given its nature, there are intriguing problems raised by ripeness theory. One, among many, is its dependence on conflict. Odd and banal as that may sound, its implications are sobering. It means, on one hand, that pre-emptive conflict resolution and preventive diplomacy are unpromising, since ripeness is hard to achieve so far ahead. On the other hand, it means that to ripen a conflict one must raise the level of conflict until the stalemate is reached and then further until it begins to hurt – and even then, work toward a perception of an impending catastrophe as well. The ripe moment becomes the godchild of brinkmanship.

Another limitation to the theory – seemingly unrelated to the above – is that it only addresses the opening of negotiations, as noted at the outset and often missed by the critics. Now that the theory of ripeness is available to explain the initiation of negotiation, people would like to see a theory that explains the successful conclusion of negotiations once opened. Can ripeness be extended in some way to cover the entire process, or does successful conclusion of negotiations require a different explanatory logic?

Practitioners and students of conflict management would like to think that there could be a more positive prelude to negotiation, without the push of a mutually Hurting Stalemate but through the pull of an attractive outcome; or, in other words, the replacement of a Hurting Stalemate by the Enticing Opportunity and hence the distinction between two types of ripeness, one "negative" and one "positive." But the positive mechanisms are still unclear, in part because the cases are so few. At best, positive occasions might provide an opportunity for improvement, but from a tiring rather than a painful deadlock (Mitchell 1995; Zartman 1995c). In some views, the attraction lies in a newly discovered possibility either of sharing power or of winning (paradoxically, a sahred perception) more cheaply than through conflict (Bueno de Mesquita and Lalman 1992; Mitchell 1995; Mason *et al.* 1999). In other views, enticement comes in the form of a new ingredient provided by a persistent mediator, and that new ingredient is the chance for improved relations with the mediating third party itself (Touval and Zartman 1989). Such openings might be seen as an expansion of the other component of ripeness, the Way Out, but the fact is that they do not seem to pay a major or frequent role in the ripening of conflict and initiation of negotiations.

But MEO is important in the broader negotiation process and has its place in extending ripeness theory into the agreement and post-agreement phases. As indicated, ripeness theory refers to the decision to negotiate; it is not self-implementing and does not guarantee results. At most it can be extended into the negotiations themselves by recognizing that the perception of ripeness has to continue during the process if the parties are not to reevaluate their positions and drop out, in the revived hopes of being able to find a unilateral solution through escalation. But negotiations completed under the shadow – or the pressure – of an MHS alone are likely to be unstable and unlikely to lead to a more enduring settlement; they will represent only an attempt to cut the costs of conflict, get the bug off the back of the parties, arrive at an agreeing formula for a ceasefire, and then stop, unmotivated to move on to a search for resolution, to get the bear off the parties' backs. The agreement is likely to break down as soon as one or both parties think they can break the stalemate, as the 1973–5 evolution of the situation in Vietnam or the 1984 Lusaka agreement in southern Africa, among others, illustrate (Zartman 1978, 1995d). A negative shadow can begin the process, but not provide for the change of calculations and mentalities to reconciliation. As Ohlson (1998) and Pruitt and Olczak (1995) have pointed out, that is the function of the MEO.

An MEO is a resolving formula that is seen by the parties as meeting their needs and interests better than the status quo. While MHS is the necessary if insufficient condition for negotiations to begin, during the process the negotiators must provide the prospects for a more attractive future to pull themselves out of their negotiations into an agreement to end the conflict. The push factor has to be accompanied by a pull factor, in the form of a formula for resolution and a prospect of transformation that the negotiating parties design during negotiations. Here the substantive aspect of the negotiation pulls ahead of the procedural element: the

Way Out or Enticing Opportunity takes over from the Hurting Stalemate in producing movement. The seeds of the pull factor begin with the Way Out that the parties vaguely perceive as part of the initial ripeness, but this general sense of possibility needs to be developed and fleshed out to be the vehicle for an agreement. Thus, the perception of an MEO is a necessary, but not sufficient, condition for the continuation of negotiations beyond simple agreement to a successful conclusion of the conflict.

Characterizing the MEO in terms of resolution, needs, interests and status quo provides an unavoidably soft, judgmental and conclusionary definition. In this, it is much like many definitions in social science; the standard behavioral definition of power – the ability to move another party in an intended direction (Tawney 1931; Simon 1952; Thibaut and Kelley 1959) – is also conclusionary, and tautological to boot. Its value lies, not in its predictability, but in the fact that it identifies the necessary elements that explain the adoption of an MEO and lead the negotiator and mediator to the necessary elements to achieve in negotiation.

In establishing the terms of trade that constitute a resolving formula, the rebels make *demands*, procedural and substantive, and they *supply* armed conflict, the insertion of violence into the country's politics; in their negotiations, they trade off the abstention from violence against the obtention of satisfactions to their two types of demands. Violence is the only money of exchange that they have, and its cessation is the major demand of the government side. The government may have additional lesser demands, ranging from the rebels' recognition of government primacy to simple disappearance of the rebels, but these are generally ancillary to the demand for the end of violence.

The demand side of the rebellion has its procedural and substantive aspects, procedural because the rebels no longer trust the procedures of government and substantive because they are moved to rebellion by substantive grievances. Parties demand procedural solutions when they have lost faith in someone else's ability to make the necessary substantive corrections; that is, they demand a share – possibly even a total "share" – in governing power when they no longer trust others to use power to deal with their particular needs. Negotiations themselves are the first step in this power-sharing, for they grant recognition to the rebel party and give it voice and legitimacy.

On the substantive side to the rebels' demands are the grievances that began the conflict. While it is too late for the resolution of grievances alone to end it, there must be attention to them in the resolving formula for it to constitute an MEO. It is not enough to leave the resolution of issue to the procedural mechanisms of power-sharing; the problems need to be addressed in their substance. It is impossible to make generalizations about the ways of handling such problems, since they are idiosyncratic to the individual conflicts. Often, however, they too relate back to equal or compensatory treatment of identity groups in society that the rebels represent, whether these groups be ethnic, religious, national, or class. This need in turn reinforces the need for continued recognition of the rebels after the conflict is over and their involvement in the procedures of power.

Thus, a resolving formula involves a trade-off between the rebels' violence and the government's concessions to their procedural and substantive demands. The details of the agreement, that is, how much violence is needed to buy how many concessions, are obviously as idiosyncratic and manipulable an equation as any bargain about prices. It is however unlikely that the rebels renounce their supply of violence, laying down their arms, without gaining any concessions in return. Equally variable is the balance between procedural and substantive demands. At one extreme is total government accession to procedural demands, making substantive concessions unnecessary and leaving grievances to be handled by the new rulers, to the elimination of the current government; at the other extreme would be concentration on grievances but leaving no share in power for the rebels. Both are unlikely to constitute a resolving formula in negotiations to end internal violent conflict.

Whether a particular resolving formula is enticing to the parties or not is for them to perceive and decide; the best an external analyst or practitioner can say is whether the formula fits the past and future extensions of the conflict, that is, whether the parties "should" see their interest in taking it, but not whether they will. A resolving formula is the objectively necessary, if insufficient, condition for durable agreements; subjectively, the parties need to see it as such for it to constitute an opportunity that will pull them out of the conflict and into new, positive relations. While external parties can do much to create a resolving formula and bring the parties to accept it, the durability of the outcome is ultimately in the hands of the parties themselves, as it should be.

But there are some guidelines for evaluating how much any particular resolving formula will be seen as an enticing opportunity. In judging the attractiveness of any posited formula, or in proposing one, conflicting parties compare the value of the proposed solution to two other images: their own needs and interests, and the value of the status quo (their security point or reservation price) (Raiffa *et al.* 2002). The first relates to the way the parties define their conflict, their goals and interests in it, and their expectations of an attainable solution, now or later. These elements form a composite package, rigid on the outside but malleable in its components. The core elements are the parties' needs and interests, less manipulable than their definition of the conflict and their estimations of attainable solution. When parties can tailor their goals and estimations to fit attainable objectives, while maintaining their sense of their needs and interests, an MEO can be possible.

The second is the payoff from continued conflict, either as active violence, as a hurting stalemate, or simply as a non-solution, often in the form of a soft, stable, self-serving stalemate ("S^5 Situation"). Unless a non-solution is actually painful, it may constitute a viable situation that leaves the future open, creates no pressure for a search for a solution, and requires no risky decision. The decision to seize a negotiating opportunity and turn it into a search for a solution depends not merely on a judgment of how well that or any solution meets the parties' needs and interests or objectively resolves the conflict, but how its uncertainty compares with the better known value of the status quo. Thus, the value of the status quo can serve as an effective pressure point for mediators. Spoilers, on the other hand, are those for whom nothing except winning is better than the status quo, and whose only demand is power, with no program for handling substantive grievances. These calculations will be determinant in deciding whether any resolving formula will or can constitute an MEO.

The process and outcome of negotiation

The analytical question then becomes: how are MEOs achieved? How is the search for a resolving formula conducted, where do their ingredients come from, when do they appear in the negotiating process? What is the relation between an agreeing formula for a ceasefire and a resolving formula for a solution to the conflict? How are the parties kept on track to a solution, how is the perception of an MHS itself maintained throughout the negotiations? What turns conflicting positions into joint formulas for agreement? How does a particular resolving formula become an enticing opportunity for the parties? To answer these questions, one must get inside the negotiation processes.

To constitute a resolving formula that in turn becomes an MEO, the agreement must meet both procedural and substantive demands, in exchange for an end to violence. The reason why violence is so high is that it has a lot to buy. Violence is not only a money of exchange, however; it is also a measure of strength of the parties, in the absence of other measures. This is why the initiating MHS is so important, for it establishes the equality of the parties that is so helpful to negotiations.

The most frequent feature in resolving formulas concerns future procedural political mechanisms for determining parties' strength, as a replacement for combat as a test of strength. Three such mechanisms are prominent: elections, power-sharing and power-dividing (autonomy, federalism, etc). Elections carry the higher risk and delay, and demand a high degree of confidence in the mechanism and trust in the fairness of the outcome. Executive power-sharing gives immediate payoffs, to be verified later with elections, and is the most prevalent procedural mechanism in MEOs). Legislative power-sharing (constitutional provisions for reserved seats, weighted majorities, vetoes, etc) are longer term and less risky, but may have finite limits. Both mechanisms are conflict management solutions, not resolving the conflict but turning it from violent to political means of pursuit. As a result, there is a built-in impediment to the cooperation that full resolution would require: power-sharing means back-stabbing and governmental paralysis; power-division carry the hidden threat of the outright secession that it was supposed to prevent; and elections mean wariness, if not distrust, of the mechanism and a tendency to confuse results with procedures as a test of freeness and failures. The power-sharing institutions of Lebanon produced a collapsed state; different forms of autonomy in Macedonia and Sudan are not trusted by the government; and Savimbi, among others, did not consider the elections free and fair unless he won.

All three methods provide continuing existence for the rebels. Plenty of literature has underscored the rebels' need for standing (as well as the government's difficulty in according it), to the point where it might be thought that standing is enough (Zartman 1995c, pp. 10, 339). Rebels need the recognition that negotiation brings, but they also need iron-clad assurances of continuing existence and recognition once the combat is terminated. Formulas that dissolve the rebels into the current political and military structures deny the basic need of the rebels and are non-starters. Before the conflict, the grievances were disembodied issues; afterward, they are incarnate in a rebel organization that has fought hard for recognition.

The vulnerability gap between ceasefire and full integration into the power structures of the state, when rebel disarmament leaves them open to attacks from the government forces, has been identified as a crucial moment in peace agreement implementation requiring external guarantors to fill the gap (Walter 2001). Resolving formulas can also help fill this gap by incorporating immediate power-sharing and power-dividing in their provisions, so that the rebels are already placed in positions of authority, particularly over the newly integrated armed forces. Obviously it is difficult to distinguish between guarantees of future involvement and return to past combat, since both are assured by continuing existence of rebel forces. But it is, after all, the possibility of revived combat that keeps the implementation process on track, just as it was the presence of armed rebellion that brought the conflict to negotiation in the first place. It is the potential for renewed hostilities that keeps the MHS current and the peace process honest.

Power-sharing, however, means sharing power, not monopolizing it. Parties, government or rebellion, that demand total power are most likely playing a spoiler role and are not open to compromise (Stedman 2000; Zahar 2003). Total victory is a matter for war, not negotiation, and a spoiler is a party who confuses the two. Procedural aspects of the rebels' demands, however, are not all the rebellion is about; if they are, the rebels (or rebel leader) is also headed for a spoiler role, looking for Time at the Trough rather than a reform of the political system. Time at the Trough and loot-seeking are greed-based rebellions and need different strategies for handling than need- or creed-based rebellion (Berdal and Malone 2000; Ballentine and Sherman 2003; Arnson and Zartman 2005).

Resolving formulas have to provide ways of dealing with substantive problems as well, as the other part of the problem-solving side of the formula. Despite the fact that grievances vary from case to case, several features are suggested by the cases. One is that grievances accumulate as the conflict goes on, quite the opposite of the frequent claim that the conflict simplifies and clarifies the options. As the parties escalate their combat, they compound grievances and add new layers of problems to be resolved, making resolution more and more difficult and complex. The shari'a issue in Sudan, Turkish army occupation and settler implantation in Cyprus, and language enclaves in Macedonia and Sri Lanka all appeared and became salient as the conflict worsened without resolution. The methods of violence themselves make atrocities, reprisals and resentment a further grievance to add to those that require and resist reconciliation and resolution from the beginning, as the longstanding conflicts in Sri Lanka, Liberia, Sierra Leone, Sudan, Angola and Mozambique show.

Full structural solutions tend to be necessitated by a long conflict, whereas more manageable and specific grievances would have sufficed earlier. Economic restructuring, state rebuilding, aid packages, and complex DDRRR programs became necessary parts of an MEO in long-running conflict cases. While specific grievances lie at the root of the conflict, they are no longer sufficient basis for resolution once the conflict has turned violent. Not only are procedural remedies required; so also are broad structural substantive measures.

The other side of the terms of trade that compose a resolving formula is constituted by the violence of the rebellion itself. Resolving formulas without exception involve the cession of hostilities in exchange for a role in power and resolution of grievances. Hostilities are the only money rebellions have, and they are not going to give it up until they have bought the concessions they need. Temporary and unilateral truces may be offered in the process, to show the other side how pleasant peace can be, but it is usually necessary to return to combat a few times to keep the process moving, to show how compelling war can be. Ceasefires will not be granted on mere faith, and will be part of the concluding elements of the bargain. In this lies a significant difference between interstate and intrastate conflicts. Violence is the life of the rebellion, whereas states in conflict have an existence – and a legitimate existence – independent of the conflict. States can makes truces without endangering their existence; rebellions are more vulnerable. But so are the governments they fight; for a state to make a ceasefire with its internal rebellion would be to grant it recognition and legitimacy without receiving anything in exchange, since the ceasefire is only a temporary suspension of its term of trade.

Thus, arrival at an enticing and resolving formula depends on keeping alive the supply side of the rebels' terms of trade – the conflict violence –

until the demand side is firmly in place. The rebels' supply side is already limited by the characteristic MHS; if they were not stalemated they would simply continue the war, ultimately to the point of eliminating the government side, as they threatened to do in Costa Rica in 1948 and as they have done in Angola, Liberia, Sudan, Sierra Leone, Sri Lanka and Lebanon. The current literature on uncertainty in decisions to use violence thus fits directly into ripeness theory. The rebels' challenge is to keep the element of violence alive throughout the negotiations in sufficient quantity to buy the required concessions on the demand side. As in any bargaining problem, the agreement is determined by the intersection of supply and demand, so the supply of at least potential violence must be raised to cover the demands, or the demands must be lowered to correspond to the available threats of violence. It is therefore most likely that the rebels brandish a little violence from time to time, to keep their "supply side" credible. For the most part, however, the supply of violence is latent and contingent (as is the other side's supply of concessions, as in any negotiation, until the deal is closed), as a threat to be used if negotiations break down (Schelling 1960).

Therefore negotiations, and especially mediation, work on both sides of the equation, keeping the supply of violence under control and seeking to tailor demands to meet the amount of concessions acceptable to the other side. As in any negotiation, there is no telling where the lines will cross; parties and mediators alike make their estimates of the firmness and softness of demands and supplies on either side (Bueno de Mesquita and Lalman 1992; Mason *et al.* 1999 (note 15); Raiffa *et al.* 2002). If the mediators can show how continued or renewed violence would lose a party international respect and support, the violence can be kept at the threat level in case of failure rather than at the actual level during negotiations. If parties start out with already less than total demands as initial positions – total replacement of the government, total disbanding of the rebels, secession and independence, total state unity and integration – it is easier to effectuate further softening than if demands are absolute, as the Macedonian and South African cases illustrate (Stedman 2000).

This challenge is generally beyond the grasp of mere bargaining or concession-convergence behavior, zero-sum reductions of demands on a single item until a mid-point agreement is reached. Of the three types of negotiation – *concession, compensation, construction*, it takes at least compensation, the introduction of additional items of trade, and the construction and reframing of issues meet both sides' needs to produce the positive-sum outcome that constitutes an MEO. As usual, in line with prospect theory (Farnham 1994), threats of losses work better than inducements, as the cases unfortunately show. Where development was part of the original formula, even though unattained, it may be used as an enticing prospect since dropping it would mean a loss, but in general aid packages and other inducements come into the negotiations only in adjunct with negative pressures and are not as widely used or effective as sanctions (including their threat). The tension between the effectiveness of implied losses and the need for positive compensations and constructions to produce an MEO underscores the narrow field of play open to those who would prepare an attractive resolving formula, and deserves further investigation.

If the ingredients of a resolving formula and an MEO and the process by which they are obtained are identified, why were they not achieved in cases of failure? A quick review of cases show both internal and external reasons that are evident only when the process itself is examined.

1   Inside the failed process, the rebels (and sometimes the governments) were spoilers, interested only in winning but unable to escalate to victory. But the government could not escalate to victory either, until the end when it eliminated the spoiler leader and made a negotiated settlement possible. The classic illustrations are Savimbi in Angola and Foday Sankoh and his lieutenants in Sierra Leone.

2   Spoilers or not, in failed negotiations, parties preferred the status quo to any resolving formula, even when an objectively good and fair one was offered. For them, the status quo of conflict was always preferable to the terms offered or conceivable, and the stalemate in which they found themselves was an S^5 situation, without any pain that they could not absorb. No MHS was present to bring the parties to negotiations or, once in negotiations, to give a full consideration to the formulas offered. In Angola, Mozambique, Sudan, El Salvador, Lebanon, Macedonia and Costa Rica, comfort in the status quo led one or both parties to reject the formula that they eventually accepted to end the conflict; in most – perhaps all – cases this perception was not one of eventual victory but simply the ability to endure continuing conflict in preference to the terms offered. Even before they could get to the delicate details, objectively good and fair formulas for resolution, such as federation/autonomy in Cyprus (offered in 2004), Karabagh (mooted on occasion), Sudan (tried in 1973–83) and Sri Lanka (negotiated in 2003), and institutional reforms in Lebanon (discussed since 1975), were rejected by the parties in favor of continued conflict that did not hurt the leadership too badly (although it hurt the population mightily). In addition, in many of these cases, external support kept the status quo alive, enabling the hold-outs to continue the conflict and not feel the pain in doing so.

3   An entirely different element that prevented perception of a resolving formula, let alone an MEO, was the absence of a coherent organization with a sense of goals and an ability to achieve consensus and make decisions about them within the parties. This problem took several related forms. In some cases, a party was merely a congeries of bandits and marauders with no clear idea of their political goals and

no central organization to pursue them. Mozambique and Macedonia present good cases: ReNaMo's party congress, not possible before 1990, and the FLN's 4 Points and Privzen Declaration (actually mediated by the US) were crucial to their ability actually to negotiate at all. In Liberia, Lebanon, Sudan and Sierra Leone, the closer negotiations got to an agreement, the more they posed a challenge to individual leaders to break away from the main group, form their own organizations, and sprint to capture a piece of the goal on their own. Similarly, the governments in Costa Rica, Sri Lanka and Lebanon were often so weak and fractioned that they could not perceive and seize an enticing opportunity.

4   Finally, external to the parties, the mediation efforts were often insufficient. Mediators lacked persistence, were satisfied (and exhausted) with superficial agreements and merely agreeing formulas, neglected substantive demands and failed to pursue procedural details, and were loath to provide incentives and sanctions to keep the parties on track, make the status quo uncomfortable and the temptation to return to violence unattractive. Cyprus, Lebanon, Liberia and Sudan until 2001 were examples of flabby mediation, compared with the firm efforts expended in Angola, Macedonia, Mozambique and El Salvador.

MEOs make for durable agreements because they resolve problems and start parties on the road of cooperation. The elements of resolving formulas and enticing opportunities are generally present at the beginning of negotiations, although they need tinkering and tailoring, and persistence and pressure, to constitute a final agreement. They provide substantive as well as procedural elements to meet the parties' needs, interests and demands, but they also need to be supported by external incentives to stay on track, and external constraints not to stray off track, in comparison with the status quo of the conflict. These are process elements that are visible only through an examination of the course of interaction between the parties and among the parties and mediators. How to achieve desired results is the crucial element in an explanation of success and durability, both for analysts and for practitioners.

15 Negotiating with terrorists
When, how and why?[44]

Officially, the subject does not exist: we do not negotiate with terrorists. Practically, however, there are negotiations and negotiations, and terrorists and terrorists. The subject is currently topical, but also analytically challenging, occurring more frequently than it is studied. What, then, does the fact of dealing with terrorists have to do with the negotiation process? When (and when not) can negotiations take place with terrorists? How does one negotiate with terrorists if one does (must, can)?

Terrorism is defined by the UN Security Council (UNSCr 1373) as "violent or criminal acts designed to create a state of terror in the general public," and by the US Government (US Department of State 2004) as "premeditated, politically motivated violence perpetrated against noncombatant targets by subnational groups or clandestine agents, usually intended to influence an audience." In either version, this is an acceptable approximate characterizations of the subject. One may argue a bit with the second definition around the edges (as with any other), perhaps because the definition is made by a government agency; in that it specifically excludes and therefore implicitly supports state terrorism.

Terror is a weapon of the weak, designed to redress the asymmetry of both justice and power in which they see themselves. Either personally or more broadly, they feel oppressed and devprived in their current situation, and powerless to change it by conventional means. Often terror is designed merely to get attention, using demonstrative violence so that the world will notice their plight. Other times it is more directly instrumental, in the service of a goal that can be so broad as to be millennial or so specific as to be tradeable. In their structurally weak position, they seize a part of the opponent as their weapon, imposing pain to make the powerful adversary give up. Thus they equalize suffering and power at the same time; terror injures and empowers. To be able to do so, terrorists must believe in their own right, whether that sense of justice that counterbalances their asymmetrical power position comes from God (as in the case of fundamentalists), from ideology (as in the case of social revolutionaries), or from their belief that the world owes them this right as a result of its own basic discrimination or corruption (nationalists and criminals, respectively).

All terrorists are hostage-takers and all are their own hostages. The standard hostage-taking terrorist takes identifiable hostages. The suicidal terrorist holds the people around them hostage, compounding the mental terror by the fact that they never know when they have chosen physical victims; the terrorist uses fear to hold the whole population hostage, among whom some are the specific victims at any specific time. But all terrorists are also their own victims. The suicider kills themself along with their victims, just as the hostage-taker has taken themself hostage along with their prisoners; they cannot escape from the barricade, kidnap hideout or hijacked planes anymore than can their captives.

Making distinctions

Finding the negotiability of this situation depends on an analysis (etymology: "taking apart") that draws distinctions within the broad concept. A basic difference separates absolute from contingent or instrumental terrorists. Absolute terrorists' action is non-instrumentalist and self-contained, an act that is completed when it has occurred and is not a means to obtain some other goal (not to be confused of course with a broader cause), whereas contingents use the victims' lives as exchange currency for other goals (Faure 2003; Hayes *et al.* 2003). Terrorist suiciders are absolute terrorists, and so are beyond negotiation, and probably even beyond dissuasion, unlike non-terrorist suicides, whose end is without broader purpose and is not intended to influence behavior beyond their own. Of course, a distinction need be made between the terrorists themselves (the suiciders) and their bosses or organizers. The organizers do not blow themselves up. They are not mad but highly rational and strategic calculators (Crenshaw 1981; Horgan and Taylor 2003; Altran 2003). But their purpose is so broad that it is unlikely to lend itself to negotiation, and indeed negotiation and the compromises involved are likely to be seen as damaging to the galvanizing purpose of the terrorist organizer in a desperate, asymmetrical situation.

A further distinction among absolutes can be made between conditionals and totals (or revolutionaries). It is not just the suicidal tactics but the unlimited cause that makes for totally absolute terrorism. Whether the cause is world social and political revolution or immediate access to a heavenly reward, it becomes an terrestrially unattainable millennial dream used to justify total indiscriminate tactics – "unlimited ends lead to unlimited means" (Crenshaw 2000).[45] Although social revolutionaries are often considered to be of a previous era and religious militants are the current brand of terrorists, it would be wrong to ignore their more important similarities. Whether their inspiration comes from revolution or revelation, both types of total absolutes want to overthrow the given social system and build a new world in the image of their dreams, and as terrorists are willing both to kill others and to die themselves to achieve their goal. Camus' *Les Justes* gives as important insights into religious as into ideological motivations. Conditional absolutes, on the other hand, use the same suicidal tactics for goals that are finite, dividable, exchangeable – aspects that will be relevant to later parts of this discussion – even though their act itself is as self-contained and absolute as any other suiciders'.

Instrumental or contingent (or demonstrative) terrorism covers much of the literature of the past century on negotiating with terrorists, referring mainly to hostage-taking. "Contingent" or even "instrumental" is preferable as a term to "demonstrative" terrorism (used by Pape 2003, p. 345), both because of the usual distinction between demonstrative/ expressive violence (to get it off your chest) and instrumental violence (to accomplish something) and because "non-absolute" terrorism seeks much more than demonstration. Its whole purpose is to exchange its victims for something – publicity, ransom, release of friends. Indeed, it is absolute terrorism, if anything, that is demonstrative, in the sense that it expresses the frustration of the suicider with the situation and their inability to change it by any other means. Contingent terror's violence is not definitive or absolute; only part of it is accomplished in the act of hostage taking, and the rest is threatened or contingent, in the fate promised for the hostages if the demands are not met.

Most hostage-takers are not suiciders, but those that are, such as airline suiciders, are absolute, not contingent, terrorists; their goal is their own sacrifice as well as the sacrifice of their hostages, and there is no way of negotiating a compromise. Among contingent terrorists, further distinctions between barricade and kidnapping terrorists and non-suicidal aerial hijackers highlights an important difference over the sustainability and vulnerability of the situation (Dolnik 2003; Faure 2003; Donahue 2003). Analysts also distinguish between motivational types, such as criminals, militants (nationalists or revolutionaries), fundamentalists, and mentally unstable cases, categories that can often overlap but make a difference in regard to negotiability. Barricaders are more frequently mentally imbalanced and kidnappers either extortionists (criminals) or militants (see Arnson and Zartman 2005 for distinctions between need, creed, and greed in conflict).

Conducting negotiations

These distinctions are of importance in addressing the issue: when, how and why negotiate with terrorists? Governments generally try to establish contact with contingent terrorists such as hostage takers, and even with absolutes – however discreetly or indirectly – to find out their real terms and motives and to see if there is something negotiable in them. It is obliged to in regard to contingents, in order to obtain release of the hostages, but also in regard o absolutes, to find out if there are any conditions among them. Despite disclaimers, such contacts usually do occur, and indeed they must. Whether such contacts lead to actual negotiations – exchange of offers in order to find mutually acceptable terms of trade – or not depends on estimates of negotiability as a result of the communication.

Any attempt to negotiate with total absolute terrorists only encourages them; it achieves no other purpose (Pape 2003). They have nothing to negotiate about, they have nothing to negotiate with. Indeed, it is notoriously difficult even to contact them and to talk them out of their act, once they are up in the air or even on the street heading toward their target. Since contact and communication are basic conditions of negotiation, inaccessibility is another component of absolute terrorism.

On the other hand, contingent terrorists are seeking to negotiate. They want to get full price for their hostages, and for the most part live hostages are better bargaining material than dead ones. A hostage-taker who has killed their hostage(s) verges on the absolutist, for they have little left to negotiate about or with. Hostages are negotiation capital, as Faure (2003) puts it, or bargaining chips, that is, items of no intrinsic value to the bargainer but created for the purpose of bargaining away. Contingent terrorists try to overcome their essentially weak position by appropriating a part of the other side and trying to get the best deal out of the other side's efforts to get that part back, to make itself whole again. Absolute terrorists do not want society to be whole again; they want it wounded and bleeding.

In between the two types are the conditional absolute terrorists, who do have something to negotiate about – territory, independence, conditions – even if their suicidal tactics are absolute. Conditional absolutes are not contingents; they do not seek negotiation as part of their act and their tactics are not divisible into two parts, grasping hostage capital and spending it. But their demands are potentially negotiable, leaving that potentiality to be developed by the negotiating partner. Here the distinction between agent and organizer adds to the speciality of the conditional absolute case. The agent is still likely to be totally absolute, and partial absoluteness refers only to the organizer. But the distinction suggests appropriate negotiating – or pre-negotiating – tactics. It is important to divide the terrorists, pulling the contingents and conditional absolutes away from the absolutes, which means giving the prospect of something real and attainable, as was done in the case of the IRA in Ulster as Hayes *et al.* (2003) note.

The problem in the case of contingent terrorists is not that they are not interested in negotiating but that the world does not accept their deal. Conditional absolutes may be in the same situation, which needs to be clarified by contacts if not negotiations. But that is merely an extreme case of a typical negotiating situation. In that situation there are two appropriate negotiating strategies – lower their terms or change their terms. The two must be carried out in tandem, indicating that while one avenue or problem is closed to discussion, the other is open and personally more compelling. Terrorists tend to focus on their original terms of trade –

release of hostages in exchange for fulfillment of demands – and are little open to looking for reductions and alternatives, options that need to be developed in negotiations are to succeed.

The first strategy is a reduction in the terms of trade, lowering their demands as a price for the hostages' release. Bargaining will begin with communication, to clarify those demands, and then continue with a search by the negotiator to see if any of them can be met or if the initial persuasion has to start with demands lowered to zero. The alternative strategy is to change the terrorists' terms of trade from their demands to their fate. When they see that there is no chance of their demands being met but that their future personal situation is open to discussion, new details become available for negotiation.

These two strategies may or may not be in contradiction with each other. On one hand, one strategy helps the terrorists look for a lesser form of an outcome on the terms that interest them, whereas the other helps them look for other terms. The second option also reinforces the position of the authorities as holders of the upper hand – one-up negotiators, in Donohue's (Donohue and Taylor 2003) terms – rather than full equals. On the other hand, both strategies depend on removing obstacles to creative negotiating, indicating the legitimacy and interest of both parties in finding a solution, and developing a range of options.

As in any negotiations, when the parties become convinced that a search for a solution is legitimate and acceptable to both sides, they become joint searchers for a solution to a problem rather than adversaries. To entice the terrorists into this common pursuit, they need to be convinced that the other side is willing to consider their interests. "If state leaders have the political will to promote negotiation as a response to terrorism, they will need to attend to terrorists' interests, not only their actions, strategies and tactics … To overcome the no-negotiation impediment, state leaders will need to respond in a special way, seek to understand terrorist interests, translate those interests into politically acceptable terms, and respond to them appropriately," notes Spector (2003).

The structural asymmetry of the situation points to a frequently neglected link between status and outcomes. Low status leads to unproductive tactics, position politics, and hostile bargaining that is unproductive of integrative outcomes. They bring out the "need to achieve a gradual process of creating conditions which will enable the terrorists to securely conclude the crisis, … undermining the terrorists' psychological safe-zone, constructing legitimacy for the negotiated agreement and building the terrorists' independent decision making capabilities," in Crystal's (2003) words. Treatment as equals, development of the legitimacy of a solution, expansion of options are all ways of moving the hostage takers off position bargaining and opening the possibility of a fruitful search for mutually satisfactory solutions, only available when they can think in terms of lowered expectations and so of lowered demands.

There is room for a wide range of tactics by the official negotiator, who needs to lead the terrorist against their will into the give and take of negotiation. Invitations to further refinement and creative thinking are useful at some times whereas take-it-or-leave-it offers are appropriate at others, and at some points parties can explore alternatives and options whereas at others firmness is in order. Structurally, time is on the side of the negotiator, a situation that the terrorist may seek to reverse by either killing or releasing some of his hostages and by demanding food or transportation. Once relations with terrorists get into the bargaining mode, however, they are open to the same shifts and requirements of tactics as any other negotiation.

All this is not to suggest either that terrorists' demands are to be considered legitimate in principle and only require some tailoring around the edges, or that concessions do not encourage contingent as well as absolute terrorists. Although the answer to the question of whether negotiations can be conducted with terrorists is that contingent terrorists in fact are looking for negotiations and that even conditional absolute have something negotiable in mind, the answer to the next question of how much of their demands can be considered acceptable depends on their content and on the importance of freeing the hostages. Furthermore, it is as the payment for abandonment of violent terrorism that concessions to the demands of the conditional absolute terrorist can to be offered and not as concessions to the pressure of the terrorism itself. If the negotiator should make concessions to the terrorist as part of the negotiation process, so must the terrorist too, and the absolute terrorist organizer does have something to offer as payment – their choice of terrorist tactics.

These considerations relate in turn to the danger of encouragement. It is not the matter of negotiation per se that encourages contingent terrorism but rather the degree of their demands that they are able to achieve by negotiation. If negotiating leads the terrorist to a purely symbolic result – a radio broadcast or a newspaper advert presenting their position, they are more likely to decide that the result is not worth the effort rather than to feel encouraged to do it again. Or if negotiating leads the terrorist to a bargain for their escape and totally neglect their original demands, they are not likely to feel encouraged to make another try.[46] Thus the answer of the negotiator, to their public's fears of appeasing and legitimizing terrorism, lies in the deal they are able to extract from the terrorist and in their need to focus on the fate of the victims. Any encouragement would come from the results but not from the act of negotiating itself. Basically, the official negotiator is faced with the task of giving a little in order to get the terrorist to give a lot, a return to the initial asymmetry and a particularly difficult imbalance to obtain given the highly committed and desperate nature of terrorists as they following rational but highly unconventional tactics.

Choosing negotiation

Thus far the discussion has focused on terrorists as individuals. But terrorists also come in groups, and governments frequently label all rebel groups as terrorists, then using the label as a justification for not negotiating with them. Behind the label stand rebel tactics that fit the definition, so that the justification may have some empirical support. Yet in most such cases, the government ends up negotiating.[47] So why do governments, mediators and others who brand their opponents as terrorists end up negotiating with them? Tentative answers can be drawn from a few select cases – Rwanda 1993, Israel 1993, Bosnia 1998, Macedonia 2001, Sierra Leone 1996–9[48] – to provide hypotheses with enough support to warrant further investigation.

The first answer is, because and when they have to, i.e. when they have to end violence and need the agreement of the terrorists to do so. When NATO had to negotiate with the Macedonian National Liberation Army (NLA) to reestablish a ceasefire or organize a disarmament, it overcame its objections and rose to the occasion; it did not, however, negotiate directly with the NLA to produce the Ohrid agreement. When the Kosovar Liberation Army (KLA) proved itself necessary to a final settlement, whether as a partner or as a bait for Serbian president Slobodan Milosovic' participation, the US began the difficult job of locating valid spokespeople for the rebels and talking to them. This reasoning also holds for negotiations with individual terrorists, where the only alternative to talking is a military rescue operation that is not always possible.

When a sufficient agreement could not be achieved with moderate rebels without the terrorist extremists, governments may have to turn to negotiation with extremist factions. Both the KLA and the NLA had to prove their indispensability to an agreement to be included; the Rwandan Patriotic Front (RPF) and the government of Rwanda thought the hardline Hutu Coalition for the Defense of the Republic (CDR) dispensable and excluded it, despite mediator pressure to the contrary. Israeli Prime Minister Itzhaq Rabin negotiated with the Palestine Liberation Organization (PLO), it was because he saw it as the only way to deliver on his electoral promise to bring peace within the year, Syria having proven obdurate and the Washington/Madrid talks without the PLO, sterile.

Sometimes it takes a change in the government to admit the necessity of negotiating with terrorists. When the government is too publicly committed to exclusion, it may need to change its incumbents in order to change its position, even if the previous government would have liked to end the conflict through negotiation. Rwanda shifted its position and began to negotiate with RPF rebels under the coalition government in the summer of 1992, not because a sea-change in thinking had occurred within the old guard concerning the proper tactical treatment of the RPF, but because once the coalition government came into being, ultimate decision-making power passed out of Habyarimana's hands and out of the hands of the old guard. A change in the Israeli government leadership from Shamir to Rabin made possible the Oslo negotiations, as did changes in the French government leadership to Pierre Mendes France and to Charles de Gaulle in regard to Tunisia and Algeria, among others.

Government change may in turn be brought about when public support for a "hard" stance against the terrorist camp weakens. A perceptual shift concerning the nature of the conflict or a reframing of the conflict against competing concerns may allow negotiations to take place. The first *Intifada* convinced many Israeli citizens that Palestinian nationalism was in fact real. Shifting economic, geopolitical and regional security concerns brought about by the ending of the Cold War forced many Israelis to view the domestic conflict within a broader context. The severity of the government's crackdown also helped to feed a domestic peace movement in Israel. Battle fatigue among the Israeli public helped to bring Rabin to power in 1991 under a pledge to bring peace to the region within a year. Sometimes, however, it may take a back channel or a secret venue to make negotiation possible, when channels can be opened to explore talks away from public scrutiny, so that the government can claim detachment from the process if negotiations fail. The facilitators behind the Oslo process created a safe avenue for both parties to open discussions without having to modify their positions publicly, which would have made them open to charges of inconsistency or weakness ahead of a negotiated solution.

A second answer, behind the first, is, when there is a mutually hurting stalemate. Governments and mediators negotiate when they have to because both sides were stymied and suffering if they did not negotiate. As in any ripe situation, both parties have to be unable to escalate their way out of a painful deadlock, to be able to perceive the possibility of a way out, and to have valid spokesmen for their negotiations. In Sierra Leone, Macedonia, and Kosovo, the parties finally realized they were cornered, although it took a while in Kosovo; in Rwanda, they did not, with horrible results. In the Middle East, Israel and the PLO were painfully stalemated, not in Palestine but in the Madrid Talks in Washington, and needed a way to meet their own campaign pledges and to face the common external enemy, Hamas, the "real" terrorist (Pruitt 1997). Of course, the stalemate with individual contingent terrorists also creates a hurting stalemate for both parties.

The third answer is, when the mediators lead the way. The mediators' presence and activity was absolutely crucial in the cases examined, and is often helpful in dealing with individual terrorists as well. They help the parties see the necessity and opportunity born of stalemate, for productive negotiations. In the cases, the various mediators were always more ready to open negotiations – cautiously – with the accused terrorists and urged the governments to do so, often preparing the way with their own mediation, conditions, and actions. But the mediators were not simply soft on terrorists: they worked on the extremists to fulfill the conditions helpful to the terrorists' being accepted as negotiation partners. When the mediators did not, the government held firm on a policy of exclusion. It was the mediators who produced unity in Macedonia and Kosovo, by helping to provide security to assuage the rebel groups' fears that their government opponents would not abide by a negotiated commitment; the US tried for Rwandan (Hutu) unity but was unable to achieve it.

Thus, governments may also turn to negotiation when the international pressure of the mediators builds to move toward an agreeing (though not necessarily resolving) formula, giving in to the pressures only in form. When the Cold War ended, Israel came under pressure from Washington as well as its regional neighbors to show that it was making progress toward a negotiated solution; Israel attended Madrid only to meet Washington's demand to be there, not to negotiate. Milsovic gave in to the Rambouillet terms after the mediators turned on their muscle and bombed. The Sierra Leonean government came to Lomé only under pressure from the neighboring states of the region. Indeed, Governments may even accept to negotiate not to resolve the conflict at all but rather in order to stall the process until a time when it will be able to press for its demands more unilaterally – as may have been the case with the 1998 Milosevic–Holbrooke agreement.

A fourth answer is, when unity of goals is achieved among the various rebel groups, moderate and radical. Unity, almost by definition, pulls the terrorists away from their extreme stands, although governments tend to fear that it will radicalize the moderates instead and legitimize the goals of the terrorists, a logical possibility considered below. However, the cases, even though few, show that unity made negotiation possible, as in Macedonia and Kosovo, and that the absence of unity merely set up the extremists to conduct their terror, as in Rwanda. The key to the Macedonian Albanians' negotiations with the government was their unity, so that moderates could speak for all, after the Prizren Document was created. The mediators again worked for unity among the Kosovar, even if they switched the focus of their strategies to Milosovic on occasion; getting the latter on board at Rambouillet depended on Kosovar unity as a negotiating partner. The jury is still out in Palestine; Oslo was a tactic to steal victory from Hamas and was unsustained, but the tactic of the PLO under President Mahmoud Abbas is to seek unity with Hamas in order to curb terrorism and gain legitimacy for broader goals.

A major impediment to the mediators' strategy of unite-and-resolve is the mediators' own unclarity of an acceptable outcome, including their sense of the popular legitimacy locally, regionally or globally of the rebels' demands as opposed to the resistance capabilities on the government side. Whereas Macedonia was a case of a single salient solution, autonomy, Kosovo was a case of a two-solution problem, integration vs independence; objectively, there is no stable intermediate solution as in Macedonia.

Rwanda is a curious intermediate case: there was a single salient solution –
a multiparty government, as provided at Arusha – but it was not stable,
given the terrorists' unshakable option for another salient solution, ethnic
cleansing and political takeover. For the mediator or opponent to press
for the necessary factional coalescence, there must be a single salient
acceptable solution about which the rebels can unite and on which both
sides can agree.

Indeed, governments may even turn to negotiation with extremist factions when it is the extremists who can unite the factions and deliver an
agreement, when the government feels that extremist leaders have the
capacity to enforce a negotiated peace among their ranks, or, tactically,
when the ensuing agreement will shift responsibility for future security
failures onto extremist leaders without opening its own population to
excessive security risks. The futility of the Washington Process in absence
of the PLO demonstrated to everyone that a deal could not be made
without them. The details of the Oslo accord made the PLO responsible
for keeping the peace when an agreement was signed, even though it
failed to provide it with the capacity to do so. The Sierra Leonean government and neighboring intermediaries negotiated with the Revolutionary
United Front (RUF) in 1999, although with unsustainable results, but the
ensuing agreement did obligate the RUF to run as a political party in the
next election, where they were decisively defeated.

However, complex strategic calculations, such as divide-and-defeat or
exclude-and-split, do not fare well. Sophisticated tactics such as testing a
leader's control by exclusion do not hold up in most cases. Excluding the
akazu (extreme faction) CDR proved to be the undoing of he Arusha
agreement on Rwanda. Even Israel's test of Arafat's ability to control terrorism seems to be straightforward, and indeed Rabin sought to pull
Arafat into a peace agreement as an ally against Hamas, a strategy that his
successor, Benyamin Netanyahu, could not conceive of.[49] Instead, exclusion becomes a self-proving hypothesis: one cannot negotiate with a
faction because they are terrorists, and so they become real terrorist
because they are excluded. The CDR in Rwanda is a poignant case in
point, although whether the *ukazu* faction coud have been committed to
an Arusha agreement will never be known. The Kosovar KLA is another
case in point. The mediator never sought to follow a tactic of split and
isolate, but Milosovic did, with unrewarding results. In the process, the
moderates are left unable to deliver on a deal because the excluded
faction is able to upset the deal. While not all excluded factions are strong
enough to be effective as spoilers, they will be cast as spoilers if excluded.
This preliminary study based on five cases, however, can in no way answer
the conundrum, were the terrorists radical enough to warrant exclusion,
as posited in Rwanda, or were they radicalized – turned into terrorists –
because of exclusion, as suggested in Kosovo?

Once a total absolute terrorist group is identified, tactical choices must include plans for dealing with the eventuality that the spoiler spoils. Though the choice to exclude the CDR was logical from the perspective of the assessment that the CDR was not includable, exclusion as a tactic depends on a second assessment as to whether the party that is deemed to be beyond inclusion is also excludable without upsetting the agreement. Here the coalition partners either failed to make the necessary calculations as to what was needed to ensure the CDR *could* be excluded, or else calculated incorrectly. At the same time, governments should also be aware of the potential for spoilers within their own ranks. It was the *akazu* that was sidelined when the first coalition government was formed. Once Arusha began, ongoing extremist rhetoric by CDR spokesmen convinced the coalition and the RPF that the CDR could never accept a power sharing arrangement with the RPF. In other words the coalition concluded, somewhat ironically, that though the original terrorists, the RPF terrorists, *would* be capable of making a deal, the ex-government terrorists would not.

The final answer is the most tentative: when the terrorists revise their goals or their nature. It is tentative because it is not clear how much revision is necessary or whether inclusion or the possibility of inclusion triggers revision or revision triggers the decision to include. The PLO had already recognized Israel before Oslo and it revised its statutes and agreed to formal mutual recognition at the end of the negotiations; Hamas has not, a year after its elections. Macedonian Albanians at Prizren made plain their willingness to accept a democratic solution, dropping a geographic solution as a threatened goal; but Kosovar Albanians were quite imprecise about their softening of the demand for an immediate promise of independence. The *akazu* retained their opposition to ethnic or party power-sharing, justifying the exclusion to which they were subjected. The RUF changed its demands very little, and the ensuing agreement had to be pushed aside when they reverted to their original tactics.

But the conditions of negotiation (compromise, persuasion, positive-sum outcomes) and of democracy (legitimacy of all parties, need to appeal widely, acceptance of popular judgment) themselves impose limitations on terrorists that can mark the beginning of the socialization process toward inclusion. Moderation is a process, not a status; a party seeking a solution must be able to see indication of a change in goals or nature in the terrorists that it feels can be encouraged by engaging the terrorists in negotiations. To the extent that the terrorists engage, the very process of negotiation tends to teach and induce moderation. Ambassador Christopher Hill has indicated that negotiations with North Korea are designed to show that there incorporation into the norms and practices of the community is a surer way of achieving national security than hostile unilateralism. There must be some empirical indication of change to lead to negotiation and some analytical estimation that negotiation will intensify the change. Initially, the erstwhile terrorist is unlikely to change its ends, only its means, and in dealing with individual terrorists that is what negotiation is all about. But engagement in negotiation and the new situation it produces can gradually produce deeper changes, as the PLO in Palestine, the NLA in Macedonia, and, complicatedly, the RUF in Sierra Leone show.[50] But how much moderation is a necessary precondition to negotiation and how much negotiation is a necessary precondition to moderation remains uncertain. It is still a chicken-and-egg process, until more research is done, and even then may ultimately be a matter of political or diplomatic "feel."

16 Methods of analysis
Case studies[51]

Case studies are one of, if not the, most frequently used methods for conducting research on negotiation. They can vary from purely historical studies that seek to establish all the relevant facts of the encounter, to analytical studies chosen to illustrate specific theoretical propositions. The most successful cases for the purposes of generating useful knowledge are those located somewhere in the middle of that spectrum, leaning toward the latter side of center. "Case" is used here to refer to the story of negotiations on a single conflict or problem, either as a single set of encounters or as a number of successive instances. Cases are the best way of combining empirical data (a redundant expression) with theory and concepts, but their use raises further, more interesting methodological questions. These questions concern the number of cases used by a research project and the type of data to be drawn from them, questions that are of forefront importance in the current wave of scholarship on the subject.

Any research designed to create knowledge involves a set of questions needing answers or a category of events needing an explanation, a theory embodying those answers and explanations, and a method for gathering and using data. Each step in the research process poses its challenges. Given the need to bridge idiosyncrasies and to combine depth of Weberian understanding with the breadth of multiple instances, there is much to be said for using a comparative case method to answer questions and provide explanations about negotiations, focusing on the basic question of how negotiated outcomes are obtained? For if one can explain how outcomes have been obtained (the analyst's question) one can explain how to obtain outcomes (the practitioner's question). Case studies can be exploratory or confirmatory, providing inductive ideas for generalized explanations or deductive testing of logical constructs. Case studies can show causal links; they shed light on process and allow an exploration of the dynamic path from components to results, thus satisfying the needs of both analysts and practitioners. Comparative case studies lie at the crossroads of theory and practice; they present their evidence through the eyes of a knowledgeable specialist and they test it against the hypothetical constructs of a creative conceptualist. So the Janus-faced challenge to case study authors is dual and the standards of quality are high.

Theory and data

To begin with some extremely simple basics, knowledge can be considered to be ordered and generalized data. We live by generalizations, to get us away from suffocation in a world of infinite, unique data: leaves need to be aggregated onto branches and branches onto trees, lined up in forests. Leaves are of course interesting in their own right, but unless we are innate historians, interested only in understanding correctly what happened in a single past event, data from the past are interesting only to the extent that they provide guidance in the present for the future. To be of such use, data must be aggregated into generalized knowledge as concepts and, if the concepts themselves are arranged in a dynamic relation to each other, as theories. Theories can be either concocted out of whole conceptual cloth, as a logical exercise, or built out of the record of data, generalized from idiosyncratic instances – exercises called deductive and inductive, respectively. Either way theories face two tests of internal and external validity, respectively: a logical verification to see whether they hold together and make sense, and an empirical verification to see whether they summarize regularities in the data on the ground. Although it is the second test that concerns us here, it is worth taking a small paragraph to address the first.

Building theory depends on prior identification of its components and purposes, taking us back to concepts. Phenomena or regularities in data need to be named, as concepts, and then explained, and explanation depends on the chosen terms of analysis, or concepts and categories of data to be applied to the explanation. "Theory" is a rather big and overused word; we are lucky if we can identify regularities, relations, effects, and generalizations and then – extremely important – the reasons behind them. These two elements – regularities and reasons – are the what and the why of theory-building, and the why is crucial in understanding rather than just observing the mechanisms of behavior. "What we are trying to explain" is a crucial question for analysis, and the terms of analysis chosen to pursue that explanation constitute the next crucial choice. There are many answers to that first question but an important one is "what is it in the process of negotiation that explains the outcome?" Thereafter, there are a myriad terms of analysis that can be used to pursue the answer to the question; none is trumps but a few leading ones emerge to face the test of logic as providing the most convincing reasoning.

The exciting thing about current research on negotiation is that it has produced important conceptual development and cumulative knowledge. Old effects – since the process of negotiation itself is millennia old – have been identified and given names (things only "come into existence" when they have been named). I have been associated with such concepts as *formulas* and *ripeness*, but there are plenty of others – flexibility, prenegotiation, BATNA and security points, integration and distribution, toughness dilemma, value making and value taking, among many others – that have made the understanding of the negotiation process and the answering of the crucial question move ahead. But for all their logic, concepts and effects such as these (to dodge the big word "theory" for the moment) need to be tested against data to make sure that they work and are not just figments of creative imagination. Testing logic against real data has three purposes: to see if the logic is "real," to provide an explanation of real events if it is, and to incite a search for alternative explanations – alternative logics – for exceptions. Where do these data come from? The best source of data is historical reality, from negotiations that have actually happened, recorded and analyzed in case studies.[52]

Case data are authoritative; they record what happened, not what could or might have happened (although there is value in counterfactual analysis as well).[53] There are many good historical case studies of negotiation that seek no particular conceptual guidance or verification but work merely to establish a good record and understanding of the event itself, finding an explanation of outcomes in the events (and often personalities) of the case itself. Fine examples of such historical studies are numerous, ranging from Nicolson (1946) to Preeg (1970).[54] Often such accounts do provide generalized bits of wisdom that emerge from the events and can be helpful in understanding and producing successes or failures in other (or the same) cases, beginning the inductive process of theory- and concept-building, as in the very studies just cited. The contrast in evident in the two oldest accounts of negotiations: the negotiations recorded in Genesis between God and Abraham over Sodom, which is rich in concepts but only implicitly, and the negotiations recorded in Thucydides (1960/–411) between Sparta and Athens, where the purported lessons are made most explicitly. Other essentially historical studies refer to concepts already formulated, either induced from other cases or deduced from logical premises.

But whether one is the writer of Genesis, Thucydides, Preeg, Nicolson, or any other author of quality about cases of negotiation, they have been steeped in the ambience and context of the case, as a participant observer (as in the case of the first three names cited) or as a diligent researcher, and has developed a feel for the subject that makes a deep understanding analysis of the case possible. Whatever the level of conceptual sophistication, a case study writer never stops being a diligent historian too if they do a good job, and that feel for the case allows the writer to get behind the data to give it context and meaning and achieve a Weberian understanding of its dynamics (Skocpol and Somers 1980/1994).

If the theory fits the historical data (never the reverse), a presumptive explanation is provided; if not, an alternative explanation is needed. As philosophers of science tell us, the theory is never proven in the sense of being fully verified; it merely gains support, even though exceptions can always take place. Beyond that, as social scientists (should) know, humans have a happy capacity of free choice, the ability to do what they please, including wildly stupid and gloriously creative things, and can never be caught inescapably in theories, mechanisms and regularities. But all that said, general regularities in events, contexts and behavior do occur, to be expressed in concepts and illustrated through data. The question remains, what cases, and what data to draw from them?

Choice of cases

The simplest answer to the choice of data sources is to pick the case in which the analyst is interested, and to seek guidance in an explanation of its outcome from the available concepts and theories. In single case studies, the choice is generally directed by considerations external to the concept; the purpose is to find explanations for the case, not tests of the concept. The case is the dependent variable or explanans, the thing being explained, whereas the concept is the independent variable or explanandum, the thing explaining. Such use of cases assumes either that the concepts are already well established or that the case can be used inductively to derive them. Two excellent examples are studies of multilateral negotiations, one by Bunn (1992) on arms control negotiations and the other by Winham (1986) on the GATT Tokyo Round of negotiations. While focusing on their subject per se, both found the concept of formulas useful in their analysis. Another insightful pair is Rubin's (1981) collection of interpretations of the Kissinger shuttle negotiations in the Arab–Israeli conflict and Pruitt's (1997) collection of analyses of the Oslo negotiations on the Palestine–Israeli conflict; in these cases, the concepts tested and applied varied among contributing authors.

However, single case studies are of inherently limited utility in producing knowledge about negotiation as opposed to data on the unique case. Things that happened once, however engrossing as a story, have no way of telling us whether they represent regularities or exceptions; truth is stranger than fiction not because it is exceptional but because the story leaves us wondering whether it is really normal or indeed an exception to normality. The only way to test and reinforce concepts' and theories' claims to normal regularity rather than exceptionality is to look at a number of cases, not just one, and the more the better (knowing, as noted, that the generality can never be proved or expected to be universal). Zartman (1994) and Hampson (1995) are the first works to attempt a theoretical analysis of multilateral negotiations, each using cases somewhat differently; the first subjects two cases (the Single Europe Act and the GATT Uruguay Round) to a competition among six different theoretical approaches (game, decision, small group, leadership, coalition, and organization theories) to try to draw out a common analytical perspective, whereas the second examines nine cases from which to draw conceptual characteristics and insights.[55] Controlled comparisons of cases exhibit the advantages of in-depth analysis of reality while overcoming the weaknesses of focusing on one case alone. But how and what to compare?

There is a large literature on case studies, starting with Mill (1843/1967) and going on to the most authoritative recent statement made by Alexander George (1979; George and McKeown 1985). With limited space and an argument make, cases are unlikely to be chosen at random, if indeed there were a notion of randomness that was operationalizable and applicable. Most likely the analyst will begin by choosing a number of cases that are salient and relevant. Saliency involves importance in the general discourse about negotiation problems, including simply current events. Relevance concerns applicability to the conceptual issues involved. The more cases can be chosen to focus on variations relevant to the conceptual issues and hold other features constant, the more explanatory factors can be isolated and identified, a condition termed structured, focused comparisons. It would also be useful to bring in negative cases as a control, rather than including only positive cases, although comparing why it didn't happen with why it happened significantly increases the difficulty of holding constant the elements to be analyzed.

The simplest way to achieve controlled comparison is to examine multiple instances in the same case. Instances of failure can be compared with instance(s) of success in the same country in a comparative analysis that uses specific concepts to provide an explanation of outcomes, as was well and explicitly done in Touval (1982) examining nine attempts to mediate the Arab–Israeli conflict, and in Stedman (1991) comparing three failures and one success in mediating the Zimbabwe anticolonial war. Interestingly but only coincidentally, both works focus on ripeness as a major explanatory variable, making important contributions to an understanding of the concept. Another comparative single-cases analysis can be provided by examining the role of various components of a single set of negotiations, as is done in the first study of European integration as negotiation (Meerts and Cede 2004), which analyzes negotiations in each of the major institutions of the European Union. If multiple instances or segments within a single case are not available or chosen, then similar cases can be the corpus of analysis, following the same rules of structured, focused comparison. As one moves away from multiple instances within a single case, it becomes more difficult to hold elements constant in order to focus on particular explanatory aspects of negotiation.

The problem with multiple case studies is that the more the cases, the bigger the book, and the further the account gets from the important details of reality. Some excellent multiple case studies guided by or testing concepts get rather voluminous, such as Crocker *et al.* (1999, 21 cases in 735 pp.) on mediation or Stedman *et al.* (2002, nine cases in 728 pp.) on post-agreement settlement, leaving in the dust behind them other studies such as Ali and Matthews (1999, eight cases in 322 pp.) on negotiating African civil wars and Zartman (1995, 11 cases in 353 pp.) on the difficulties of negotiating centralist and regionalist civil conflict. Yet the ability to make comparisons across a number of negotiations gives a rich harvest of lessons and insights. In addition to their supporting case material, such studies also contain varying amounts of conceptual or theoretical knowledge drawn and tested from the cases. Obviously support is not measured by the number of pages, but more and longer case accounts can provide more data to test and apply the theory and concepts.

It might be worthwhile examining the last-mentioned work (Zartman 1995) in greater detail, as an example of the process and advantages (and disadvantages) of a comparative set of case studies. Cases were chosen, not "scientifically," but by the criteria of saliency and interest already mentioned. Most cases were significant and unresolved at the time the project started – Sri Lanka, Sudan, Eritrea, Lebanon, South Africa, Angola, Mozambique, Afghanistan, Colombia – plus two other cases, also unresolved but less well known – Euskadi and Philippines. The challenge was to analyze the negotiations to date and then provide conceptually-derived prescriptions on ways to bring them to success. Interestingly, a number of cases (Eritrea, Lebanon, South Africa, Mozambique) came to a conclusion while the project was underway, while some others (Angola and Afghanistan) reached a successful conclusion of the current phase of the conflict, only to be followed by a new phase. The cases further divided into conflicts for control of the central government and conflicts for control of a region. A conceptual framework, built on contrasting notions of stalemate and on characteristics of internal wars (asymmetry, phases, agendas, escalation) and mediator tactics, was set up at the beginning and refined inductively in interaction with the case authors, providing the basis at the end for a review of factors in failure and success and two parts of a bottom line (weakness of both parties that hinders ripeness, and weakness of mediators that impedes patronage or relationship) to give a final account for failure. It was above all the repeated interaction between the inductive and deductive parts and people of the project that made the study so effective. On the other hand, it is worth recalling that nothing was "proven"; old and new propositions and concepts were supported and proposed, open for further testing.

Multiple case accounts allow the analyst to develop a deeper understanding of the details and idiosyncrasies of the case, so that the fit between the generalizations and the data can be fully explored, explained, and understood. This analytical formula has been an integral part of the studies of the Processes of International Negotiation (PIN) Program of the International Institute of Applied Systems Analysis (IIASA) in Austria. These works include comparative case-and-concept studies of negotiations on such issues as civilian and military use of nuclear material in order to test a number of propositions regarding the impact of the world's most dangerous substance on the process of negotiation (Avenhaus *et al.* 2002), economic issues in order to compare the strength of economic vs negotiation explanations of outcomes (Sjöstedt and Kremenyuk 2000), symmetric and asymmetric cases in order to derive strategies and employ a new concept of power (Zartman and Rubin 2000), environmental issues in order to develop analytical and strategic concepts (Sjöstedt 1993), and a broad range of historic and contemporary encounters in order to answer some major conundrums about management vs transformation and peace vs justice (Zartman and Kremenyuk 2005).

But events, unlike concepts, do not naturally come in boxes, with sharp sides and square corners, and calling an event one thing or another has to be done with extreme care and support. To evoke the concepts mentioned above, was there really a formula in the negotiations; what was it, specifically; and when did negotiations pass from diagnosis to formulation? Or was there really a Mutually Hurting Stalemate (MHS); how do we know and how did they (the participants) know, and how long did that perception last (even if they didn't say so)? Debates about the existence and effects of the concepts and theories in reality can only be resolved by evidence from reality, and that can only be supplied by detailed case studies.

Beyond cases and back

But if eight cases are better than one and 21 cases better than eight, what about going to truly large sets containing many tens and even hundreds of cases? How to provide even larger collections of comparative data for more conclusive application and testing? Ostensibly, the answer seems to be found in aggregate data, large collections of precisely identified statistical indicators applicable to all cases and associated with characteristics treated in relevant theories and concepts. If the analysis can enter into truly large data sets, firm generalizations and regularities can be established, both for knowledge and for appropriate policymaking. Usually, there is no unanimity of support for a theory or concept, but merely statistically significant correlations among a number of variables.[56]

A number of recent works have taken up the challenge of combining case data into large wads that can then be subjected to statistical significance tests. This research uses aggregate data on the largest number of cases possible either to test deductive propositions or generate inductive findings through correlation or factoring. Despite careful coding, it needs to group large numbers of diverse cases together into types, and is more interested in showing statistically significant correlations than in finding causality or in explaining the category of exceptional cases. Recent works by Walter (2002)[57] and Fortna (2004) have turned to a particular aspect of negotiation of contemporary concern, the question of durability of negotiated agreements. Hampson (1999, five cases) and Stedman *et al.* (2002) previously sought explanations based on selected, structured, focused comparisons, but the new wave of studies took on an N of 72 and 24 respectively.

But in the process of doing so, they raise a number of significant methodological questions (for a fuller development, see Brady and Collier 2004; Sambanis 2004; and Ragin 1997). First, in seeking to compress events into statistics, the data move far away from the subtleties of reality, as coders make sharp judgments on the nature or category of complex events. Many events do not lend themselves to binary (yes-no) or even plural statistics. To cite one example, in a recent preliminary study involving 60 instances of negotiation in 12 cases (Zartman 2004), I ran into frequent coding problems: how long does an MHS have to last to be coded an MHS?[58] Which (power-sharing, power-division, elections) was the significant procedural provision when more than one occurred? When and for how long was a ceasefire a ceasefire? When was an instance of conflict autonomous rather than a continuation/revival of the previous instance? Concepts are clean, statistics are sharp, but events are messy. Yet they require procrustean sharpening to be subjected to statistical analysis. Such analysis can only handle data that are quantitatively, objectively measurable and can explain only that for which it has data, and in the interest of precision it must make inflexibly quantitative definitions.

Second, not only do the statistical data turn difficult evaluations into absolute indicators but they also hide the reasoning and details that support those choices. The basis of individual categorizations is always open to question when the evidence is not given, and an assurance of intercoder reliability is simply not adequate to relieve questions. Should they use an established data set, such as Correlates of War, about which questions still exist, or a new one, about which questions have not even been explored? Case study accounts may be compressed, but at least one can spot missing data and questionable judgments.

Third, direct data are often not available, only indicators, sometimes termed proxies. Since the method can only handle comparable, quantifiable data, and so, because it has no "feel" for its subject, it has to rely on indicators or "proxies"; subjective elements must be objectified to become data. As a result, its indicators, such as percapita income or economic growth, are often far away from the effect they are proxying, such as proneness to the breakdown of order. Inequalities (in household incomes and in land ownership) are used as indicators of "grievance," as if there were some universal threshold of envy or economic inequalities were the only and direct cause of protest and revolt (Collier and Hoeffler 2002; Collier *et al.* 2003, p. 66).

Fourth, what cannot be measured or proxied is not analyzed. Since it is difficult to objectify intensity of feelings, such as nationalism or commitment, or degree of satisfaction with outcomes, these phenomena become ignored in analysis, even though they have been identified as crucial elements in negotiation.

Fifth, as a result of the above, data become no longer data but are themselves events squeezed into generalizations. They become shorthand for the event and so enter into a tangling tautology: they become theoretical generalizations required to test theoretical generalizations. If household incomes are used to "proxy" grievance in order to test its role in causing conflict, they contain the unproven theory that income inequality directly causes or relates to grievance. But whether or how it does so, or operates, is outside the analysis. Of course, the research is not as simple-minded as that; the analyst looks for evidence or at least an indicator for the effect being evaluated, but the notation that appears on the correlation chart sets the tautology trap.

Finally, there is remarkably little process in this analysis. Outcomes and conditions are noted but they are static road signs, neither roads nor driving skills. Getting there doesn't tell how, and so the dynamic of the process is lost. That loss is serious indeed, and marks a step backward in the analysis of negotiation. When the analysis was in the hands of the historians, attention tended to be focused on results, with much less on the way in which they were obtained. Process analysis in social science has been working to correct the aim, building on the historical analysis. It would be a step backward to focus simply on correlations between conditions and results.

Conclusion

This is a rich list of problems; an equally full list can be made for case studies as well. Case studies exchange feel for precision and thrive on it; their strength is an understanding of the situation(s) they analyze, even if it is hard to place numbered pieces of those situations into columns in a chart. Such studies are more interested in arguing and illustrating how perceptions, processes, communications, and grievances operate in known instances of negotiation than in correlating inputs and outcomes, and they spend little time on absent effects, non-instances, or control cases. Case students may be satisfied to understand one case well and produce some lessons for someone else to test on other cases, rather than finding correlations in universes of cases of varying importance. They are even happier when comparative case studies can be undertaken, either through successive negotiation attempts in the same conflict or through several negotiations of several problems or conflicts. Yet their data suffer from loose formalization, necessarily small numbers of cases, deference to case idiosyncrasy, and absence of "scientific" quantification.

At the other extreme of one or a few cases lie studies involving many, many cases, summarized in aggregate data analyzed by statistical methods. While useful for establishing correlations, this method has its own problems: apples and oranges are often crammed into the same indicator, sensitive concepts are crudely operationalized, the variables used for analysis are often so distant from the phenomena named in the theory that it is hard to be sure the theory is being tested, and process dynamics are almost invariably lost. All this is not to say that such studies and their methodology are useless, as this critique may imply. It does indicate that enormous refinement is still awaited, that conceptual links and assumptions still need analysis, that subjective data still call for their place in the analysis, and that the statistical correlations can well be used to provide hypotheses that closer analysis can test.

Yet the balance of advantages and weaknesses, inevitable in any method of analysis, places case studies in the midst of a search for breadth and depth, for data and theory. Much of the greatly expanded understanding of the negotiation process made available over the past four decades involves from case studies – largely comparative case studies – used either to generate or to test conceptual and theoretical generalizations. Empirical soundness, including a feel for the subject, harnessed to a concern for usefulness through accurate generalizations and concepts, can be achieved – perhaps even best achieved – through comparative case studies.

Notes

1 Specifically, conflict management refers to efforts to move a conflict from violent to political means of pursuit, whereas conflict resolution refers to the settlement of issues at contest; see Zartman 2006a.
2 I would like to acknowledge the support of the Blaustein Foundation, the Hewlett Foundation, the US Institute of Peace, the Hollings Center for Intercultural Dialog, the International Institute forApplied Systems Analysis, and The Johns Hopkins University for their support of these various activities.
3 See the final chapter in Zartman 1971.
4 Even if non-quantitative priorities are used, they are often difficult to establish. There is more usefulness in metrical reasoning for deciding whether to negotiate or not, than in analyzing outcomes, despite the obvious relation between the two. See Rapoport 1966, p. 130. Since Ikle and our own theorems suggest that negotiations pose a continual choice between agreement and no agreement, however, this may be a worthwhile time to attempt a more direct application of the game theory, although this would seem to lead to an unmanageable number of plays that would not clarify the process.
5 Rapoport 1966, has gone far in seeking out other "rationalities," an important step.
6 Thus the following analysis may not be adequate for disarmament or security negotiations, which may need their own special type of approach.
7 There have been two significant, if incomplete, attempts to grapple with this question: Ikle 1964, and Sawyer and Guetzkow 1965. See Zartman 1974.
8 Note that this is what the Six tried to do with East Africa in 1965 – bypass the deadlock on principle by creating a crest on details that would make balking on principle either unthinkable or at least anticlimactic.
9 However, on the Nigerian negotiations, Bridget Bloom 1969, pp. 18, 25, estimates that the value of the EEC concessions to Nigeria was "hardly enough to cover the cost of sending the successive Nigerian delegations to Brussels," whereas the value of the reciprocal concessions was "probably somewhat in excess of the Community's expenditure on its negotiating team in Brussels"; respective figures are £50,000 and £175,000, but do not count non-monetary values. Despite the limitations inherent in the last phrase, this evaluation does help explain the ease both of agreement and of expiration.
10 See "Introduction", Zartman (ed.) 1987e.
11 Zartman 1978c.
12 Coalition is used here in a narrower ("total conflict of interest") sense than in Axelrod, (1970, chapter 8) referring to a decision-making process and not simply a matter of forming a government.

13 I know of no theoretical work that probes the nature of this process (this includes the works on judicial decision-making cited in Zartman 1974, p. 385).

14 One such notion of justice among many is the formula for "fairness" used by Bartos 1978.

15 Off-the-record Middle East study-group session, 1976.

16 The Project for the Stimulation of International Negotiating Skills (SINS) of the Academy for Educational Development, Inc., New York, funded by the Rockefeller Foundation.) In this work, I am most grateful for the skillful assistance of Maureen Berman, who conducted the interviews. The scenarios can be obtained by writing to the author. Full results are published in Zartman and Berman 1982.

17 See Zartman *et al.* 1996.

18 The categorization used here is similar, among others, to that of HP Young 1994; however, the terms "equality" and "inequality" are used here instead of "parity" and "proportionality," respectively, because they express the contrast more sharply.

19 FBIS, SADCC meeting. I am grateful to Frederick Ehrenreich for the reference.

20 See Zartman 1997a.

21 See Zartman 1997b. This study is drawn from a project of the Processes of International Negotiation (PIN) Program based at the International Institute of Applied Systems Analysis (IIASA) in Laxenburg, Austria. The full work is Zartman and Rubin 2000. I wish to thank the members of the Washington Interest in Negotiation (WIN) Group – Lance Antrim, Francis Deng, Daniel Druckman, Lloyd Jensen, Dean Pruitt, Donald Rothchild, Timothy Sisk, Bertram Spector, and Saadia Touval – for their helpful comments on this manuscript.

22 Admittedly, "ability" might be taken to mean "skill and will," two components of power discussed below, although it have never been identified explicitly in this sense. Were it to be so, it would only be a partial definition, since it would exclude another component, resources, also discussed below

23 See Zartman 1988.

24 Selection 2 identifies eight approaches, some of which are combined here for greater coherence.

25 See Zartman 1997c.

26 This is the other side of the same coin as discussed by Amatrya Sen and not in contradiction with his position; Sen 1999, chapter X, especially 244–8. I am grateful to Guy Olivier Faure of the Sorbonne for useful suggestions in this area.

27 See Touval and Zartman 2001.

28 See Zartman 1989.

29 See Zartman 2005c. Also see Zartman and Aurik 1991 for fuller cases studies.

30 This is not to ignore all the problems of misperception and miscalculation that the introduction and previous chapters have identified, nor the effects of intransitive escalation, which carry the parties away in vicious cycles. But it does emphasize the essential role of escalation in the pursuit of conflict, and it highlights the basic rationality of increasing effort in order to win. cf. the discussion of rationality in escalation in Waltz 1954, pp. 191–2; HP Young 1991, pp. 102–4, 115–16.

31 This is not to imply that all escalation is a purposeful exercise of power. It may well be designed simply to hurt the other party, with no further relation to intended outcomes. Since, as the introductory chapter discusses, escalation can refer to many dimensions, there are aspects that escape the focus of this inquiry. On the other hand, such "purposeless" escalation may well also have the same effects in producing negotiations, even if it was only intended to produce pain.

32 Snyder and Diesing's (1977, p.181) contention that "the escalation ladder as a series of preexisting escalation options usually does not exist for bargainers and is not used in crisis decision-making" seems both descriptively and prescriptively wrong. In many situations, including some of those considered as cases in this chapter, future escalations were in fact considered, and in any case, in general, if they were not they should have been. Situations concerned in the entrapment literature arise because the escalation ladder was not fully surveyed before the first (or third) step.

33 See Zartman 2003b.

34 Only Young 1989, and Young and Osherenko 1993 give importance to the bargaining process of regime formation.

35 The one author who recognized this evolutionary nature was, not surprisingly, the same author who brought negotiations into the process of regime creation, Oran Young; see specifically Young 1983, pp.105–7.

> International regimes do not become static constructs even after they are fully articulated. Rather they undergo continuous transformation in response to their own inner dynamics as well as to changes in their political, economic and social environments. In this connection, I use the term "transformation ..."

Here the term used is "evolution," which includes both minor tinkering and major alterations, a distinction that Young understandably finds difficult and that is not required, at least for present purposes. The analysis in this chapter carries further some of the ideas initiated in O Young 1983 and 1989.

36 It could quite well be argued that regimes have been around for a long time and many studies of them as ongoing negotiations could well have informed the study of regimes (cf. Preeg 1970; Malgren 1973; Winham 1977a, 1977b on economic regimes, none of which were noted in the original work on regimes; and, in the subsequent period, Winham 1986, 1994 on GATT; Sjöstedt 1993 on environmental regimes; Spector *et al.* 1994 on UNCED; Zartman 1994 and Hampson 1995 on multilateral negotiations.

37 For a discussion of another case of polysemy, referring to both product and process, on the word "thought," see Geertz 1983, pp.147–8. Similarly, Ruggie (1983, p.196) discusses regime as a consummatory rather than a merely instrumental value, relating to Weber's (1978, pp.24–6) distinction between value- and purpose-rationality, although it might seem that the distinction could run either way .

38 Two of these were foreshadowed by processes identified in Young 1983, pp. 106–13, as part of regime transformation: "internal contradictions" is similar to the present second factor of regime adjustment, and "exogenous forces" is similar to the fourth exogenous factor. Young's other process, "shifts in the underlying structure of power," is reflected in the inputs of power, interest and values that are involved in any negotiations. It is the addition of the other two factors, system maintenance and cybernetic loops, that distinguishes the two approaches.

39 Roles are related to, but quite different from, Young's (1989, 1991) discussion of leadership. Roles are a typology which allow classification, with implications, but not any statement of causative hypotheses. Leadership discussions are based on a tautological hypothesis. "Institutional bargaining is likely to succeed when *effective* leadership emerges ... [and] fail in the absence of such leadership"; (Young 1989, p.373, emphasis added) and does not break into a very clear typology, other than effective/ineffective.

40 Unlike his discussion in 1983, p.110, Young (1989a), pp.371–2 assigns a positive direction to the effects of exogenous shocks "for the most part." The

original discussion seems more convincing, although the differences may lie in the difference between broader and more ambiguous exogenous "forces" (1983, p. 110) and narrower and more specific exogenous "shocks or crises" (1989a, p. 371).

41   I am grateful to John Odell for triggering some key ideas in this conclusion.

42   Hayashi (1999) has elegantly shown that parties will bolt peacekeeping obligations when the costs of compliance are higher than the costs of bolting.

43   See Zartman 2006b.

44   See Zartman and Alfredson 2006. An earlier version of part of this chapter appeared as Zartman 2003a.

45   Pape (2003) lumps together negotiable and non-negotiable goals, which is a mistake. The European Commission for the Prevention of Torture appears to use representativity, but it is unoperationalizable; see Palma 2003.

46   In a few cases, of course, they may be led to try to do it better or not make the same mistakes next time.

47   A quick count indicates that 21 of the 26 cases of negotiation in civil wars between 1900 and 1989 (including negotiated surrender and unstable negotiations) in Stedman 1991, pp. 6–7, were instances where governments negotiated with former terrorists.

48   I am grateful to Tania Alfredson for research on the cases and input on the conclusions.

49   Kydd and Walter 2002 and Bueno de Mesquita 2004 to the contrary.

50   Recalling the change in means of the National Party under FW de Klerk, which eventually led to a change in ends under the new political system (Zartman 1995).

51   See Zartman 2005d.

52   Experimental data are useful to generate solid hypotheses but they are not empirical data and their controlled conditions necessitate verification against actual events.

53   Too little work is done on historic possibilities at particular decision points, comparing the possible against the actual, and analyzing why a particular decision was made. For some such case studies, see Tuchman (1984), Parker (1993), Jentleson (2000), and Zartman (2005).

54   I have tried to cite significant case studies to illustrate my analysis. There are many more of them than those cited here and I apologize to their authors for the omissions.

55   Ten years later, the 1994 book was then used as the basis for further case studies in Crump and Zartman (2003) and Crump (2003), expanding the conceptual and empirical development

56   For a serious effort to bridge this gap, see Sambanis 2004.

57   Walter (2002) combines both methods by examining two cases (Zimbabwe and Rwanda) in addition to the 72 sets of data.

58   Although Walter (2002) at 56 says it does not matter.

References

Adams, JS, 1965. "Inequality in Social Exchange," in Berkowitz, L, *Advances in Experimental Psychology*. Academic Press.

Adorno, TW, Frenkel-Brunswick, E, Levinson, DJ and Sanford, RN, 1950. *The Authoritarian Personality*. New York: Harper

Aggarwal, VK, 1983. "The unraveling of the Multi-Fiber Arrangement 1981: an examination of international regime change," *International Organization* 37:4, pp. 617–45.

Albin, C, 1992. *Fairness Issues in Negotiation*. Laxenburg: International Institute of Applied Systems Analysis, working paper 92–88.

Ali, TM. and Matthews, RO (eds), 1999. *Civil Wars in Africa*. Montreal: McGill-Queens University Press.

Allison, GT, 1971. *Essence of Decision*. Boston: Little, Brown.

Alwin, D, 1987. "Distributive Justice and Satisfaction with Material Well-Being," *American Sociological Review* 52: 1, pp.83–95.

Apter, DE, 1971. *Choice and the Politics of Allocation*. New Haven: Yale University Press.

Aristotle, 1911. *Nichomachean Ethics*. New York: Dutton.

Arnson, C and Zartman, IW (eds), 2005. *Rethinking the Economics of War: The Intersection of Need, Creed, and Greed*. Baltimore: The Johns Hopkins University Press.

Aron, R, 1965. "The Anarchical Order of Power," in Hoffman, S (ed.), 1965.

—— 1969. *Peace and War*. New York: Doubleday.

Arrow, K, 1963. *Social Choice and Individual Values*. New Haven: Yale University Press.

Arrow, K, 1974. *The Limits of Organization*. New York: WW Norton.

Assefa, H, 1987. *Mediation of Civil Wars*. Boulder, CO: Westview.

Atran, S, 2003. "Genesis of Suicide Terrorism," *Science* CCCIC, pp.1534–39 (7 March).

Avenhaus, R and Zartman, IW (eds), 2006. *Diplomacy Games: Formal Models of, in and for Negotiation*. Springer Verlag.

Avenhaus, R, Kremenyuk, V, and Sjöstedt, G (eds), 2002. *Containing the Atom: Nuclear Negotiations for Safety and Security*. Lexington, MA: Lexington Books.

Axelrod, R, 1970. *The Conflict of Interest*. Chicago: Markham.

—— 1984. *The Evolution of Cooperation*. New York: Basic Books.

Axelrod, R and Dion, D, 1988. "The Further Evolution of Cooperation," *Science* 242:4884, pp.1385–90.

Bacharach, P and Baratz, M, 1970. *Power and Poverty*. Oxford: Oxford University Press.

Bacharach, SB and Lawler, E, 1980. *Power and Politics in Organizations*. Hoboken, NJ: Jossey-Bass.

Baldwin, DA, 1965. "The International Bank in Political Perspective," *World Politics* 8:1, pp. 68–81.

—— 1971a. "Thinking about Threats," *Journal of Conflict Resolution* 15:1, pp. 71–8.

—— 1971b. "The Costs of Power," *Journal of Conflict Resolution* 15:2, pp. 145–55.

—— 1971c. "The Power of Positive Sanctions," *World Politics* 24:1, pp. 19–38.

—— 1987, "Bargaining with Airline Hijackers," in Zartman 1987b.

Ballentine, K and Sherman, J, 2003. *Beyond Greed and Grievance: The Political Economy of Armed Conflict*. Boulder: Lynne Rienner Publishers.

Barclay, S and Petterson, C, 1976, *Multi-Attribute Utility Models*. McLean: Designs & Decision, technical report 76–1.

Barrett, S, 1998. "On the Theory and Diplomacy of Environmental Treaty-Making," *Environmental and Resource Economics* 11:3–4, pp. 317–33.

—— 2003. *Environment and Statecraft*. Oxford: Oxford University Press.

Barry, B, 1989. *Theories of Justice*. Berkeley: University of California Press.

Bartos, OJ, 1967a. "How Predictable are Negotiations?" *Journal of Conflict Resolution* 11:4481–195, reprinted in Zartman 1978b.

—— 1967b. *Simple Models of Group Behavior*. New York: Columbia University Press.

—— 1974. *Process and Outcome of Negotiation*. New York: Columbia University Press.

—— 1987a. "A Simple Model of Negotiation," in Zartman (ed.), 1987b.

—— 1987b. "How Predictable are Negotiations?" in Zartman (ed.), 1987b.

Bazerman, M and Neale, MA, 1992. *Negotiating Rationally*. New York: The Free Press.

Bazerman, M, Magliozi, T and Neale, MA, 1985. "The Acquisition of an Integrative Response in a Competitive Market," *Organizational Behavior and Human Performance* 34:2, pp. 294–313.

Beetham, D, 1991. *The Legitimation of Power*. London: MacMillan.

Bell, R, Edwards, D, Harrison Wagner, R (eds), 1969. *Political Power*. New York: The Free Press.

Bendahmane, D and McDonald, J (eds), 1984. *International Negotiation*. Washington: State Department Foreign Service Institute.

Bendahmane, D and McDonald, J (eds), 1986. *Perspectives on Negotiation*. Washington: State Department Foreign Service Institute.

Ben-Dor, G and Dewitt, D (eds), 1987. *Conflict Management in the Middle East*. Lexington, MA: Lexington Books.

Benedick, R, 1991. *Ozone Diplomacy*. Cambridge, MA: Harvard University Press.

Benedick, R, Chayes, A, Lashof, DA, Matthews, JT and Nitze, WA, 1991. "Greenhouse Warming: Negotiating a Global Regime." Washington: World Resources Institute.

Benton, AA and Druckman, D, 1973. "Salient Solutions and the Bargaining Behavior of Representatives and Nonrepresentatives," *International Journal of Group Tensions* 3:1, pp. 28–39.

Benton, AA, Kelley, HH and Liebling, B, 1972. "Effects of Extremity of Offers and Concession Rates on the Outcomes of Bargaining," *Journal of Personality and Social Psychology* 23:1, pp. 78–83.

Bercovitch, J (ed.), 1996. *Resolving International Conflicts*. Boulder: Lynne Rienner Publishers.

Bercovitch, J (ed.), 2002. *Studies in International Mediation*. New York: Palgrave.

Bercovitch, J and Rubin, JZ (eds), 1992. *Mediation in International Relations: Multiple Approaches to Conflict Management* . London: Macmillan.

Berdal, M and Malone, D, 2000. *Greed and Grievance: Economic Agendas in Civil War.* Boulder: Lynne Rienner Publishers.

Bernstein, BJ, 1976. "We Almost Went to War," *Bulletin of Atomic Scientists* 2, pp. 13–21.

Bies, B, Lewicki, R, and Sheppard, B (eds), 1997. *Research on Negotiations in Organization.* Newbury Park: Sage.

Bloom, B, 1966. Unpublished paper, NISER, 25 August.

Bodansky, D, 1993. "The United Nations Convention on Climate Change: A Commentary," *Yale Journal of International Law* 28, pp. 451–558.

Bonoma, T 1975. *Conflict: Escalation and Deescalation.* Beverley Hills: Sage.

Borawski, J, 1992. *From the Atlantic to the Urals.* New York: Pergamon.

—— 1992a. *Security for a New Europe.* Macmillan.

—— 1992b. *From the Atlantic to the Urals.* Pergamon.

Boulding, K, 1956. *The Image.* Ann Arbor, MI: University of Michigan Press.

Boyer, B, 1996. "Positional Bargaining and Coalition Structures" in *International Environmental Organization.* Geneva: Graduate School in International Relations, doctoral thesis.

Brady, HE and Collier, D, 2004. *Social Inquiry: Diverse Tool, Shared Standards.* Lanham, MD: Roman & Littlefield.

Braithwaite, RB, 1955. *Theory of Games as a Tool for the Moral Philosopher.* Cambridge: Cambridge University Press.

Brams, SJ, 1975. *Game Theory and Politics.* New York: The Free Press.

—— 1985. *Superpower Games.* New Haven: Yale University Press.

—— 1990. *Negotiation Games.* London: Routledge.

—— 1994. *Theory of Moves.* Cambridge: Cambridge University Press.

Brams, SJ and Kilgour, DM, 1988. *Games and National Security.* New York: Basil Blackwell.

—— 1999. "Fallback Bargaining," presented to the International Studies Association.

Brams, SJ and Taylor, A, 1996. *Fair Division.* Cambridge: Cambridge University Press.

Bueno de Mesquita, B and Lalman, D, 1992. *War and Reason.* New Haven: Yale University Press.

Bull, H, 1977. *The Anarchical Society.* New York: Columbia University Press.

Bunn, G, 1992. *Arms Control by Committee.* Stanford: Stanford University Press.

—— (ed.), 1995. "Justice and Negotiation in Global Security," *American Behavioral Science* 38:6.

Burton, J, 1969. *Communication and Conflict.* New York: The Free Press.

Byrne, H, 1996. *El Salvador's Civil War: A Study in Revolution.* Boulder: Lynne Rienner Publishers.

Camazine, S, Deneubourg, JL, Franks, N, Sneyd, J, Theraulaz, G and Bonabeau, E, 2001. *Self-Organization in Biological Systems.* Princeton: Princeton University Press.

Carlson, L, 1995. "A Theory of Escalation and International Conflict," Journal of Conflict Resolution 39:3, pp. 511–34.

Carr, EH, 1949. *The Twenty Years' Crisis.* Macmillan.

Carrington, Lord, 1980. *Negotiating UN Security Council Resolution 242.* Washington: Center for the Study of Diplomacy.

Casper, G and Taylor, MM, 1996. *Negotiated Democracy: Transitions from Authoritarian Rule.* Pittsburgh: University of Pittsburgh Press.

Chasek, P, 1994. "The Negotiating System of Environment and Development," in Spector, NI, Sjöstedt, G and Zartman, IW (eds). *Negotiating International Regimes.* London: Graham & Trotman.

—— 2003. "The Ozone Depletion Regime," in Spector, BI and Zartman, IW (eds), 2003. *Getting it Done: Post-Agreement Negotiation and International Regimes.* Washington: USIP.

Chasek, P, Wagner, L and Zartman, IW, 1996. "Le Maghreb dans les negociations internationales de l'environnement," in Bencherifa, A and Swearingen, W (eds). *L'environnement Maghrébin en Danger.* Rabat: Editions Université Mohammed V, Faculté des Sciences Sociales; also in Swearingen, W and Bencherifa A, (eds). *North African Environment at Risk.* Boulder, CO: Westview.

Chayes, A and Chayes, AH, 1993. "On Compliance," *International Organization* 47:2, pp. 175–206.

Cline, WR *et al.*, 1978. *Trade Negotiations in the Tokyo Round.* Brookings.

Coddington, A, 1968. *Theories of the Bargaining Process.* Aldine.

—— 1973. "Bargaining as a Decision-Making Process," *Swedish Journal of Economics* 75:3, pp. 397–403.

Collier, P, 2003. *Breaking the Conflict Trap: Civil War and Development Policy.* World Bank Research Reports.

Collier, P and Hoeffler, A, 2002. "Greed and Grievance in Civil Wars." Working Paper Series 2002–01. Oxford Center for the Study of African Economies. See www.csae.ox.ac.uk

Cook, KS, 1975. "Expectations, Evaluation and Equity," *American Sociological Review* 30:2, pp. 372–88.

Cook, KS and Hegtvedt, K, 1983. "Distributive Justice, Equity and Equality," in Inkeles, A (ed.). *Annual Review of Sociology* 9, pp. 217–41.

Coplin, W, 1969. *The Functions of International Law.* Chicago, IL: University of Chicago Press.

Crawford, B, 1984. "Stabilizing factors in international conflict resolution," *Negotiation Journal* 3:4, pp. 333–45.

Crawford, B and Hegtvedt, K, 1983. "Distributive Justice, Equity & Equality," in Inkeles, A (ed.). *Annual Review of Sociology* 9. Palo Alto: Annual Review.

Crenshaw, M 2000. "The Psychology of Terrorism: An Agenda for the 21st Century" Political Psychology, 21:2, pp. 405–20.

Cristal, M, 2003. "Negotiating under the Cross," *International Negotiation* 8:3, pp. 549–76.

Crocker, C, 1992. *High Noon in Southern Africa.* New York: WW Norton.

Crocker, C, Hampson, FO and Aall, P (eds), 1999. *Herding Cats: Multiparty Mediation in a Complex World.* . Washington: US Institute of Peace.

Crocker, C, Hampson, FO and Aall, P, 2005. *Taming Intractable Conflicts: Mediation in the Hardest Cases.* Washington: US Institute of Peace.

Cross, JG, 1969. *The Economics of Bargaining.* New York: Basic.

—— 1978. "Negotiation as a Learning Process," in Zartman, IW (ed.), 1978b.

Crozier, M 1964. "Pouvoir et organisation," *Européennes de Sociologie* 5:1, pp. 55–8.

Crump, L, (ed.), 2003. "Multiparty Negotiation and the Management of Complexity," *International Negotiation* 8:2, pp. 189–95.

Crump, L and Zartman, IW (eds), 2003. "Multilateral Negotiation and Complexity", special issue of International Negotiation 8:1.

Curzon, G, 1965. *Multilateral Commercial Diplomacy*. New York: Praeger.

Cutler, C and Zacher, M (eds), 1992. *Canadian Foreign Policy and International Economic Regimes*. Vancouver: UBC Press.

Dahl, R, 1955. "Hierarchy, Democracy and Bargaining in Politics and Economics," *Research Frontiers in Politics and Government*. Brookings.

—— 1957. " The concept of power," Behavioral Science 2:2, pp.201–15.

—— 1971. *Polyarchy: Participation and Opposition*. New Haven: Yale University Press.

—— 1976. *Political Analysis*. Englewood Cliffs: Prentice Hall.

Davidow, J, 1984. *A Peace In Southern Africa*. Boulder, CO: Westview.

de Callières, F, 1963[1716]. *On the Manner of Negotiating with Princes*. Notre Dame, IN: University of Notre Dame Press.

de Felice, FB, 1978[1778]. "Des négociations ou l'Art de négocier," in von Martens, K, *Le Guide Diplomatique* 1. Paris: Gavelot.

Deng, F, *et al.*, 1996. *Sovereignty as Responsibility*. Brookings.

de Soto, A, 1999. "Ending Violent Conflict in El Salvador," in Crocker, C, Hampson, FO and Aall, P (eds). *Herding Cats: Multiparty Mediation in a Complex World*. Washington: USIP.

deTocqueville, A, 1850. *De la démocratie en Amérique*. Paris: Pagnerre.

Deutsch, M, 1973. *The Resolution of Conflict*. New Haven: Yale University Press.

—— 1975. "Equity, Equality and Need," *Journal of Social Issues* 31:3, pp. 137–49.

—— 1985. *Distributive Justice*. New Haven: Yale University Press.

de Waal, FBM, 1992. Chimpanzee Politics. Cape.

Dolnik, A, 2003. "Contrasting Dynamics of Crisis Negotiations," *Internaional Negotiation* 8:3, pp. 495–526.

Donohue, W and Taylor, P, 2003. "Testing Role Effect in Terrorist Negotiations," *International Negotiation* 8:3, pp. 527–47.

Doran, CF, 1991. *Systems in Crisis: New Imperatives of High Politics at the Century's End*. New York: Cambridge University Press.

—— 2000. " Confronting the Principles of the Power Cycle," in Midlarsky, M (ed.). *Handbook of War Studies* 2. Ann Arbor, MI: University of Michigan Press.

Douglas, A, 1957. "The Peaceful Settlement of Industrial and Intergroup Disputes,"*Journal of Conflict Resolution* 1:1, pp. 69–81.

Dreyer, JT, 1999. "China, The Monocultural Paradigm," *Orbis* 43:4, pp. 581–98.

Druckman, D, 1973. *Human Factors in International Negotiation*. Sage.

—— (ed.), 1977. *Negotiations: A Social-Psychological Perspective*. Halstead.

—— 1986. "Stages, Turning Points and Crises: Negotiating Military Base Rights, Spain and the US," *Journal of Conflict Resolution* 30:3, pp. 327–60.

—— 1990. "The Social Psychology of Arms Control and Reciprocation," *Political Psychology* 9:4, pp. 553–81.

Druckman, D and Bonoma, TV, 1976. "Determinants of Bargaining Behavior in Bilateral Monopoly 2," *Behavioral Science* 21:3, pp. 252–62.

Druckman, D and Harris, R, 1990. "Alternative Models of Responsiveness in International Negotiation," *Journal of Conflict Resolution* 43:2, pp. 234–51.

Druckman, D, Benton, A, Faizunisa, A and Bagur, JS, 1976. "Cultural Differences in Bargaining Behavior," *Journal of Conflict Resolution* 20:3, pp. 413–51.

Druckman, D, Broome, BJ and Korper, SH, 1988. "Value Differences and Conflict Resolution: Facilitation or Delinking?" *Journal of Conflict Resolution* 32:4, pp. 489–510.

Dugatkin, LA, 1997. *Cooperation among Animals.*New York: Oxford University Press.

Dunnoff, J, 1995. "Toward the Transformation of International Environmental Law," *Harvard Environmental Law Review* 19:2, pp. 241–311.

Dupont, C, 1994. "Coalition Theory," in Zartman (ed), 1994.

Eckhoff, T, 1974. *Justice: Its Determinants in Social Action.* Rotteredam: Rotterdam University Press.

Eden, L and Hampson, FO, 1990. *Clubs are Trumps: Towards a Taxonomy of International Regimes.* Ottawa, Canada: Carleton University Center for International Trade and Investment Policy Studies, paper 90–02.

Edgeworth, FY. 1881. *Mathematical Physics.* London: Kegan Paul; reprinted. Kelley 1967.

Edmead, F, 1971. *Analysis and Prediction in International Mediation.* New York: UNITAR Study PS-2.

Eisenstadt, S, 1966. *Modernization: Protest and Change.* Englewood Cliffs, NJ: Prentice-Hall.

Elias, N, 1970. *Qu'est-ce que c'est la sociologie?* Aix-en-Provence: Pandora.

Ellsberg, D, 1975. "Theory and Practice of Blackmail," in Young, O (ed.), 1975.

Elster, J, 1992. *Local Justice.* New York: Russell Sage.

Emerson, R, 1960. *From Empire to Nation.* Cambridge, MA: Harvard University Press.

Evans, JW, 1971. *The Kennedy Round in American Trade Policy.* Cambridge, MA: Harvard University Press.

Evans, R, Jacobson, HK and Putnam, R (eds), 1993. *Double-Edged Diplomacy.* Berkeley: University of California Press.

Faber, M, 1990. "The Volta River Project: For Whom the Smelter Tolled," in Pickett, J and Singer, H (eds). *Towards Economic Recovery in Sub-Saharan Africa.* Routledge.

Fagen, RR (ed.), 1979. *Capitalism and the State in US-Latin American Relations.* Stanford: Stanford University Press.

Fagen, RR and Nau, HR, 1979. "Mexican Gas: The Northern Connection," in Fagen, RR (ed.), 1979. *Capitalism and the State in US-Latin American Relations.* Stanford: Stanford University Press.

Fan, X, 2000. "Seeking Honor under Strong Symmetry in the Korean War Armistice Negotiations," in Zartman, IW and Rubin, JZ (eds), 2000.

Farnham, B (ed.), 1994. *Avoiding Losses/Taking Risks.* Ann Arbor, MI: University of Michigan Press.

Faure, GO, 2003. "Negotiating with Terrorists: The Hostage Case," *International Negotiation* 8:3, pp. 469–94.

Faure, GO and Kolb, D, 1994. "Organizational Theory," in Zartman, IW (ed.), 1994. *International Multilateral Negotiations.* Hoboken, NJ: Jossey Bass.

Faure, GO and Rubin, JZ (eds), 1993. *Culture and Negotiation.* Newbury Park: Sage.

Favret, J, 1973. "Traditionalism Through Ultra-Modernising," in Micaud, C and Gellner, E. *Arabs and Berbers.* Lexington, MA: Lexington Books.

Feith, H, 1962. *The Decline of Constitutional Democracy in Indonesia.* Ithaca, NY: Cornell University Press.

Feiwel, G (ed.), 1989. *The Economics of Imperfect Competition and Employment.* London: Macmillan.

Feld, W, 1966. "External Relations of the Common Market and Group Leadership Attitudes in the Member States," *Orbis* 10:2, pp. 564–87.

Filley, AC, 1975. *Interpersonal Conflict Resolution.* Glenview: Scott Fores-man.

Fisher, R, 1969. *International Conflict for Beginners.* New York: Harper and Row.

Fisher, R and Ury, W, 1981. *Getting to Yes.* Boston: Houghton Mifflin.

Fliess, B, 1987. "The World Administrative Radio Conference 1979," in Zartman, IW (ed.), 1987c.

Floweree, C and Aberle, R, 1993. *The Chemical Weapons Ban Negotiations.* Washington DC: School of Advanced International Studies Case Studies.

Fortna, VP, 2004. *Peace Time: Ceasefire Agreements and the Durability of Peace.* Princeton: Princeton University Press.

Forward, N, 1971. *The Field of Nations.* Boston: Little, Brown.

Foucault, M, 1984. *Un Parcours Philosophique.* Paris: Gallimard.

Friedheim, R, 1965. "The 'Satisfied' and 'Dissatisfied' States Negotiate International Law," *World Politics* 18:1, pp. 20–41.

—— 1987. "The Third United Nations Conference on the Law of the Sea," in Zartman, IW (ed.), 1987c.

—— 1993. Negotiating an Ocean Regime. Columbia: University of South Carolina Press.

Gardner, R, 1992. *Negotiating Survival.* Council on Foreign Relations.

Gauthier, D, 1986. *Morals by Agreement.* New York: Oxford University Press.

Geertz, C, 1983. *Local Knowledge.* New York: Basic Books.

Genesis 18:16–33.

George, A, 1979. "Case Studies and Theory Development," in Lauren, P (ed.). *Diplomacy: New Approaches in Theory, History and Policy.* New York: The Free Press.

—— (ed.), 1991. *Avoiding War.* Boulder, CO: Westview.

George, A and McKeown, T, 1985. "Case Studies and Theories of Organizational Decision-Making," in Coulam, R and Smith, R (eds). *Advances in Information Processing in Organizations* 2. JAI Press.

George, A, Hall, D and Simons, W, 1971. *The Limits of Coercive Diplomacy.* Boston: Little, Brown.

Gerth, HH and Mills, CW (eds), 1946. *From Max Weber.* Oxford: Galaxy.

Ghali, BB, 1995. *Agenda for Peace.* UN.

Ghebali, Y, 1989. *La Diplomatie de la Détente.* Bruylant.

Gilpin, R, 1981. *War and Change in World Politics.* Cambridge: Cambridge University Press.

Goldstein, J, 2007. "The Game of Chicken in International Relations," in Touval, S and Zartman, IW (eds), 2007.

Goodby, J, 1988. "Stockholm Conference," in George, A, Farley, P and Dallin, A (eds). *US-Soviet Security Cooperation.* Boulder, CO: Westview.

Gouldner, A, 1960. "The Norm of Reciprocity; A Preliminary Statement," *American Sociological Review* 25:2.

Granger, C and Morgenstern, O, 1970. *Predictability of Stock Market Prices.* Lexington, MA: Heath.

Grayson, GW, 1980. *The Politics of Mexican Oil.* Pittsburgh: University of Pittsburgh Press.

Green, D and Schapiro, I, 1994. *The Pathologies of Rational Choice.* New Haven: Yale University Press.

Grieco, J, 1988. "Anarchy and the Limits of Cooperation," *International Organization* 32:3, pp. 485–508.

—— 1990. *Cooperation among Nations.* Ithaca, NY: Cornell University Press.

Griffiths, F, 1989. "The Soviet Experience of Arms Control," in Stein, JG (ed.), 1989. *Getting to the Table*. Baltimore: The Johns Hopkins University Press.

Gross, L, 1962. "Some Observations on the International Court of Justice," *American Journal of International Law* 56:1, pp. 40–2.

Guinier, L, 1994. *The Tyranny of the Majority: Fundamental Fairness and Representative Democracy*. New York: The Free Press.

Gulliver, PH, 1979. *Disputes and Negotiations*. New York: Academic.

—— 1997. "On mediators," in Hammett, I (ed.). *Social Anthropology and Law*. London: Academic.

Gyawali, D, 1989. "Water in Nepal". Honolulu: East-West Center, occasional paper 8.

Haas, P, 1990. *Saving the Mediterranean*. New York: Columbia University Press.

Habeeb, WM, 1988. *Power and Tactics in International Negotiation*. Baltimore: The Johns Hopkins University Press.

—— 2000. " Frustrated Asymmetry in US-Egyptian Aid Negotiations" in Zartman, IW and Rubin, JZ (eds), 2000.

Hamermesh, DS, 1978. "Who 'Wins' in Wage Bargaining?" in Zartman, IW, 1987d.

Hammer, WC and Baird, LS, 1978. "The Effect of Strategy, Pressure to Reach Agreement, and Relative Power on Bargaining Behavior," in Sauermann, H (ed.). *Contributions to Experimental Economics* 7. Mohr.

Hampson, FO, 1989. "Headed for the Table," in Stein, JG (ed), 1989. *Getting to the Table*. Baltimore: The Johns Hopkins University Press.

—— 1995. *Multilateral Negotiation*. Baltimore: The Johns Hopkins University Press.

—— 1996. *Nurturing Peace: Why Peace Settlements Succeed or Fail*. Washington: USIP.

Hao, Y and Zhai, Z 1990. "China's Decision to Enter the Korean War," *China Quarterly* 121 (March).

Harsanyi, J, 1975[1956]. "Approaches to the Bargaining Problem Before and After the Theory of Games," in Young, O (ed.), 1975. *Bargaining*. University of Illinois Press.

—— 1977. *Rational Behavior and Bargaining Equilibrium in Games and Social Situations*. Cambridge: Cambridge University Press.

Hasenclever, A, Mayer, P and Rittberger, V, 1997. *Theories of International Regimes*. Cambridge: Cambridge University Press.

Hayashi, H, 1999. "Game Theoretic Model of Peacekeeping," presented to the American Political Science Association Annual Meeting.

Hayek, F, 1973. *Rules and Order*. Chicago: University of Chicago Press.

Hayes, R, Kaminski, S, Beres, S, 2003. "Negotiating the Non-Negotiable," *International Negotiation* 8:3, pp. 451–67.

Hicks, JR, 1932. *Theory of Wages*. Macmillan.

Hipel, K and Fraser, N, 1984. *Conflict Analysis*. London: Elsevier.

Hirschman, AO, 1970. *Exit, Voice, and Loyalty*. Cambridge, MA: Harvard University Press.

Hobbes, T. (1998[1651]) *The Leviathan*. Oxford: Oxford Paperbacks.

Hoffmann, S, 1960. *Contemporary Theory in International Relations*. Englewood Cliffs, NJ: Prentice-Hall.

—— 1965. *Conditions of World Order*. Simon & Schuster.

Holbrooke, R, 1997. *To End a War*. Random House.

Holsti, OR, 1972. *Crisis, Escalation and War*. Montreal: McGill-Queens University Press.

Homans, G, 1961. *Social Behavior.* Harcourt, Brace and World.

Hopkins, R, 1987. "The Wheat Negotiations," in Zartman, IW (ed.), 1987c.

Hopmann, PT, 1978, "An Application of the Richardson Process Model," in Zartman, IW (ed.), 1978b.

—— 1993. *'I Cut You Choose': A Model for Negotiating Trade-Offs in Complex Multi-Issue Negotiations.* Design and Decision.

—— 1996. *The Negotiation process and the Resolution of International Conflicts.* Columbia: University of South Carolina Press.

—— 2001. "Disintegrating States: Separating without Violence," in Zartman, IW (ed.), 2001.

Hopmann, PT and Smith, TC, 1978. "An Application of the Richardson Process Model: Soviet-American Interactions in the Test-Ban Process," in Zartman (ed.), 1978.

Horgan, J and Taylor, M, 2003. *The Psychology of Terrorism.* Frank Cass.

Houben, PH, 1967. "Principles of International Law Concerning Friendly Relations and Cooperation among States," *American Journal of International Law* 61:3, pp. 703–36.

Huntington, SP, 1969. *Political Order in Changing Societies* New Haven: Yale University Press.

—— 1991. *The Third Wave: Democratization in the Late Twentieth Century.* Oklahoma: University of Oklahoma Press.

Hurrell, A and Kingsbury, B, 1992. *The International Politics of the Environment.* Clarendon.

Ikle, FC, 1964. *How Nations Negotiate.* New York: Praeger.

—— 1968, "Negotiation," in *International Encyclopedia of the Social Sciences*, vol. XI, 117–120. Macmillan and Free Press.

Ikle, FC and Leites, N, 1962, 'Political Negotiation as a Process of Modifying Utilities," *Journal of Conflict Resolution* 6:1, pp. 19–28.

Jasso, G, 1980. "A New Theory of Distributive Justice," *American Sociological Review* 45:l, pp. 3–32.

Jensen, L, 1987. "Soviet-American Bargaining Behavior in Postwar Arms Control Negotiations," in Zartman, IW (ed.), 1987b.

—— 1988. *Negotiating Disarmament.* Columbia: University of South Carolina Press.

Jentleson, B (ed.), 2000. *Opportunities Missed, Opportunities Seized.* Lanham: Rowman & Littlefield.

Jervis, R, 1985, *World Politics* 38:1.

Johnston, A, 1996. "Cultural Realism and Strategy in Modern China," in *The Culture of National Security: Norms and Identity in World Politics.*

Johnston, D, and Sampson, C (eds), 1994. *Religion: The Missing Dimension of Statecraft.* New York: Oxford University Press.

Jones, EL, 1987. *The European Miracle: Environments, Economies and Geopolitics in the History of Europe and Asia.* Cambridge: Cambridge University Press.

Jorden, W, 1984. *Panama Canal Odessy.* University of Texas Press.

Joseph, L and Wills, M, 1963. "An Experimental Analog to Two-Person Bargaining," *Behavioral Science* 8:1, pp. 11–27.

Kahneman, D and Tversky, A, 1979. "Prospect Theory," *Econometrica* 47:3, pp. 263–91.

Kanet, R and Kolodziej, E (ed.), 1991. *The Cold War as Cooperation.* Macmillan.

Karass, C, 1970. *The Negotiation Game.* World.

Keenan, J and Wilson, R, 1999. *Journal of Applied Economics.*

Kelley, EW, 1970. "Bargaining in Coalition Situations," in Kelley, EW *et al., The Study of Coalition Behavior.* Holt, Rinehart & Winston.

Kelley, HH, Beckman, LL and Fisher, CS, 1967. "Negotiating the Division of a Reward under Incomplete Information," *Journal of Experimental Psychology* 3:3, pp. 361–98.

Kendell, F and Louw, L, 1987. *South Africa: The Solution.* Berkeley: University of California, Institute for Policy Studies.

Kennedy, RF, 1969. *Thirteen Days: A Memoir of the Cuban Missile Crisis.* WW Norton.

Keohane, R, 1986. "Reciprocity in International Relations," *International Organization* 40:1, pp. 1–28.

Khrushchev, N, 1962. "Messages exchanged by President Kennedy and Chairman Khrushchev during the Cuban Missile Crisis 1962," Department of State Bulletin (19 November).

—— 1970. *Khrushchev Remembers.* Boston: Little, Brown.

—— 1974. *Khrushchev Remembers.* Boston: Little, Brown.

Khury, F, 1968. "The Etiquette of Bargaining in the Middle East," *American Anthropologist* 70:4, pp. 698–706.

Kimball, L, 1992. *Forging International Agreement.* World Resources Institute.

Kissinger, H, 1969. "The Vietnam Negotiations," *Foreign Affairs* IIL:2, pp. 211–34.

—— 1991. "False Dreams of a New World Order," *Washington Post,* 26 February.

Kivimäki, T, 1993. *Distribution of Benefits in Bargaining between a Developing Country and a Superpower.* Helsinki: University of Helsinki, doctoral dissertation.

—— 2000. "US-Indonesian Negotiations over the Embargo of the Communist Bloc 1950–54," in Zartman, IW and Rubin, JZ (eds), 2000.

Klir, GJ, 1985. "The Many Faces of Complexity," in Aida, S *et al., Science and Praxis of Complexity.* UN University Press.

Knorr, K, 1975. *Military Power and Potential.* Lexington, MA: Heath Lexington.

Knutsen, T, 1997. *A History of International Relations Theory.* Manchester: Manchester University Press.

Kolb, D and Faure, GO, 1994. "Organization Theory: The Interface of Structure, Culture, Procedures and Negotiation Processes," in Zartman, IW (ed.), 1994. *International Multilateral Negotiation: Approaches to the Management of Complexity.* Hoboken, NJ: Jossey-Bass.

Kolm, SC, 1992. "Reciprocity," *Political Economy of the Good Society Newsletter* 2:2, pp. 1–6.

Korula, A, 2003. "The Regime Against Torture," in Spector, B and Zartman, IW (eds), 2003. *Getting it Done: Post-Agreement Negotiations and International Regimes.* Washington: USIP.

Krasner, S (ed.), 1983. *International Regimes.* Ithaca, NY: Cornell University Press.

Kratochwil, F, 1989. *Rules, Norms and Decisions.* Cambridge: Cambridge University Press.

Kremenyuk, V (ed.), 2002a. *International Negotiation: Analysis, Approaches, Issues* 2nd ed. Hoboken, NJ: Jossey-Bass.

—— 2002b. "Systems of International Negotiations," in Kremenyuk, V (ed.). *International Negotiations: Analysis, Approaches, Issues.* Hoboken, NJ: Jossey-Bass.

Kressel, K and Pruitt, DG (eds). *Mediation Research.* Hoboken, NJ: Jossey-Bass.

Kuhn, TS, 1962. *The Structure of Scientific Revolutions.* Chicago, IL: University of Chicago Press.

Kumar, K (ed.), 1998. *Post-Conflict Elections, Democratization, and International Assistance.* Boulder: Lynne Rienner Publishers.

Laitin, DD, 1987. "South Africa: Violence, Myths, and Democratic Reform," *World Politics* 39:2, pp. 258–79.

Lall, A, 1966. *Modern International Negotiation.* New York: Columbia University Press.

Lamm, H and Kayser, E, 1978. "An Analysis of negotiation concerning the Allocation of Jointly Produced Profit or Loss: The Role of Justice Norms, Politeness,.Profit Maximization, and Tactics." *International Journal of Group Tensions* :1, pp. 64–80.

Lamm, H and Rosch, E, 1972. "Information and Competitiveness of Incentive Structure as Factors in Two-Person Negotiation," *European Journal of Sociology* 2:4pp. 459–62.

Landsberger, HA, 1955. "Interim Report on a Research Project on Mediation," *Labor Law Review* 6:4, pp. 552–60.

Lang, W, 1989. *Internationaler Unweltschutz.* Vienna: Orac.

Larson, D, 1988. "The Psychology of Reciprocity in International Relations," *Negotiation Journal* 4:3, pp. 281–301.

Lasswell, H and Kaplan, A, 1951. *Power and Society,* New Haven: Yale University Press.

Lax, D and Sebenius, J, 1986. *The Manager as Negotiator.* New York: The Free Press.

—— 1991. "Thinking Coalitionally," in Young, HP (ed.). *Negotiation Analysis.* Ann Arbor, MI: University of Michigan Press.

—— 1996. *Principles and Paradoxes of Peaceful Change.* Syracuse, NY: Syracuse University Press.

Leatherman, J, 2003. "The Challenges of Regime Adjustment and Governance in the OSCE," in Spector, B and Zartman, IW (eds), 2003. *Getting it Done: Post-Agreement Negotiations and International Regimes.* Washington: USIP.

—— 2004. *From the Cold War to Democratic Peace: Third Parties, Peaceful Change and the OSCE.* Syracuse, NY: Syracuse University Press.

Leib, D, 1985. "Iran and Iraq at Algiers 1975," in Touval, S and Zartman, IW (eds), 1985.

Levy, M, Young, O and Zürn, M, 1994. *The Study of International Regimes: International Institute for Applied Systems Analysis,* WP94–113.

Lewicki, RJ, Barry, B, Minton, J and Saunders, D, 2003. *Negotiation, 4th edition.* New York: McGraw-Hill.

Lewicki, RJ, Sheppard, B and Bies, R (eds), 1986–1997. *Research on Negotiation in Organizations* 1–6. Greenwich CN: JAI Press.

Lewin, K, Lippitt, R and White, RK 1939. "Patterns of Aggressive Behavior in Experimentally Created Social Climate," *Journal of Social Psychology* 10:2, pp. 271–99.

Lieberfield, D, 1999a. "Conflict 'ripeness' revisited," *Negotiation Journal* 15:1, pp. 63–82.

—— 1999b. *Talking with the Enemy.* New York: Praeger.

Lieberthal, K, 1995. *Governing China: From Revolution to Reform.*

Lijphart, A, 1977. *Democracy in Plural Societies.* New Haven: Yale University Press.

—— 1985. *Power-Sharing in South Africa, Policy Paper in International Affairs, No. 24.* Berkeley: University of California, Institute of International Studies.

Lind, EA and Taylor, TR, 1988. *The Social Psychology of Procedural Justice.* Plenum.

Linz, J, 1975. "Totalitarian and Authoritarian Regimes," in Greenstein, FI and Polsby, NW (eds). *Handbook of Political Science* 3. Addison-Wesley.

Lipset, SM, 1981. *Political Man: The Social Basis of Politics.* Baltimore: The Johns Hopkins University Press.

Lipson, C, 1985. "Bankers' Dilemma," *World Politics* 38:2, pp. 200–25.

——— 1991. "Why are some international agreements informal?" *International Organization* 45:4, pp. 495–538.

Locke, J, Mill, JS, 1947. *On Liberty* (ed.). Alburey Castell: Appleton-Century-Crofts.

Lockhart, C, 1974. *The Efficacy of Threats.* Sage.

——— 1979. *Bargaining in International Conflicts.* New York: Columbia University Press.

Low, S, 1985. "The Zimbabwe Settlement 1976–1979," in Touval, S and Zartman, IW (eds), 1985.

Lyons, G and Mastanduno, M (eds), 1995. *Beyond Westphalia: State Sovereignty and International Intervention.* Baltimore: The Johns Hopkins University Press.

McDermott, R, 2007. "Prospect Theory and Negotiation Risks," in Avenhaus, R and Sjösted, G (eds). *Negotiating Risks.* Laxenburg: IIASA.

McWhinney, E, 1966. "The 'New' Countries and the 'New' International Law," *American Journal of International Law* 60:1, pp. 1–34.

Mahler, V, 1984. "The Political Economy of North-South Commodity Bargaining: the Case of the International Sugar Agreement," *International Organization* 38:4, pp. 709–32.

——— 1985. *Liberal Protectionism.* Berkeley: University of California Press.

Malmgren, H, 1973. *International Economic Peacekeeping in Phase II.* Quadrangle.

Markovsky, B, 1986. "Toward a Multilevel Distributive Justice Theory," *American Sociological Review* 50:4, pp. 822–39.

Marshall, CB, 1965. *The Exercise of Sovereignty.* Baltimore: The Johns Hopkins University Press.

Mason, T D, Weingarten, JP and Fett, PJ, 1999. "Win, Lose or Draw: Predicting the Outcome of Civil Wars," *Political Research Quarterly* 52:2, pp. 239–68.

Maundi, M, Zartman, IW, Khadiagala, G and Nuameh, K, 2006. *Getting In: Mediator's Entry into African Conflicts.* Washington: US Institute of Peace.

Meerts, PJ, 2005. "Entrapment," in Zartman, IW and Faure, GO (eds), 2005.

Meerts, P and Cede, F (eds), 2004. *Negotiating European Union.* Palgrave.

Messe, L, 1971. "Equity in Bilateral Bargaining," *Journal of Personality and Social Psychology* 17:3, pp. 287–91.

Micaud, C, Moore, CH, and Brown, LC, 1964. *Tunisia: The Politics of Modernization.* New York: Praeger.

Michels, R, 1962. *Political Parties.* New York: The Free Press.

Midgaard, K, 1968. "Some Comments on the Meaning and Use of Game Theory," *Cooperation and Conflict.* 3:2, pp. 108–30 .

Mill, JS, 1967 (1843). *A System of Logic.* Toronto: University of Toronto Press.

Mitchell, CR 1995a. "Asymmetry in Regional Conflicts" in Zartman, IW and Kremenyuk (eds), 1995.

——— 1995b. *Cutting Losses.* Fairfax, VA: George Mason University, Institute for Conflict Analysis and Resolution, working paper 9.

Modelski, G and Thompson, WR, 1996. *Leading Sectors and World Powers: The Coevolution of Global Economics and Politics.* New York: Columbia: University of South Carolina Press.

Mooradian, M and Druckman, D, 1999. "Hurting Stalemate or Mediation?" *Journal of Peace Research* 35:6, pp. 706–27.

Moravcsik, A, 1994. "A Liberal Intergovernmentalist Approach to the EC," in Bulmer, S and Scott, A (eds). *Economic and Political Integration of Europe*. Blackwell.

Morgan, TC, 1994. *Untying the Knot of War*. Ann Arbor, MI: University of Michigan Press.

Morgenthau, HJ, 1960. *Politics Among Nation, 3rd edn*. Random House.

Mosca, G, 1939. *The Ruling Class*. New York: McGraw-Hill.

Moussalli, AS (ed.), 1998. *Islamic Fundamentalism: Myths and Realities*. Ithaca Press.

Munton, D and Castle, G, 1992. "Air, Water and Political Fire: Building a North American Environmental Regime," in Cutler, C and Zacher, M (eds), 1992. *Canadian Foreign Policy and International Economic Regimes*. Vancouver: UBC Press.

Myers, N, 1995. "Environmental Unknowns," *Science* 269: 5222, pp. 358–60.

Nash, J, 1950. "The Bargaining Problem," *Econometrica* 8:2, pp. 155–62, reprinted in Young, O (ed.), 1975. *Bargaining*. University of Illinois Press.

Neufeld, M, 1993. "Interpretation and the 'Science' of International Relations," *Review of International Studies* 19:1, pp. 39–61.

Newhouse, J, 1974. *Cold Dawn*. London: Holt, Rinehart and Winston.

Nicolson, H, 1946. *The Congress of Vienna: A Study in Allied Unity 1812–1822*. New York: Harcourt, Brace and Company.

—— 1964. *Diplomacy*. New York: Oxford University Press.

Nierenberg, G, 1973, *Fundamentals of Negotiating*. Hawthorn.

Nogee, J, 1963. "Propaganda and Negotiation: The Case of the Ten-Nation Disarmament Commission," *Journal of Conflict Resolution* 7:3, pp. 510–21.

North, D, 1991. *Institutions, Institutional Change, and Economic Performance*. Cambridge: Cambridge University Press.

Norton, AR (ed.), 1995, 1996, 2005. *Civil Society in the Middle East*. 2 vols. Brill.

Odell, J, 2000. *Negotiating the World Economy*. Ithaca, NY: Cornell University Press.

O'Donnell, G and Schmitter, PC, 1986. *Transitions from Authoritarian Rule: Tentative Conclusions about Uncertain Democracies*. Baltimore: The Johns Hopkins University Press.

Olson, M, 1965. *The Logic of Collective Action*. Cambridge, MA: Harvard University Press.

Ohlson, T, 1998. *Power Politics and Peace Policies*. Uppsala: Uppsala University.

Ohlson, T and Stedman, SJ, 1994. *The New is Not Yet Born*. Brookings.

Organski, AFK, 1968. *World Politics*. Knopf.

Ottaway, M, 1995. "Negotiating a Conflict in Transition: The Ethiopian Civil War," Zartman, IW (ed.), 1995c. *Elusive Peace: Negotiating an End to Civil Wars*. Washington, DC: Brookings Institution.

Palma, M, 2003. "European Strategy Against Terrorist Insurgency and Local Armed Conflict." Gino Germani Research Center.

Pape, RA, 2003. "The Strategic Logic of Suicide Terrorism," *American Political Science Review* 97:3, pp. 343–61.

Parker, R, 1993. *The Politics of Miscalculation in the Middle East*. Indiana University Press.

Patchen, M, 1988. *Resolving Disputes Between Nations*. Duke University Press.

Patterson, M and Grubb, M, 1992. "The International Politics of Climate Change," *International Affairs* 68:2, pp. 293–310.

Paul, TV, 1994. *Asymmetric Conflicts: War Initiation by Weaker Powers.* Cambridge: Cambridge University Press.

Pecquet, A, 1738. *De l'Art de Négocier avec les Souverains.* The Hague: van Duren.

Pen, J, 1975[1952]. "A General Theory of Bargaining," in Young, O (ed.), 1975. *Bargaining.* University of Illinois Press.

Piaget, J, 1948. *The Moral Development of the Child.* New York: The Free Press.

Pillar, P, 1983. *Negotiating Peace.* Princeton: Princeton University Press.

Pomeranz, K, 2000. *The Great Divergence: China, Europe and the Making of the Modern World.* Princeton: Princeton University Press.

Pondi, JE, 2000. "Compensating for Weak Asymmetry in the Mali-Burkina Faso Conflict 1985–86" in Zartman & Rubin (eds), 2000. *Power and International Negotiation.* Ann Arbor, MI: University of Michigan Press.

Porter, G and Brown, J, 1995. *Global Environmental Politics* 2nd ed. Boulder, CO: Westview.

Porter, G and Brown, JW, 1996. *Environmental Politics.* Boulder, CO: Westview Press.

Powell, R, 1994. "Anarchy in International Relations Theory," *International Organization* 48:3, pp. 313–44.

Prasnikar, V and Roth, A, 1992. "Considerations of Fairness and Strategy: Experimental Data from Sequential Games," *Quarterly Journal of Economics* 107:3:865–88.

Preeg, E, 1970. *Traders and Diplomats: An Analysis of the Kennedy Round of Negotiations under the GATT.* Brookings.

Princen, T, 1992. *Intermediaries in International Conflict.* Princeton: Princeton University Press.

Pruitt, DG, 1972. "Methods for Resolving Differences of Interest: A Theoretical Analysis," *Journal of Social Issues* 28:1, pp. 133–54.

—— 1981. *Negotiation Behavior.* Academic.

—— (ed.), 1997. *Lessons Learned from the Middle East Peace Process.* International Negotiation 2:2, pp. 175–6.

Pruitt, DG and Carnevale, P, 1993. *Negotiation in Social Conflict.* Brooks/Cole.

Pruitt, DG and Kim, SH, 2004. *Social Conflict.* New York: McGraw-Hill.

Pruitt, DG and Olczak, P, 1995. "Beyond Hope: Approaches of Resolving Seemingly Intractable Conflict," in Bunker, B and Rubin, J (eds). *Conflict, Cooperation, and Justice.* Hoboken, NJ: Jossey-Bass.

Przeworski, A, 1970. *States and Markets.* Cambridge University Press.

Putnam, R, 1976. *The Comparative Study of Political Elites.* Englewood Cliffs: Prentice Hall.

—— 1988. "Diplomacy and domestic politics: the logic of two-level games," *International Organization* 32:3, pp. 427–60.

Pye, L, 1978. *China: An Introduction.* Boston: Little, Brown.

—— 1988. *The Mandarin and the Cadre: China's Political Culture.*

Quandt, WB, 1970. *Revolution and Political Leadership.* MIT Press.

—— 1977. *Decade of Decisions.* Berkeley: University of California Press.

—— (ed.), 1988. *The Middle East Ten Years after Camp David.* Brookings.

—— 1990. *The US and Egypt.* Brookings.

—— 1993. *The Peace Process.* Brookings.

Rae, D and Taylor, M, 1970. *The Analysis of Political Cleavages.* New Haven, CT: Yale University Press.

Ragin, CC, 1997. "Turning the Tables: How Case-Oriented Research Challenges Variable-Oriented Research," *Social Research* 16:1, pp. 27–42.

Raiffa, H, 1953. "Arbitration Scheme for generalize 2-person games," in Kuhn, HW and Tucker, AW (ed.). *Contribution to the Theory of Games* 2. Princeton: Princeton University Press.

—— Raiffa, H, 1982. *The Art and Science of Negotiation.* Cambridge, MA: Harvard University Press.

Raiffa, H, Richardson, J and Metcalfe, D, 2002. *Negotiation Analysis.* Cambridge, MA: Harvard Belknap Press.

Randle, R, 1973. *The Origins of Peace.* New York: The Free Press.

Rapoport, A, 1960. *Fights, Games and Debates.* Ann Arbor, MI: University of Michigan Press.

—— 1966. *Two Person Game Theory.* Ann Arbor, MI: University of Michigan Press.

—— 1974. *Conflict in Man-Made Environment.* Penguin.

Raven, BH and Kuglanski, AW, 1970. "Conflict and Power: The Structure of Conflict," in Swingle, P (ed.). *The Structure of Conflict.* Academic Press.

Raven, BH and Rubin, JZ, 1983. *Social Psychology.* Wiley.

Rawls, J, 1971. *A Theory of Justice.* Cambridge, MA: Harvard University Press.

Reich, W, 1990. *Origins of Terrorism: Psychologies, Ideologies, Theologies, States of Mind.* Woodrow Wilson Center Press.

Riker, W, 1962. *The Theory of Political Coalitions.* New Haven, CT: Yale University.

Rittberger, V and Mayer, P (eds), 1993. *Regime Theory and International Relations.* Clarendon.

Rittberger, V and Zürn, P, 1990. "Towards Regulated Anarchy in East-West Relations: Causes and Consequeces of East-West Regimes," in Rittberger, V (ed.). *International Regimes in East-West Politics.* Pinter.

Robson, P, 1965. "Africa and EEC: A Quantitative Note on Trade Benefits," *Bulletin of the Oxford University Institute of Statistics* 27:4, pp. 299–303.

Rogowski, R, 1974. *Rational Legitimacy.* Princeton: Princeton University Press.

Rosenau, J, 1967. "A Pre-Theory of Foreign Policy," in Farrell, RB (ed.). *Comparative Foreign and Domestic Policy.* Evanston: Northwestern University Press.

Rosenau, J and Czempiel, EO (eds), 1992. *Governance without Government.* Cambridge: Cambridge University Press.

Ross, J, 1998. "Escalation Theory in Labor-Management Negotiations," in, Wagner, JA *Advances in Qualitative Organization Research, volume 1.* St Louis, MO: Elsevier Science.

Rossi, P, 1958. "Community Decision-Making," in Young, R (ed.). *Approaches to the Study of Politics.* Evanston: Northwestern University Press.

Ross, L and Stillinger, C, 1991. " Barriers to Conflict Resolution," *Negotiation Journal* 7:4, pp. 389–404.

Roth, A (ed.), 1985. *Game Theoretic Models of Bargaining.* New York: Cambridge University Press.

Roth, G and Wittich, C (eds), 1968. *Max Weber: Economy and Society.* Berkeley: University of California Press.

Rothstein, R, 1977. *The Weak in the World of the Strong.* New York: Columbia University Press.

—— 1979. *Global Bargaining: UNCTAD and the Quest for a New International Economic Order.* Princeton: Princeton University Press .

Rubin, JZ (ed.), 1981. *The Dynamics of Third Party Intervention: Kissinger in the Middle East.* New York: Praeger.

Rubin, JZ and Brown, B, 1975. *The Social Psychology of Bargaining and Negotiation.* Academic.

Rubin, JZ and Salacuse, JW 1990. "The problem of power in international negotiations," *International Affairs* April, pp. 24–34.

Rubinstein, A, 1982. "Perfect Equilibrium in a Bargaining Model," *Ecometrica* 50:1, pp. 97–109.

Ruggie, JG, 1983. "International Regimes, Transactions and Change," in Krasner, S (ed.), 1983. *International Regimes.* Ithaca, NY: Cornell University Press.

Sambanis, N, 2004. "Using Case Studies to Expand Economic Models of Civil War," *Perspectives on Politics* 2:2, pp. 259–79.

Sand, P, 1990. *Lessons Learned in Global Environmental Governance.* World Resources Institute.

Saunders, H, 1985a. "We Need a Larger Theory of Negotiation: The Importance of Pre-Negotiating Phases," *Negotiation Journal* 1:3, p. 250.

—— 1985b. *The Other Walls.* Washington: AEI.

—— 1988. "International relationships," *Negotiation Journal* 3:3, pp. 245–74.

Sawyer, J and Guetzkow, H, 1965. "Bargaining and Negotiations in International Relations," in Kelman, H (ed.). *International Behavior.* London: Holt, Rinehart and Winston.

Sawyerr, A, 2000. "Renegotiation of the VALCO Agreement in Ghana," in Kremenyuk, V and Sjöstedt, G (eds). *International Economic Negotiations: Model vs Reality.* London: Edward Elgar, p. 100.

Scapple, K, 1996. "The Helsinki and Sofia Protocols: Can They Be as Effective as the Montreal Protocol?" Paper presented to the International Studies Association, San Diego CA.

Schapiro, I and Hardin, R, 1993. *Political Order (Nomos XXXVIII).* New York: New York University Press.

Scharpf, F, 1989. "Decision Rules, Decision Styles, and Policy Choices," *Journal of Theoretical Politics* 1:1, pp. 149–76.

Schelling, T, 1960. *The Strategy of Conflict.* Cambridge, MA: Harvard University Press.

—— 1966. *Arms and Influence.* New Haven: Yale University Press.

—— 1978. *Micromotives and Microbehavior.* New York: WW Norton.

Schneider, A and Honeyman C (eds), 2006. *The Negotiator's Fieldbook.* American Bar Association.

Schopenhauer, A, 1896. *The Art of Controversy.* Allen & Unwin.

Sebenius, J, 1984. *Negotiating the Law of the Sea.* Cambridge, MA: Harvard University Press.

Sen, A, 1970. *Collective Choice and Social Welfare.* Holden-Day.

—— 1999. *Development as Freedom.* Penguin.

Shalev, C, "Escalation in Israel," Maariv, 3 April, quoted in Sontag, D, "In Absence of Talk, Israeli-Palestinian Violence Speaks," *New York Times,* 4 April 2001.

Shapley, LS, 1953. "A Value for N-Person Games," *Annals of Mathematical Studies* 28:4, pp. 307–17.

Shell, GR, 1999. *Bargaining for Advantage.* Penguin.

Siegel, S and Fouraker, L, 1960. *Bargaining and Group Decision-Making.* New York: McGraw-Hill.

—— 1963. *Bargaining Behavior.* New York: McGraw-Hill.

Simon, H, 1953. "Notes on the observation and measurement of power." *Journal of Politics* 15:3, pp. 500–16.

—— 1957. *Models of Man*. New York: Wiley.

Sisk, T, 1995. *Democratization in South Africa*. Princeton: Princeton University Press.

Sjöstedt, G (ed.), 1993. *International Environmental Negotiations*. Newbury Park: Sage.

Sjöstedt, G and Kremenyuk, V (eds), 1996. *International Economic Negotiations*. London: Edward Elgar.

Skocpol, T (ed.), 1994. *Social Revolutions in the Modern World*. Cambridge: Cambridge University Press.

Skocpol, T and Somers, M, 1980. "The Uses of Comparative History in Macrosocial Analysis," *Comparative Studies in Society and History* 22:2, pp. 174–97.

Smith, M, 1996. "The European Union and a Changing Europe: Establishing the Boundaries of Order," *Journal of Common Market Studies* 34:1, pp. 5–28.

Smith, DL, Pruitt, DG and Carnevale, PJD, 1962. "Matching and Mismatching: The Effect of Own Limit, Other's Toughness and Time Pressure on Concession Rates in Negotiation," *Journal of Personality and Social Psychology* 40:4, pp. 876–83.

Smoke, R, 1977. *War: Controlling Escalation*. Cambridge, MA: Harvard University Press.

Smoker, P, 1964. "Fear in the Arms Race," *Journal of Peace Research* 1:1, pp. 55–63.

Snidel, D, 1985. "The Limits of Hegemonic Stability Theory," *International Organization* 39:4, pp. 579–614.

Snyder, G and Diesing, P, 1977. *Conflict Among Nations*. Princeton: Princeton University Press.

Solomon, D and Druckman, D, 1972. "Age, Representatives' Prior Performance, and the Distribution of Winnings with Teammates," *Human Development* 15:2, pp. 244–52.

Spar, D, 1993. "Co-developing the FSX Fighter," in Stein, JG and Pauly, L (eds). *Choosing to Cooperate*. Baltimore: The Johns Hopkins University Press.

Spector, BI, 1978. "Negotiation as a Psychological Process," in Zartman, IW (ed.), 1978b.

—— 1994. "Decision Analysis," in Zartman, IW (ed.), 1994.

—— 2003. "Negotiating with Villains Revisited," *International Negotiation* 8:3, pp. 613–21.

Spector, BI and Zartman, IW (eds), 2003. *Getting it Done: Post-Agreement Negotiations and International Regimes*. Washington: USIP.

Spector, BI, Sjöstedt, G and Zartman, IW (eds), 1994. *Negotiating an Environmental Regime: Lessons from UNCED*. London: Graham & Trottman.

Sprinz, D and Vaahtoranta, T, 1994. "The interest-based explanation of international environmental policy," *International Organization* 38:1, pp. 77–106.

Staw, BM, 1997. "The Escalation of Commitment," in Shapiro, Z (ed.). *Organizational Decision-Making*. Cambridge: Cambridge University Press.

Stedman, SJ, 1991. *Peacemaking in Civil War*. Boulder: Lynne Rienner Publishers.

—— 2000. "Spoiler Problems in Peace Processes," in Stern, P and Druckman, D (eds), 2000.

Stedman, SJ, Rothchild, D and Cousens, E (eds), 2002. *Ending Civil Wars: The Implementation of Peace Agreements*. Boulder: Lynne Rienner Publishers.

Stein, JG (ed), 1989. *Getting to the Table*. Baltimore: The Johns Hopkins University Press.

Stein, J and Pauly, L (eds), 1993. *Choosing to Cooperate: How States Avoid Loss*. Baltimore: The Johns Hopkins University Press.

Stern, P and Druckman, D (eds), 2000. *International Conflict Management after the Cold War*. Washington, DC: National Academy Press.

Stern, P, Axelrod, R, Jervis, R and Radner, R (eds), 1989. *Perspectives on Deterrence*. New York: Oxford University Press.

Stoll, RJ and McAndrew, W, 1986. "Negotiating Strategic Arms Control 1969–1979," *Journal of Conflict Resolution* 30:3, pp. 315–26.

Stolte, JF, 1987. "The Formation of Justice Norms," *American Sociological Review* 52:4, pp. 774–84.

Strange, S, 1983. "Cave! Hic Dragones," in Krasner, S, (ed.). *International Regimes*. Ithaca, NY: Cornell University Press.

Strauss, A, Schatzman, L, Ehrlich, D, Bucher, R and Sabshin, M (1963) "The Hospital as a Negotiated Order" in Friedson, E (ed.). *The Hospital in Modern Society*. New York: The Free Press.

Susskind, L, 1995. *Environmental Diplomacy*. New York: Oxford University Press.

Swingle, P (ed.), 1970. *The Structure of Conflict*. Academic.

Szulc, T, 1974. "How Kissinger Did It," *Foreign Policy* 15:21–69.

Talbott, S, 1979. *Endgame: The Inside Story of SALT II*. New York: Harper & Row.

Tawney, RH, 1931. *Equality*. Unwin.

Thibaut, JW and Kelley, HH, 1959. *The Social Psychology of Groups*. Wiley.

Thomas, K and Kilmann, R, "Developing a Forced-Choice Measure of Conflict-Handling Behavior," *Educational and Psychological Measurement* 37, pp. 309–25.

Thornton, TP, 1985. "Tashkent," in Touval and Zartman (eds), 1985. *International Mediation in Theory and Practice*. Boulder, CO: Westview.

Thucydides, 1960[– 411]. *The Peloponnesian Wars*. Oxford: Oxford University Press.

Tomlin, BW, 1989 "The Stages of Pre-Negotiation: The Decision to Negotiate North American Free Trade," in Stein, JG (ed.), 1989.

Touré, S, 1962. *The International Policy of the Democratic Party of Guinea* 7, p. 21. Conakry: PDG.

Touval, S, 1982. *The Peace Brokers*. Princeton: Princeton University Press.

—— 1992. "The Superpowers as Mediators." in Bercovitch, J and Rubin JZ (eds). *Mediation in International Relations: Multiple Approaches to Conflict Management*. Macmillan/St. Martin's Press.

—— 2001. "International Mediation in the Post-Cold War Era," in Crocker, CA, Hampson, FO and Aall, P (eds). *Turbulent Peace: The Challenges of Managing International Conflict*. Washington: US Institute of Peace.

—— 2002. *Mediation in the Yugoslav Wars: The Critical Years 1990–95*. Palgrave.

Touval, S and Zartman, IW (eds), 1985. *International Mediation in Theory and Practice*. Boulder, CO: Westview.

—— 1989. "Mediation in International Conflicts," in Kressel, K and Pruitt, DG (eds), 1989. *Mediation Research*. Hoboken, NJ: Jossey-Bass.

—— 2007. *Cooperation and Multilateralism Revisited*. Lanham: Roman & Littlefield.

Trachtenberg, M. (ed.), 1985. "White House Tapes and Minutes of the Cuban Missiles Crisis," *International Security* 10:1, pp. 164–203.

Tracy, BH, 1978. "Bargaining and Trial and Error: The Case of the Spanish Base Negotiations 1963–70," in Zartman, IW (ed.), 1978b.

Tsikata, FS (ed.), 1990. *Essays from the Ghana-VALCO Negotiations*. Accra: Ghana Publishing House.

Tuchman, B, 1984. *The March of Folly*. Knopf.

Udalov, V, 1995. "National Interests and Conflict Reduction." Zartman, IW and Kremenyuk, V (eds), 1995.

US Department of State, 2002. *Patterns of Global Terrorism 2001*. Office of the Coordinator for Counterterrorism.

Valavanis, S, 1958. "Resolution of Conflict When Utililes Interact," *Journal of Conflict Resolution* 2, pp. 256–68.

Vatcher, WH, 1958. *Panmunjon*. New York: Praeger.

Victor, D, Raustiala, K and Skolnikoff, E (eds), 1998. *International Environmental Commitments*. MIT Press.

von Haldenwang, C, 1999. "The State and Political Regulation: On the Legitimacy of Political Order in the 21st Century," *Politische Vierteljahrsschrift* 40:3, p. 365.

Wade, LL and Curry, RL, 1971. "An economic model of socio-political bargaining," *American Journal of Economics and Sociology* 30:4, pp. 383–93.

Wagner, H, 1975[1957]. "A Unified Treatment of Bargaining Theory," in Young, (ed.).

Wallerstein, I, 1966. *Social Change*. Wiley.

Walter, B, 2001. *Committing to Peace: The Successful Settlement of Civil Wars*. Princeton: Princeton University Press .

Walton, RE, 1970. "A Problem-Solving Workshop on Border Conflicts in East Africa," *Journal of Applied Behavioral Sciences* 6, pp. 453–89.

Walton, R and McKersie, R, 1965. *A Behavioral Theory of Negotiation*. New York: McGraw-Hill.

Waltz, K, 1954. *Man, the State and War*. New York: Columbia University Press.

——— 1979. *Theory of International Politics*. Random House.

Weber, M, 1978. *Economy and Society*, in Roth, G and Wittich, C (eds). Berkeley: University of California Press.

Weinbaum. M, 1986. *Egypt and the Politics of US Economic Aid*. Boulder, CO: Westview.

Whelan, J, 1979. *Soviet Diplomacy and Negotiating Behavior*. Government Printing Office.

Wills, ML, 1963. "An experimental analog to two-person bargaining," *Behavioral Science* 8:1, pp. 11–27.

Wilson, JQ, 1993. "The Moral Sense," *American Political Science* 87:1, pp. 1–11.

Winham, G, 1986. *International Trade and The Tokyo Round. Negotiations*. Princeton: Princeton University Press.

Winham, G and DeBoer, EC, 2003. "Asymmetry in Negotiating the Canada-US Free Trade Agreement 1985–87," in Zartman, IW and Rubin, JZ (eds), 2000.

Winham, GR, 1977a. "Complexity in International Negotiation," in Druckman, D (ed.). *Negotiations: A Social-Psychological Perspective*. Halstead.

——— 1977b. "Negotiation as a Management Process," *World Politics* 30:1, pp. 87–114.

——— 1988. *Trading with Canada*. New York: Priority.

——— 1990. "The Prenegotiation Phase of the Uruguay Round," in Stein (ed.), 1989.

Witkin, R, 1969. "The Straphangers' Cliff-Hanger," *New York Times*, 31 December 1969.

Wolf, A, 1997. *Quotas in International Environmental Agreements*. Earthscan.

Wolfe, TE, 1979. *The SALT Experience*. Ballinger.

Wriggins, H. 1987. "Up for Auction: Malta Bargains with Britain, 1971," in Zartman, I. W (ed.), 1987b.

Wriggins, H, 1995. "Negotiating Peace in Sri Lanka," in Zartman, IW (ed.), 1995

Young, HP (ed.), 1991. *Negotiation Analysis*. Ann Arbor, MI: University of Michigan Press.

—— 1994. *Equity*. Princeton: Princeton University Press.

Young, HP and Wolf, A, 1992. "Global Warming Negotiations: Does Fairness Matter?" *Brookings Review* 10:2, pp. 46–50.

Young, O, 1967. *The Intermediaries*. Princeton: Princeton University Press.

—— 1968. *The Politics of Force*. Princeton: Princeton University Press.

—— (ed.), 1975. *Bargaining*. University of Illinois Press.

—— 1983. "Regime Dynamics," in Krasner, S (ed.). *International Regimes*. Ithaca, NY: Cornell University Press.

—— 1986. "International Regimes: Toward a New Theory of Institutions," *World Politics* 44:1, pp. 104–22.

—— 1989a "Politics of Regime Formation," *International Organization* 33:3, pp. 349–76.

—— 1989b. *International Cooperation*. Ithaca, NY: Cornell University Press.

—— 1991. "Political Leadership and Regime Formation," *International Organization* 35:3, pp. 281–308.

Young, O, Demko, G and Ramakrishna, K, 1996. "Global Environmental Change and International Governance." Hanover, NH: Dartmouth College.

Young, R, 1992. "Egalitarianism and Personal Desert," *Ethics* 102:2, pp. 319–41.

Zagare, F, 1978, "Game Theoretic Analysis of the Vietnam negotiations," in Zartman, IW (ed.), 1978b.

Zahar, MJ, 2003. "Reframing the Spoiler Debate in Peace Processes," in Darby, J and MacGinty, J (eds). *Contemporary Peacemaking*. Palgrave.

Zartman, IW, 1964a. "The Moroccan-American Base Negotiations," *Middle East Journal* 18:1, pp. 27–40 and in expanded form in *Problems of New Power* Atherton, 1964b).

—— 1964b. "Les Relations entre la France et l'Algérie," *Revue Française de Science Politique* 14:6, pp. 1087–113.

—— 1971. *The Politics of Trade Negotiations between Africa and the European Common Market: The Weak Confront the Strong*. Princeton: Princeton University Press.

—— 1974. "The Political Analysis of Negotiation: Who Gets What When How?" *World Politics* 26:3, pp. 33–7.

—— 1978a. "Negotiation as a Joint Decision-Making Process," in Zartman, IW (ed.). *The Negotiation Process*. London: SAGE Publications.

—— (ed.), 1978b. *The Negotiation Process*. London: SAGE Publications.

—— 1978c "Negotiation as a Joint Decision-Making Process," *Journal of Conflict Resolution* 21:4, pp. 619–38, also published in Zartman, IW (ed.). *The Negotiation Process*. Thousand Oaks: SAGE Publications.

—— 1983. "The Strategy of Preventive Diplomacy in Third World Conflicts," in George, A (ed.). *Managing US-Soviet Rivalry*. Boulder, CO: Westview.

—— 1985 "Negotiating from Asymmetry," *Negotiation Journal*, 2, pp. 121–38.

—— (ed.), 1987a. *Positive Sum: Improving North-South Negotiations*. Edison, NJ: Transaction.

—— (ed.), 1987b. *The 50% Solution*. New Haven: Yale University Press.

—— 1988 "Common Elements inte Analysis of the Negotiation Process," *Negotiation Journal* 4:1 pp. 31–44.

—— 1989a. *Ripe for Resolution*. New York: Oxford University Press.

—— 1989b. "Negotiations and Prenegotiations in Ethnic Conflict: The Beginning,

The Middle, and the Ends," in Montville, J (ed.). *Conflict and Peacemaking in Multiethnic Societies.* Lexington, MA: Lexington Books.

—— 1989c. "Pr-Negotiation: Phases and Functions," in Stein, JG (ed.), 1989. *Getting to the Table.* Baltimore: The Johns Hopkins University Press.

—— 1990. "Negotiating Effectively With Terrorists" in Rubin, B (ed.), 1990. *The Politics of Counterterrorism.* Washington.: The Johns Hopkins Foreign Policy Institute.

—— (ed.), 1991. *Tunisia: The Political Economy of Reform.* Boulder: Lynne Rienner Publishers.

—— (ed.), 1994. *International Multilateral Negotiations.* Hoboken, NJ: Jossey Bass.

—— 1995a. "The Role of Justice in Security Negotiations," *American Behavioral Scientist* 38:6, pp. 889–903.

—— 1995b. "Negotiations to End Conflict in South Africa," in Zartman, IW *Elusive Peace: Negotiating an End to Civil Wars.* Washington, D.C.: Brookings Institution.

—— (ed.), 1995c. *Elusive Peace: Negotiating an End to Civil Wars.* Washington, D.C.: Brookings Institution.

—— 1997. "The Structuralist Dilemma in Negotiation," in Lewicki, R (ed.). *Research on Negotiation in Organization.* JAI.

—— 2000. "Ripeness: The Hurting Stalemate and Beyond," in Stern, P and Druckman, D (eds), 2000. *International Conflict Management after the Cold War.* Washington, DC: National Academy Press.

—— 2003a. "Negotiating with Terrorists." *International Negotiation* 8:3 pp. 443–450.

—— 2003b "Negotiating the Rapids: The Dynamics of Regime Formation," in Spector, BI and Zartman, IW (eds), 2003.

—— 2004. "MEOs and Durable Settlements: A Theoretical and Empirical Evaluation of the Reasons for Durability of Peaceful Settlements in Civil Wars." Paper delivered at the American Political Science Association, Chicago.

—— 2005. "Resolving the Toughness Dilemma," in Faure, GO (ed.). *La Négociation: regards sur sa diversité.* Paris: Editions Publibook Université.

—— 2005a. "Analyzing Intractibility," in Crocker, C, Hampson, FO and Aall,P (eds). *Grasping the Nettle.* Washington: USIP.

—— 2005b. *Cowardly Lions: Missed Opportunities to Prevent Deadly Conflict and State Collapse.* Boulder: Lynne Rienner Publishers.

—— 2005c "Structures of Escalation and Negotiation" in Zartman, IW and Faure, GO (eds), 2005.

—— 2005d "Methods of Analysis: Case Studies," *International Negotiation* 10:1 pp. 3–15.

—— 2006a "Ripeness Revisited: The Push and Pull of Conflict Management," in Hauswedell, C (ed.). *Deeskalation von Gewaltkonflikt seit 1945.* Essen: Klartext-verlag.

—— 2007a, *Peacemaking in International Conflicts: Methods and Techniques, 2nd edn.* Washington, DC: US Institute of Peace.

—— 2007b. "Process Explanations," in Faure, GO and Cede, F, (eds). *Explaining Negotiation Failures.* Washington: US Institute of Peace.

Zartman, IW and Alfredson, T, 2007. "Negotiating with Terrorists: When, How and Why?" in Dupont, C (ed.). *Transformations du Monde et Négociation: implications, défis et opportunités.* Paris: Publibook.

Zartman, IW and Aurik, J, 1991. "Power Strategies in De-escalation," in Kriesberg, L and Thorson, S (eds). *Timing the De-escalation of International Conflicts.* Syracuse, NY: Syracuse University Press.

Zartman, IW and Bassani, A, 1987. *The Algerian Gas Negotiations.* Washington: Foreign Policy Institute, The Johns Hopkins University.

Zartman, IW and Berman, M, 1982. *The Practical Negotiator.* New Haven, CT: Yale University Press.

Zartman, IW and Faure, GO (eds), 2005. *Escalation and Negotiation in International Conflicts.* Cambridge: Cambridge University Press.

Zartman, IW and Faure, GO, 2007. *Negotiating with and against Terrorists: a Handbook.* Washington: USIP and PIN/IIASA.

Zartman, IW and Kremenyuk, V (eds), 1995. *Reducing International Conflict.* Syracuse University Press.

—— 2005. *Peace vs Justice: Negotiating Forward- and Backward-Looking Outcomes.* Lanham, MD: Rowman & Littlefield.

Zartman, IW and Rubin, JZ (eds), 1995. *Power and Negotiation.* Ann Arbor, MI: University of Michigan Press.

Zartman, IW and Rubin, JZ, (eds), 2000. *Power and International Negotiation.* Ann Arbor, MI: University of Michigan Press.

Zartman, IW, Druckman, D, Jensen, L, Pruitt, D and Young, P, 1996. "Negotiation as a Search for Justice," *International Negotiation Journal* 1:1, pp. 79–98.

Zartman, IW, Saunders, H, and Azar, E, 1987. *Mediation in Middle East Conflicts.* Syracuse, NY: Syracuse University Press.

Zeuthen, F, 1930. *Problems of Monopoly and Economic Welfare.* London: Routledge and Kegan Paul.

Index